# The Dynamics of Managing Diversit

# The Dynamics of Managing Diversity

## A critical approach

Gill Kirton and Anne-Marie Greene

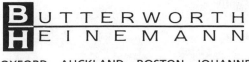

BUTTERWORTH
HEINEMANN

OXFORD   AUCKLAND   BOSTON   JOHANNESBURG   MELBOURNE   NEW DELHI

Butterworth-Heinemann
Linacre House, Jordan Hill, Oxford OX2 8DP
225 Wildwood Avenue, Woburn, MA 01801-2041
A division of Reed Educational and Professional Publishing Ltd

℞ A member of the Reed Elsevier plc group

First published 2000
Reprinted 2001

**British Library Cataloguing in Publication Data**
Kirton, Gill
    The dynamics of managing diversity
    1.  Diversity in the workplace – Great Britain      2.  Diversity in
    the workplace – Great Britain – Statistics      3.  Diversity in
    the workplace – Government policy – Great Britain
    4.  Discrimination in employment – Great Britain
    5.  Discrimination in employment – Law and legislation –
    Great Britain
    I.  Title      II.  Greene, Anne-Marie
    331.1'33'0941

ISBN 0 7506 4417 6

For more information on all Butterworth-Heinemann
publications please visit our website at www.bh.com

Composition by Genesis Typesetting, Laser Quay, Rochester, Kent
Printed and bound in Great Britain

FOR EVERY TITLE THAT WE PUBLISH, BUTTERWORTH-HEINEMANN
WILL PAY FOR BTCV TO PLANT AND CARE FOR A TREE.

# Contents

# Acknowledgements

The authors and publishers wish to thank the following for permission to reproduce copyright material: Commission for Racial Equality, *Equal Opportunities Review* (published by Industrial Relations Services), Institute of Employment Studies, Office for National Statistics, Gender, Work and Organization, Mark Whitehead. The authors wish to thank Butterworth-Heinemann's Commissioning Editor, Clare Slater, for supporting the writing of this book, and Development Editor, Sally North, for advice and assistance in the writing stages. Thanks are also due to the anonymous reviewers for their valuable comments on and criticisms of earlier drafts.

# About the authors and contributors

**Gill Kirton** BA, MA, LicIPD, is Senior Lecturer in HRM and Industrial Relations at the University of North London. She has a long-standing interest in equality issues and has published articles on women's roles in trade unions.

**Anne-Marie Greene** BA, MA, PhD, GradIPD, is Lecturer in Industrial Relations at Aston University. Her research interests include gender and workplace trade unionism and she has published articles in these areas.

**Linda Johnson** LLM, LLB, DipASHE, Cert Ed., is Principal Lecturer in Business and European Law at the University of North London. Her research interests include discrimination law, employment and industrial relations law, and consumer protection law.

**Sue Johnstone** LLM, BA, is Principal Lecturer in Employment and Industrial Relations Law at the University of North London. Her research interests include trade union law, equality law and comparative employment law.

# List of tables and exhibits

## Tables

## Exhibits

# List of figures

# Part One
# Contexts and concepts

# Chapter 1

# Introduction: mapping the diversity and equality territory

## Aim

To introduce the reader to the central themes and tenets of the book.

## Objectives

- To define the terms of reference and outline the parameters of the book.
- To provide guidance on using the book.

## Background

The idea for writing this book arose from one author's experiences of planning and teaching a final year undergraduate module entitled 'Managing Diversity'. Unusually perhaps, this module is core, and therefore compulsory, for students taking the University of North London's 'Human resource studies' pathway. As a core module 'Managing Diversity' is of central importance within the pathway and it is intended that the module will situate current and emerging equality and diversity debates and issues within the context of the UK labour market. It is also intended that it will provide the theoretical and conceptual underpinning necessary to understand the policies and practices of organizations, line managers and human resource practitioners. Thus the module has a broad agenda, pointing away from a narrow focus on equality practice or on the functional activities of human resource practitioners, towards an examination of the social and economic contexts within which labour market activity takes place. Difficulties were found in selecting a suitable textbook to support the programme of teaching and learning, this despite an abundance of research-based literature contained in texts and journals. A prescriptive or management textbook would not provide the theoretical and conceptual substance, whilst a US-based textbook (of which there are many) would not provide the appropriate contextual backdrop for a discussion of the UK situation. Following in-depth student evaluation of the module, involving questionnaires and focus groups, the conclusion arrived at was that it was timely to consider writing a textbook that would map the diversity and equality territories, and provide a solid basis for the study thereof.

This book's overall aim is to fill the gap identified, to act as a supporting textbook to modules centred on equality, diversity or discrimination in employment and to allow students to acquire the contextual, theoretical and conceptual tools necessary to access and understand the rich variety of research-based literature in the field. It is not intended as a replacement of that literature. As is the case with any textbook, it should be regarded as a departure point, rather than as a whole package of study and programme of learning in itself. Our aim is to stimulate students' interest in this field of study by mapping the territory, such that the further reading we suggest and references we provide will be consulted in order to deepen and broaden understanding. We also expect that students will cascade to other texts and articles, for the references we provide are not exhaustive.

# Defining terms

The chosen title of this book reflects the recent changes in thinking on equality issues and the shift towards conceptualizing workforces as composed of diverse social groups which share many employment experiences, but which simultaneously are also treated differentially, and at times require different treatment, by the labour market. We use the term 'diversity' within a conceptual framework which is not wholly in line with the way in which the term is used in the US literature and much of the UK management literature, where it is firmly tied to individualistic, utilitarian, instrumental models. We reject the appropriation of the diversity concept by the orthodox management literature. In our view, the shift away from conceptualizing social groups as homogeneous, hermetically sealed units, leads towards a perspective which views social groups as heterogeneous, overlapping and non-fixed. From this perspective a diversity paradigm has the important ability to highlight intragroup as well as intergroup difference, enabling issues of social identity to be drawn out which have been neglected within traditional equality debates.

Highlighting the heterogeneity and diversity of social groups assists in the task of recognizing and understanding that discrimination and disadvantage are multifaceted and that it is important to draw on the experiences of, and reflect the needs of, all social groups within the workforce when developing or analysing employment policy (Liff and Dale, 1994). Thus, unlike much of the diversity literature, we use the term in a broad sense and do not place it firmly within a 'human resource management' (HRM) or 'business case' framework. However, on occasion within the book we talk about 'managing diversity' as a business-oriented catch phrase for employer-led initiatives designed to value workforce diversity, and which is more concerned with utility than justice. For clarity, where we employ the term in this sense, we encapsulate it in inverted commas. The book's title, *The Dynamics of Managing Diversity*, is intended as a *double entendre*. On the one hand it can be taken to suggest an examination of the dynamic context in which employers seek to manage workforce diversity. On the other hand, and from the student perspective, it can be understood as referring to the dynamics of attempting to 'manage', that is, to make sense of, the study of diversity. We believe the book and its contents are sufficiently broad to enable it to be utilized on a range of modules not bearing its title, since it deals with issues of diversity, equality, discrimination and disadvantage.

The book's overall focus is on employment and labour market structures and outcomes, the treatment of diverse social groups therein and on policy interventions at the level of the state and of organizations. However, by focusing our analysis on five social groups – women, minority ethnic people, older people, disabled people and lesbians and gay men – we also seek to inject a subjectivist dimension into the study of equality and diversity issues. In other words, we attempt to highlight the ways in which different groups and individuals experience the world of work, rather than viewing the topics from a one-dimensional management or employer perspective.

# The UK, European and US contexts

Whilst intercountry comparisons make interesting reading in the employment arena, and in this sense comparative study is worthwhile in itself, there are also important and marked differences in the social, economic and historical contexts of countries. These shape employment policy and practice at both organizational and institutional levels, as well as impacting on individuals' and social groups' labour market experiences. The consequence is that debates centred on employment policy and practice must be contextualized if the causes and effects of failure or success of various interventions are to be understood. It is for this reason that we have chosen to situate our discussion largely within the UK context.

However, as much of the diversity literature emanates from the USA it is worth briefly considering the case for not extending our analysis as far as the USA. Debates within the US diversity literature reflect the social, economic and historical contexts of the USA and the concerns preoccupying organizational and institutional policy-makers in the USA are not entirely transferable to the UK context. For example, it has been established that by 2000, white males will no longer be the dominant demographic group *entering* the US labour market (Arvey et al., 1996). This is because women and minority ethnic groups are projected to comprise a larger proportion of new entrants than formerly. This means that US employers are required to make adjustments to employment policy and practice to attract new 'types' of worker. Although similar arguments are proffered in the UK context, especially in the case of women, of particular note when comparing the USA and the UK, is the sizes of the two countries' minority ethnic populations, which are 26 per cent and 5.5 per cent respectively (Edwards, 1995). It is argued (Edwards, 1995) that these overall figures shape government policy and concerns. In other words, with a larger minority ethnic population, US policy-makers have paid more attention to redressing ethnic disadvantage. This has been achieved via policies such as 'affirmative action', whereas in the UK the legislation all but prohibits what is termed here 'positive discrimination' (the policy equivalent of the USA's 'affirmative action').

Also, in the US context, the past denial of civil rights for the black population has influenced the perceived need to 'right' the 'wrongs' of the past. Within the UK the growth of a multiracial society has very different origins, its provenance being postwar immigration (Solomos, 1989). This is not to say, however, that minority ethnic disadvantage is not a significant feature of the societies of both the USA and the UK. This notwithstanding, the origins of such disadvantage are rather different and the consequences are therefore not identical.

Another important difference between the US and UK contexts is the circumstances surrounding the promulgation of a diversity discourse. In the USA, the seemingly less threatening discourse of 'valuing diversity' has risen to the fore because of backlash and resistance to affirmative action programmes. Critics of affirmative action programmes argue that such 'preferential policies' violate the rights of others to positions under the 'merit principle' (Edwards, 1995: 179). A concern has been mooted in the US that the 'wrong' people are paying the costs of past discriminatory practice, that is, it is argued by some that white American men cannot get jobs (Edwards, 1995: 184). This is certainly a spurious claim lacking empirical support, but it has nevertheless been powerful enough to cause the less threatening and less controversial diversity paradigm to emerge. With its emphasis on valuing individuals, 'managing diversity' does not seek to engineer employment outcomes in the way that affirmative action does, and it may therefore be capable of winning the approval of white American males (Yakura, 1996). In the UK, the 'managing diversity' approach emanates from the widespread perceived need to anchor equality objectives to broader business and organizational objectives. It is argued that failure to do so has been one of the key weaknesses of the traditional 'equal opportunity' approach.

Thus, we have chosen to situate this book within the UK context. However, it is self-evident that as a member of the European Union the UK context is influenced by developments within Europe, especially those towards the creation of a single European market. Therefore, our examination of the law framing equality and diversity policies, and emerging developments thereof, draws some attention to the broader

European context within which UK equality legislation is enacted. We also dedicate a chapter to European comparisons, in order that salient contrasts and similarities may be drawn between the UK and its European social partners.

Our examination of the macro and micro structures of inequality, and the theoretical explanations thereof, are situated within debates about equality and diversity and whether recognition and acclamation of workforce diversity offers a new way forward in terms of employment policy formulation and implementation. Our reading of the existing research-based literature leads us to a rather negative conclusion on this point. As shown in Chapters 5 and 8, most academic commentators are sceptical about 'managing diversity' as linked to 'business case' arguments for equality and the ability of this approach to redress material inequalities. This is because of the contingent and partial nature of business case arguments with their reliance on the functional rationality of management (Webb, 1997) as drivers of employment policy. Therefore, in the context of the UK labour market, it remains apposite to examine efforts to effect equality and not solely those to value diversity. It also remains important for diversity policy levers to grow from and on to, existing equal opportunity policies, rather than replace them.

# The social construction of inequalities

It is a widespread myth that employment inequalities have been eradicated and that any status or earnings differentials that exist among the workforce, simply reflect individual merit or choice. Human capital and rational choice theorists would favour this argument, whilst sociologists (especially those writing in the feminist tradition) favour structural explanations for continuing inequalities. In terms of this book's terrain, the consequence of the belief that equality has been achieved, is that it is now time for employers to stop worrying about group-based equality issues and start lending their thoughts to how to motivate and reward individuals or to how to value diversity.

If aggregate labour market data are only cursorily examined, it can be seen that certain social groups are disproportionately represented among those employees who are low status and low paid – women, minority ethnic, disabled and older people. Social group membership is salient in the sense that a group's relationship with social institutions influences the individual members' interaction with, and experiences and perceptions of, those institutions, which in turn impact upon the choices and opportunities individuals are faced with. We are gendered, racialized, aged, sexualized beings and are viewed, and often judged, as such by social actors. This is not to say that individuals are not also subjects in the making of their own histories. Some individuals can and do overcome the socially constructed barriers and obstacles generally encountered by their social group. For example women can become powerful figures in business or industry, defying the general trend for women to be concentrated in lower status occupations, but individuals can never entirely escape their socially constructed positioning (Cockburn, 1991). As stated previously, empirical evidence shows that, on average, some social groups have greater difficulty than other groups in realizing their work goals and in achieving a reasonable standard of living. Not least because in the employment context, members of dominant social groups or members of those groups already privileged by their disproportionate representation in high-status positions, are likely to be favoured by those making decisions within organizations.

Social group membership is usually conceptualized in juxtaposition to the dominant majority group (Roberts, 1996), which, in the UK employment context, is usually white, non-disabled, heterosexual, male. That is not to say that all men falling into this category are privileged: class is also an important factor. However, if we compare social groups within their own social milieu we can uncover patterns of inequality between them: for example, women manual workers earn on average less than male manual workers, whilst black manual workers earn on average less than white manual workers.

The book's focus on certain social groups is predicated upon the premise that there are five main sources of labour market disadvantage – gender, race, disability, age and sexual orientation. Class mediates these sources of discrimination, in the sense that the situation in the UK labour market is not one of, for example, all men at the top and all women at the bottom (Cockburn, 1991). The picture is far more complex than this, with educational attainment and occupational classification also playing a role in determining the work opportunities and experiences of individual working men and women in the UK. Nevertheless, it can be argued that in a capitalist, patriarchal society with an imperialist history, such as the UK, gender and race are the principal determinants of a person's structural position within that society. This is because sexism and racism both cut across class (Anthias and Yuval-Davis, 1992), such that middle-class women and minority ethnic people suffer discrimination despite their relatively privileged class position, whilst working-class women and minority ethnic people suffer the deprivations of their class as well as gender and race specific deprivations. As Hall (1978, quoted in Cockburn, 1991: 60) puts it: 'Race is the modality in which class is lived. It is also the medium in which class relations are experienced.' The same could be said of gender. Thus, we do not offer an explicit class analysis of inequalities, because of the intersection of class with other sources of labour market disadvantage, rather we concentrate on gender-, race-, age-, disability- and sexual orientation-specific forms of disadvantage.

This disadvantage arises from the embeddedness in the fabric of society of prejudice and discrimination against those groups we focus on and is reflected in employment and in organizational life. Therefore, certain categories of people enter employment and organizations already disadvantaged by social inequalities as reflected in, for example, the education system and by their social group membership(s). The discrimination they meet therein reinforces their disadvantaged position and militates against their progress. In fact, it may be argued that inequality is both a prerequisite for and outcome of, capitalist labour relations (Cockburn, 1991). In other words, a system of production based upon the principles of market competition inherently creates winners and losers. The point is that winners and losers are not randomly distributed throughout the working-age population, rather they are concentrated in and among segments of that population. The five groups we identify – women, minority ethnic people, disabled people, older people and lesbians and gay men – represent groups among whom 'losers' are concentrated. Thus, in our view it is not appropriate to focus solely on the organizational benefits to be derived from diversity unless and until equality of opportunity, condition and outcome (Miller, 1996) exist for all social groups. This cannot be said of the UK at the present time.

# The social construction of identity

The importance of social group in the construction of identity is that social group membership influences both how individuals perceive themselves and how others perceive them (Roberts, 1996). Thus, identity can be imposed (by others) and assumed (by self-identification). Gender and race are especially salient in the construction of identity, in that as characteristics they fix people in an immutable and, usually, visible category to which traits are ascribed by various social actors, including employers. Frequently, there are negative consequences associated with such ascription. Jenkins (1996: 61) argues that 'gender is one of the most pervasive classificatory principles, arguably, the most pervasive, with myriad implications for the life-chances and experiences of whole categories of people, and one of the most consistent identificatory themes in human history'. On the question of ethnicity, Jenkins (1996: 65) holds that 'ethnic identity . . . is often an important and early dimension of self-identification. Individuals may learn frameworks for classifying themselves and others by ethnicity and 'race' during childhood . . . Ethnicity, when it matters to people, really matters'.

Other sources of identity are more fluid and often less visible, but not necessarily and in all circumstances less salient. For example, disability takes many different forms: it can be temporary or permanent; it can occur to anyone at any stage in the life course; it is infinitely graduated. Similarly, sexual orientation is not necessarily fixed, and age discrimination affects people to different extents and in different ways over the life course. It can be argued that other sources of identity and the experiences arising from them, are mediated by gender and race. From this perspective, it follows that it is appropriate to accord more attention to issues of gender and race, as we do in this book. This is not to say that we do not believe that all sources of identity are important in contributing to who or what a person is and who or what others perceive a person to be.

On the contrary, we firmly subscribe to the view that social group membership helps to construct a sense of self anchored in social and cultural meaning, and in this sense has positive as well as negative consequences.

# The book's contents

The book is divided into two parts. Part One 'Contexts and concepts' situates equality and diversity within the UK employment and organizational contexts. It also explores theoretical explanations for labour market inequalities and presents conceptual frameworks and models for understanding equality and diversity policy. Chapter 2 sets the scene for exploring and understanding equality and diversity within the context of the UK labour market. It outlines the social and economic factors which shape the labour market position and employment experiences of women, black and minority ethnic people, disabled people, lesbians and gay men and older people. The chapter draws on macrolevel labour market statistics to reveal trends and patterns of inequality between and among social groups. Chapter 3 presents the main theoretical explanations for occupational segregation and segmentation, which characterize the British labour market. The strengths and weaknesses of the various conceptual frameworks are critically appraised. Importantly, the chapter also injects identity issues into the discussion. Chapter 4 examines diversity, equality and discrimination issues at the level of the organization, focusing on organizational cultures and the way in which they are infused with values constructed around an archetypal, white, non-disabled, heterosexual masculine norm. The consequences of this are explored from the perspectives of diverse social groups. Chapter 5 presents chronological developments in the meaning and understanding of different approaches to equality and diversity policy. The chapter provides the conceptual and theoretical underpinning necessary to develop a critical analysis of institutional and organizational policy approaches.

Part Two 'Policy and practice' explores contemporary approaches to equality and diversity policy and practice. It considers the role of key actors in both perpetuating and seeking to challenge disadvantage and discrimination in the labour market and organizations. Chapter 6 examines the nature and content of equality legislation, including recent developments emanating from the European Union. The chapter provides a critical appraisal of the law as an instrument for overcoming inequalities in employment. Chapter 7 posits that as one of the three key industrial relations actors, trade unions have a central role to play in the challenging of discriminatory employment policy and practice, and in the promotion of equality and diversity issues. Issues of equality and diversity within trade unions are also explored. Chapter 8 explores and critically analyses, variations in approach to the formulation and implementation of equality and diversity policy at the level of the organization. The ideology underpinning policy approaches is discussed, namely social justice and business case arguments. The role of key organizational actors is also considered. Chapter 9 evaluates human resource management and what it offers the equality and diversity projects. The analysis focuses on the central tenets of HRM, namely strategic integration, employee commitment, flexibility and quality. Chapter 10 draws on some examples of European countries which have made a significant contribution to the promotion of equality and diversity in employment, and examines similarities and differences among European Union member states, thus situating the UK in a European context. The importance of social and employment policy in promoting equality is underscored. The concluding chapter provides a summary of the issues raised in Chapters 2 to 10, seeking to demonstrate how they interconnect and discussing the prospects for a diversity paradigm in eclipsing the present equality paradigm.

# Using the book

This is a textbook and in our view this means that it should be capable of supporting a programme of teaching and learning. As stated above, we seek to map the territory of equality and diversity, and thereby provide a solid basis for students to progress to research-based texts and articles. With this aim in mind, it is necessary for us to attempt to achieve an appropriate balance between description and analysis. Description is essential to any 'mapping' exercise, whilst analysis is necessary to make sense of the landscape depicted. Our intention is to provide relevant information and summarize different arguments. What we hope to have produced is a valuable resource for students, which will underpin their study in the field.

We believe it would be wrong to claim academic writing as entirely objective and unbiased. Our choice of literature sources inevitably reflects our own beliefs and values, as is the case with any academic text or textbook. However, we try to present the material we have gathered in as detached a manner as possible and to consider alternative and competing perspectives and understandings of the social phenomena we describe and analyse. We do not always draw firm conclusions from our discussions and we do not make recommendations, rather we leave it to readers to make up their own minds based on the information we present and that to be gleaned from further reading. Although we do not make explicit recommendations, clear and fairly transparent implications can be drawn from the overall contents of the book for readers with a vocational or practitioner orientation.

Each chapter commences with an overall aim and a set of objectives to inform the reader of the territory covered by the chapter and to indicate what the chapter is attempting to achieve. Key learning points are provided at the end of each section within chapters. These summarize and draw out the principal messages of the section. Where appropriate, tables and diagrams are presented to reinforce the explanations and discussions contained within the text. We intend that the review and discussion questions at the end of each chapter encourage further reading, reflection and discussion. The questions can be used by students working alone, in study groups or in seminar sessions. The suggested further reading we provide in each chapter will help those discussions to be more in depth and fruitful. As is the case with any such questions, they can be treated simply as checks on understanding of the contents of a chapter, or subjected to rigorous debate and analysis. Some of the review and discussion questions lend themselves to essay questions – we leave this to tutor discretion. We also provide activities within each chapter. These are intended to develop students' analytical abilities by requiring that the themes of the chapter in question are reflected upon in order to understand, interpret and analyse the situations, circumstances and questions in the activity. Again, these short activities can be attempted by students working independently of classes, or within seminar sessions. At the end of the book there is a glossary of terms and abbreviations with the aim of illuminating key concepts. There is also a subject index which will assist students in searching for information.

Although we believe the chapters are organized in a logical sequence, each can also be read in isolation. Therefore, there is a high degree of flexibility in how students and tutors approach the topics covered by the book. In any subject field with a large literature, it is always necessary for authors to make decisions about what to include and what to exclude. This book is no different and doubtless there are omissions, which can be remedied by wider reading and by tutor input.

# References

Anthias, F. and Yuval-Davis, N. (1992). *Racialized Boundaries*. Routledge.

Arvey, R., Azevedo, R., Ostgaard, D. and Raghuram, S. (1996). The implications of a diverse labour market on human resource planning. In *Managing Diversity* (E. Kossek and S. Lobel, eds). Blackwell.

Cockburn, C. (1991). *In the Way of Women*. Macmillan.

Edwards, J. (1995). *When Race Counts: The Morality of Racial Preference in Britain and America*. Routledge.

Jenkins, R. (1996). *Social Identity*. Routledge.

Liff, S. and Dale, K. (1994). Formal opportunity, informal barriers. *Work, Employment and Society*, **8** (2), 177–198.

Miller, D. (1996). Equality management: towards a materialist approach. *Gender, Work and Organization*, **3** (4), 202–214.

Roberts, K. (1996). Managing disability-based diversity. In *Managing Diversity: Human Resource Strategies for Transforming the Workplace* (E. Kossek and S. Lobel, eds). Blackwell, 310–331.

Solomos, J. (1989). The politics of immigration since 1945. In *Racism And Antiracism: Inequalities, Opportunities and Policies*. (P. Braham, A. Rattansi and R. Skellington, eds). Sage, 7–29.

Webb, J. (1997). The politics of equal opportunity. *Gender, Work and Organization*, **4** (3), 159–170.

Yakura, E. (1996). EEO law and managing diversity. In *Managing Diversity* (E. Kossek and S. Lobel). Blackwell.

# Chapter 2
# The social and economic landscape

## Aim

To demonstrate that the UK workforce is composed of diverse social groups with differential patterns and experiences of labour market participation.

## Objectives

- To outline the changing extent and nature of women's labour market participation.
- To outline the employment patterns of minority ethnic groups and to place these within the context of the legacy of immigration policy.
- To outline some of the employment trends and patterns among disabled people.
- To discuss the impact of age on labour market participation and on employment experiences.
- To highlight some of the employment experiences of lesbians and gay men.

## Introduction

This chapter constitutes the contemporary structural context for understanding the dynamics of managing diversity. It outlines the social and economic factors, which shape the labour market position and employment experiences of women, black and minority ethnic people, disabled people, lesbians and gay men, and older people. This sketch of macrolevel labour market trends and patterns demonstrates the existence of inequalities of outcome between and within social groups. The chapter is a presentation of data, with some commentary, although detailed analysis and theoretical explanations are reserved for subsequent chapters. Thus, the contents of this chapter represent a valuable resource for students to consult in order to contextualize discussions on the themes of equality and diversity.

The approach we take is to examine the employment trends and patterns of the five social groups that are this book's focus. It must be noted that it is impossible to consider any of these groups entirely separately for three reasons: individuals can self-evidently fall into more than one category, social group membership is not fixed and the groups themselves are not homogeneous. Attention is drawn, for example, to ethnic differences in women's employment to reinforce the point that the category 'women' is not a unitary one and that diversity among women exists. Similarly, diversity exists among minority ethnic groups' experiences of the labour market and between male and female members of these groups.

Although the data presented in this chapter are correct at the time of writing, there may have been some changes by the time of publication. However, we are concerned primarily with the *trends and patterns* revealed by the data. Change will be slow and incremental rather than rapid and revolutionary, therefore the trends and patterns described and analysed below are likely to remain valid for some time to come. For up-to-date statistics the Equal Opportunities Commission and the Commission for Racial Equality are reliable sources, as are the journals and publications (such as *Equal Opportunities Review, Labour Market Trends*) which report the results of the latest Labour Force Surveys.

# Patterns and trends in women's employment

Over the past thirty or forty years one of the major social and economic changes has been the increase in women's employment, especially that of mothers. Women now make up 46 per cent of the UK labour force (EOC, 1997a), compared with under 30 per cent in 1954 (Wilson, 1994). Between 1951 and 1981 the rate of increase escalated so that women's participation rate more than doubled in the thirty-year period (Joshi, Layard and Owen, 1985). As we enter the new millennium it is now the norm for women to be in paid employment, with the traditional family composition of full-time male breadwinner and full-time 'housewife' caring for the home and children now the exception rather than the norm (Wilson, 1994). The reasons for this enormous social change are complex and multilayered: there exist both demand- and supply-side dimensions, which we explore below.

Although women's labour market participation has increased rapidly and dramatically, this tends to be concentrated in certain occupations and industries. The terms 'occupational sex segregation' or 'gender segregation' are used to describe the tendency for men and women to be employed in different occupations. It is not entirely clear whether demand- or supply-side factors explain occupational sex segregation: it is likely that both contribute to the phenomenon.

Women form the majority of workers in three major occupational groups (EOR, 1998a). These are 'clerical and secretarial' (75 per cent women), 'personal and protective services' (66 per cent women) and sales (62 per cent women), and over half (53 per cent) of all working women are employed in these three occupational groups alone. Women also predominate in other occupational groups, including 'health and social work' (81 per cent women), 'education' (69 per cent), hotels and restaurants' (59 per cent), retail trade (60 per cent) and clothing manufacture (71 per cent) (EOR, 1998a). Occupational sex segregation is particularly pronounced in part-time work (Hakim, 1993). What cannot be overlooked, is the fact that female dominated occupations and industries attract lower pay, which we discuss below.

Women and men are not divided purely along the horizontal lines described above; they are also vertically segregated. Men continue to dominate the higher levels of organizational hierarchies including the two occupational groups 'managers and administrators' (67 per cent men) and 'professional' (60 per cent men) (EOC, 1997a). Therefore, women have made only limited qualitative gains, the pace of change being very slow when we look at women's share of managerial and professional jobs, which has increased from 34 per cent in 1984 to 40 per cent in 1997 (EOR, 1998a). Women are more likely to be found in the professions than in management, partly because a greater number and a wider range of professional than managerial jobs are available on a part-time basis. Women and men also tend to be employed in different professions, with for example, men dominating the traditionally male preserves of engineering and technology (93 per cent men) and women dominating the feminized teaching profession (64 per cent women). Women have increased their share of professional and managerial occupations at the same time as increasing their share of lower level jobs. The consequence of this is that women as a group are becoming polarized as small numbers gain access to the higher echelons of occupational hierarchies and the vast majority remain concentrated at the lower end (Rubery and Fagan, 1994). Occupational segregation is a theme we return to in Chapter 3, where we consider different theoretical explanations for the phenomenon.

There is a strong relationship between occupational sex segregation and lower pay for women (Anker, 1997; Lim, 1996). Millward and Woodland (1995) refer to this as the 'wage penalty' associated with working in organizations and occupations dominated by women. Women who work full time currently earn 80 per cent of the average hourly earnings of male full-time workers (EOC, 1997a). Since 1975 (and the consolidation of equal pay legislation) the gender pay gap has narrowed by just 9 per cent and has closed by only 1 per cent since 1992 (EOC, 1996). A closer look at the available data reveals further differences between women and men and among women. Women who work part time have much lower hourly earnings than men who work full time: they earn 58 per cent of men's average hourly pay. This has remained almost unchanged since the mid-1970s, so although levels of pay have improved for full-time working women when compared to men, the substantial minority of women who work part time (45 per cent) have made very little progress towards parity with men. The corollary of this is that women, who work part time, in any industry, also earn far less (73 per cent) than women who work full time. Thus, women face a higher wage penalty for working part time. This is a phenomenon partly explained by the fact that part-time jobs tend to be concentrated in

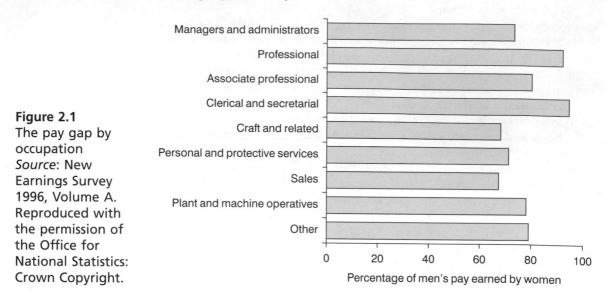

**Figure 2.1**
The pay gap by occupation
*Source*: New Earnings Survey 1996, Volume A. Reproduced with the permission of the Office for National Statistics: Crown Copyright.

low-skill, female-dominated sectors of the economy (Rubery and Fagan, 1994). It should also be noted that the above are aggregate figures. The gender pay gap varies considerably from sector to sector and occupation to occupation (see Figure 2.1 and EOC, 1997a).

## Demand-side explanations

There is an interesting debate to be had around whether trends and patterns in women's labour market participation can be explained by women's preferences, the nature and level of their skills and qualifications (supply-side factors), or by employers' strategies towards labour (demand-side factors). Demand-side factors include employers' requirements for labour, both in the sense of numbers and 'types' of employees required and the skills and qualifications required.

Changes in the labour market participation of both men and women have come about to some extent because of the restructuring of the UK economy (Wilson, 1994): demand-side factors. There has been a substantial decline in the manufacturing industry and in the jobs traditionally done by men, and a significant growth in the service industry and jobs traditionally done by women (EOC, 1997b). Accompanying these structural changes have been labour shortages in some industries, compelling employers to adopt new strategies to recruit and retain hitherto underutilized labour sources, such as women. Structural changes, combined with global competitive pressures, have also led to the increased demand for cheap, flexible labour. As discussed above, women's pay is lower than men's and they have a greater propensity to work part time: therefore many employers have sought to attract part-time women workers into their workforces. Overall, then, men's participation in paid employment is declining (EOC, 1997b), although they are presently employed in greater numbers than are women.

The labour market participation rates of men and women are expected to move closer together as the men's rate stabilizes and the women's rate increases further, as a consequence of economic growth in the service sector where women are employed in the greatest numbers. However, a note of caution here in the interpretation of the economic activity rates of men and women. The 'economic activity rate' is measured by a headcount of those participating in the formal economy. Hakim (1993) alerts us to one of the pitfalls of this approach, arguing that it has become a misleading measurement of men's and women's participation since it fails to distinguish between those in full-time and those in part-time employment. If the measure of work hours is used, men still dominate the workforce, accounting for 67 per cent of all work hours, whilst women account for the remaining 33 per cent (Hakim, 1993).

In fact, the expansion of women's employment has mainly been in part-time jobs and this trend is expected to continue (Crompton, 1994). Indeed, there was a slight decrease in the proportion of women working full time in the twenty-year period between 1971, when 42 per cent of women did so, and 1991, when the figure was 41 per cent (Webb, 1994). This can by accounted for partly by the demand-side factors we are discussing here, in that the expanded service industry has created mainly part-time jobs and most of these are filled by women. Eighty-one per cent of all people of working age who work part time are women (Sly, Thair and Risdon, 1998). The growth in part-time work has been most concentrated among women with dependent children (Webb, 1994), underscoring the point made below that women's labour market participation is closely bound up with their childcare role (Lim, 1996). Since the majority of women still leave the workforce for a period after the birth of their first child (McRae, 1993), part-time work is an option often taken up by women returners (Crompton, 1994).

## Supply-side explanations

Supply-side factors are also important in shaping women's labour market participation. Coupled with economic restructuring, some economists argue (Joshi, Layard and Owen, 1985) that the dramatic fall during the postwar period in the prices of domestic, labour-saving appliances has reduced the time women spend on housework and released them to take on paid employment outside the home. However, there are other important factors, which centre on women's role within the family. Women's employment patterns are closely bound up with their childcare role and linked to the availability of affordable childcare. In 1995 only 36 per cent of employed, working-age women had children under the age of sixteen (Sly, 1996) and the majority of those worked part time (61 per cent, EOR, 1998a), compared with less than one-third of women without dependent children (Sly, 1996).

Some economists explain this trend by arguing that women prefer to prioritize their childcare and domestic roles, therefore they prefer to return to work when children are older and no longer dependent and/or they prefer to work part time so that they can juggle their multiple roles more easily. Whereas, writers in the sociological tradition tend to highlight the lack of affordable childcare in the UK, together with the powerful influence of gender socialization, which continues to accord women the primary responsibility for the family. Wherever the explanation lies, social trends shaping the composition of the family are important determinants of women's labour market participation (see Figure 2.2). For example, the general trend towards smaller families means that women spend a smaller proportion of their lives caring for children. In their study Joshi, Layard and Owen (1985) found that each child reduces the years a mother works by almost three, so that women who have two children work about six years less than childless women.

**Figure 2.2**
Economic activity rates by highest qualification and age of youngest dependent child
*Source*: Labour Force Survey, Office for National Statistics. Reproduced with the permission of the Office for National Statistics, Crown copyright.

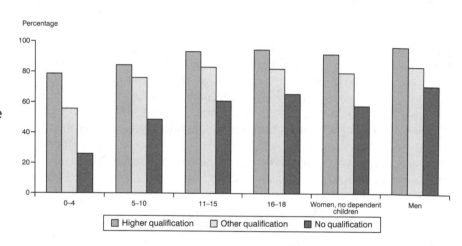

Also, marriage rates have fallen and divorce rates have risen, with the consequence of an increase in lone-parent families, the majority of which are headed by women. It might be expected that changes such as these in personal circumstances would propel women into paid employment out of financial need. However, the economic activity rate of lone mothers was 51 per cent in 1996, compared to 70 per cent for mothers in couples (EOC, 1997b). In addition, lone mothers' participation in *full-time* employment is particularly low (JRF, 1996). Thus, the evidence suggests that the rise in women's paid employment is concentrated within households in which there is a couple living in partnership (Elias and Hogarth, 1994). Although there may be a strong financial need for paid work among lone mothers, their lack of labour market participation can be assumed to be related to the constraints of caring single-handedly for young children. These constraints prevent lone mothers from competing for jobs on an equal basis with childless women and women living with a partner (Elias and Hogarth, 1994)

Family responsibilities affect women's labour market participation in another significant way. Brannen and Moss's (1991) in-depth study of 'dual earner households' after maternity leave found that women were at risk of 'downward occupational mobility': that is, they typically return to lower paid, lower status jobs. This trend particularly affects women who leave the labour market for a period after childbirth and return later to new jobs and to a lesser extent those who resign after returning from maternity leave and then take new jobs (Brannen and Moss, 1991: 57). In other words, women who remain with the same employer after childbirth and maternity leave tend to retain their previous status. This factor may affect the choices women make about returning to work: for example, in the absence of financial need some women may prefer not to engage in paid employment rather than take a lower status and possibly less satisfying job.

The rise in women's educational levels is also a significant factor in the growth of women's participation in the labour market. The percentage of women without qualifications has fallen from 46 per cent in 1984 to 22 per cent in 1997 (EOR, 1998a). Jacobsen (1994) argues that education turns unskilled labour into skilled labour, the corollary of which is that highly educated, skilled women can demand higher wages, which makes it more profitable to enter and stay in the labour market, the cost of childcare notwithstanding. This is borne out by the available evidence. Women qualified above A level have the highest economic activity rates – as shown in Figure 2.2. Eighty-six per cent of this group is in paid employment compared to 52 per cent of women not qualified to this level (EOR, 1998a). This is a pattern particularly marked among those with children under five: of this group, 77 per cent of highly qualified women are in paid employment, compared with 26 per cent of women without higher level qualifications (EOR, 1998a). This underscores the point made above that when work is more extrinsically and intrinsically satisfying, the motivation to continue throughout the child-rearing years is likely to be stronger. Highly qualified women are also in greater demand: there are more jobs available to this group than to lower skilled women. This is because another feature of economic restructuring has been the growth in white-collar, non-manual and highly skilled jobs (EOC, 1997a; EOR, 1998a; Wilson, 1994). Thus, demand-side factors interact with supply-side factors to create a dynamic in which women's labour market participation is both enabled and constrained. Structural changes, particularly the growth of part-time work, have resulted in women making quantitative gains in the labour market: that is, they have taken a disproportionate share of the total growth in employment, but qualitative gains have been restricted.

---

**Key learning points**

1 One of the significant and dominant features of the contemporary UK labour market is women's increased participation. This increase can be attributed to a complex combination of economic and social causes. These include the shift from an industrial to a service economy, compositional changes in the family, the rise in women's qualification levels and the availability of part-time work.
2 Women are heavily concentrated in a narrow range of occupations. Occupational sex segregation operates along both a horizontal and a vertical dimension, such that women are under-represented among managers and professionals.
3 On average, women earn less than men. The gender pay gap is particularly wide between women in part-time work and men in full-time work.

## Activity 2.1: Superwoman's coming home – to the family

The ink on her resignation letter had barely dried before the carping began. Yet another leading businesswoman was leaving her job to concentrate on being a mother. The death knell of the superwoman was sounded.

This time it was Brenda Barnes, one of America's most powerful women executives, who announced she was standing down from her $2 million (£1.25 million) a year job as president and chief executive of Pepsi-Cola's North American operation to spend more time with her husband and three sons.

The interminable 'Can women have it all?' debate reared its head again. Undoubtedly, such high-profile resignations highlight the dilemmas all parents – particularly women – face in combining work and children. But, as Anna Coote, deputy director of the Institute for Public Policy Research, points out, Brenda Barnes and the other so-called superwomen are far from typical and cannot be used to draw any conclusions about women and work.

*Source*: *Guardian*, 26 September 1997.

*Questions*

Consider the statement, made by Anna Coote, that 'so-called superwomen are far from typical and cannot be used to draw any conclusions about women and work'.

1 To what extent is this true?
2 What evidence is there in support of this statement?

# Minority ethnic employment patterns and trends

## Defining race and ethnicity

The defining of different racial and ethnic groups is a complex and controversial area. The somewhat confusing terminology used in the different data and literature sources underscores this. Different sources employ different classifications and this can make comparisons between them problematic. For example the category 'black' can include people of Caribbean, African and Asian origins, whilst on other occasions separate categories of Black Caribbean, Black African and Asian are used. Brown (1992: 46) reminds us that 'there has been a substantial black presence in the British labour market for over thirty-five years, so it is inappropriate to discuss today's scene in terms of "immigrants" and "newcomers"'. This view is reflected in the various classifications used in the available sources. This chapter uses the original definitions employed by the data and literature sources cited to ensure that the data is not skewed by reclassification. For convenience, the term 'minority ethnic groups' is used here and encompasses people who cannot be described as white.

## Historical background

Brown argues that 'we can only understand the present position and experience of minority workers if we remember that only one generation ago most blacks and Asians in Britain were immigrants, and if we know the causes of and conditions of their migration' (Brown, 1992: 46). This section draws on Brown's account of migration to Britain and the original patterns of employment among immigrant workers. Most of the jobs available to immigrant workers in the 1950s and 1960s were in public service employment, with lower wage levels than private industry, and in industrial jobs with long hours, shift work and poor conditions. Anthias and Yuval-Davis (1992) argue that these were jobs that the indigenous population did not want. In the early phase of postwar immigration men typically arrived in the UK without their wives and other female relatives. This was especially true of Pakistani men (Brah, 1994), which had a subsequent impact on the job opportunities available to Pakistani women. They arrived in the UK later than men and other Asian women in the late 1960s and early 1970s, when the economic context had altered. Ethnic differences in women's employment are further explored below.

Statistics from 1966 show that immigrant workers were concentrated in certain sectors of the economy: manufacturing, transport and communications. This early recruitment pattern laid the foundations for subsequent employment segregation by race. By the mid-1970s one of the most significant features of black and Asian employment was their low representation in white-collar work and continuing high concentration in manual work (Brown, 1992: 52). This trend was partly determined by immigrants' earlier patterns of geographical settlement and the industrial differences between the regions. However, the minority ethnic workforce also occupied inferior positions within the regions and industries where they were concentrated, suggesting that employer discrimination also played a role. For example, in the mid-1970s, 24 per cent of minority ethnic men in the South-East had non-manual jobs compared with 47 per cent of white men (Brown, 1992: 53). Historically, minority ethnic workers have also been disproportionately affected by unemployment as shown by Brown's (1992: 54) charting of the period 1963–80, partly because of their concentration in the industries most affected by the economic restructuring and by the recessions of the period. Employer discrimination also interacted with structural and economic forces to place minority ethnic groups in inferior and vulnerable labour market positions. It is important to remember that race discrimination was not unlawful until 1968 and that employers did until this time openly discriminate (Brown, 1992).

## Contemporary minority ethnic employment trends and patterns

In the UK, minority ethnic groups have lower economic activity rates than white people (as shown by Table 2.1) and minority ethnic groups of both sexes continue to experience higher rates of unemployment than the white population (Brown, 1992; DfEE, 1997; EOC, 1997b; TUC, 1996). Thus, minority ethnic groups remain disadvantaged in the labour market.

In 1996 the rate of unemployment for the minority ethnic population (16 per cent) was more than twice that for the white population (8 per cent) (TUC, 1996). There are also differences within and among minority ethnic groups. Generally, women of all ethnic origins experience lower rates of unemployment than men. This is partly a consequence of economic restructuring – the growth of service sector and part-time jobs.

The gap between white and minority ethnic job levels is still large, particularly if levels of unemployment and pay are taken into account. Black and Asian workers are still disproportionately found among semi-skilled and unskilled manual workers (Brown, 1992). In 1996, 51 per cent of the white population worked in non-manual jobs compared with 42 per cent of minority ethnic groups. This gap both narrows and widens according to the particular minority ethnic group. For example, in 1996 about 51 per cent of the Indian population were in non-manual jobs (the same proportion as white employees) compared with 43 per cent of the Pakistani/Bangladeshi population (DfEE, 1997). The gap is almost closed in management and the professions: the proportion of black employees who work in managerial and professional jobs is 33 per cent compared with 34 per cent of white employees. This suggests that, like women's employment patterns, minority ethnic people's employment patterns may be polarized between the highly qualified, where there is little objective difference between their own and the white majority group's pattern, and the low qualified, where the differences are quite marked. However, it is important to note that jobs within any occupational classification may be located within low-paying sectors and industries, and this works to the detriment of the labour market position of minority ethnic employees. Pay is discussed below.

**Table 2.1** Economic activity rates 1985 and 1996

|  | 1985 | | 1996 | |
|  | Women % | Men % | Women % | Men % |
| --- | --- | --- | --- | --- |
| White | 68 | 89 | 72 | 85 |
| Black | 70 | 84 | 69 | 78 |
| Indian | 53 | 84 | 60 | 80 |
| Pakistani/Bangladeshi | 16 | 79 | 19 | 71 |
| Chinese | 60 | 73 | 56 | 62 |

*Source*: Labour Force Surveys 1985 and 1996, Office for National Statistics.

Brown (1992) argues that, although entry to management and the professions has been gained by many minority ethnic workers, once there, progress within these categories has been limited. Their high-level work experience or qualifications does not, therefore, fully insulate them against the effects of employer discrimination. For example, a National Health Service report (EOR, 1996) found that black nurses were less likely than white staff with similar personal profiles to be in the higher grades. A Commission for Racial Equality (CRE) report on the graduate labour market found that minority ethnic groups made more job applications, but received fewer job offers (Brennan and McGeevor, 1990). The same study also found evidence suggesting that fewer Black Caribbean graduates were in jobs that had long-term career prospects.

## English language, education and qualifications

A large proportion of Asian migrants had very limited English language skills at the time of migration: they acquired facility in English as they became settled in Britain. Today, fluency in English is associated with age, gender and length of residence, but age on arrival in Britain and gender are the most critical factors determining fluency in English (Modood et al., 1997). More than three-quarters of Asian men speak English fluently or fairly well, but for women the picture is not uniform. There is little gender difference among African Asians and the Chinese, but fewer Indian women than men and considerably fewer Pakistani and Bangladeshi women speak English well (Modood et al., 1997). Fluency in English will undoubtedly have an impact upon the job opportunities of minority ethnic people, but from the available evidence the conclusion can be drawn that, since the vast majority of minority ethnic people now have such fluency, there is little difference in this respect between them and the indigenous population. In other words, poor labour market prospects can be explained by lack of fluency in English in only a small proportion of cases.

Among those aged sixteen to fifty-nine, taken together, minority ethnic people are similarly qualified to the white population. However, this pattern conceals considerable diversity among and between minority ethnic groups. The Chinese, African Asians and Indians are the most well qualified minority ethnic groups, and the least likely among minority ethnic women to be unemployed, with Caribbeans and Pakistanis being less qualified and Bangladeshis the least so (Modood et al., 1997). Looking further at women, Caribbean women are more likely to have qualifications at O level or higher, but are less likely to have a degree than white women: 3 per cent of Caribbean women have a degree, compared with 8 per cent of white (Modood et al., 1997). The groups of women least likely to have qualifications are Bangladeshi and Pakistani women, of whom 73 per cent and 60 per cent, respectively, are without qualifications. Among women this is also the group most likely to be unemployed (28 per cent).

When different age cohorts are examined, change in overall qualification levels of minority ethnic groups can be observed. Progress has been made in most groups by the second generation (those aged twenty-five to forty-four years who were born in Britain or migrated as children). This is especially the case for Caribbean men, with Bangladeshis remaining the exception. In terms of the new generation (those aged sixteen to twenty-four years), far fewer are without qualifications. Minority ethnic women in this age group have made particular progress (Modood et al., 1997). Improvements in qualification levels among minority ethnic groups suggest that in the future patterns of employment and unemployment will also change, since level of education and qualifications are linked to opportunities, prospects and attainment in employment, especially within the context of a service economy.

## Minority ethnic trends in pay

Minority ethnic full-time employees earn on average 5 per cent less than white full-time employees (TUC, 1996). Pakistani/Bangladeshi men have lower average earnings than men from all other ethnic groups (EOC, 1996). They earned 28 per cent less than did white employees in 1995 (TUC, 1996). Some of the black–white earnings disparity can be accounted for by differences in occupational and age structures, levels of unemployment, qualification levels and geographical residence (EOC, 1996). However, these factors do not offer a full explanation (TUC, 1996), especially since there is significant diversity between minority ethnic groups. For example, the Pakistani/Bangladeshi population is significantly less well qualified than the white population and also significantly less well paid, whilst the black (Caribbean, African) population is more highly qualified than the white, yet more poorly paid. Interestingly, comparing black and white full-time employees, earnings differentials are greatest at the top of the earnings distribution amongst better-paid workers (TUC, 1996): black managers and professionals earn significantly less than do white. Thus, although, as shown earlier, black people have made progress in the higher echelons of occupational and organizational hierarchies, they are differentially and deleteriously rewarded. The conclusion to be drawn is that institutional racism is embedded in the fabric of UK society and that it plays itself out in the dynamics of the labour market.

## Ethnic differences in women's employment

In a previous section we examined overall patterns in women's employment. There are, however, significant ethnic differences in women's employment, which aggregate data do not expose. Differences exist when comparing minority ethnic women with white women, and diversity *among* minority ethnic women also exists. As shown earlier, the economic activity rate for women and men in most minority ethnic groups is lower than that for the white population (EOC, 1997a; see Table 2.1). In other words, minority ethnic women are more likely than white women to experience unemployment. However, the gap in job levels between black and white women is narrower than that between black and white men (Phizacklea, 1994).

When we compare white women with minority ethnic women, part-time work is one area where we can uncover significant ethnic differences in women's employment patterns. Holdsworth and Dale's (1997: 436) research finds that levels of part-time working are consistently higher among white women than other ethnic groups. They therefore describe what is commonly thought of as the 'British' pattern of women's employment as a 'white' pattern, which cannot be generalized to other ethnic groups. Levels of full-time working among minority ethnic women (with the exception of Pakistani and Bangladeshi women) with young children and a partner are much higher than among white women (Holdsworth and Dale, 1997). Holdsworth and Dale (1997: 437) seek to explain this by examining social and economic factors which 'mediate culturally ascribed gender roles'. The economic imperatives can be summarized as financial need. In the case of Black Caribbean women, their high rate of full-time employment may be partly explained by the greater likelihood of their being the sole breadwinner for the family (Anthias and Yuval-Davis, 1992). In addition, the concentration in low-paid employment of both men and women from minority ethnic groups ensures that women's wages are an important source of income for the family, perhaps more so than in many white households. However, Holdsworth and Dale note that Pakistani and Bangladeshi women have the lowest levels of economic activity despite their concentration in low-income households. A note of caution here as homeworking is commonplace among these two groups of women, but official figures of economic activity may not reveal this.

Another area of economic activity not revealed by official data is unpaid participation in a family business, which women from some minority ethnic groups have a tendency towards (Anthias and Yuval-Davis, 1992). Again, this practice can skew the data on minority ethnic women's labour market participation.

It is interesting to note that UK-born Pakistani and Bangladeshi women aged under thirty-five, with no children and no partner, are almost as likely as all other ethnic groups to be economically active. This underscores once again the significance of the presence of children in determining women's labour market participation but, as shown above, the presence of children does not have a uniform impact on all women. This also alerts us to the importance of avoiding crude, stereotypical explanations, which are insensitive to intergenerational social changes. In other words, later generations of minority ethnic women exhibit labour market behaviour much more like their white counterparts than their older female relatives (Anthias and Yuval-Davis, 1992). When compared with white women, minority ethnic women's employment is polarized between those in full-time work and those not in paid work (Bruegel, 1994). Those minority ethnic women in paid work are marginally more highly qualified than white women. As stated earlier, level of qualification is an important determinant of women's continued full-time employment during the early child-rearing years. Nevertheless, proportionately fewer black women than white are employed in management and the professions (EOC, 1997a). Asian women are overrepresented in low-paid, semi-skilled and unskilled work in the manufacturing sector, unlike white women who are concentrated in the service industries (Brah, 1994).

## Key learning points

1 Minority ethnic employment patterns have been shaped by early employer recruitment strategies and by patterns of geographical settlement among the immigrant workers of the 1950s and 1960s, which combined to result in the concentration of minority ethnic employees in certain industries and occupations.

2 All minority ethnic groups of both sexes experience higher rates of unemployment than the white population. These disparities cannot be explained simply by qualification levels, age profiles and geographical residence.

3 There is now more employment and occupational diversity than ever before among the minority ethnic population of the UK. Nevertheless, the overall gap between white and minority ethnic job levels is still large.

4 Women do not constitute a unitary category of employees. Ethnic differences in women's employment patterns were outlined. Particularly notable among these was the tendency for minority ethnic women to work full-time, compared to a high part-time rate among white women. Again, economic circumstances and social phenomena interact to determine such differences among women.

## Activity

### Activity 2.2: Broadcasters 'are failing to promote ethnic minorities'

Britain's leading broadcasters are increasingly failing to employ staff from ethnic minority backgrounds, says a report published in October 1998. The situation is described as 'a national disgrace'.

The study shows that broadcasters such as the British Broadcasting Corporation (BBC) and the Independent Television (ITV) network have failed to promote minorities. Independent Television managed to employ an extra twenty-six black workers last year, but the proportion employed in nine regional franchises fell. Only at the BBC's World Service was there change; ethnic minority employees doubled in 1997.

Co-ordinated by the European Institute for the Media, in Dusseldorf, the study, 'More colour in the media', looks mainly at freelancers and the BBC, Channel 4 and ITV. It shows minorities have been denied an equal chance to gain a foothold. The report found that at the BBC in London the number of people from minorities employed by the corporation fell last year from 7.5 per cent to 7.4 per cent. Independent Television has an even worse record. Of 8033 staff employed by the network companies and Channel 4 in 1996, only 3.7 per cent were from ethnic minority backgrounds. And only a hundred of them were employed in programme departments.

*Source*: *Guardian*, 6 October 1998

*Questions*

1 To what extent does the position of minority ethnic groups in broadcasting mirror their overall labour market position?

2 How can the study's findings be accounted for?

3 Consider the role of the media in promoting equality at work.

# Patterns and trends in disabled people's employment

## Defining disability

The definition and classification of types of disability is a complex and controversial area (Honey, Meager and Williams, 1993). The data on disabled people's labour market participation vary according to the definition of 'disability' adopted. Some surveys use a broad definition, which includes 'limiting health problems' caused perhaps by long-term illness; whilst others use a narrower definition, which tends to exclude this category. For example, the Department for Education and Employment (DfEE) definition (figures cited below) includes those with 'limiting health problems', with the consequence that the disabled population of working age is larger than that of other surveys (e.g. Office of Population Censuses and Surveys – OPCS) and that the unemployment rate of disabled people is lower. That is, people with limiting health problems are more likely to be in employment than are those with more severe disabilities.

Nevertheless, the different sources accord with the view that disabled people are disadvantaged in the labour market. According to government research, only 75 per cent of respondents representing employers in both the public and private sectors said that they would not discriminate against disabled people. Thirteen per cent said that they would only employ disabled people for certain types of jobs, and 6 per cent said they would not employ disabled people under any circumstances (Barnes, 1992). The same research found that employers provide broadly paternalistic justifications and rationalizations of their discriminatory practices, namely the unsuitability for disabled people of jobs in their firm, the unsuitability of premises, access problems and shift work. The lack of disabled applicants was also a popular explanation for the absence of disabled employees, one which might provide a partial, but not full, explanation given the hostile environment that disabled people encounter within workplaces (Barnes, 1992).

## Research data

A review of research and development initiatives aimed at promoting disabled people's employment found that there remain many gaps in knowledge (Barnes et al., 1998). In particular, despite surveys on disability and employment there is still an unmet need for facts and figures to fully illuminate the labour market activity of disabled people. Thus the attitudes of non-disabled people as employers and colleagues are identified as a priority area for research. Such research would help shed light on some of the barriers encountered by disabled people seeking to find and retain employment. Hyde (1996: 686) holds that 'equality and integration can only be effectively promoted if disabled people have access to adequately remunerated employment', in the absence of which poverty and social exclusion are likely to be experienced.

## Employment and unemployment levels among disabled people

Labour Force Survey data show that disabled people's level of unemployment is almost three times higher than that of non-disabled (DfEE, 1997). Of the 1.6 million economically active people of working age described as disabled in 1996, 21.2 per cent were unemployed, compared with only 7.6 per cent of non-disabled people. High levels of unemployment prevent disabled people from taking a full part in mainstream society and from achieving a reasonable standard of living.

The category 'economically active' excludes disabled people who are neither in employment nor registered as unemployed. It excludes, therefore, those capable of and willing to work, who in anticipation of employer discrimination prefer the alternative of long-term social security benefits (Hyde, 1996). Smith (1992) refers to this group of disabled people as 'discouraged workers': people who experience the labour market as hostile; those who are aware of the obstacles facing them in their search for employment and of the type of low-level jobs they are likely to be assigned to, when they do find employment (Barnes, 1992). The size of this group is unknown (DfEE, 1997). Thus, although economic activity rates are related to disability (that is, disabled people of all ages are less likely to be active than non-disabled) we cannot assume that all those disabled people who are classified as inactive are neither able nor willing to work (Thornton and Lunt, 1995). Indeed, evidence from one national study found that 85 per cent of disabled men and 65 per cent of disabled women who described themselves as unable to work, had tried to find employment, but had given up (Barnes, 1992).

Table 2.2 shows a distinctive age effect on the economic activity rate of disabled people. Younger disabled people in the age group twenty to twenty-four have the highest rate, whilst for non-disabled people the

**Table 2.2** Activity rates for people with and without disabilities

| Age group | People without disabilities % | People with disabilities % |
|-----------|-------------------------------|----------------------------|
| 16–19 | 63.0 | 53.8 |
| 20–24 | 79.2 | 56.6 |
| 25–34 | 84.9 | 53.0 |
| 35–49 | 89.5 | 46.8 |
| 50–59 | 80.7 | 27.8 |
| 16–59 | 83.0 | 40.0 |

*Source*: Labour Force Survey 1996, Office for National Statistics.

highest rate is in the thirty-five to forty-nine age group. The reasons for this are unclear, but may include the greater likelihood of younger, non-disabled people being in full-time education. People with disabilities tend to have lower levels of education and qualification than the average (Honey, Meager and Williams, 1993), suggesting that discrimination against disabled people is embedded in social institutions, including the education system. There is also a discernible gender effect: economic activity rates are lower for disabled women (35 per cent) than for disabled men (44 per cent). This mirrors the situation among non-disabled people, although the activity rates of both non-disabled men and women are higher.

# Occupations and industries

Disabled people are over-represented in low-skilled, low-status jobs (DfEE, 1997). Only 12 per cent are in professional or managerial positions compared with 21 per cent of non-disabled employees, whilst 31 per cent are in low-skilled manual jobs, compared with 21 per cent of non-disabled employees (RADAR, 1993). This may be related to the older age profile of the manual workforce (DfEE, 1997) and the greater incidence of disability among older people. Disabled women tend to be found in routine clerical work, cleaning and catering (Barnes, 1992). Generally, disabled people are more likely to work part time or be self-employed (Barnes et al., 1998). It is not entirely clear whether this is because of the limiting nature of the disability itself or from choice, or because they are excluded from a broader range of work opportunities. For example, Barnes posits that in certain circumstances when 'good appearance' is deemed an important attribute for the job, disabled people may be disadvantaged by the emphasis, 'placed by many male employers on physical desirability and attractiveness. Some employers in the service sector feel that the sight of a disabled woman disturbs clients' (Barnes, 1992: 66).

Moving from the occupational to the industrial distribution of disabled workers, some clear patterns can be identified. First, the likelihood of an organization employing disabled people appears to increase with size. Honey, Meager and Williams's extensive survey (using a broad definition of disability including limiting health problems) found that although only 15 per cent of organizations with ten employees or less employed people with disabilities, all organizations with over 500 employees did so (Honey, Meager and Williams, 1993: 17). The incidence of the employment of disabled people also varied according to sector with the manufacturing industry most likely to employ disabled people and the financial and 'other services' sectors least likely. The full picture is shown in Table 2.3.

The sectoral effect may be a simple reflection of the larger size of organizations in the manufacturing industry: size was found to be by far the most significant influence on whether or not an organization employs disabled people (Honey, Meager and Williams, 1993: 18). This could be related to higher staff turnover in larger organizations and greater financial resources to make any necessary access arrangements. Another factor,

**Table 2.3** Employment of people with disabilities, by size and sector (percentage)

|  | Yes | No | Do not know | N = |
|---|---|---|---|---|
| **Total** | **56.7** | **41.5** | **1.8** | **1116** |
| *Sector* | | | | |
| Energy/water supply | 88.9 | 11.1 | 0.0 | 27 |
| Metals/minerals | 74.4 | 25.6 | 0.0 | 78 |
| Engineering | 64.9 | 32.7 | 2.4 | 211 |
| Other manufacturing | 70.8 | 27.8 | 1.4 | 72 |
| Construction | 43.8 | 56.2 | 0.0 | 73 |
| Distribution/hotels | 52.8 | 45.0 | 2.2 | 180 |
| Transport/communication | 40.4 | 55.3 | 4.4 | 114 |
| Financial and business services | 53.7 | 44.8 | 1.5 | 201 |
| Other services | 51.3 | 48.1 | 0.6 | 160 |
| *Number of employees* | | | | |
| 1–10 | 14.7 | 83.4 | 1.9 | 211 |
| 11–49 | 30.4 | 66.7 | 2.9 | 207 |
| 50–199 | 59.0 | 40.5 | 0.5 | 222 |
| 200–499 | 76.5 | 20.9 | 2.7 | 187 |
| 500–4999 | 95.6 | 3.1 | 1.3 | 159 |
| 5000+ | 100.0 | 0.0 | 0.0 | 92 |

*Source*: Honey, Meager and Williams (1993).

which influenced the propensity of organizations to employ disabled people, was the existence of a policy on disability and employment: equal opportunity policies are associated with larger employers.

In terms of disabled employees' share of organizational workforces, Honey, Meager and Williams's survey paints a bleak picture. Employees with disabilities comprised less than 3 per cent of the workforce in more than half of the organizations surveyed. This is in contrast to disabled people's 13 per cent share of the working-age population (Honey, Meager and Williams, 1993: 141). There is also evidence that disabled workers earn considerably less than non-disabled workers. On average, disabled men in full-time employment earn almost a quarter less per week than their non-disabled peers (Barnes, 1992), demonstrating that disabled people's over-representation in part-time work does not account for the earnings disparity between them and non-disabled people.

## Key learning points

1 When examining the economic activity rate of disabled people, it is important to remember that this classification excludes those neither in employment nor registered as unemployed. A group of disabled people of an unknown size is willing and able to work, but is discouraged from doing so by a hostile labour market.

2 The economic activity rate of disabled people is related to age and gender, but the effects of these demographic variables are different when compared with their effects on non-disabled people's rate.

3 Disabled people are far more likely to experience unemployment than are non-disabled people. Disabled workers are concentrated in low-skilled, low-status jobs and they are also more likely to work part time or be self-employed.
4 Size appears to be the most significant influence on whether or not an organization employs disabled people.

## Activity

### Activity 2.3: Personal advisers to help disabled find jobs

From this week, disabled people looking for work can get extra help in finding jobs. In six pilot schemes, every local disabled person on incapacity benefits will receive dedicated help. The Personal Adviser service for disabled people will provide personal advice and support with training, jobs and access to funds which can help with any adaptation necessary to support an individual at work. The first six schemes, run by the Employment Service, opened for business this week, with a budget of £5 million. More than a quarter of a million people on incapacity benefits will gain from the schemes when all 12 are running.

*Source*: *Guardian*, 3 October 1998.

*Questions*

1 Consider the possible barriers and limitations to the success of the Personal Adviser Scheme in terms of assisting disabled people in finding work.

2 How might 'success' be measured from the perspectives of the government and of disabled people?

# Older people and labour market participation

## Ageism

Ageism is sometimes described as the fourth main form of discrimination (EOR, 1998a). Employer attitudes, rooted in stereotypes of and myths about older people, represent the main barriers to the employment of older people. According to the DfEE (1997) more than a quarter of employers consider people too old to recruit at the age of fifty, whilst 60 per cent consider people too old at age sixty (Taylor and Walker, 1994). Further, there is some evidence that for black workers employer ageism could begin as young as age forty. Ageism also has a gendered dimension in that youth is frequently an implicit, if not explicit, prerequisite for many of the jobs dominated by women: for example, secretary, receptionist or airline attendant. Nevertheless, young workers between the ages of sixteen and twenty-one may also encounter discriminatory practice in the labour market. However, the causes of such discrimination relate more to lack of qualifications and experience, rather than to age *per se*.

According to recent survey evidence (EOR, 1998b) only around 10 per cent of job adverts use numerical age limits compared with 35 per cent five years ago. This reduction in overt discrimination has occurred against a background of government campaigns against ageism and the subsequent voluntary restraint among some employers and parts of the advertising and recruitment industries. For example, the Institute of Personnel Development (IPD) no longer accepts job advertisements containing age limits. Nevertheless, thinly veiled messages about the desired age groups continue to litter recruitment advertisements, arguably deterring older people from applying for jobs for which they possess the requisite experience, skills and qualifications (Taylor and Walker, 1994). A 1996 survey found that 80 per cent of people aged over fifty believed they had been refused a job because of their age (EOR, 1998b). The age of fifty appears to be a turning point in people's work histories (McKay, 1998), therefore those over fifty are described here as older workers.

## Older people and unemployment

Older people are less likely to be unemployed than the very young (DfEE, 1997), but the corollary of employer discrimination against older people is that they find it more difficult to return to employment (McKay, 1998) once out of the labour force. In spring 1996 over half of unemployed people between the age of fifty and the state retirement age had been without work for more than a year, compared with a quarter of the sixteen to twenty-four age group and just under 40 per cent of the unemployed population as a whole (DfEE, 1997).

There is also a marked race effect: the unemployment rate of black people over forty (the Trade Union Congress's – TUC's– definition of the older worker) is nearly twice the rate of their white counterparts (Labour Research, 1998). The intersection of race and age can create what is sometimes described as the 'double bias' or 'double discrimination' faced by older black workers. Further, when we compare the employment rates of older black women with older white women, there also appears to be a gender effect: 56 per cent of older black women have jobs, compared with 72 per cent of older white women (Labour Research, 1998). Is this evidence of 'triple discrimination' in operation in the labour market? It can also be argued that as well as facing discrimination on more than one 'count', the nature of the discrimination encountered by older black workers is qualitatively different from that met by older white workers.

## Older people's employment patterns

The majority of men aged over fifty work full-time (64 per cent) whilst the majority of women in this age group work part time (72 per cent): therefore, we can see that women's propensity to work part time persists over the life course. This may be attributable to personal preferences or to

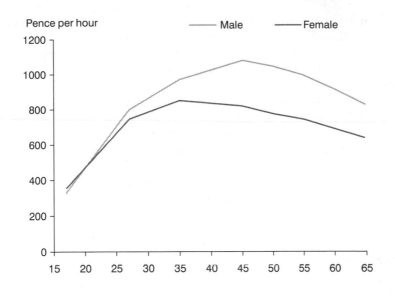

**Figure 2.3**
Hourly earnings by age
*Source*: New Earnings Survey 1996, Volume A. Reproduced with the permission of the Office for National Statistics, Crown copyright.

structural obstacles to full-time employment. The older men are, the more likely they are to be working in clerical jobs and in jobs classified as 'other occupations' such as labourers, porters, road-sweepers and shelf-fillers. Women in this age group are more likely to be employed in 'other occupations' such as cleaning and selling (McKay, 1998). Thus, men and women continue to be concentrated in different types of jobs for the duration of the lifecycle, although both older men and women are generally located in lower-level work. Age discrimination, then, operates against both sexes. It is also worth noting that the gender pay gap widens after the age of thirty and is particularly marked between the ages of forty-five and fifty-five (see Figure 2.3) (EOC, 1996). It is possible to postulate that women never recover the earning potential they lose earlier in their working lives when they tend to opt to work in low-level part-time employment.

## Training and education

Older people are typically less well qualified than younger people, partly due to changes in the training and education system over time (DfEE, 1997). For example, the provision of further and higher education has expanded rapidly and, consequently, younger people are likely to be more highly qualified than are older people. There is also evidence that older people generally receive less training from their employers than do younger people (DfEE, 1997; McKay, 1998). This is thought to be because of employers' negative attitudes towards older people, including the view that they are less trainable, less interested in developing their careers and suitable only for low-skill, low-responsibility jobs (Taylor and Walker, 1994). Thus, older people's lack of formal (academic or vocational) qualifications, and the consequent restricted employment opportunities, is further compounded by employers' reluctance to train them to adjust to the skill demands of a restructured labour market. Taylor and Walker's study found that 13 per cent of employers did not train management past the age of fifty, while 17 per cent did not train other staff past the age of sixty (Taylor and Walker, 1994: 577). This was despite the fact that employees in this age group still have another fifteen years before state retirement age. It is important to note that this employer reluctance to invest in older people in terms of recruitment and training is set against a background of labour and skills shortages in some sectors and occupations.

Employers' preferred strategic response to this problem may be to recruit young, female or migrant labour rather than older people. This is borne out by the findings of Taylor and Walker's study, which found that the employment of greater numbers of older people was not a priority for most employers. Nevertheless, some organizations in the service sector, such as 'do-it-yourself' stores and supermarkets do actively recruit older people, although mostly into part-time employment (Taylor and Walker, 1994).

## Older women's employment

We have seen earlier that women's career trajectories are different from men's in that women's labour market participation is bound up with their childcare role. Yet it is the case that fewer women in their fifties than in their forties are in paid work, contrary to what might be expected, in view of the fact that most women do not have dependent children when they reach their fifties. Women in their fifties are, in theory at least, released from earlier responsibilities constraining their labour market participation. Instead of rising, the proportion of women in employment declines steeply in the fifteen years before reaching state retirement age (Ginn and Arber, 1995). Part of the explanation lies in the fact that older women often assume new domestic responsibilities including caring for grandchildren, elderly relatives or adult children. These responsibilities reduce older women's propensity to be in employment.

Other factors that contribute to older women's reduced employment are low financial and intrinsic rewards, an unemployed husband or a high-earning husband (Ginn and Arber, 1995). Older women without educational qualifications and who have a manual occupational class have lower rates of employment. They are also likely to be low paid and reap fewer intrinsic rewards from work. Older women with husbands in receipt of some state benefits are unlikely to be in work. This is because of means testing and the taking into account of a couple's combined income, creating a disincentive to engage in paid labour. Conversely, older women with high-earning husbands are also unlikely to be in work, perhaps because the financial necessity is reduced (Ginn and Arber, 1995). These factors combine to suggest that varied financial circumstances shape older women's labour market circumstances, but these are likely to intersect with negative employment experiences and employer attitudes, to militate against the likelihood of older women continuing to work.

1 Negative attitudes towards older people's employment exist. This is reflected in employer's reluctance to recruit and train older people and the consequent difficulties older people have in finding employment and continuing to participate in the labour market until state retirement age.
2 Older people, particularly women, are over-represented in low-pay, low-status forms of employment and in self-employment.
3 Older women's labour market participation is shaped by a combination of varied financial circumstances and negative employment experiences.

**Key learning points**

## Activity

### Activity 2.4: Make short work of your career

When the Cabinet meets tomorrow to discuss the manifesto for the general election, it will be a very unrepresentative group.

Few other office meetings these days are largely composed of people in their fifties and sixties. About a third of men between the ages of 50 and 64 are unemployed – more than four times the rate for men as a whole.

Yet the Cabinet is unlikely to act on calls this week by the Carnegie Third Age Programme to 'put age issues high on their manifesto agenda'.

One of Carnegie's main concerns is the way people as young as 40 are being edged out of the labour market. Whereas our fathers often worked for 50 years – from 15 to 65 – our children could work for only 20 or 25 years. Many aspects of the workplace and home life will have to change.

*Source*: *Observer*, 1 January 1987.

*Questions*

1 To what extent are the points made in this article still valid today and should the issue of older people's employment be a concern for government?
2 What are these 'aspects of the workplace and home life' that will have to change?

# Lesbians and gay men in employment

The issues for lesbians and gay men in employment are somewhat different than those for the other groups we have so far considered. First, it is not possible to set out the employment locations and concentrations (if any) of lesbians and gay men, because the main data sources do not ask questions about sexual orientation. Second, sexual orientation can be concealed far more easily than can gender, race, disability or age. Concealment represents a choice for individuals that may be made in order to avoid discrimination. Nevertheless, there are ways in which lesbians and gay men are disadvantaged and discriminated against in employment. Cockburn (1991) holds that gender relations in organizations are both sexualized and heterosexualized. Therefore, to be a lesbian woman or a gay man is to be outside the concomitant organizational culture. Such culture can give rise to indirect and covert forms of discrimination. We explore these themes in greater detail in Chapter 4. For the moment we are concerned with what Cockburn (1991) describes as the tangible employment disadvantages of being lesbian or gay: discrimination in recruitment, promotion and in access to certain employee benefits.

## Discrimination in recruitment and promotion

Women and men who are either openly lesbian or gay commonly experience discrimination by employers based on their sexual orientation (EOR, 1997). This is confirmed by survey evidence (for example, Palmer, 1993; Snape, Thomson and Chetwynd, 1995) which reveals that between 10 and 14 per cent of lesbians and gay men believe they have either been refused a job or denied promotion because of their sexuality. More than a third more suspect this to be the case (Palmer, 1993). These findings are underscored by the widespread belief among heterosexual people that employers treat gay men and lesbians less favourably (Snape, Thomson and Chetwynd, 1995). It is important to note that in anticipation of discrimination and unequal treatment at work many lesbians and gay men may conceal their sexual orientation. One survey (Palmer, 1993) suggests that high earners find it more difficult to be open about their sexuality at work. In another survey (Snape, Thomson and Chetwynd, 1995) respondents believed that it was considered unacceptable to be openly lesbian or gay in certain professional fields such as teaching, the health service and the military.

Individuals who conceal their sexual orientation are less likely to experience the direct forms of discrimination being discussed here. Indeed, concealment may be a deliberate strategy to avoid discrimination, although the perceived need to conceal sexual identity could be considered an indirect form of discrimination or disadvantage in itself. There is evidence of widespread concealment of sexuality among lesbians and gay men. In one survey over half of the lesbian and gay respondents reported that none of their work colleagues knew about their sexuality and only two-fifths said that all their colleagues knew, whilst some people confide in a few trusted colleagues (Snape, Thomson and Chetwynd, 1995). In the same survey over 40 per cent of respondents said that when applying for a job they would behave in such a way as to ensure that the employer did not discover their sexuality (Snape, Thomson and Chetwynd, 1992: 63). The fact of the widespread concealment of sexual orientation suggests that discrimination in employment against lesbians and gay men is a potentially larger problem than the reports of instances of discrimination would lead us to believe. In other words, if lesbians and gay men did not take action to avoid discrimination it is likely that reported cases would be far higher.

## Access to employee benefits

There is another significant way in which lesbians and gay men are disadvantaged in employment: in unequal access to employee benefits such as special leave arrangements, health insurance, pensions, staff discounts and so on. This is because such benefits are often extended to spouses or to opposite-sex partners only. In the case of special leave, this can mean, for example, that time off to care for a sick partner or compassionate leave following the death of a partner may only apply to employees with opposite-sex partners. Employees with same-sex partners may either be denied special leave or may have to use annual leave. This, of course, effectively results in the lower remuneration of lesbians and gay men.

Similarly, the remunerative loss to lesbians and gay men of not having access to certain other employee benefits can be considerable. For example, dependants' benefits from pension schemes usually specify that the widow's or widower's pension can only be paid to a married partner (EOR, 1997). There are exceptions and the TUC has campaigned for same-sex partners to be eligible for such benefits. However, in order to claim any such benefits, lesbians and gay men may need to be prepared to disclose their sexual orientation. To do this, they will need to be confident that this will not have adverse effects on their employment security and prospects. The above survey evidence suggests that this is not currently the case.

**Key learning points**

1 There is evidence to suggest that lesbians and gay men experience discrimination and disadvantage in employment. Those who are open about their sexual orientation risk discrimination at the point of recruitment and in promotion.

2 To avoid discrimination many lesbians and gay men actively seek to conceal their sexuality from employers and colleagues.

3 Lesbians and gay men are also frequently treated unequally in terms of access to certain employee benefits, resulting in a loss to the total remuneration package.

## Activity

### Activity 2.5: Lesbian couple lose test case on perks at work

A lesbian couple lost a test case over access to perks at work yesterday, dealing a severe blow to the campaign for equal rights for gays in the workplace.

The European Court of Justice in Luxembourg ruled that South West Trains did not breach European equality laws in refusing a railway worker, Lisa Grant, travel concessions for her partner.

A victory for Ms Grant would have had major implications for Britain's employment, pensions and social security systems. Ms Grant claimed that company rules at South West Trains limiting the perk of free or reduced travel worth £1000 a year to spouses or opposite-sex partners breached European equal pay laws, which cover perks as well as salary. The judges said the EU had not yet adopted rules treating gay relationships as equal to marriage or stable opposite-sex partnerships.

*Source*: *Guardian*, 2 February 1998

*Questions*

1 What are the 'major implications for Britain's employment' systems referred to in the article?
2 Consider the implications for the employment of lesbians and gay men of the absence of rules 'treating gay relationships as equal to marriage or opposite-sex partnerships'.

# Conclusion

By examining macrolevel data, this chapter has shown that the labour market differentiates between different groups of employees. We can assume this to be on the basis of the characteristics ascribed to or possessed by the different groups. The result for employees is unequal outcomes and opportunities, and from an employer perspective the underutilization of certain segments of the workforce. Claims made by employers to treat everyone the same or as individuals are likely to prove naive or unfounded. The data presented here reveal significant and distinctive employment trends and patterns among disadvantaged social groups. Thus, labour market opportunities are mediated and constrained by gender, race, age, disability and sexual orientation, albeit in qualitatively different ways. By examining labour market trends and patterns along the lines of social group membership, a complex picture emerges, which is ever changing partly in response to wider social and economic changes.

The remaining chapters in Part One explore alternative theoretical and conceptual explanations for, and different interpretations of, labour market trends and patterns, whilst Part Two investigates the strategies and policies of the key industrial relations actors and how they seek to manage equality and diversity.

# Review and discussion questions

1 Why is it that gender can be held to be a constitutive element in the formation of labour markets?
2 Brah (1994) argues that it is crucial 'to conceptualize the labour market as mediated by race, class, gender, ethnicity, age, disability and sexuality'. Consider the evidence that supports this proposition.
3 How can the gender pay gap be explained?
4 'Structural changes in the economy and moves towards more flexible forms of work and its organization have failed to challenge many orthodox notions surrounding work' (Thornton and Lunt, 1995: 3). Consider what this statement means and explore how it relates to the labour market experiences of women, people from minority ethnic groups, disabled people and older people.

# Further reading

Anthias, F. and Yuval-Davis, N. (1992). *Racialised Boundaries*. Routledge.
Examines the issue of race and the labour market. Critically evaluates conceptual and theoretical frameworks as they relate to race.
EOC (1997a). *Briefings on Women and Men in Britain*. Equal Opportunities Commission.
Provides data on women and men in the spheres of employment and education. Produced yearly. Free from the EOC.
Honey, S., Meager, N. and Williams, M. (1993). *Employers' Attitudes towards People with Disabilities*. Institute of Manpower Studies.
Survey findings and literature review on disabled people in employment.
Lindley, R. (1994). *Labour Market Structures and Prospects for Women*. Equal Opportunities Commission.
A collection of articles analysing women's labour market participation from a range of perspectives. Draws out ethnic differences.
Modood, T., Berthoud, R., Lakey, J., Nazroo, J., Smith, P., Virdee, S. and Beishon, S. *Ethnic Minorities in Britain: Diversity and Disadvantage*. Policy Studies Institute.
A comprehensive study of ethnic minorities in Britain, concentrating on disadvantage and discrimination in education, employment and housing.
Snape, D., Thomson, K. and Chetwynd, M. (1995). *Discrimination against Gay Men and Lesbians*. SCPR.
A comprehensive survey of the experiences of lesbians and gay men. Includes the views of heterosexual respondents.

# References

Anker, R. (1997). Theories of occupational segregation by sex: an overview. *International Labour Review*, **136** (7), 315–340.

Anthias, F. and Yuval-Davis, N. (1992). *Racialised Boundaries*. Routledge.

Barnes, C. (1992). Disability and employment. *Personnel Review*, **21** (6), 55–73.

Barnes, H., Thornton, P. and Maynard Campbell, S. (1998). *Disabled People and Employment: A Review of Research and Development Work*. Policy Press.

Brah, A. (1994). South Asian young Muslim women and the labour market. In *The Dynamics of 'Race' and Gender* (H. Afshar and M. Maynard, eds). Taylor Francis.

Brannen, J. and Moss, P. (1991). *Managing Mothers*. Unwin Hyman.

Brennan, J. and McGeevor, P. (1990). *Ethnic Minorities and the Graduate Labour Market*. Commission for Racial Equality.

Brown, C. (1992). 'Same difference': the persistence of racial disadvantage in the British employment market. In *Racism and Antiracism: Inequalities, Opportunities and Policies* (P. Braham, A. Rattansi and R. Skellington, eds). Sage.

Bruegel, I. (1994). Labour market prospects for women from ethnic minorities. In *Labour Market Structures and Prospects for Women* (R. Lindley, ed.). Equal Opportunities Commission.

Cockburn, C. (1991). *In the Way of Women*. Macmillan.

Crompton, R. (1994). *Occupational Trends and Women's Employment Trends*. In *Labour Market Structures and Prospects for Women* (R. Lindley, ed.). Equal Opportunities Commission.

DfEE (Department for Education and Employment) (1997) *Labour Market and Skill Trends 1997/8*. DfEE.

Elias, P. and Hogarth, T. (1994). Families, jobs and unemployment: the changing pattern of economic dependency in Britain. In *Labour Market Structures and Prospects for Women* (R. Lindley, ed.). Equal Opportunities Commission.

EOC (Equal Opportunities Commission) (1996). *Briefings on Women and Men in Britain*. EOC.

EOC (Equal Opportunities Commission) (1997a). *Briefings on Women and Men in Britain*. EOC.

EOC (Equal Opportunities Commission) (1997b). *Facts about Women and Men in Great Britain 1997*. EOC.

EOR (Equal Opportunities Review) (1996). Racial harassment in NHS 'widespread', says report. *Equal Opportunities Review*, (65), January–February, 8–9.

EOR (Equal Opportunities Review) (1997). Equality for lesbians and gay men in the workplace. *Equal Opportunities Review*, (74), July–August, 20–28.

EOR (Equal Opportunities Review) (1998a). Women in the labour market. *Equal Opportunities Review*, (79), May–June, 30–31.

EOR (Equal Opportunities Review) (1998b). Tackling age bias: code or law? *Equal Opportunities Review*, (80), July–August, 32–37.

Ginn, J. and Arber, S. (1995). Exploring mid-life women's employment. *Sociolog,* **29**, (1), 73–94.

Hakim, C. (1993). The myth of rising female employment. *Work, Employment and Society,* **7**, (1), 97–120.

Holdsworth, C. and Dale, A. (1997). Ethnic differences in women's employment. *Work, Employment and Society,* **11**, (3), 435–457.

Honey, S., Meager, N. and Williams, M. (1993). *Employers' Attitudes towards People with Disabilities.* Institute of Manpower Studies.

Hyde, M. (1996). Fifty years of failure: employment services for disabled people in the UK. *Work, Employment and Society,* **10**, (4), 683–700.

Jacobsen, J. (1994). *The Economics of Gender.* Blackwell.

Joshi, H., Layard, R. and Owen, S. (1985). Why are more women working in Britain? In *Gender and Economics* (J. Humphries, ed.). Edward Elgar.

JRF (Joseph Rowntree Foundation) (1996). *Lone Mothers and Work.* Findings, May.

Labour Research (1998). *Black over 40s Hit by Double Bias.* September, Labour Research Department.

Lim, L. (1996). *More and Better Jobs for Women: An Action Guide.* International Labour Office.

McKay, S. (1998). Older workers in the labour market. *Labour Market Trends,* July, 365–369.

McRae, S. (1993). *Maternity Rights in Britain.* Policy Studies Institute.

Millward, N. and Woodland, S. (1995). Gender segregation and male/female wage differences. In *Economics of Equal Opportunities* (J. Humphries and J. Rubery, eds). Equal Opportunities Commission.

Modood, T., Berthoud, R., Lakey, J., Nazroo, J., Smith, P., Virdee, S. and Beishon, S. *Ethnic Minorities in Britain: Diversity and Disadvantage.* Policy Studies Institute.

Palmer, A. (1993). *Less equal than others.* Stonewall.

Phizacklea, A. (1994). *A Single or Segregated Market.* In *The Dynamics of 'Race' and Gender* (H. Afshar and M. Maynard, eds). Taylor Francis.

RADAR (Royal Association for Disability and Rehabilitation) (1993). *Disability and Discrimination in Employment.* RADAR.

Rubery, J. and Fagan, C. (1994). *Occupational Segregation: Plus ca change . . .?* In *Labour Market Structures and Prospects for Women* (R. Lindley, ed.). Equal Opportunities Commission.

Sly, F. (1996). Women in the labour market: results from the spring 1995 Labour Force Surve. *Labour Market Trends,* March, 91–100.

Sly, F., Thair, T. and Risdon, A. (1998). Women in the labour market: results from the Spring 1997 Labour Force Survey. *Labour Market Trends,* March, 97–105.

Smith, S. (1992). *Disabled in the Labour Market.* Employment Policy Institute.

Snape, D., Thomson, K. and Chetwynd, M. (1995). *Discrimination against Gay Men and Lesbians.* SCPR.

Taylor, P. and Walker, A. (1994). The ageing workforce: employers' attitudes towards older people. *Work, Employment and Society,* **8**, (4), 569–591.

Thornton, P. and Lunt, N. (1995). *Employment for Disabled People: Social Obligation or Individual Responsibility?* Social Policy Research Unit.

TUC (Trade Union Congress) (1996). *The Wages of Discrimination: Black Workers and Low Pay in 1995*. TUC.

Webb, S. (1994). Women and the UK income distribution: past, present and prospects. In *Labour Market Structures and Prospects for Women* (R. Lindley, ed.). Equal Opportunities Commission.

Wilson, R. (1994). Sectoral and occupational change: prospects for women's employment. In *Labour Market Structures and Prospects for Women* (R. Lindley, ed.). Equal Opportunities Commission.

# Chapter 3
# Theorizing labour market segmentation and identity issues

## Aim

To provide the conceptual and theoretical underpinning which is necessary to develop a critical analysis of both the differentiation which exists within the labour market outlined in Chapter 2 and the diversity policies and practices which will be discussed in Part Two.

## Objectives

- To present the main theoretical explanations for the occupational segregation, pay differentials and segmentation, which characterize the British labour market.
- To provide a critical analysis of these theoretical explanations, highlighting the strengths and weaknesses of the various approaches as explanatory tools.
- To highlight issues of identity, aiming to unpack concepts of homogeneous groups into which people are placed.

## Introduction

The previous chapter outlined the segmented nature of the British labour market, where there is differentiation between groups of employees resulting in unequal outcomes and opportunities. While it is important to recognize that groups within the labour market are not homogeneous (discussed later), some groups on average experience more disadvantage than others. This chapter aims to present the various and competing theories about the structures and processes which give rise to these differential patterns and trends. It draws on both demand- and supply-side arguments, and critically appraises their ability to offer explanations for the segmentation and segregation of the labour market. For utility, a distinction is made between neoclassical and human capital theories, labour market segmentation theories and social identity theories. It should be recognized that these overlap and interconnect, but the distinction provides a useful classificatory tool for discussion and analysis. This prepares the reader for the discussions at a microlevel in the following chapters, exploring how people within and between different social groups experience discrimination and disadvantage in employment.

# The existence of occupational segregation

Chapter 2 provided an overview of the occupational segregation, which exists within the British labour market. The five social groups that are discussed throughout this book are identified as disproportionately suffering from occupational segregation. This involves both vertical and horizontal segregation where women, minority ethnic workers, workers with disabilities and older workers are far more likely to hold lower status, lower paid jobs with less chances of promotion, training and career opportunities than the white man without disabilities, aged twenty-five to forty. Given the necessity of widespread concealment of sexual orientation, the occupational segregation of gay and lesbian workers is more difficult to identify. It is certain that this concealment occurs in order to avoid discrimination, which disadvantages gay and lesbian workers in the labour market; for example, for access to employment benefits and opportunities for promotion and career advancement.

The Equal Opportunities Commission's (EOC's) position on occupational segregation is that it is inequitable because it places restrictions on people's freedom to choose the job that they do (Hakim, 1992). Occupational segregation is a force for labour market rigidity and inefficiency; it is wasteful of human resources and a source of inflexibility within a context of globalization, where flexibility is stressed (Anker, 1997). More importantly, it is obviously detrimental to some groups of workers, having a negative effect on how they are viewed in the workplace and on their own status and income. Occupational segregation is significant as it is generally agreed that segregation, particularly vertically, is by far the most important explanation of the sex differential in earnings and women's weak position in the labour market generally (Anker, 1997; OECD, 1988; Treiman and Hartmann, 1981).

| **Key learning points** | 1 It is clear that a segmented and segregated labour market exists in Britain where some groups on average are more disadvantaged than others. |
| | 2 This occupational segregation is an important influence on the disadvantaged position faced by many categories of workers, and is linked directly to lower pay, lower status and increased vulnerability of employment. |

# The neoclassical approach

## Supply-side arguments

The focus here is on the perspective of employees: what labour skills they can supply. The neoclassical approach derives from economics, where the emphasis is placed on the rational and efficient functioning of the labour market (for a summary see Beardwell and Holden, 1997: 81–94). Within neoclassical economic theory, irrational and prejudicial discrimination against certain groups of workers runs counter to the neoclassical view of this rational market. Discrimination would theoretically be seen as uncompetitive and, therefore, as a matter of course, should be competed away. However, in recognizing that there are groups of workers who face a disproportionately disadvantaged position in the labour market, this is explained by focusing on the preferences of workers and employers, which market forces have to then accommodate. Workers thus seek out the best-paying jobs after taking into consideration their own personal abilities, responsibilities and preferences (Anker, 1997; Lee and Loveridge, 1987).

From the labour supply point of view, a neoclassical approach to explaining occupational segregation stresses that it is due to differences in workers' human capital (Becker, 1971). The occupation that a person has is seen as the outcome of individual agency and rational human capital investment decisions. Thus, for example, women and workers from minority ethnic groups are situated in lower paid jobs and particular occupations because of their different levels of human capital to white male workers. This involves the human capital that they bring to the labour market (most notably education and training), and the human capital that they acquire after joining the labour market (most notably the record of experience of labour market participation). Chapter 2 highlighted that there is not a level playing field before entry to the labour market, as there is also segregation and segmentation within the education system. This means, for instance, that there is a gender and race imbalance with regard to the level and subject area of education (Haggerty and Johnson, 1995). Thus, certain groups are said to come to the labour market with less human capital.

Chapter 2 also highlighted that while the 'traditional' family structure is on the decline, women around the world are almost exclusively responsible for housework and childcare. These family responsibilities mean that women gain less experience than men owing either to their early and permanent withdrawal, or a temporary absence, from the labour market in order to care for young children. Thus, according to human capital theory, women would rationally choose occupations with relatively high starting pay, relatively low returns to experience and relatively low penalties for temporary withdrawal from the labour force (Anker, 1997; England, 1982). This would also make occupations that are flexible in terms of entry and working hours, more attractive to women. The disproportionate representation of women in lower skilled occupations and part-time work is seen as due to women's own preferences: the differentials are accepted as compensations for the other responsibilities that women have (Anker, 1997: 4). Thus, women engage in less training because they expect to work less and choose occupations where interruptions are not costly. In addition, a woman's career is severely affected by the sexual division of domestic and parental responsibilities. While women's employment is typically characterized by one or more career breaks, this is found to have a particularly detrimental effect on women's job prospects (Newell, 1993). Two main factors positively influencing career progression are a full-time uninterrupted working life and being seen as promotable through having the ability and commitment to appear a long-term prospect, particularly through being able to work long hours (Colgan and Tomlinson, 1991). Thus women are commonly disadvantaged, when the model of employment is based on that of a male full-time employee.

There is some support for the human capital thesis of occupational segregation. Catherine Hakim's (1991) assertions to this effect have been the subject of controversy. Her research indicated significant support for a human capital explanation of occupational segregation by sex and was an attempt to counter accounts that saw women as 'victims' of social structures and attitudes. The main proposition was that while women were disproportionately in the lowest status and lowest paid jobs, they were also disproportionately satisfied with their jobs.(see also Cully et al., 1999). Hakim explained this by the fact that the majority of women aimed for a 'homemaker' career and work was seen as of peripheral importance. Her findings indicated that only a minority of women was committed to work as a central life goal. Hakim distinguished between two groups of women workers: those few who worked full time and had stronger work commitment, and the majority of part-time women workers who had lower levels of work commitment than men. Drawing on longitudinal evidence in the USA, looking at work plans, Hakim concluded that very few women had unplanned careers, and that their plans for their careers (of which having a family was a choice), were seen as significant predictors of actual work behaviour. In other words, occupational segregation was not imposed upon women. It derived from women's work orientations and life priorities. Thus Hakim goes so far as to state: 'most women have actively colluded in their own imprisonment in unpaid work in the home and low-paid, low status jobs in the workforce' (Hakim, 1991: 110).

## Demand-side arguments

Many of the factors influencing individual preferences for particular occupations also influence employers' preferences for particular types of worker. Thus, jobs requiring a relatively high level of education, and those where experience and on-the-job training are relatively important, are more likely to be offered to men than women (Anker, 1997). Another reason for this is that women are also considered to be higher cost workers because they are assumed to demand higher indirect labour costs. These can include statutory costs such as maternity leave, but also women are said to have higher rates of absenteeism and lateness, largely due to family responsibilities. Women are also said to have higher turnover rates (again due to family responsibilities), meaning that employers have to find and train new workers.

This role stereotyping is particularly relevant in a discussion of why older workers are seen to have disadvantages in human capital terms. The education system in Britain is seen as playing an important part in the relationship between age and employment (Branine and Glover, 1997: 239). The education system is based on making career decisions at an early age, and mature graduates and people who gain qualifications later in life are generally disadvantaged when they seek employment, training and promotion. There is also a perceived belief, similar to the higher indirect costs women are felt to bring with them, that older workers cost companies more due to higher healthcare costs.

Such stereotypes are also attached to ethnicity. West Indians are defined as 'slow', 'lazy', 'happy-go-lucky', 'aggressive' or 'excitable'. Asians are stereotyped as hard workers, ambitious, 'stand-offish' (Jenkins, 1986: 114). While human capital issues of women's domestic responsibilities are seen as a key to their disadvantaged position in the labour market, for women from ethnic minority groups supposed 'language' difficulties and 'lack of skills' are seen as *doubly disadvantaging* women from ethnic minority groups (Phizacklea, 1994: 179).

According to a model of employer behaviour developed by Becker (1971), employers are prejudiced against certain groups of workers. Because of this prejudice, employers are said to sustain a cost when they hire someone from the group discriminated against (see also Jenkins, 1986: 235). Therefore, according to this theory, employers act rationally when they hire fewer people from that group since they wish to avoid this 'cost'. This is seen as statistical discrimination, where employers discriminate against groups of workers (such as women, ethnic minorities, disabled, gays and lesbians or older people), due to the perceived characteristics of that particular group (Anker, 1997). Such stereotypes are bound up with perceptions of what is acceptable in an employee and generally lead to a preference for a white man or woman over a person of minority ethnic origin (Cockburn, 1991), for a younger worker over an older one or for a person without, rather than with disabilities and so on. Thus, occupational segregation is perpetuated and jobs become stereotyped through a combination of institutional discrimination and limited expectations.

# Institutional and labour market segmentation theories

This section focuses on another way in which employers actively encourage segregation. Here employers are seen as acting to fragment the collective power of labour. Employer choices ensure that disadvantaged groups only rarely gain the opportunity to improve their circumstances.

One can extend this theory also to recognize that institutions like trade unions as well as employers play an important role in determining who is recruited, promoted and made redundant, and how much people are paid for their work. Thus, capital accumulation is seen as predicated on the exploitation of resources, including women and minority ethnic labour, relating back to the theories of 'reserve armies' (Mies, in Cockburn, 1991: 84). Labour markets are seen as being segmented, where different groups of labour market participants are compartmentalized and isolated, and receive different rewards and opportunities for otherwise comparable attributes (Watts and Rich, 1993: 160).

Perhaps the best known of the segmentation theories is that of dual labour market theory (Doeringer and Piore, 1971). They emphasize that there is an overall duality present within any economy due to the segmented labour markets within specific firms. Here, a primary sector is distinguished from the secondary sector. Jobs in the primary sector are relatively good in terms of pay, security, opportunities for advancement and working conditions. In contrast, secondary sector jobs tend to be relatively poor as regards pay, chances for promotion, working conditions and job security. As Anker (1997) points out, it is obvious that the concept of dual markets can be adapted to occupational segregation, where the primary labour market holds mainly 'male' 'white' jobs, and the secondary sector 'female', 'older worker' and 'ethnic' jobs. For men, given their generally more continuous work experience and the fact that primary sector jobs will tend to accord a relatively high value to firm-specific experience and low labour turnover, male workers will tend to be favoured by primary sector employers.

Alternatively, Edwards (1975, in Lee and Loveridge, 1987), from a Marxist perspective, pointed to the dual labour market as deriving from clear control strategies by employers. In the face of a highly organized and highly skilled workforce, employers' consciously exploited race, ethnic and sex antagonisms to undercut trade union strength. With regard to race, there is evidence that there was a clear strategy from the government and employers to deliberately segment the market in employing people from minority ethnic groups. Black workers were specifically recruited to fill jobs at the lower end of the labour market, within the 'secondary' sector (Cockburn, 1991).

Chapter 2 emphasized that a historical analysis is required to understand the development of this 'underclass' where immigrants and migrant workers form the lowest strata of the British class system (Phizacklea, 1994). The migration of labour is linked to labour demand during the period of economic development in the postwar era. The economic boom from 1945 to the late 1960s, which saw a growing number of white women enter the British labour market, also led to the recruitment of workers from Britain's former colonies. British employers experiencing a labour shortage in the postwar period advertised for labour in the West Indies and the Indian subcontinent (Cockburn, 1991). Migrant workers thus provided a 'reserve army of labour', taking on jobs that indigenous workers did not want (Anthias and Yuval-Davis, 1993). Migrant workers are seen as providing vast population movements between less developed and more developed economies. The nature of this underclass is constituted by its inferior position within the wider working class and by the fact that people within it are politically separate from the organized labour movement. This is linked to the way in which colonialism stigmatized workers from ethnic minorities as 'outsiders'. While the acceptance status of these 'reserve armies' varies from country to country and between different ethnic groups, what is more significant is the way in which the existing labour force assigned them to an inferior position in Britain (Lee and Loveridge, 1987). Migrant workers thus came to form a defining part of the British class system.

The method of entry of migrant workers into the British labour market is also significant from a gender point of view. Brah (1994), points to the fact that the way in which men from ethnic minority groups entered the British labour market had a crucial effect on the nature and type of employment on offer to women when they arrived. The class position of ethnic minority men was as low-waged workers resident in declining inner areas of British cities, thus continuing to stigmatize their female relations similarly.

The issue of significance is that once entrenched within the secondary labour market sectors, it is difficult to move out. People become trapped by stigmatization and, thus, labour market segregation is perpetuated into the next generation. The segmentation process becomes self-reinforcing (Watts and Rich, 1993). For example, a vicious cycle of insecure employment and unemployment is disproportionately the experience of workers from minority ethnic groups.

---

**Key learning points**

1 The neoclassical approach to explaining occupational segregation stresses that it is due to differences in workers' human capital. The supply-side argument looks at differences in education and training and the division of childcare responsibilities. The demand-side argument stresses the rational preferences of employers for low-cost employees based on views of characteristics of certain groups and statistical discrimination.
2 Labour market segmentation theories point out that indeed labour markets are segmented and this segmentation leads to a disadvantaged position for certain groups of workers. This segmentation is felt partly to have come about due to clear control strategies of employers.
3 Historical analysis of the movements of labour from developing to developed world has led to segmentation of the labour market based on ethnicity, which is perpetuated through generations.

---

# Weaknesses of economic and market theories

Neoclassical and labour market segmentation theories can make some contribution to an understanding of occupational segregation and the lower pay of women and ethnic minority workers. The neoclassical approach highlights the important role that is played by systematic differences in the human capital accumulated by different people. Labour market segmentation theories are useful for understanding inequality in the labour market, stressing the existence of segregated occupations and markets. However, there are also strong criticisms. In particular, several problems arise if these approaches are taken as the only explanations of occupational segmentation.

## Gaps in the evidence

Chapter 2 pointed to the fact that women's labour market activity has increased rapidly during the 1960s to 1990s. Additionally, there is evidence for the breakdown of so-called 'traditional' family structures where there has been a decline in the amount of housework and the increase in the number of female-headed households all over the world (Buvini, 1995). These changes imply that women are gaining greater labour market experience which, according to neoclassical theory, means that women have increased human capital and this should lead to overall changes in the types of occupation women are offered, but this obviously has not occurred (Anker, 1997: 320). In addition, the fact that the bulk of occupational segregation by sex cannot be explained by sex-based differentials is a problem for neoclassical economists. For example, the human capital approach would state that the higher income spouse would specialize in paid employment while the other ought to specialize in domestic production. In the majority of cases, the lower income spouse would be the female partner. But the theory is challenged by non-traditional couples (where the woman earns more than the man) who do not fit into this rational choice model, where the woman still predominantly holds the domestic role (Corcoran and Courant, 1987).

It is also not clear to what extent a focus on a differentiated workforce finding expression through the marketplace indicates a 'real' difference in skills or experience. In other words, rather than 'real' difference, the difference in skills is based on social evaluation (Blackburn and Mann, 1979). There is little evidence to suggest that people from ethnic minority groups have ended up at the lowest end of the labour market because of limited occupational goals or social aspirations (Jenkins, 1988). Indeed, as Chapter 2 highlighted, while workers from ethnic minorities are markedly less successful in obtaining the kind of job that they want, this is not due to a lesser level of education and qualifications. Brown (1992) indicates that while Asian children, for example, receive at least as much as white children in terms of qualifications, this does not translate into comparably favourable positions in the labour market. Formal education does not seem to act as the buffer against unemployment for people from minority ethnic groups as it might for whites.

Additionally, the view that primary sector jobs are seen as requiring more continuity of experience does not seem to be the case. Many primary sector and male-dominated occupations do not require more experience or continuity of employment than do many female-dominated jobs. Anker (1997: 320) compares the male job of a delivery truck driver with that of the female job of a secretary, where he asserts that the latter requires considerably more knowledge and skills. In addition, one can criticize an underlying assumption in theories which, in seeing women as having lesser work commitment, make the assumption that part-time work is less demanding than full time (Hakim, 1991). In contrast, Scheibl (1996) finds that part-time work can be just as, if not more, demanding than full-time work and criticizes the view that work commitment should be measured primarily in terms of work hours, which automatically disadvantages women. Women are particularly 'time poor' as a consequence of the disproportionate responsibility they hold for household and childcare tasks (Turner, Grieco and Apt, 1998).

On another supply-side issue, there is evidence that jobs in the secondary sector are not a rational choice for women, bearing in mind human capital theory which states that women who plan to spend a lot of time out of the labour market will choose jobs with low penalties for intermittent employment – predominantly those jobs in the secondary sector. On the contrary, England (1982) found that occupations employing a larger proportion of women did not consistently show lower penalties for intermittent employment than did predominantly male occupations. In other words, the supply-side theory of occupational segregation cannot explain women's predominance in these jobs, particularly their concentration within a small number of female occupations at each skill level (Watts and Rich, 1993).

With regard to demand factor explanations, one can question whether there are higher direct and indirect labour costs associated with female workers. Labour laws and regulations can increase the comparative cost of employing female workers if they decide to have children, for example, maternity leave costs. (This, of course, ignores that men have families too and women should not be discriminated against on the basis of biological ability to have children!) However on other points of higher cost, there does not seem to be a gender difference, for example, survey evidence indicates that there are similar turnover and absenteeism rates for women and men (Anker, 1997).

Similarly, the stereotyping of older workers finds little evidence. A review of studies of age and job performance (Lackzo and Philopson, 1991) found older workers to be as productive as their younger counterparts, despite the fact that older workers face much stereotyping about their lack of energy, flexibility, and ability and willingness to learn (Branine and Glover, 1997: 240). In addition, the evidence for older workers leading to higher indirect costs is also refuted in the main (Capowski and Peak, 1994).

This discussion places a different tenor on Hakim's (1991) argument, pointing to the positive relationship between women's long-term career plans and labour market outcomes. In agreement with Scheibl (1996), we would assert that the issue appears more complex than this, where some peoples' aspirations have little chance of being actualized within the constraints of existing organizational and societal structures. The women in Scheibl's study had to accept reluctantly a domestic career path despite their earlier intentions to have a career in the labour market. It is not so much a question of releasing women from the attitude that they are passive victims of societal constraints, but that these very same constraints restrict the actualization of these career aspirations, or that these are never seen as possible aspirations to begin with.

## Questions that still remain

In general, the human capital and labour market segmentation theories provide only an incomplete explanation. Human capital theories point out how women are less well qualified than men for certain occupations, looking at differences in education and years of experience. Labour market segmentation theories point out that labour markets are segmented and this segmentation leads to a disadvantaged position for women and workers from ethnic minorities. However, questions remain: why do women and workers from ethnic minority groups come to the labour market with lower levels of education and in less relevant subjects? Why is housework and childcare almost always the sole responsibility of women? Why does labour market segregation persist despite a wide overlap in the abilities of those advantaged and disadvantaged groups in the labour market? Perhaps more significantly, why are the disadvantaged position of three other significant groups of people – namely disabled workers, gay and lesbian workers and older workers – within the labour market not dealt with specifically as part of human capital and dual labour market explanations. This silence is significant in highlighting the inability of economic theories to provide a full explanation for occupational segmentation.

**Key learning points**

1 Clear weaknesses are apparent if human capital and institutional approaches are used as the only explanations for occupational segmentation. There is a lack of evidence for the negative characteristics ascribed to certain groups of workers and the theories do not explain why such attitudes have come about in the first place and continue to be perpetuated in changed economic and sociological conditions.
2 Neoclassical and institutional approaches are almost exclusively focused on gender and race segmentation and do not adequately explain the disadvantaged position of disabled, older and gay and lesbian workers.

# Social identity explanations

In his book, *Social Identity*, Richard Jenkins relates an incident where he meets the daughter of his neighbour and her little daughter Helena for the first time:

> I cannot . . . forget that Mrs. Oswald's daughter is female. Otherwise she would be Mrs. Oswald's son, and she could not possibly be Helena's mother. And the relevance of gender depends upon the point of view: whether 'I' am male or female . . . nor is ethnicity

disregardable: 'my' ethnic point of view matters depending on context. When I first encountered the woman who I now know to be Helena's mother, that she was Afro-Caribbean may have been the first significant thing that I noticed about her. And is Mrs. Oswald Afro-Caribbean? And what might tell me if she were not? Similarly, the fact that her daughter owns a red Mazda tells me something about her class, which in itself may call up knowledge about her profession . . . (Jenkins, 1996: 116)

Such an example illustrates a process of categorization that occurs continually in our interactions with other people and which, therefore, in a similar way has consequences for the categorizations and choices made by employers and employees within the labour market. Concepts of social identity are necessary to query and confirm who we are and who others are. As Jenkins (1996: 6) asserts, social identity is an integral part of society: 'Without frameworks for delineating social identity and identities, I would be the same as you and neither of us could relate to the other meaningfully or consistently. Without social identity, there is in fact, no society'.

What is significant from such a perspective for our discussion (of inequality, equality and diversity in the labour market) is that if we recognize that social identity is integral to society, we also recognize that some groups are disproportionately affected by the social identities ascribed to and achieved by them. The question for discussion in this next section is, therefore, what leads to the differential impact of that delineation and categorisation, in terms of outcomes and balance of rewards and opportunities for different groups? In comparison to the neoclassical explanations, social identity perspectives highlight that whatever group of workers we are looking at, it must be acknowledged that choices and life goals are defined by the opportunity structures that exist in society. Choices are enabled and constrained within the limits set by rules and expectations, and people need material and social resources to challenge these social constraints.

# Feminist and gender theories

Jenkins is keen to inform that a preoccupation with social identity has been apparent in philosophical writings for many hundreds of years. However, it has become a particularly 'modern' project whose origins can arguably be traced back to the women's movement of the 1960s (Jenkins, 1996: 13; see also Giddens, 1991). Feminist and gender theories have primarily been concerned with explaining the subordinate position of women; however, as this chapter will demonstrate, the premises and arguments made have pertinence for the explanation of the disadvantaged position of other groups within the labour market also.

Feminist theories emerged out of a critique of Marxist theories as failing to take account of the gendered nature of the labour force (see Beechey, 1980; Hartmann, 1979; Walby, 1990). Marxist approaches, focusing on the oppression of the working class by capitalists, fail to distinguish individuals by gender when evidence seemed to point to the obvious distinction made by employers between the two sexes and, as we have pointed out earlier, between different ethnic groups. While Marxist thinkers such as Lenin and Engels stated that women would be emancipated from the oppression of family life by their entry into the productive labour force, the experience of women in the twentieth century showed that women's oppression as a sex continued (Cockburn, 1991: 22). Thus, feminist analysis has challenged and developed Marxist theory in new directions.

## Patriarchy

The most significant of these new directions has been the approach based on the concept of patriarchy which is seen as existing long before the capitalist modes of production. Patriarchy is an analytical and empirical tool, and different approaches use the concept in various ways. Walby (1990: 20) defines patriarchy as 'a system of social structures and practices in which men dominate, oppress and exploit women'. Thus the patriarchal relations experienced both at home and in the workplace oppress women. The domestic mode of production was seen as the 'super-exploitation' of women (Cockburn, 1991: 23), first, because women's work in the home can be seen as a form of production and because all the tasks of domestic labour could be purchased in the market. However this labour is uncompensated by pay and thus women are the exploited labourers of men in the home. Second, women subsidize the employer by maintaining those male employees (husbands and sons who needed to be clothed and fed). Third, women continue to suffer the effects that this domestic labour has when entering the paid workplace. Women's wages came to be seen as a secondary income to the male breadwinner wage, which encouraged the wage differential and lack of solidarity in the workplace between male and female workers. This overarching system of patriarchal relations structures the way in which women and men are treated as workers.

Feminist studies focusing on the practices and ideologies of male workers and employers point to the need to look at structures of patriarchy as well as those of capitalist markets in order to understand gender inequality in the labour market (Cockburn, 1983; Hartmann, 1979; Walby, 1990). Patriarchal structures and attitudes within society places a distinction between the female as the 'homemaker' and the male as the 'breadwinner', thus enforcing a view of childcare and housework (domestic labour) as the chief responsibility of the woman. As Cockburn (1991: 100) highlights, the sexual division of roles intensifies with parenthood, and evidence indicates that men with young families work the longest hours. This directly relates to the provision of childcare facilities in Britain, which are relatively poor compared with many other countries. Public and domestic spheres are thus separated, with womanhood being related to the gendered division of labour where women are ascribed to domestic life and men to public life. The image of womanhood is associated with child bearing, child rearing and domestic life (Mills, 1989). There is an asymmetrical relationship in this gendered idea of skill, where the public sphere is accorded greater cultural worth than the domestic sphere, thus disadvantaging women disproportionately (Mills, 1989). However, it also relates more significantly to wider social attitudes, discussed in the next section.

---

1 Feminist and gender theories look at non-economic variables and explore the way in which a disadvantaged position in the labour market is caused by, and is a reflection of, societal structures and attitudes. While the focus has primarily been concentrated on the subordinate position of women, the premises and arguments made have pertinence for the explanation of the disadvantaged position of other groups within the labour market.
2 The patriarchal structure of society is seen as an important determinant of women's subordinate position in the labour market, leading to the development of a distinction between the public and domestic sphere where women are primarily characterized as workers with domestic ties.

**Key learning points**

---

# Attitudes

Linking back to the last chapter, alongside the increasing level of economic activity by women, there is also some evidence of changing social attitudes towards women in paid work. A synthesis of some of the nationwide attitude survey evidence (Newell, 1993) indicates that compared with the 1960s there has been a significant fall in the number of women who feel mothers with children under five years old *should* stay at home. However, there is also evidence of upholding traditional attitudes, with a large proportion of women agreeing that a husband's job was to earn money and a wife's to care for the home and family (supporting the traditional 'homemaker/breadwinner' distinction). For women, therefore, paid work is still something that has to be accommodated alongside domestic demands. The continued segregation of household work is clear (Newell, 1993) and there is little evidence that the 'new man' of the 1990s has been expanding his role to encompass a more egalitarian sharing of domestic work.

Men in Newell's sample were found to have more traditional ideas about a woman's role in the workplace and in the home than do women. For women to break out of this structured subordination there needs to be a radical transformation of the relationship between the domestic and public sphere. However, the above attitudinal evidence does not bode well for this transformation. In addition, evidence from empirical studies indicates that even if the provision and opportunity were there for men to take an increased domestic role, there would be opposition or unwillingness. Only a small minority of men welcome the idea of a greater share of parental work and the extension of provisions, such as exist in Sweden (see Chapter 10 for a detailed discussion) and many acknowledge that they would not want to play a more domestic role (Cockburn, 1991: 99). The sex-role stereotyping within society is therefore deeply embedded and is continually perpetuated.

Much of the stereotyping occurs before entering the labour market. The idea of sex socialization from childhood is not a new one, with psychological literature suggesting that boys and girls are raised in ways that tend to foster consistency with traditional sex roles (Jenkins, 1996: 58). Corcoran and Courant's (1987) study provides a summary of this literature as well as empirical evidence that families treat boys and girls differently in a way that advantages boys once they enter the labour market. Thus human capital differences arise from this socialization and provide an alternative explanation for why boys and girls choose different subjects at school and why girls might value characteristics that are less profitable in the labour market. This also leads men to devalue a woman's attributes and produces motivation for future discrimination (England and McCreary, 1986).

There is also a view of skill as gendered, which links back to the earlier discussion about whether or not employers' views of women are based on a 'real' skill difference. The characteristics of those jobs segmented as 'women's jobs' mirror the common stereotypes of women and their supposed abilities. Anker (1997) draws up a list of such characteristics: for example, a caring nature, greater manual dexterity, greater honesty, attractive physical appearance, disinclination to supervise, lesser physical strength, lesser ability in mathematics and science, greater willingness to take orders, greater interests in working at home and greater tolerance of repetitive work. These stereotypes would seem to have a great influence on the general characteristics that typify 'female' occupations. The neoclassical economic theorists would place this characterization as due to women's preferences and biological differences. However, feminist theory suggests an alternative, that sex stereotyping is the outcome of organizational power relations and social, economic and ideological forces governing the sex-segregated nature of labour market practices (Collinson, Knights and Collinson, 1990).

Thus, the view that the occupational position of women derives from rational choice, is: 'a construction of reality that shifts the blame for women's difficulties to themselves rather than recognising the socially instituted and internalised stereotypes that underpin those choices' (Newell, 1993: 287). This relates back to the previous discussion of human capital theory and the idea that women have less work commitment than men and thus predominantly *choose* part-time work. Alternatively, the complexity of any choices made is emphasized, pointing out that part-time work and homeworking are not freely chosen (Cockburn, 1991: 82; Scheibl, 1996). Women are thus forced to occupy two roles which are to some extent incompatible, particularly in a labour market where promotion and earning potential are based on issues of longevity of employment, ability to work long hours and uninterrupted careers.

This has particular significance for older women workers, where Branine and Glover (1997) emphasize the connections between patriarchy and its embodiment through domination on the basis of age and gender. Making links between women and age, Pringle (1989: 170) pointed to the overtly discriminatory attitudes of managers responsible for recruitment. They made decisions based on stereotyping which cast women over the age of forty years as being increasingly domesticated and uninterested in business issues. Thus the role stereotyping which is prominent for women in general becomes exacerbated as women get older.

Overall, this division of responsibility between the sexes and patriarchal ordering of society is instrumental in explaining why women usually accumulate less human capital compared with men in terms of level and subject area of education. It also accounts for the statistical discrimination faced by women from employers, once in the labour market. Finally, it explains why women are perceived as having less need for labour market skills and acquire less human capital once in the labour market through occupational experience, as many of them withdraw from the labour market early or temporarily. As Anker highlights: 'the fact that these societal norms and perceptions bear little relation to the daily lives of may women, men and families does not detract from their influence on people's behaviour and their contribution to gender-based discrimination against women' (Anker, 1997: 326).

# Action of employers, employees and trade unions

Theories of patriarchy also lay the responsibility for the exclusion of those groups most commonly disadvantaged and their segregation into the secondary labour market on men's active behaviour. Cockburn (1983) subjected craft trade unions to an extensive feminist critique, identifying how the exclusionary practices of male dominated trade unionists reproduced and protected segmented work patterns. This involved the great influence of men (and white, heterosexual, non-disabled men) over recruitment and training and in defining the skill content of jobs. Similarly, Walby (1990) identified the role of trade unions in the reproduction of job segregation through empirical work in engineering, cotton textile and clerical work. Thus in cotton textiles, from the nineteenth century, women were actively excluded from union membership and the entry of women into the highly skilled spinning jobs was resisted. Other studies have pointed to the sexualization of roles and masculine cultures within trade unions which have marginalized and oppressed women who take an active role in modern trade unions (Collinson and Collinson, 1989; Kirton and Healy, 1999).

---

1 Societal attitudes relating to the gendered distinction between breadwinner/homemaker, public/domestic roles are deeply embedded and there is clear evidence that much sex stereotyping occurs before entry to the labour market. There is also little evidence of widespread change in these attitudes, even in more egalitarian societies.

**Key learning points**

2 The division of responsibility between the sexes and patriarchal ordering of society is instrumental in explaining why women accumulate less human capital compared with men, and accounts for the statistical discrimination experienced by women.

### Activity 3.1: What's your problem?

Ten years ago, the Institute of Practitioners in Advertising conducted a comprehensive survey into women in advertising. It examined the number of female employees that were in the business, the nature of their jobs and how senior they were. It made for depressing reading. Women were not climbing the corporate ladder. They were noticeably absent from key senior positions. They were almost totally unrepresented in many departments.

A decade on, the picture looks alarmingly similar. Out of the line-up of leading agencies, none today can claim a female chairman, and only two have a woman in the position of chief executive. Most disturbing is the fact that there are still, as ten years ago, no female creative heads . . . Where women do better are in the traditional support roles of planning, strategic thinking area of advertising, as well as PR and marketing, new business and account management, which involves directly looking after clients.

Here the traditional issues of having families and fundamental questions about ambition come into play. M. T. Rainey, chief executive at Rainey Kelly Campbell Roalfe/Y&R says: 'You have to work inordinately hard, not only at what you do but where you are going. It is utterly consuming and women are very good at caring about what they are doing rather than planning a career. It's less important to them.' Interestingly, Rainey doesn't have a family and she believes that because she hasn't had to balance children with work, she has been able to channel her energies into her career.

*Source*: Edited extract from the *Guardian*, 13 September 1999.

*Questions*

1 Discuss possible different explanations for this occupational sex segregation drawing on neoclassical, institutional and social identity approaches and identifying weaknesses and strengths.
2 Discuss Rainey's comments about women having lesser career ambitions, drawing on human capital explanations and Hakim (1991). How convincing do you find this explanation?

# Ascribed and achieved identities

It is important here to note the kind of identities that become most relevant in organizational settings. *Ascribed* identities are socially constructed on the basis of contingencies of birth (which account for the collective identities of our five social groups: gender, race, age, disability and sexual orientation). *Achieved* identities are assumed through the life course (Jenkins, 1996: 142). In competitive organizational recruitment, *ascriptive* identities are most likely to influence the identification of *acceptability* (whether or not a person will 'fit in' to the social networks and relationships of the organization – the 'right kind of person'). This is in comparison to *suitability*, usually based on achieved characteristics (for example, skills, education and interests).

As Jenkins (1996: 148) asserts, it is within acceptability criteria that stereotypes become important; being 'suitable' for a job does not guarantee a person's recruitment to it (discussed in greater detail in Chapter 4). As Cockburn (1991: 175) points out, in most cases an *acceptable* worker is one who is trouble free, and racist reactions from the existing workforce will want to be avoided. Similarly, women are seen primarily as people with domestic ties, regardless of their individual experiences. This identity casts women as workers with disadvantages, while the lower earning capacity of women and their subordination to men in the workplace also diminishes their standing within the domestic sphere (Cockburn, 1991: 76). Collinson, Knights and Collinson (1990) provide examples of discriminatory practices as part of their research within the insurance industry, highlighting that organizations may be nominally open to all, but virtually closed to many categories of the population who are excluded on the basis of this ascription. Here, the routine conditions and consequences of recruitment were the means for the legitimization of race and sex discrimination practices, with interviewers making decisions based on taken for granted beliefs about stereotypical roles.

The self-reinforcing nature of the position of women in the labour market is highlighted by the fact that wider societal attitudes and the fact that women do predominantly take responsibility for childcare mean that women are often seen as meeting the stereotype in practice, though certainly this is not a free or rational choice. Women in Cockburn's (1991: 86) study found that the difficulty of combining a demanding paid job and family responsibilities meant that women are prevented from taking promotion opportunities. Women are often forced to unilaterally state they will not put their family first if they want to progress, which is an inequitable statement to have to make, particularly as a man would not be asked to make the same decision regardless of the fact that men have families too.

This discussion highlights the complexity of the debates surrounding occupational segregation. We have moved on from the initial position where patriarchy was seen as primarily a system of exploitation, meeting the criticism made by Collinson, Knights and Collinson (1990) that the influence of the patriarchal system extends beyond exploitation to include the role of biology, familial ideology and issues of gender identity. It is important to recognize that material realities, which impact upon women's labour market position, emerge from this interaction of ideology, stereotype and socialized roles. The mutually reinforcing nature of patriarchal labour market practices and domestic subordination can be identified, where the position of women is both a consequence and a condition. Through social agency and resistance of men and women, biological differences can lead to material differences where there is identity formation that reproduces and reinforces gender roles. It is important to avoid biological determinism; just because women can have children does not automatically lead to gendered roles. As Armstrong and Armstrong (1985: 32) point out: 'That women have babies, albeit under a variety of conditions, does not necessarily mean that they will rear the children or clean the toilets.'

Such discussion has clear relevance for the position of other groups of workers commonly disadvantaged in the labour market, for example, the position of workers with disabilities. The gender and feminist perspectives point out the importance of wider societal attitudes and stereotyping that lead to the exclusion and subordination of certain groups of workers. Thus, disabled workers are seen as an extra cost that the employer wants to avoid paying. Cockburn (1991) points to the fact that disabled people still seldom get short-listed for jobs, while certain managers in her study had overtly discriminatory attitudes towards workers with disabilities. Issues that were seen as contributing to discriminatory practices towards other categories of workers are applicable here also. For example, the existence of informal methods of recruitment, for example, internal labour markets can be seen as encouraging the perpetuation of a workforce that may not include disabled workers. In the recent BBC documentary, *Disabled Century,* in answer to the question from the floor 'what defines disability', a woman on the panel commented that she did not consider herself disabled, it was non-disabled people who defined her in that way. For her, the way in which she lived her life was simply different. It seems that such an attitude could apply to many of the groups of people who continue to face discrimination and societal barriers within the labour market and illustrates the explanatory power that social identity perspectives have in understanding the ways in which the labour market becomes segmented.

| **Key learning points** | 1 The active behaviour of employers, employees and trade unions also encourages the occupational segregation of different groups. Material realities that impact upon the labour market position of individuals emerge from the interaction between ideology, stereotype, socialized roles and the agency of individuals. |
|---|---|
| | 2 A distinction can be made between ascribed and achieved social identities, of which the former is highlighted as having most effect on whether an individual is seen as 'acceptable' for a job, and where there is the greatest chance of stereotypes negatively influencing recruitment processes. |

# Connecting race and gender

The black feminist critique of white feminism is central to developing thoughts about the intricate links between gender, race, ethnicity and class (Anthias and Yuval-Davis, (1993). Black feminists have pointed to the ethnocentric nature of Western feminism where certain priorities are posited which do not take into account the experiences of black or third world women. As feminism assumes a unity on the basis of white experiences, the minority ethnic woman is rendered invisible and denied a voice. There is an inherent racism in analyses and practices that assume the white experience to be the norm.

On the other hand, gender and ethnic divisions can be linked (Anthias and Yuval-Davis, 1993: 111). Both divisions involve practices of exclusion and structuring of disadvantage in favour of a dominant group. Race and gender divisions both involve differential access to resources and processes of exclusion and inclusion. While gender relates to the social construction, representation and organization of sexual difference and biological reproduction, gender cannot be reduced to biology. The practices around gender originate in social relations, which include race. We cannot understand racism except in its interconnection with ethnicity, nationalism, class, gender and state. The conditions of the reproduction of ethnic groups are centrally linked to other primary social divisions of class and gender. While the particular discourses of sexism and racism can be separated, the experiences of the groups affected are interconnected. Thus Brah (1994: 151) talks of the 'racialized gendering of labour markets'.

Citizenship is one such gendered and racialized concept which affects labour market position. In her analysis of British identity, Allen (1994: 99) points out that in the imperial phase of British government, the state defined all those living in the UK as British subjects with varying rights according to gender and race/ethnicity. Thus, differences in immigration and nationality laws casts women as dependants on men, and ethnicity and racialism function to exclude access to full citizenship to certain groups of people (Anthias and Yuval-Davis, 1993: 127). This has an impact on societal stereotypes of different groups and the jobs they will be seen as suitable for. Brah points to the discriminatory impact that immigration legislation has on the status of ethnic minority workers:

> Social constructions of Asian marriage and family systems as a 'problem for British society' have been pivotal in the legitimation of British immigration policy. Images of 'tidal waves' of Asian men scheming to circumvent immigration restrictions through the arranged marriage system were commonly invoked in the justification of immigration control. Whilst the Asian male was defined as a prospective worker posing a threat to the employment prospects of white men, Asian women were defined in immigration law as 'dependants'. The social imagery of Asian women as hapless dependants who would most likely be married off at the earliest opportunity has played an important role in shaping the views that teachers or careers officers might hold of young Muslim women's education and employment prospects. (Brah, 1994: 157)

Brah (1994) also provides a summary of the extensive literature, which documents direct and indirect discrimination in the labour market against workers from ethnic minorities. Here, the social agency highlighted in feminist and gender theories about occupational segmentation is emphasized. Discriminatory practices are socially constructed and involve a racialized discourse which stereotypes and stigmatizes ethnic minority workers as 'different' or the 'other', in the same way that patriarchal discourses stigmatize women. Thus racialized discourses have relevance for the general suitability of a group for certain types of jobs and positions (Brah, 1994: 157). The actions of male employers, employees and trade unions can also be found to have actively subordinated the position of workers from minority ethnic groups in the same way as for women (Cockburn, 1991: 180). This relates back to our previous discussion of the 'double disadvantage' of women workers from minority ethnic groups. Many studies have pointed to evidence of discrimination against black workers at ports of entry to and exit from the labour market. Ageism is linked in here, where younger workers from minority ethnic groups are most severely affected.

Sex stereotyping interacts with ethnic boundaries; indeed, cultural restrictions can contribute to the establishment of what is seen as acceptable work for women. This relates to the idea of purdah – 'a series of norms and practices which limit women's participation in public life' (Brah, 1994: 158). This cultural constraint is most commonly invoked for Muslim women, but different versions of purdah have been found among other ethnic groups such as Hindus and Sikhs. Sharma (1983) suggests that purdah can be applied in a wider context, applicable in all societies. One can see the direct link between gender and race here, where women in all societies face ideologies and practices that influence the ways in which they can participate in the public sphere. Thus, these patriarchal ideologies and practices can be seen as forms of purdah. This approach is important in emphasizing that the patriarchal discourses and practices, which influence the British labour market, are not race blind in that the racialized discourses and practices are embedded within the context of British society.

**Key learning points**

1 While black feminism has criticized Western feminism for its assumption that the white experience is the norm, gender and race divisions can be linked. Both involve differential access to resources and policies of exclusion, and are inevitably linked together in wider social relations of ethnicity, class, gender and state.

2 There is an extensive literature which documents direct and indirect discrimination against workers from ethnic minority groups reflecting conclusions drawn from the feminist and gender theories about the interaction between attitudes, childhood socialization, levels of human capital and individual experiences of labour market practices, as explanations for occupational segmentation.

# The sexuality of the workplace

It is also important to recognize the sexualized character of the workplace. The role stereotyping of 'women's jobs' often includes the harnessing of sexuality in certain jobs and the subtle pressures for women to behave in a sexual manner at work. For example, women in positions such as receptionists, secretaries, sales people and airline attendants find themselves expected to 'sell their sexuality' as part of their job in a way that men would not be called upon to do. Thus the sexual aspects of the female role are carried over to work and can override a view of a woman as a capable, committed worker (Gutek, 1989). Not burdened with the stereotype of domestication, the situation for a man is different where men are seen as works oriented and the natural inhabitants of organizations.

This has relevance for the discussion of the position of gay and lesbian workers in organizations. Predominantly, the workplace is heterosexualized (see discussion in Chapter 4). Pringle (1989: 164) highlights that the normality of sexuality in daily life is heterosexual, involving both the domination of male heterosexuality over women's and the subordination of other forms of sexuality. First, homosexuals are not protected from discrimination in employment by law as are women and workers from minority ethnic groups, which was discussed in the previous chapter. Pringle (1989) noted how striking it was that they found examples of few homosexuals in their study and that this reflected a view (as discussed in the previous chapter) that often latent homophobia from employers and other employees leads to homosexuals being driven underground. Hall (1989) summarizes the possible strategy choices that homosexuals have within organizational settings, and that while there is an argument that a person's sexuality is a private affair and need not be publicly disclosed, many homosexuals related how non-disclosure led to 'living a lie' and feelings of betrayal. On the other hand, many gay and lesbian workers also point to the view that being open about their sexuality was felt to lead to the loss of promotion opportunities. Thus like the stereotyping of women and ethnic minority workers, sexualized discourses could also have material consequences in terms of resources. Cockburn (1991: 188–91) provides a discussion of the tensions within male sexuality which finds male homosexuality particularly threatening to male identity, male authority and, because of the heterosexualized nature of the workplace, the culture of organizations. Again drawing on the feminist and gender perspective, wider embedded societal attitudes are seen to have significant consequences for the position and prospects of homosexual workers within the labour market.

1 The heterosexualized nature of the workplace has consequences in terms of the perpetuation of the gendered stereotyping of work, where women are commonly called upon to harness their sexuality in their work in a way that men are not.

2 The heterosexuality of organizational identities also has consequences for the position of homosexual workers who are disadvantaged by the supposed threat they pose to the heterosexualized organization and patriarchal authority structures, leading to discrimination and loss of opportunities.

**Key learning points**

# Conclusion

It is important to recognize the enormous diversity within the different groups of workers who have been discussed. The discussion throughout this book has emphasized that women, homosexuals, older workers, workers from ethnic minorities and disabled workers are not mutually exclusive categories. More importantly, neither are they homogeneous categories. Women are not a homogeneous group, and here is where the danger of theories and explanations lies. Individual women differ in their material and social resources, in their individual aspirations and career plans. The ethnocentric nature of Western feminism has also been discussed, rejecting an assumption that there is a unity of women's interests on the basis of white experience (Anthias and Yuval-Davis, 1993). The issue of feminism is complex and multifaceted, where other social divisions cut across gender, thus meaning that only some women share a common basis with which to identify and act (Allen, 1994: 96).

The social identity perspectives allow us to focus more closely on the social agency within the segmentation of labour markets and within wider societal positions. As Collinson, Knights and Collinson (1990: 192–212) summarize, stereotyping and discriminatory practices can be seen as a process of individual agency and identity formation. Different groups within the workplace are constructed as different threats and opportunities to other groups. Thus there is no common experience of subordination; for example, it should be recognized that female workers from minority ethnic groups cannot just be seen as 'doubly discriminated' as their experience is likely to be qualitatively different and not just an issue of amount of discrimination (Maynard, 1994: 13). Nor is the white male the common enemy of all the other types of worker in the British labour market. For example, Collinson, Knights and Collinson (1990) illustrate how female personnel managers did not intervene in cases of overt discrimination against women because of the need to maintain their own identities and statuses within the heterosexualized organization. Racism and ethnic relations cut across other societal categories and can unite women with men on racial grounds (Anthias and Yuval-Davis, 1993: 106). Thus men from ethnic minorities can be sexist, women can be racist, and people from many groups can be heterosexist and ignore the plight of disabled workers. Cockburn (1991: 188) points to the elements of male gay culture, which reinforce the subordination of women.

Issues of identity formation and identity politics are too broad to be discussed in detail here, but at least a limited understanding of identity issues are pertinent and relevant to the overall discussion of diversity. They relate to the quest for equality and whether this is an issue of cultural assimilation and demands the dilution of difference, or whether the maintenance of diversity is an important political and social issue in itself. The discussion moves from the more theoretical and macrolevel analysis of this chapter, to the level of the organization in the next chapter where some of these issues of identity are dealt with in terms of organizational cultures.

## Activity 3.2: Welcome to the world of opportunity knocks

It is a truism among graduate recruiters that they make up their minds about you within 20 seconds of you walking through the interview room door. Just think – your hairstyle, your eye contact and the warmth of your handshake can all count for more than your degree. Add to that your Birmingham accent, your 'female-ness', the fact you're only 21 and you're wearing a nose ring. Handshake getting cooler? Now factor in a wheelchair or the fact that you're black. I'm sorry, but your 20 seconds are up.

Ask any medium or large employer in the UK what their reaction would be and they will tell you that none of these things would make any difference to their decision. They would tell you in fact that to do so would be illegal. Yet the figures seem to tell a different tale.

According to employers' organizations, companies are doing everything they should be to ensure that they treat workers fairly. Nearly three-quarters have an equality policy and many monitor recruitment by category. Yet often it is not the intake of women, black or Asian people or other 'minorities' which is weak, but their subsequent rise through the ranks . . .

*Source*: Edited extract from the *Guardian*, 20 March 1999.

*Questions*

1 Think about the social identity issues involved in this example. Discuss ascribed and achieved identities and the impact of such categorizations on the employment patterns of different groups of workers.
2 Discuss whether you think employers are 'doing everything they should to ensure that workers are treated fairly'.
3 What explanations of occupational segregation would be most helpful in making sense of the situation described above?

# Review and discussion questions

1 Identify and summarize the central tenets of each of the main explanatory approaches: neoclassical, institutional and social identity.
2 What contribution can each approach make to explain the existence of occupational segmentation in the British labour market and what are the weaknesses of each approach?
3 Discuss how the premises and arguments made as part of the feminist and gender approach can help to explain the occupational segregation and disadvantage experienced by groups of workers other than women.

# Further reading

Afshar, H. and Maynard, M. (eds) (1994). *The Dynamics of Race and Gender: Some Feminist Interventions*. Taylor and Francis.
  Extends discussion of feminist theory, indicating the links between gender, class, race and ethnicity.

Anker, R. (1997). Theories of occupational segregation be sex: an overview. *International Labour Review*, Autumn, **136**, (7), 315–340.
  A clear summary of theories of occupational segregation by sex, outlining the strengths and weaknesses of human capital, institutional and feminist and gender theories.

Anthias, F. and Yuval-Davis, N. (eds) (1993). *Racialised Boundaries: Race, Nation, Gender, Colour and Class and the Anti-Racist Struggle*. Routledge.
  A collection of chapters examining the issue of race and the labour market. Provides examples of empirical evidence of labour market segmentation.

Cockburn, C. (1991). *In the Way of Women: Men's Resistance to Sex Equality in Organisations*. Macmillan.
  Comprehensive analysis of labour market disadvantage of women focusing on feminist and gender theory. Links theory and evidence to a discussion of other groups in the labour market including ethnic minorities, disabled and gay and lesbian workers.

Collinson, D., Knights, D. and Collinson, M. (1990). *Managing to Discriminate*. Routledge.
  Good summary and critical analysis of feminist and gender theories, particularly in the concluding chapter.

Hearn, J., Sheppard, D., Tancred-Sheriff, P. and Burrell, G. (eds) (1989). *The Sexuality of Organisation*. Sage.
  Collection of papers examining the sexualized nature of the workplace through both theoretical and empirical analysis.

Jenkins, R. (1996). *Social Identity*. Routledge.
  Key theoretical text examining conceptualizations of social identity and processes of social identity construction.

# References

Allen, S. (1994). Some questions of identity. In *The Dynamics of Race and Gender: Some Feminist Interventions* (H. Afshar and M. Maynard, eds). Taylor and Francis.

Anker, R. (1997). Theories of occupational segregation by sex: an overview. *International Labour Review*, Autumn, **136**, (7), 315–340.

Anthias, F. and Yuval-Davis, N. (eds) (1993). *Racialised Boundaries: Race, Nation, Gender, Colour and Class and the Anti-Racist Struggle*. Routledge.

Armstrong, P. and Armstrong, H. (1985). Beyond sexless class and classless sex: towards feminist Marxism. In *Feminist Marxism and Marxist Feminism: A Debate* (P. Armstrong, A. Connelly and A. Miles, eds). Garamond Press.

Beardwell, I. and Holden, L. (1997). *Human Resource Management Textbook: A Contemporary Perspective*, Financial Times Management.

Becker, G. (1971). *The Economics of Discrimination*. Chicago University Press.

Beechey, V. (1980). *Unequal Work*. Verso.

Blackburn R. M. and Mann, M. (1979). *The Working Class in the Labour Market*. Macmillan.

Brah, A. (1994). 'Race' and 'culture' in the gendering of labour markets: South Asian young Muslim women and the labour market. In *The Dynamics of Race and Gender: Some Feminist Interventions* (H. Afshar and M. Maynard, eds). Taylor and Francis.

Branine, M. and Glover, I. (1997). Ageism in work and employment: thinking about connections. *Personnel Review*, **26**, (4), 233–244.

Brown, C. (1992). 'Same difference': the persistence of racial disadvantage in the British employment market. In *Racism and Antiracism: Inequalities, Opportunities and Policies* (P. Braham, A. Rattansi and R. Skellington, eds). Sage.

Buvini, M. (1995). The feminisation of poverty? Research and policy needs. In *Reducing Poverty through Labour Market Policies: New Approaches to Poverty Analysis and Policy* (J. Figueiredo and Z. Shaheed, eds). International Labour Organization, International Institute for Labour Studies.

Capowski, G. and Peak, M. (1994). Ageism: the new diversity issue. *Management Review*, **83**, (10), 10–17.

Cockburn, C. (1983). *Brothers: Male Dominance and Technological Change*. Pluto.

Cockburn, C. (1991). *In the Way of Women: Men's Resistance to Sex Equality in Organisations*. Macmillan.

Colgan, F. and Tomlinson, F. (1991). Women in publishing: jobs or careers? *Personnel Review*, **20**, (5), 16–26.

Collinson, D. and Collinson, M. (1989). *Sexuality in the Workplace: The Domination of Men's Sexuality*. In *The Sexuality of Organisation* (J. Hearn, D. Sheppard, P. Tancred-Sheriff and G. Burrell, eds). Sage.

Collinson, D., Knights, D. and Collinson, M. (1990). *Managing to Discriminate*. Routledge.

Corcoran, M. and Courant, P. (1987). Sex role socialisation and occupational segregation: an exploratory investigation', *Journal of Post Keynesian Economics*, Spring, **9**, (3), 330–346.

Cully, M., Woodland, S., O'Reilly, A. and Dix, G. (1999). *Britain at Work*. Routledge.

Doeringer, P. and Piore, M. (1971). *Internal Labour Markets and Manpower Analysis*. D. C. Heath and Co.

England, P. (1982). The failure of human capital theory to explain occupational sex segregation. In *Gender and Economics* (J. Humphries and E. Elgar (1995)). Cambridge University Press.

England, P. and McCreary, L. (1986). Gender inequality in paid employment. In *Analyzing Gender* (M. Ferre and B. Hess, eds). Sage.

Giddens, A. (1991). *Modernity and Self-Identity: Self and Society in the Late Modern Age*. Polity Press.

Gutek, B. (1989). Sexuality in the workplace: key issues in social research and organisational practice. In *The Sexuality of Organisation* (J. Hearn, D. Sheppard, P. Tancred-Sheriff and G. Burrell, eds). Sage.

Haggerty, M. and Johnson, C. (1995). The hidden barriers of occupational segregation. *Journal of Economic Issues*, **29**, (1), 211–222.

Hakim, C. (1991). Grateful slaves and self made women: fact and fantasy in women's work orientations. *European Sociological Review*, **7**, (2), 101–118.

Hakim, C. (1992). Explaining trends in occupational segregation: the measurement, causes and consequences of the sexual division of labour. *European Sociological Review*, **8**, (2), 127–152.

Hall, M. (1989). private experiences in the public domain: lesbians in organisations. In *The Sexuality of Organisation* (J. Hearn, D. Sheppard, P. Tancred-Sheriff and G. Burrell, eds). Sage.

Hartmann, H. (1979). Capitalism, patriarchy and job segregation by sex. In *Capitalist Patriarchy and the Case for Socialist Feminism* (Z. Eisenstein, ed.). Monthly Review Press.

Jenkins, R. (1986). *Racism and Recruitment*. Cambridge University Press.

Jenkins, R. (1988). Discrimination and equal opportunities. In *Employment in Britain* (D. Gallie, ed.). Blackwell.

Jenkins, R. (1996). *Social Identity*. Routledge.

Kirton, G. and Healy, G. (1999). Transforming union women: the role of women trade union officials in union renewal. *Industrial Relations Journal*, **30**, (1), 31–46.

Lackzo, F. and Philopson, C. (1991). *Changing Work and Retirement*. Open University Press.

Lee, G. and Loveridge, R. (eds) (1987). *The Manufacture of Disadvantage*. Oxford University Press.

Maynard, M. (1994). 'Race', gender and the concept of 'difference' in feminist thought. In *The Dynamics of Race and Gender: Some Feminist Interventions* (H. Afshar and M. Maynard, eds). Taylor and Francis.

Mills, A. (1989). Gender, sexuality and organisation theory. In *The Sexuality of Organisation* (J. Hearn, D. Sheppard, P. Tancred-Sheriff and G. Burrell, eds). Sage.

Newell, S. (1993). The superwoman syndrome: gender differences in attitudes towards equal opportunities at work and towards domestic responsibilities at home. *Work Employment and Society*, **7**, (2), 275–289.

OECD (Organization for Economic Co-operation and Development) (1988). Women's activity employment and earnings: a review of recent developments. *OECD Employment Outlook*, Paris, September, 129–172.

Phizacklea, A. (1994). A single or segregated market? Gendered and racialised divisions. In *The Dynamics of Race and Gender: Some Feminist Interventions* (H. Afshar and M. Maynard, eds). Taylor and Francis.

Pringle, R. (1989). Bureaucracy, rationality and sexuality: the case of secretaries. In *The Sexuality of Organisation* (J. Hearn, D. Sheppard, P. Tancred-Sheriff and G. Burrell, eds). Sage.

Scheibl, F. (1996). *Part Time Workers: Grateful Slaves or Rational Time Maximising Individuals? An Examination of Fact and Fiction in Recent Explanations of Women's Preferences for Part Time Working.* Employment Studies Unit Paper 4, University of Hertfordshire.

Sharma, U. (1983). *Women, Work and Property in North-West India.* Tavistock Publications.

Treimann, D. and Hartmann, H. (1981). *Women, Work and Wages: Equal Pay for Work of Equal Value.* National Academic Press.

Turner, J., Grieco, M. and Apt, N. (1998). Gender, transport and the new deal: the social policy implications of gendered time, transport and travel. Paper presented at the Social Policy Association Conference, Lincoln, July.

Walby, S. (1990). *Theorizing Patriarchy.* Blackwell.

Watts, M. and Rich, J. (1993). Occupational sex segregation in Britain 1979–1989: the persistence of sexual stereotyping. *Cambridge Journal of Economics,* **17**, 159–177.

# Chapter 4

# Diversity, equality and discrimination in organizations

## Aim

To examine diversity, equality and discrimination issues at the level of the organization, in particular the way in which organizational cultures give rise to (indirect and often subtle forms of) discrimination and inequality.

## Objectives

■ To outline the development of approaches to organizational analysis.
■ To discuss the concept of cultural hegemony and how it contributes to the persistence of inequalities.
■ To explore organizational culture from the perspectives of diverse social groups.

## Introduction

In Chapters 2 and 3 we examined employment at a macrolevel. In Chapter 2 we outlined employment trends among diverse social groups and demonstrated that when considered as discrete categories, there are discernible patterns of unequal outcomes among women, minority ethnic groups, older people, disabled people and lesbians and gay men. In Chapter 3, we sought to explain these phenomena using a range of theoretical and critical perspectives. In this chapter, we shift the focus to the level of the organization – the microlevel. Here, we seek to understand the nature of the organization itself and how it contributes to reproducing and reinforcing traditional patterns of disadvantage.

The chapter begins by examining developments in approaches to organizational analysis, drawing attention to the importance of the emergence of gendered organizational analysis for a diversity perspective. The nature of organizational culture is discussed; especially in so far as it can be viewed as a subjective phenomenon, one that is not neutral, but laden with diverse meanings and symbolism. The remaining sections of the chapter are organized around the five social groups upon which this book focuses. This is because different aspects of organizational cultures impact on social groups in qualitatively different ways, resulting in different patterns of disadvantage and inequality. In this vein, we select some of the most salient illustrations of the consequences of organizational cultures for each social group. Before proceeding, it is important to note that we do not wish to give the impression that organizational life has only negative consequences for the social groups we focus on. On the contrary, work and organizations can offer opportunities for socialization, personal growth and development, and of course economic security.

# A 'new' approach to organizational analysis

The past fifty years has witnessed the development of a distinctive sociology of organizations (Tancred-Sheriff and Campbell, 1992). Organizational analysis is concerned with 'the process and dynamics that create and maintain given organizational realities and, from a radical perspective, the impact of those realities upon the construction of social relationships' (Mills and Tancred, 1992: 49). The traditional approach to organizational analysis has been criticized by a number of contemporary organizational theorists (examples are cited in this chapter), writing from a feminist or pro-feminist perspective, for its neglect of gender, sexuality and race. There is, then, widespread acceptance that organizational analysis has traditionally 'occurred through a lens which is primarily white and male' (Cianni and Romberger, 1997: 116), the consequence of which is that organizational knowledge has hegemonic characteristics, (the concept of hegemony is discussed further below). Consider, for example, the influential Hawthorne studies, which explored the relationship between motivation and performance, and involved research with a group of women and a group of men. Contemporary commentaries and analyses of the studies still often fail to draw attention to salient gender differentials in the research findings (Acker and Van Houten, 1992; Mills, 1992). This type of 'gender-blind' approach to and interpretation of research fails to acknowledge gender as a critical feature or significant dynamic of organizational behaviour, which many writers now argue it to be (for example, Acker, 1992; Cockburn, 1991; Gherardi, 1996; Mills, 1992; Pringle, 1989). Thus, the consequence of the neglect of gender and diversity in organizational analysis has been the acceptance (particularly in the management literature) of white, non-disabled, heterosexual men's experiences and interpretations of organizational life as generally valid and universally applicable (Alvesson and Billing, 1997).

In contrast to the neutral approach, many writers are now seeking to redirect organizational analysis towards uncovering the gendered, heterosexualized and racialized nature of organizational structures, cultures and processes, and the causes and consequences thereof. However, although there now exists a plethora of literature examining gender and organization, there remains a greater or lesser research and knowledge gap in terms of understanding organizations from the perspectives of minority ethnic groups, older people, disabled people and lesbians and gay men. The gap is particularly notable in the case of disability. The neglect of the study of gender and diversity within organizations has occurred, first, because of the traditional research focus on senior levels of occupational and organizational hierarchies (Acker and Van Houten, 1992), in which white, non-disabled men predominate and which are, therefore, relatively homogeneous. Second, they occurred because of white, non-disabled male domination of the research process itself (Alvesson and Billing, 1997; Hearn and Parkin, 1992; Tancred-Sheriff and Campbell, 1992) until fairly recently, which arguably resulted in a lack of interest in women and other social groups. Further, the recent focus on gender and organizations has occurred partly because gender and gendered relations within organizations are now widely believed to be ubiquitous (Burrell and Hearn, 1989), as is male power (Hearn and Parkin, 1992). From this perspective, the question of how men relate to each other and to women (Hearn and Parkin, 1992) – that is, gender relations – is central to understanding organizations and the nature of authority and power relationships therein. It can be argued that a focus on gender can also extend to embrace a multiplicity of overlapping diversity issues, including those of race, disability, age and sexual orientation, as these all intersect with gender relations.

In the face of this research and knowledge gap, students of organization theory are required to make intergroup connections, for which empirical support may be lacking. Nevertheless, the body of research on gender and organization has importantly drawn attention to the masculine bias of organizations and exposed the variety of subjective experiences of organizations that do not accord with the male-biased interpretations traditionally presented. The burgeoning 'women in management' literature is an example of this (see also Chapter 9). Thus, the insights into organizations, which have been provided by researching gender, can be drawn upon in seeking to understand diverse experiences of organizations.

## Key learning points

1 Historically, organizational analysis has tended to view organizations as neutral and objective realities. More recently a new approach has emerged, which places gender and gendered relations at the centre of analysis and understanding, with a large body of literature now available. However, there persists a greater or lesser research gap in the analysis of organizations from the perspectives of other diverse social groups.

# Understanding organizational culture

The central focus of this chapter is organizational culture, which is usually defined in terms of shared symbols, language, practices and deeply embedded beliefs and values (Newman, 1995). Newman is among the many writers who argue that each of these manifestations of organizational culture is gendered, in that organizations are important sites in which gendered meanings, identities, practices and power relations are sustained (Newman, 1995: 11). It can also be added that organizations are sites for the creation, reproduction and enactment of *multiple* (or diverse) meanings and identities. Thus, the notion of 'shared values' within organizations is called into question, as is the assumption that culture change can be manufactured or managed (Legge, 1995). Nevertheless, organizational power-holders occupy a structural position from which to manipulate the cultural signals and messages, which the organization projects both internally and externally. Thus, the values of the dominant group come to be seen as those of the organization. An understanding of power, its locations and its exercise is, then, essential in order to understand how dominant cultures are produced and reproduced (Newman, 1995).

Newman criticizes models of organizational culture as found in management texts, on the grounds that spurious assumptions underpin them. These assumptions are, first, that cultures are 'closed societies', an assumption which leads to neglect of the impact of the external environment, including discrimination and social disadvantages in wider society. Second, 'cultures are integrated wholes' in which a unitary concept of 'corporate culture' is drawn upon. Third, 'cultures are consensual', therefore, very little attention is paid to conflict and resistance. Fourth, 'culture is objective reality', with a distinct set of uncontested and incontestable characteristics, an assumption which ignores differentiated subjective experiences of organizational cultures. Fifth, 'culture is static', in other words a phenomenon that can be managed and changed in an unproblematic fashion. Finally, 'culture can be changed through new symbols', an assumption which suggests management intervention at a superficial level will create new values (Newman, 1995: 22). The point to draw out here is that it is necessary to reconceptualize organizational culture if the embedded nature of inequalities is to be understood.

Similarly critical of traditional approaches, Mills (1992: 98) identifies three crucial factors, which a focus on organizational culture should highlight. These are the relationship between societal values and organizational behaviour, the importance of powerful actors in the development of value systems and the significance of organization as a subjective experience. Importantly, the study of organizational cultures is concerned with the qualitative and symbolic aspects of organizational life (Mills, 1992), which require interpretation. This chapter seeks to avoid the kind of reification of the organization found within the traditional approach, which both Newman and Mills criticize, an approach which results in organizational cultures, structures and processes being treated as neutral, even rational, objectivities.

| **Key learning points** | 1 The orthodox managerialist and essentially unitarist concept of 'shared values' is weakened when organizations are analysed and understood from a gendered or diversity perspective. |
|---|---|
| | 2 The study of organizational culture is concerned with investigating and exploring the qualitative and symbolic aspects of organizational life. These cannot be measured objectively, but require interpretation. |

# The hegemony of organizational culture

In the introduction to this book we describe the categories of women, men, minority ethnic, lesbian, gay, disabled, older workers as social groups. Membership of social groups rests partly on the possession of a single or set of characteristics associated with that group. Social group membership is not entirely voluntary, in that classificatory characteristics may be ascribed by others. When those 'others' are in powerful positions, for example, managers and employers, such ascription can have negative consequences for individuals. Therefore, individuals cannot always escape their social group membership. This discussion has particular salience when seeking to explore the reasons for the persistence of inequality in employment and organizations. For example, in occupational or organizational settings where feminine characteristics are regarded as inappropriate or even detrimental, fewer women than men will be able to meet the requirements imposed, especially by male managers, even if overt or conscious gender-based discrimination does not take place. Collinson, Knights and Collinson (1990) show this in their case study of the insurance industry where women were excluded from sales jobs, through both the conscious and unconscious practices of male managers, and for similar reasons channelled into office clerical work, for which feminine characteristics were deemed more appropriate. Cockburn describes processes such as these as masculine hegemony. She says that masculine hegemony is 'sway exerted over *women and men alike*, not by legal coercion or economic compulsion but by cultural means, by force of ideas' (Cockburn, 1991: 168, emphasis added). Cockburn argues that explanations for women's inequality, such as their presumed preference for and prioritizing of domestic life, represent hegemonic ideas in the sense that they appear as truth or reality to most people. It is this hegemonic force that renders popular explanations for gender inequality difficult to contest, resist or defy, so that both women and men are bound or guided in their behaviours by a hegemonic cultural force.

Notions of masculinity and femininity are, then, central to understanding the sexual division of labour (or occupational sex segregation) and the sex-typing of jobs. Most types of work and occupations are associated with masculine or feminine characteristics. (For a detailed discussion of masculinities and femininities see, for example, Alvesson and Billing, 1997; Collinson and Collinson, 1997) Alvesson and Billing (1997) argue that work and occupations are also infused with gender symbolism. They suggest examples of occupations with a strong masculine symbolism include firefighter (despite the recent name change from 'fireman') and army officer. Examples they give of occupations with a strong feminine symbolism include secretary and nurse (Alvesson and Billing, 1997: 90). Cockburn's (1991) and Collinson, Knights and Collinson (1990) work draws similar conclusions, with the jobs of trade union official and insurance sales person permeated with masculine meaning and the jobs of retail sales assistant and clerical support worker permeated with feminine meaning. The consequence of such powerful gender symbolism is that individual men or women who transcend traditional occupational boundaries often find themselves in a precarious and isolated position, with adverse consequences, which we discuss below. Further, there are of course economic disadvantages associated with work constructed as feminine, in that it is generally low paid and affords fewer opportunities for advancement. There are then 'vertical' consequences associated with sex-typing, in that management and leadership are traditionally constructed as masculine (Collinson and Hearn, 1994). Similarly, the stereotyping of other social groups is reflected and manifest in organizational cultures, often with adverse consequences for the group concerned.

For example, Cockburn applies her ideas on hegemonic culture to the issue of ethnicity, arguing that a 'national hegemony' is created by 'a white ruling group' (Cockburn, 1991: 185). According to this account, minority ethnic groups must integrate and become acceptable to the white 'host' society. In a similar vein, so too must homosexuals conceal or suppress their sexual orientation in order to be acceptable within a dominant or hegemonic heterosexualized culture. Thus, it should not be assumed that men represent a unitary category – there are status differences between men, especially along the lines of race and ethnicity, sexual orientation, age and disability. Nevertheless, a discourse is created in which organizational cultures are constructed and legitimated as monocultures, from which deviants or those regarded as 'other' (Gherardi, 1996) are excluded if not literally, then symbolically. Gherardi suggests that there are various types of organizational cultures whose gender relations are characterized by a 'guest–host' dynamic, in which women are constructed and understood as the guests and men are the hosts (Gherardi, 1996: 199). Again, this argument can be applied to other social groups, who may also be constructed as 'guests' for failing to conform to the expected norm and thereby challenging the social order.

Alvesson and Billing (1997: 107) talk about the 'pressure for homogeneity and culturally competent behaviour'. This involves individuals, consciously or unconsciously, conforming and adapting to organization norms, for example, by adopting the expected and desired language, style, appearance and so on. Even from this perspective the demand for 'cultural competence' serves the self-perpetuating functions of both reinforcing and reproducing the dominant monoculture. It is those people most likely to be constructed as 'other' who are required to make the most adaptations. This is likely to include women, minority ethnic workers, lesbians and gay men. Age and disability are also likely to matter in this respect. Cockburn's (1991) research finds that managers and other non-disabled employees fear disability, yet at the same time disabled people are often deemed worthy of sympathy, unlike for example, black people or women. Nevertheless, it can be argued that both fear and sympathy responses to disability are indicators of a type of organizational culture, which constructs disabled people as 'other' and thereby as unacceptable or unwelcome.

**Key learning points**

1 Organizational culture can be understood as masculine-biased, with the consequence that women and other 'minority' groups are constructed as 'other' or as 'guests'.
2 Within organizations there are pressures for conformity, assimilation and homogeneity, which operate to marginalize or exclude those who are 'other'.

# Organizational culture: unpacking diversity issues

## Women in organizations

In this section we illustrate how organizational cultures are gendered and we explore some of the ways in which women are disadvantaged by such hegemonic organizational culture. We examine some of the actions, events, objects and language through which culture is manifested (Alvesson and Billing, 1997). These manifestations are infused to a greater or lesser extent with gendered meanings, which are often unarticulated and thus rendered invisible (Itzin, 1995a) and regarded as 'natural'. The challenge to students of organization is, then, to interpret and decipher through a gendered lens, social practices, processes and relations which are taken for granted and structures which are regarded as neutral.

The hierarchy of gender – male dominance and female subordination (Itzin, 1995b) – is enacted through or manifested in a number of 'rules' (written or unwritten, formal or informal), which frame the organizational culture. We use two examples to illustrate this. The societal and organizational hierarchy of gender is often reflected in meetings, where a senior (male) manager's authority is underscored by his domination of a meeting (Alvesson and Billing, 1997). Hierarchical and patriarchal relations may also be rendered visible at organizational meetings by formal seating arrangements – for example, the top table being reserved for the most senior members of the group, who in most organizational settings are predominantly white males. Or by the formal servicing arrangements – the minutes being taken by the female secretary and refreshments served by the female canteen worker. These are examples of the way in which the sexual division of labour produces a gendered hierarchical order. Nowhere is the gender hierarchy more evident than in the boss–secretary relationship. Pringle argues that gender and sexuality are central to all workplace power relations and that the boss–secretary relationship provides the most vivid illustration of this; it is, she says, the 'paradigm case' of gender relations in organizations (Pringle, 1989: 158). The male boss–female secretary relationship is one which is also heterosexualized. Secretaries are often described as 'office wives' – the secretary typically has a close personal relationship with her boss, reflected in the personal services she provides to him, organizing his personal as well as work life. She is also expected to be loyal to him and she derives her status from that of her boss – these are the informal 'rules'.

From a gender perspective, one of the most patent, and potent, symbols of organizational culture or the gender hierarchy is dress. Different dress norms and rules for men and women can either be formally imposed by the organization – by way of a written or unwritten dress code or by way of a uniform – or self-imposed (that is, informally) by men and women, who can be said to internalize notions of femininity and masculinity and express these through dress. It is axiomatic that different types of organizations have their differing dress norms and rules, but these are almost always gendered. This is the case even if we omit from the analysis instances where uniforms are used deliberately to sexualize or eroticize women, for example, some waitress or airline attendant uniforms. In her study of a retail company, Cockburn describes how women retail and office workers are required to adopt a feminine, though not sexual, appearance. She contrasts this with the appearance of male workers, 'The men move together, a solid mass of grey, conversing in deep tones. The women by contrast tap-tap along, chatting and laughing, colourful as a bunch of flowers. Gender differentiation is total' (Cockburn, 1991: 151). Cockburn argues that at one level the men's and women's dress is a matter of personal choice; at another, it is compulsorily differentiated by the powerful social norms governing behaviour within the organization. Moreover, dress is deeply symbolic of male authority (Cockburn, 1991: 149) in that the men's appearance and behaviour are more earnest – it is in this sense that dress both reflects and constructs a gender hierarchy. Gendered and stereotyped appearances, according to Gutek (1989), thus convey a sense of men as organizational beings and of women as sexual beings. She further argues that because it is men who are viewed as analytical, logical and assertive, women who do not adopt masculine modes of appearance and behaviour will not generally be perceived as possessing such abilities (Gutek, 1989: 60).

Dress can be viewed, then, as one dimension of a 'symbolic order of gender' (Gherardi, 1996: 190), a means of constructing and underscoring gender difference and, at the same time, women's subordination. The question of women wearing trousers to work is especially pertinent in this respect. Cockburn (1991) claims that in most organizations women are still made to feel uncomfortable wearing trousers, even if they are not explicitly forbidden to do so. On the grounds of health and safety, it could be argued that trousers are more suitable for some occupations, nurses for instance. Yet female nurses are still almost always required to wear skirts (Labour Research, 1994). This discussion leads to the race and ethnicity dimension of gendered dress codes. Labour Research (1994) cites various instances where minority ethnic women have objected on religious grounds to not being permitted to wear trousers at work.

As suggested above, dress at work is also significant in that it has the potential to purvey sexual attractiveness. There are many examples of jobs dominated by women, which implicitly, if not explicitly, require sexual attractiveness – receptionist, secretary, airline attendant. By contrast, there are very few jobs, unconnected with the sex industry, which require the same of men. Therefore, dress carries a potent symbolism for women. In her research, Gutek finds that at work women want to be recognized for their accomplishments not their sexual attractiveness (Gutek, 1989: 65), in other words, for what they do, not *what they are*. When sexual attractiveness is perceived to be the key qualification for a job, that work will be devalued and trivialized (Gutek, 1989). Because of this women managers and professionals may seek to establish, through the medium of dress, difference between themselves and lower status women (Sheppard, 1989). This involves selectively borrowing masculine modes of appearance – the muted colours, the tailored suit, short or medium-length hair – yet retaining a degree of gender appropriateness (Cianni and Romberger, 1997). Dress is often regarded as especially problematic for women managers, who walk a tightrope between appearing to be overly masculine and overly feminine, both of which could be detrimental to the exercise of managerial authority (Gutek, 1989; Sheppard, 1989). Thus, women managers are required to manage their femininity at the workplace (Gutek, 1989), whereas, Cockburn (1991) suggests that manual women have more freedom and flexibility.

We turn now to examine gendered dimensions of organizational practices and of social relations within the organization, and their ramifications. Earlier in this chapter we argued that most organizational cultures are permeated with predominantly masculine values and characteristics. One of the most significant ways in which gendered cultural assumptions permeate organizational practice relates to patterns and hours of work. For example, the so-called 'long hours culture' (Collinson and Hearn, 1994) – the requirement to demonstrate commitment to the organization by working beyond contractual hours – presents practical problems and dilemmas to women, which are not experienced by most men. This relates to the fact that it is typically women who assume responsibility for domestic matters, for example, childcare, which bring time pressures to bear on women to a far greater degree than on men. Further, it can be argued that the notion of 'career' is a masculine construct, in so far as it is usually associated with a continuous, unbroken record of full-time employment (Collinson and Hearn, 1994), a pattern to which most women's work experiences do not conform. Thus, the concept of the 'career woman' becomes synonymous with either a woman who has chosen not to have children, or a woman who has sacrificed the primacy of her mothering role to her paid work. These constraints do not apply to men, in the sense that it is generally assumed that men's primary sphere of activity will be that of paid work. Men are, then, better able to separate work from home and subordinate all other activities to that of paid employment (Collinson and Hearn, 1994).

Time constraints also come to bear on the issue of accessing social networks, as activities often take place outside normal working hours. Thus, the dynamics of organizational social life are also gendered. This has especially adverse consequences for women managers and professionals, and is partly responsible for the construction of the so-called 'glass ceiling' – the invisible barrier to women's advancement. Obvious examples include the pub or golf club cultures, where business relationships are often cemented. These activities do not formally exclude women, but because of gendered social divisions, women typically feel less comfortable in these traditionally male social settings (Cianni and Romberger, 1997). Cianni and Romberger (1997) suggest that social networks provide access to vital information and afford opportunities to form strategic alliances, both of which are essential for women managers and professionals. Therefore, exclusion or marginalization has detrimental consequences for these women.

Women are also (informally) excluded from male-dominated social networks by the behaviour and practices of male colleagues. There is a body of feminist research, which explores how men can mobilize masculine bias to control and subordinate women. Sexual humour is one such medium that both dominant and subordinate men can use to exclude, alienate and thereby control women. Collinson and Collinson's research on the shop floor uncovers the everyday utilization of sexual humour, which constructed an image of men as 'assertive, independent, powerful and sexually insatiable' (Collinson and Collinson, 1989: 95). In contrast, women were constructed as passive and dependent. In her research in a retail company, Cockburn recounts events at a team meeting of the computer division. In introducing the meeting, a senior manager produced a life-sized photograph of a bare-breasted model and proceeded with an 'ice-breaker' infused with sexual and sexist jokes, allusions and innuendo (Cockburn, 1991: 153). Cockburn argues that this example of 'male clubbing' in senior ranks produces a culture which, 'includes women *but marginalises and controls them*' (Cockburn, 1991: 153, original emphasis). In other words, stereotypical masculine sexual humour includes women on male-defined terms. Thus, sexualization of the workplace and objectification of women serves to trivialize and undermine women as organizational beings. It also creates a sense of in-group identity for men, where women are the outsiders (Cianni and Romberger, 1997). Women can, of course, join in with sexualized banter, but in so doing they risk, according to Cockburn (1991), being perceived negatively as unfeminine, lesbian or feminist. Collinson and Collinson draw attention to the consequences *for men* of non-participation in sexual banter and joking – the raising of serious questions about 'the deviants' masculinity' (Collinson and Collinson, 1989: 96). There are therefore powerful cultural forces inducing men to participate.

In addition to creating credibility problems for women at work (Itzin, 1995a), sexual humour can easily spill over and become sexual harassment. Rubenstein (1989: 226) contends that 'sexual harassment is a new term for an old phenomenon'. In making the case for legal provisions to prevent sexual harassment, Rubenstein argues that it undermines the dignity of women at work and is 'one of the most demeaning experiences an employee can suffer' (Rubenstein, 1989: 229). What distinguishes sexual harassment from consensual sexual relations is that it is unwanted and unwelcome behaviour. Further, it is likely to 'reflect broader patterns of sexual expression which are culturally acceptable in the wider society' (Collinson and Collinson, 1992: 11–12) and the phenomenon may therefore go unchallenged by both women and men. Much sexual harassment takes place within the arena of organizational social life (Collinson and Collinson, 1992), especially when alcohol is flowing, but it also takes place in the normal work environment as a brief examination of employment tribunal cases will undoubtedly demonstrate (see, for example, Equal Opportunities Review's *Discrimination Law Digest*).

From a feminist perspective, sexual harassment can be interpreted as a gendered power struggle (Cockburn, 1991). In her research, DiTomaso (1989) argues that two categories of women are particularly vulnerable to and conscious of sexual harassment. These are women who transcend either vertical and/or horizontal gendered job boundaries: first, women who climb the organizational ladder and assume positions of authority; second, women who enter traditional male (dominated) occupations. Either way, women are competing with men for jobs and in so doing are also challenging traditional gender-role stereotyping on which identity is constructed. Cockburn (1991) concurs, arguing that sexual harassment is a controlling gesture, reminding women that they remain vulnerable to men's power. Collinson and Collinson's (1997) research in the insurance industry also confirms this argument. They found men reduced women entrants to sexual objects of ridicule and in so doing reproduced the dominant masculine culture, which had traditionally excluded women from senior positions.

## Key learning points

1 Organizational cultures are infused with gendered meanings, which are often unarticulated and thus rendered invisible. The gendered hierarchy is an example, as are various unwritten codes, rules, customs and habits, which guide gendered behaviour and underpin expectations of organizational members.

2 Sexual harassment and the use of sexual humour are pervasive and the outcome of workplace gendered social relations, which are also powerful mechanisms for the control and subordination of women.

## Activity

### Activity 4.1: Championing women in British Telecom

As part of its strategy to proactively capitalize on a diverse workforce, British Telecom (BT) has developed a number of initiatives designed to raise the visibility of gender issues and change attitudes and behaviours within the organization. One of these initiatives is the BT Women's Network (BTWN), started by a group of women who attended one of the company's original women's management development programmes in 1986. The underlying belief is that the network represents an important way of alleviating women's feeling of isolation in this male-dominated company and industry, and of increasing women's sense of involvement within the company. The network is supported and resourced by BT with the aim of progressing women throughout the company.

The network encourages women's self-development through sharing experience, information and advice, and acts as a channel to communicate ideas back to the company. Membership is free and open to all BT women. The network hosts events in London and at other locations within and outside the UK. It also has its own intranet website set up by and for women in the company, which represents a tool for the women's network to achieve its overall aim of progressing women. The website's function is to give easy access to information about the women's network and it invites women to contact the network with ideas. The website is an important development because it removes the gendered barriers that may exist because of geographic boundaries and time availability. It also enables women to develop skills in technological communication.

*Source*: Edited abstract from 'BT: championing women in a man's world', *Equal Opportunities Review*, (84), March–April 1999.

### Questions

1 Discuss the significance of this initiative within the context of a male-dominated environment. What can women's networking be expected to achieve for women and for British Telecom?
2 In what sense are geographic boundaries and time availability gendered barriers?
3 This is a seemingly positive initiative in terms of encouraging women's progression. Can you identify any possible negative ramifications or obstacles to the achievement of its aims? (To answer this question you may need to draw on other chapters, including Chapters 3, 5 and 9.)

## Minority ethnic workers in organizations

'Disadvantage in the labour market does not "just happen", it is neither "natural" nor is it solely the unintended consequence of actors' practices' (Jenkins and Parker, 1987: 58). In Chapter 2 we examined employment patterns and trends among minority ethnic groups. These indicate disadvantage, which according to Jenkins and Parker (1987: 58) is a 'socially constructed phenomenon'. In this chapter we seek to understand how 'racialized' organizational cultures contribute to the social construction of disadvantage.

Many of the issues discussed earlier in relation to women and the gendering of organizational cultures have racialized dimensions. For example, we have explored in some detail the issue of dress. As we have seen, dress is an important way of underscoring difference between women and men and, thereby, the gendered hierarchy. It is also a visible feature of ethnic difference (Modood, 1997), laden with symbolism. Modood (1997: 326) suggests that the wearing of 'traditional clothes' can be resented by indigenous peoples. This is evidenced by employment tribunal cases centred on the rights of minority ethnic employees to wear traditional clothes and hairstyles at work. Modood's detailed examination of clothes and appearance among minority ethnic groups finds, for example, that only 1 per cent of men and 12 per cent of women sometimes wear Asian clothes at work. Whereas there is a generational decline in the use of traditional Asian clothes at work (especially among Hindus and Sikhs), the opposite is true for Caribbean people. This group is more likely to use dress or hair as a means of marking a cultural dimension to their ethnicity (Modood, 1997: 328). It appears that overall a significant proportion of younger Asian and Caribbean people are choosing in different settings and on different occasions to wear clothes that either display or downplay their ethnic identity. This is attributable to the perceived pressure for assimilation and the perceived links between overt projection of ethnic identity and direct and indirect discrimination in certain social contexts, employment for instance.

Cockburn argues that the system of male power that underpins organizations is 'specifically *white* male power' (Cockburn 1991: 174, original emphasis). Racial stereotypes often inform the allocation of work and employment decisions (Cockburn, 1991; Jenkins, 1985). Whilst sex stereotyping can result in a *preference* for women in certain occupations (there are numerous examples, especially in the service and 'caring' sectors), race stereotyping rarely results in a preference for minority ethnic people (Cockburn, 1991), because race stereotypes almost always connote negative characteristics. There is, however, diversity in the way different minority ethnic groups are stereotyped, suggesting that the issue is more complex than that of a crude response to skin colour. For example, as stated in Chapter 3, Jenkins (1985: 152) suggests that black Caribbean people are commonly stereotyped as 'lazy, happy-go-lucky or slow', or Asians are 'clannish and don't mix'. The explanation for this may lie in the different groups' relationship to British colonialism (Modood, 1997), but race stereotyping is almost always damaging in the employment context. According to Jenkins, racial stereotyping informs managers' and employers' conceptions of 'acceptability' and, he argues, the non-specific criteria of acceptability shape recruitment decisions (Jenkins, 1985: 149). He divides the criteria of acceptability into three categories – primary, secondary and tertiary – according to their apparent significance to managers. Primary criteria included appearance, manner, attitude and maturity; secondary criteria included 'gut feeling', speech style, age and the ability to 'fit in'; tertiary criteria were English language competence and employer references (Jenkins, 1985: 149). Jenkins shows how many of these criteria are not only highly subjective, but also racialized. It is in this sense that race discrimination in employment is socially constructed.

Different ethnic groups are ascribed cultural traits, which are praised or condemned (Modood, 1997: 149) and which will impact (in many instances negatively) on their ability to 'fit in', when such ability is judged through the eyes of a white employer or manager. One case study of a major retail organization (O'Neilly, 1995) provides an example of the complex and subtle processes of unconscious discrimination in selection and appraisal. The study examined the appraisal forms of a matched sample of ethnic minority and white staff. The white sample revealed more encouraging comments and a third more white staff were in the 'ready for promotion' grade than were minority ethnic staff – it should be noted that all line managers conducting appraisal were white.

Modood's survey confirms the damaging nature of race discrimination. It shows the majority of economically active people in all ethnic groups believe that employers refuse people jobs for racial or religious reasons (Modood, 1997: 130). The *belief* that employers discriminate is much more widespread than actual *experiences* of discrimination. This is because people do not always know that they have been discriminated against. This survey finds that a fifth of minority ethnic people, who had ever been economically active, believed that they had been refused a job for racial or religious reasons – because they would not 'fit in'.

In her US-based research DiTomaso (1989) finds that minority ethnic women's experiences of discrimination and harassment are qualitatively different from that of white women. Her data show that white and Hispanic females were most likely to attribute discrimination to their gender, whilst most black women felt they had experienced race discrimination. Both black women and black men believed they had experienced worse treatment at the hands of their supervisors than their white or Hispanic counterparts (DiTomaso, 1989: 84). This echoes Cianni and Romberger's (1997) US study, which finds all ethnic groups believing there to exist racial and ethnic barriers to success within a large organization. These barriers included language skills, accents, stereotyping, difference in cultural values, and experiences. Further, the use of racist jokes and humour served to reinforce and reproduce stereotyped beliefs about minority ethnic groups at the same time as leading to negative organizational experiences among black and Hispanic employees. In their study, women and minority ethnic employees referred to the 'automatic camaraderie' (Cianni and Romberger, 1997: 120) among white men, which conferred inclusion in important and powerful informal networks. The overwhelming majority (96 per cent) of white participants in the study reported having supervisors of the same race, whilst the same proportion of black participants had supervisors of a different race. This raises the question of sponsorship and more generally the importance of racialized social relations in the workplace, and the role they play in reproducing inequality or in constructing the so-called 'concrete ceiling' – the almost impenetrable barrier to minority ethnic workers' advancement. Although the DiTomaso and Cianni and Romberger research is situated in the US context, both studies demonstrate the importance of researching diverse experiences of organizational cultures in order to gain a complete picture. Further, both studies underscore the way in which subjective experiences are mediated by both gender and race.

| **Key learning points** | 1 'Racialized' organizational cultures contribute to the social construction of disadvantage by creating negative racial stereotypes, which are used to guide decision-making in employment. |
|---|---|
| | 2 Racist stereotypes and beliefs are further reinforced by jokes and humour, the use of which leads to negative organizational experiences among minority ethnic groups. |

# Activity

## Activity 4.2: Changing image at Lloyds TSB

In the late 1990s the financial services group, Lloyds TSB, embarked upon a programme to increase the recruitment of minority ethnic employees, particularly to management and management training grades. Focus groups were used to investigate why ethnic minorities might not see a career with the bank as an attractive option. It was revealed that one of the main barriers was the company's image. Advertising literature presented a predominantly white workforce.

Lloyds TSB set out to improve minority ethnic graduate recruitment in a number of ways. It made significant changes to its advertising literature, with employees from more diverse ethnic backgrounds being shown both in and out of work to emphasize the bank's recognition of the importance of both work and home life. More case studies of minority ethnic graduates were included and e-mail addresses given for all employees featured, and it started to advertise in the minority ethnic press.

Recently the bank completed a survey of minority ethnic managers and the issues raised have been taken to the board. The aim of the survey was to look at the barriers, which exist to the promotion of minority ethnic employees. One issue, which arose, was the lack of role models for minority ethnic managers. When they looked above them they did not see themselves reflected and this affected their confidence and therefore their ability to apply for more senior posts.

*Source*: Edited extract from 'Improving recruitment and promotion opportunities for ethnic minorities', *Equal Opportunities Review*, (85), May–June 1999.

*Questions*

1 How important is image in creating an enabling organizational culture? Explain and justify your answers.
2 Why is it important for under-represented groups to have role models?
3 Evaluate the methods Lloyds TSB used to identify the barriers to minority ethnic progression.

## Lesbians and gay men in organizations

Most organizations are dominated by heterosexual men, and most organizationally oriented studies of sexual harassment and sexuality focus on heterosexuality (Burrell and Hearn, 1989: 21–3). This has led to a research gap and lack of theorizing on the collective dimensions to homosexuality within organizations (Oerton, 1996a). Cockburn (1991: 186) argues that 'all the assumptions in everyday relationship and discourse are heterosexual'. Men, she says, negotiate male solidarity around a heterosexual principle (Cockburn, 1991: 193). Consequently, lesbians and gay men are both constructed as 'other' and in opposition to heterosexual masculine identity and discourse. Organizations tend to be sites of hostility towards lesbians and gay men (Oerton, 1996b), many of whom conceal their sexual orientation to avoid discrimination and harassment (EOR, 1997). A paradoxical situation exists wherein homosexuality in organizations is ubiquitous (Hall, 1989) yet invisible, because of widespread non-disclosure of homosexual identity.

One dimension of organizational culture is the informal 'rules of behaviour', which construct norms and values. Sexuality becomes a symbol of power relations (Mills, 1989), where heterosexuality is the norm, and in which homosexuality is subordinate and subordinated because it poses a threat to the maintenance of the gendered hierarchy (Oerton, 1996b). Thus, a type of heterosexual hegemony comes to dominate the culture and discourse of the organization (Mills, 1998; Oerton, 1996a), with various detrimental consequences for lesbians and gay men. Oerton (1996a) characterizes male-dominated hierarchies as oppressively heterosexist and homosocial. This plays itself out in workplace social relations, where, for example, sexual banter and joking are of a heterosexual nature. We have argued earlier that this serves to subordinate and objectify women, but it also marginalizes in different ways, lesbians and gay men. Men cannot easily control lesbians (Cockburn, 1991) as their sense of sexual attractiveness or femininity is not dependent on male approval: patriarchal gender relations do not impact on lesbian women in the same way as on heterosexual women. However, difficulties do arise in workplace interactions and relations between lesbians and heterosexual men (Oerton, 1996b). Lesbians are less likely to engage in sexual banter with men, yet lesbianism is often eroticized by men (Oerton, 1996a). Lesbians' rejection or lack of interest in male sexual advances violates gendered expectations and often meets with retaliation or harassment (Hall, 1989). Gay men, on the other hand, are excluded from participating in heterosexual masculine humour and are more likely to be on the receiving end of such humour. Thus, jokes about gay men reinforce notions of heterosexual masculinity.

Earlier, we discussed the gendered dynamics of organizational social life: it could be said that organizational social life is also heterosexualized. For example, despite the now widespread usage of the more neutral term 'partner' (to replace wife/husband, boyfriend/girlfriend), couples are still generally assumed to be made up of a man and a woman. Such heterosexual or heterosexist assumptions lead some lesbians and gay men to keep secret their partners, thus assisting in the task of non-disclosure of sexual identity. This is arguably one of the most insidious forms of indirect discrimination experienced by lesbians and gay men – it represents a covert attack on the group's identity and dignity (EOR, 1997). Separation between work and leisure is forced (Hall, 1989), and this can lead to exclusion from important social networks or from pleasurable social banter. Hence, fear of being exposed as homosexual may lead some lesbians and gay men to voluntarily exclude themselves from organizational social life, leading to social isolation.

Cockburn (1991) suggests that equality for lesbians and gay men is the most contested and conflictual of equality projects. It is the one area unsupported by legislation or government initiated codes of practice. This in itself is indicative of the lack of consensus over the moral worthiness of the gay rights project. Cockburn (1991) cites the Aids panic of the 1980s, as one of the primary reasons for the growth of animosity against homosexuals. She proceeds to argue that homosexuality is 'pathologized' in popular discourse and associated with alcohol and drug abuse, and with obsession with sex and molestation. Further, homosexuality is popularly assumed to be elective in a way that gender, ethnicity or disability are not (Cockburn, 1991: 192).

Although homosexuality stands in opposition to heterosexuality, lesbians and gay men do not constitute a unitary category. Lesbians and gay men may share many common experiences of organizations, for example, the fears surrounding disclosure of sexual orientation, or of being 'outed' and the consequent negative ramifications. However, their experiences may at times diverge. For example, gay men undoubtedly challenge the norms and 'rules' of gendered behaviour and the heterosexual principle, but in so doing they are sometimes mysogynistic, representing women as loathsome (Cockburn, 1991). In other words, gay men are not always united with lesbian women in opposing the norms and values generated by heterosexual men. This is because, according to Cockburn (1991), gay men want to retain their position in the gendered (masculine) hierarchy. Further, lesbianism may worry heterosexual women as well as men (Cockburn, 1991) and, therefore, lesbians may experience a female-dominated environment as equally hostile as that of a male-dominated one. Nevertheless, lesbians and gay men do constitute a category, which experience discrimination in various forms because of their sexual orientation.

| Key learning point | 1 Organizational cultures pivot around heterosexual discourse, which constructs heterosexuality as the norm and homosexuality as deviant. This is evidenced by heterosexualized workplace social relations. |

## Activity

### Activity 4.3: Heterosexualized workplace culture

Surveys have revealed that a significant proportion of lesbian and gay employees conceal their sexual identity to avoid discrimination. The issue for an organization is what it can do to create a workplace culture in which lesbian and gay employees feel able to be open about their sexuality. Formal policies prohibiting discrimination and harassment and provision for same-sex partners with respect to benefits are essential in demonstrating an organization's commitment to equal treatment. However, it is likely that measures other than formal policies are required to overcome the informal and heterosexualized social relations within organizations.

The gay rights organization, Stonewall, recommends that employers should encourage the development of lesbian and gay groups in the workplace and should consult these groups on policies and procedures affecting them. Another step is to appoint a member of staff whose brief it is to support gay and lesbian employees. This might be a member of an equalities team or a personnel officer. This person could be approached by lesbians and gay men experiencing difficulties or in need of advice. South Yorkshire Police is an example of an organization which has taken this approach. The civilian officer appointed to the role believes that her existence does contribute towards creating an environment in which officers may eventually feel able to be open about their sexuality. The officer has also set up a gay support group, which runs gay awareness training sessions for organizations.

*Source*: Edited extract from 'Equality for lesbians and gay men in the workplace', *Equal Opportunities Review*, (74), July–August 1997.

*Questions*

1 Explain why many lesbian and gay employees conceal their sexual identity and the effects this may have on the group's work lives.
2 Discuss why and how support mechanisms for lesbians and gay men can assist in breaking down cultural hegemony.
3 What role is there for gay awareness training in changing the dominant monoculture?

## Disability in organizations

Most non-disabled people have very little personal contact with disabled people (EOR, 1998a). Many disabled children are educated in segregated establishments (French, 1996b) and disabled adults are underemployed (Thornton and Lunt, 1995). It is possible, therefore, for non-disabled people to journey through childhood and adulthood with very little contact with disability. It is against this background that it is necessary to set a discussion about organizational culture in so far as it reinforces and reproduces inequalities among disabled people. Ignorance of and unfamiliarity with disability contribute to the pervasiveness of the many myths and stereotypes surrounding the issue.

There are two main approaches to understanding disability and its effects on individuals. Within the 'medical model', it is the physical disability and/or the psychological consequences thereof which prevent disabled individuals from participating in the labour market (Barnes, 1992). Opposing this approach, there is a view that disabled people are among the most excluded in society because of the *attitudes* of others rather than because of the physical barriers they encounter (EOR, 1998a). Disabled people experience society as hostile to them, with a substantial proportion believing that attitudinal barriers render it almost impossible to find employment (EOR, 1998a). Hyde (1996: 683) echoes this view arguing that 'discriminating employers are the main factor underlying disadvantage'. It is in this sense that disability can be viewed as a social construction and as a phenomenon 'caused not by the state of our bodies, but by the state of our society' (Davis, 1996: 124). From this 'social model'

(Thornton and Lunt, 1995) perspective, what is needed is the removal of the environmental and social barriers which prevent disabled people from participating fully in society (Davis, 1996). According to the social model, disadvantage does not arise inevitably because of physical impairment as in the 'medical model' (Hyde, 1996). In the employment context, then, it is work and organizations which need to change rather than disabled people needing to be 'cured' or subjected to therapeutic interventions. There are an infinite variety of causes of both mental and physical disability and the extent to which the disability will be experienced as disabling depends on the context and the demands and constraints of that context (Honey, Meager and Williams, 1993). Thus, it is not inevitable that disabled people will experience work negatively, although many do.

Employment is an important context in which access to opportunity, status and self-worth is located. Disabled people are influenced by the same expectations and aspirations towards work as are generally accepted to exist among the non-disabled population (Smith, 1996). However, with most disabled people in employment concentrated in low-paid, low-skilled, low-status jobs (Thornton and Lunt, 1995), there are few role models in senior positions who bear testimony to the intrinsic value of work. Negative employment experiences lead many disabled people to expect to fail at work (Smith, 1996), creating the 'discouraged worker' (Hyde, 1996) syndrome – disabled people, who in anticipation of discrimination, prefer not to work and to rely instead on state financial benefits.

Here we are concerned with the myths, stereotypes and attitudes that help to create negative labour market and organizational experiences among disabled people. It is thought that there exists a significant level of negative attitude in the general population towards disabled people. Those disabilities most disliked include alcoholism, mental illness, mental handicap and hunchback (French, 1996a). According to the various research that French reports on, there appears to be a preference for physical disabilities and those which are not visible. Any disability perceived to be self-inflicted (for example, disability arising from drug abuse or even Aids) carries its own particular stigma (French, 1996a) and does not attract the sympathy reserved for 'victims' of other disabilities. To the extent that organizations represent microcosms of wider society, it is possible to postulate that similar negative attitudes will be found among organizational members – in other words, among employers, managers and employees.

When evaluating the suitability for employment of a disabled person, non-disabled people tend to focus on *disability* rather than *ability*, yet disability is not the deterministic indicator of ability it is widely held to be (Honey, Meager and Williams, 1993). There are many widespread employer misconceptions surrounding the employment of disabled employees. The main ones are that disabled people represent a health and safety risk (both to themselves, other employees and customers), that they will have higher sickness absence rates, that they will be less productive, perform less well and be generally more expensive to employ (Honey, Meager and Williams, 1993; Roberts, 1996). It is also often claimed that disabled people will not fit in with other employees, who may feel unease or embarrassment at their presence (Honey, Meager and Williams, 1993). Thus, we can see how Jenkins's (1985) ideas (discussed previously in relation to race and ethnicity) on the importance of 'suitability' and 'acceptability' criteria have salience in respect of disability. Many of the perceived difficulties in employing disabled people expose stereotypical beliefs about disability – a focus on wheelchair users is commonplace for example. Alternatively, disability is equated with illness such that a disabled person cannot be perceived as healthy. What these stereotypes fail to acknowledge is the multiplicity of disability. Disability is often hidden and employees may prefer not to reveal it, for fear of encountering discrimination and negative attitudes and behaviour. Disability is also 'infinitely graduated' (Cockburn, 1991: 200): as well as taking an enormous variety of forms, it varies considerably in severity. It can also be temporary and/or recurring. The consequence of the ascription of stereotypical characteristics is the expectation that the behaviour of group members will be predictable (French, 1996a) and, therefore, that disability can be used as a criterion to frame selection decisions (in recruitment, for promotion, for training).

Disability is deeply feared by non-disabled people (Cockburn, 1991; Roberts, 1996). This is partly because illness and injury can unexpectedly cause disability to anyone at any time. It is thought that the presence of a disabled person serves as an uncomfortable reminder of this. Holding stereotypical beliefs about disability assists non-disabled people to psychologically distance themselves from the phenomenon, whilst reserving some pity or sympathy for some disabled individuals' conditions. Hence the tendency is to distinguish between those who 'deserve' their disability (that is, it is perceived to be self-inflicted by, for example, alcohol or drug abuse) and those who do not. It is the second category that is the most patent reminder that disability is not entirely within our personal control and yet paradoxically it is this group who attract greater sympathy.

Although disabled people's experiences of organizational life are differentiated according to the type and severity of disability, organizations are generally hostile sites for them because of the widely held negative attitudes towards disability. There are, however, factors other than attitudes that influence behaviour. These include habits, social norms and group pressure (French, 1996a), which may bind together in the organization to produce a hostile culture. In the organizational context, a culture that either condones or condemns (explicitly or implicitly) discriminatory attitudes and behaviour can develop. Consider, for example, humour. Jokes that ridicule difference abound and disability is often the object of such malevolent humour, as Cockburn (1991) demonstrates. Humour is often a test of an 'outsider's' ability to fit in with the prevailing culture in an unchallenging way. As we have shown earlier in relation to gender, humour is a powerful control mechanism, which can be used to bolster up the existing unequal social order.

Non-disabled people's lack of contact with disability is thought to be a potent obstacle to equality for disabled people. Contact is 'an important ingredient in bringing about positive attitude change' (French, 1996a: 159). French is mostly concerned with the relationship between health professionals and disabled people, but much of what she says has relevance for the social relations between non-disabled and disabled people within the organizational context. For example, she argues that *equal status* contact between disabled people and non-disabled people is especially important, for this is the context in which disabled people may present themselves as capable and as multifaceted (French, 1996a: 160).

## Key learning points

1 Non-disabled people's lack of contact with disability serves to reinforce the widespread fear and ignorance surrounding the issue and to perpetuate the many myths and stereotypes surrounding disabled people and their employment.
2 Many disabled people have negative experiences of organizational life because of the attitudes of others rather than because of the physical barriers they encounter.

## Activity

### Activity 4.4: Challenging disabling barriers

While the Disability Discrimination Act 1995 provides an essential legal framework for eradicating disability discrimination, the Act, for the most part, adopts a medical rather than a social model of disability, thereby focusing attention on what disabled people are unable to do. The social model, however, concentrates on tackling the external barriers encountered by disabled people, which are often the real causes of their exclusion from mainstream society. Glasgow City Council believes that disability discrimination is a social and civil rights issue, not a medical one, and has adopted a progressive approach to combating the disabling factors faced by people with impairments in the workplace.

A central plank of the council's approach is to mainstream disability issues by placing day-to-day operation of the disability policy firmly in the hands of directors and heads of departments. The policy provides detailed guidance for line managers on monitoring, recruitment and selection, and supporting disabled employees. Each director and head of department is required to prepare an annual report for submission to the personnel committee, to ensure the effectiveness of the disability employment policy. An action plan on equality, which includes disability, is also prepared by managers for incorporation in department service plans.

Another initiative has been the establishment of a disabled employees forum to enable the council to consult effectively with disabled employees and to provide the opportunity to meet and work together on policies, procedures, initiatives and concerns. The forum is run by disabled employees and meets on a quarterly basis. Disabled employees have elected their own working group, which is given administrative support by corporate personnel, and meets between forum meetings. The working group provides feedback on how policies and practices are affecting disabled staff, as well as acting as a source of new ideas.

There remain some concerns about filtering disability awareness issues down through the line management structure in an organization with such a large workforce and there are still complaints of discrimination against disabled people.

*Source*: Edited extract from 'Glasgow City Council – challenging disabling barriers', *Equal Opportunities Review*, (86), July–August 1999.

*Questions*

1 Critically evaluate the potential of the initiatives described above to transform the disabling culture of an organization. What are the strengths and weaknesses? What are the limitations?
2 How can disability awareness be filtered down through the line management structure?

## Older people in organizations

The issue of age intersects in different ways with other diversity issues, so that the effects of age on employment and organizational experiences cannot be fully understood without reference to other overlapping social groups. In Chapter 2 we examined older people's labour market participation. The age of fifty appears to be a turning point in the lifecycle in terms of employment experiences (McKay, 1998). For black people, it appears that age forty may be the turning point – this group's unemployment rate is almost double that of white over-forties (Labour Research, 1998). The incidence of disability and health problems rises with age, such that during the five years before age sixty, more than one-quarter of men and just under one-quarter of women are affected (McKay, 1998). Thus, it is likely that there are ageist dimensions to various forms of employment discrimination and disadvantage. However, it would be far too simplistic to suggest that direct employer discrimination against older people is the sole or main factor determining their labour market participation. For example, in the case of women, some research indicates that their motivation to continue working in later life may be low, especially where a woman has a retired husband (Ginn and Arber, 1995). Thus, questions of choice, preferences and social attitudes towards employment in later life influence patterns and trends. These supply-side factors are not examined here; rather we turn to consider the issue of ageist attitudes embedded in organizational cultures, which impact negatively on the subjective experiences of older workers.

As posited in Chapter 2, employer ageism is rife – evidence shows that more than 25 per cent of employers consider people too old to recruit at age fifty (DfEE, 1997), whilst 60 per cent consider people too old at age sixty (Taylor and Walker, 1994). In instances where managers have found themselves the victims of a particular economic and labour market trend, that of 'downsizing' and restructuring, and have been displaced from senior and well paid positions, many such employees are now competing for similarly senior jobs with younger candidates and encountering ageist attitudes. Employer ageism is reflected in recruitment advertisements, which often carry coded messages about the desired age range, even though the use of numerical age limits in job advertisements has sharply declined (EOR, 1998b). For example, many adverts use words or terms to describe the ideal candidate or to place that person in a young age range – 'first jobber', 'young, fast-moving entrepreneurial company' (EOR, 1998b). Such coded messages imply that a younger person would better fit in and deter older people from applying.

There are many myths and stereotypes underpinning the negative attitudes towards older employees. These centre on the perception of older people's unproductiveness, inflexibility, resistance to change and lower trainability. These views are reportedly widespread among line managers, and attitudinal research among business students suggests such views are likely to remain so (Taylor and Walker, 1994). Set against this are signs that some employers are becoming more positive towards older people, especially with regard to their perceived loyalty and reliability (Taylor and Walker, 1994). However, with negative attitudes outweighing positive, the jobs for which older employees are deemed particularly suitable are typically those which are lower skill, lower status and lower paid in, for example, the do-it-yourself stores and other parts of the service industry. Exemplars have been widely reported in the media, for instance, 'Older workers mean happier customers', *Guardian*, 17 November 1998 and 'Foundering on the rock of ageism', *Observer*, 22 November 1998. In view of present demographic trends, it could be argued that these positive signs are simply examples of employer responses to skill shortages, rather than of deep-seated cultural change.

In the organizational context, age has particular salience for women. Gendered ageism is a significant, deep-rooted cultural phenomenon. In an previous section of this chapter, we examined the heterosexual construction of certain workplace relationships and the gendered and sexualized nature of workplace social relations. In general women are perceived as being 'older' at a chronologically younger age than are men (Itzin and Phillipson, 1995). Youth comes into the frame as a gendered requirement of some types of jobs, especially those constructed as feminine or female. For example, feminine beauty and female sexual attractiveness are widely associated with youth and are required of women in certain types of jobs, creating difficulties for older women. In some instances it can be argued that female youth and beauty are 'sold' as part of the service. The female airline attendant is a good example of this. Until the early 1970s it was standard practice in the airline industry to dismiss women when they married or reached a certain age, usually thirty-two (Mills, 1998). Equality laws intervened to bring a halt to this directly discriminatory practice, but the occupation remains associated with images of femininity, youth and attractiveness.

Youth is preferred in other female occupations for different reasons, relating to women's childcare role and typically interrupted career histories. Some occupations and employers have a preference for women who are in the first phase of their working lives (before having children). For example, Pringle (1989) contends that family criteria are often used in the recruitment and selection of secretaries. Male bosses often avoid women with young children, because of the perceived difficulties in getting them to work long hours and also because of negative perceptions about such women's commitment to their work. Women managers meet a 'glass ceiling of age' (Itzin and Phillipson, 1995). The career break often takes women out of employment during the years which for men are considered to be the 'golden decade' – between ages thirty and forty. When they return, women managers frequently find themselves competing with younger men and the double bind of gender and age stereotyping, and consequent discrimination kicks in. What the above discussion and examples reveal is that gendered ageism is firmly linked to male perceptions of women. What women should be like, look like or be doing at any given age are all defined by men (Itzin and Phillipson, 1995), who predominate in organizational decision-making. However, gendered attitudes towards, and beliefs about, age are also internalized by women (Itzin and Phillipson, 1995), whose own behaviour and actions may reinforce male perceptions.

**Key learning points**

1 Employer ageism impacts on older people in different ways. In particular, it is mediated by race, gender and disability.
2 Myths and stereotypes underpin the negative attitudes towards older employees. Such views are apparently widespread among line managers and among business students, suggesting that they may be reproduced across generations.
3 Gendered ageism is a significant and deep-rooted cultural phenomenon, which is manifest in certain workplace relationships, in workplace social relations and In the requirements of some jobs.

## Activity

### Activity 4.5: Age bias reflected in job advertisements

There is evidence of a sharp decline in the use of numerical age limits in job advertisements, although the practice of stating age preferences does continue. The older the job seeker, the more likely it is that where an age range is specified, he or she will fall outside of it. The 'age of exclusion' from the London clerical, secretarial and administrative job market is much younger than that for the more senior commercial positions advertised in the *Sunday Times*.

Some advertisements, while not specifying a numerical age range for candidates, used language which clearly signalled that they were looking for someone from a particular age group. This was done in two main ways: either by using language which related to the preferred person, e.g. 'articulate youngsters', 'first jobber', 'second jobber'; or to the working environment, e.g. 'young, dynamic environment', 'young, fast-moving entrepreneurial company'. Whereas, few advertisements indicated that age was no barrier. Those that did emphasised that it was experience that was important, not age.

*Source*: Edited abstract from 'Tackling age bias: code or law?', *Equal Opportunities Review*, (80), July–August 1998.

*Questions*

1 Why is it that the 'age of exclusion' from the clerical, secretarial and administrative job market is much younger than that for more senior positions? What are the effects of this?
2 Discuss the relevance of language usage in the construction of barriers to age equality.

# Conclusion

In this chapter we have sought to demonstrate that organizational cultures are not neutral or rational. In order to fully understand organizational processes, relations and practices, an interpretative approach is required which focuses on the qualitative and symbolic aspects of organizational life. In pursuit of this aim, the chapter has focused on the qualitatively different organizational experiences of diverse social groups. We have posited that it is necessary to explore such experiences in order to understand the deeply embedded nature of inequalities at the microlevel and the consequent obstacles to advancing an equality and diversity agenda.

Three principal messages can be drawn out of our 'unpacking' of diversity issues within organizations. First, within organizations there exists a dearth of role models in senior positions and in some occupations for diverse social groups. This can create a problem in terms of accessing important work-related social networks and in receiving sponsorship within the internal and external labour markets. This is especially the case for women, minority ethnic people and disabled people who are concentrated at the lower ends of organizational hierarchies and in certain types of jobs. Second, myths and stereotypes, underpinned by deep-seated cultural norms and values, contribute to reinforcing the disadvantage and reproducing the inequalities experienced by the five social groups we focus on. Third, harassment and humour are used to subordinate those constructed as 'other'.

Part Two examines the policies and approaches of the key actors in the employment relationship, that is, government, employers and trade unions. The measures to address employment inequalities, which we describe in the forthcoming chapters, have met with varying degrees of success and the explanation for policy failures lies partly in their inability to fundamentally transform the societal value systems and organizational cultures which reproduce inequalities.

# Review and discussion questions

1 Identify the reasons for and discuss the ramifications of organizational analysis occurring 'through a lens which is primarily white and male' (Cianni and Romberger, 1997: 116).

2 To what extent do organizations reflect external social realities? Justify your answer with some examples. (Referring back to Chapter 2 would be useful.)

3 When looking at a diverse workforce, what are the limitations of traditional or orthodox conceptions of organizational culture?

4 Discuss what is meant by 'glass' and 'concrete' ceilings. How are these barriers constructed and manifest within organizations? To what extent do invisible and impenetrable barriers to the advancement of other social groups exist?

# Further reading

Cockburn, C. (1991). *In the Way of Women*. Macmillan.
  A book based on extensive qualitative research in four case study organizations. Cockburn deals effectively with gender, race, sexual orientation and disability.
Hearn, J., Sheppard, D., Tancred-Sheriff, P. and Burrell, G. (eds) (1989). *The Sexuality of Organisation*. Sage.
  An edited collection of papers covering a broad range of issues relating to organizational cultures, with strong theoretical underpinning.
Itzin, C. and Newman, J. (1995). *Gender, Culture and Organisational Change*. Routledge.
  This is an edited collection with a dual emphasis on theory and practice. It draws out issues of race, ethnicity and age in so far as they intersect with gender.

# References

Acker, J. (1992). Gendering organizational theory. In *Gendering Organizational Analysis* (A. Mills and P. Tancred, eds). Sage.
Acker, J. and Van Houton, D. (1992). Differential recruitment and control: the sex structuring of organizations. In *Gendering Organizational Analysis* (A. Mills and P. Tancred, eds). Sage.
Alvesson, M. and Billing, Y. (1997). *Understanding Gender and Organisations*. Sage.
Barnes, C. (1992). Disability and employment. *Personnel Review*, **21**, (6), 55–73.
Burrell, G. and Hearn, J. (1989). The sexuality of organization. In *The Sexuality of Organisation* (J. Hearn, D. Sheppard, P. Tancred-Sheriff and G. Burrell, eds). Sage.
Cianni, M. and Romberger, B. (1997). Life in the corporation: a multi-method study of the experiences of male and female Asian, Black, Hispanic and white employees. *Gender, Work and Organization*, **4**, (2), 116–127.
Cockburn, C. (1991). *In the Way of Women*. Macmillan.
Collinson, D. and Collinson, M. (1989). Sexuality in the workplace: the domination of men's sexuality. In *The Sexuality of Organisation* (J. Hearn, D. Sheppard, P. Tancred-Sheriff and G. Burrell, eds). Sage.

Collinson, D. and Collinson, M. (1992). Mismanaging sexual harassment. *Women in Management Review*, **7**, (7), 11–16.

Collinson, M. and Collinson, D. (1997). 'It's only Dick': the sexual harassment of women managers in insurance sales. *Work, Employment and Society*, **10**, (1), 29–56.

Collinson, D. and Hearn, J. (1994). Naming men as men: implications for work, organization and management. *Gender, Work and Organization*. **1**, (1), 3–22.

Collinson, D., Knights, D. and Collinson, M. (1990). *Managing to Discriminate*. Routledge.

Davis, K. (1996). Disability and legislation: rights and equality. In *Beyond Disability: Towards an Enabling Society* (G. Hales, ed.) Sage.

DfEE (Department for Education and Employment) (1997). *Labour Market and Skill Trends 1997/8*. DfEE.

DiTomaso, N. (1989). Sexuality in the workplace: discrimination and harassment. In *The Sexuality of Organisation* (J. Hearn, D. Sheppard, P. Tancred-Sheriff and G. Burrell, eds). Sage.

EOR (Equal Opportunities Review) (1997). Equality for lesbians and gay men in the workplace. *Equal Opportunities Review*, (74), July/August, 20–28.

EOR (Equal Opportunities Review) (1998a). Disabled people excluded from society. *Equal Opportunities Review*, (80), July/August, 11–12.

EOR (Equal Opportunities Review) (1998b) Tackling age bias: code or Law? *Equal Opportunities Review*, (80), July/August, 32–37.

French, S. (1996a). The attitudes of health professionals towards disabled people. In *Beyond Disability: Towards an Enabling Society* (G. Hales, ed.) Sage.

Gherardi, S. (1996). Gendered organisational cultures: narratives of women travellers in a male world. *Gender, Work and Organization*, **3**, (4), 187–201.

Ginn, J. and Arber, S. (1995). Exploring mid-life women's employment. *Sociology*, **29**, (1), 73–94.

Gutek, B. (1989). Sexuality in the workplace: key issues in social research and organizational practice. In *The Sexuality of Organisation* (J. Hearn, D. Sheppard, P. Tancred-Sheriff and G. Burrell, eds). Sage.

Hall, M. (1989). Private experiences in the public domain: lesbians in organizations. In *The Sexuality of Organisation* (J. Hearn, D. Sheppard, P. Tancred-Sheriff and G. Burrell, eds). Sage.

Hearn, J. and Parkin, W. (1992). Gender and organizations: a selective review and a critique of a neglected area. In *Gendering Organizational Analysis*. (A. Mills and P. Tancred, eds). Sage.

Honey, S., Meager, N. and Williams, M. (1993), *Employers' Attitudes towards People with Disabilities*. Institute of Manpower Studies.

Hyde, M. (1996). Fifty years of failure: employment services for disabled people in the UK. *Work, Employment and Society*, **10**, (4), 701–715.

Itzin, C. (1995a). The gender culture in organizations. In *Gender, Culture and Organisational Change* (C. Itzin and J. Newman, eds). Routledge.

Itzin, C. (1995b). Gender, culture, power and change: a materialist analysis. In *Gender, Culture and Organisational Change* (C. Itzin and J. Newman, eds). Routledge.

Itzin, C. and Phillipson, C. (1995). Gendered ageism: a double jeopardy for women in organizations. In *Gender, Culture and Organisational Change* (C. Itzin and J. Newman, eds). Routledge.

Jenkins, R. (1985). Black workers in the labour market: the price of recession. In *Racism and Antiracism* (P. Braham, A. Rattansi and R. Skellington, eds). Sage.

Jenkins, R. and Parker, G. (1987). Organizational politics and the recruitment of black workers. In *The Manufacture of Disadvantage* (G. Lee and R. Loveridge, eds). Oxford University Press.

Labour Research (1994). Watching what you wear at work. *Labour Research*, December, 7–8.

Labour Research (1998). Black over 40s hit by double bias. *Labour Research*, September, 16.

Legge, K. (1995). *HRM: Rhetorics and Realities*. Macmillan.

McKay, S. (1998). Older workers in the labour market. *Labour Market Trends*, July, 365–369.

Mills, A. (1989). Gender, sexuality and organization theory. In *The Sexuality of Organisation* (J. Hearn, D. Sheppard, P. Tancred-Sheriff and G. Burrell, eds). Sage.

Mills, A. (1992). Organization, gender, and culture. In *Gendering Organizational Analysis*. (A. Mills and P. Tancred, eds). Sage.

Mills, A. (1998). Cockpits, hangars, boys and galleys: corporate masculinities and the development of British Airways. *Gender, Work and Organization*, **5**, (3), 172–188.

Mills, A. and Tancred, P. (eds) (1992). *Gendering Organizational Analysis*. Sage.

Modood, T. (1997). Qualifications and English Language. In *Ethnic Minorities in Britain. Diversity and Disadvantage* (T. Modood, R. Berthoud, J. Lakey, J. Nazroo, P. Smith, S. Virdee and S. Beishon, eds). Policy Studies Institute.

Newman, J. (1995). Gender and cultural change. In *Gender, Culture and Organisational Change* (C. Itzin and J. Newman, eds). Routledge.

O'Neilly, J. (1995). When prejudice is not just skin deep. *People Management*, 23 February, 34–37.

Oerton, S. (1996a), Sexualizing the organization, lesbianizing the women: gender, sexuality and 'flat' organizations. *Gender, Work and Organization*, **3**, (1).

Oerton, S. (1996b). *Beyond Hierarchy: Gender, Sexuality and the Social Economy*. Taylor and Francis.

Pringle, R. (1989). Bureaucracy, rationality and sexuality: the case of secretaries. In *The Sexuality of Organisation* (J. Hearn, D. Sheppard, P. Tancred-Sheriff and G. Burrell, eds). Sage.

Roberts, K. (1996). Managing disability-based diversity. In *Managing Diversity: Human Resource Strategies for Transforming the Workplace* (E. Kossek and S. Lobel, eds). Blackwell

Rubenstein, M. (1989). Preventing sexual harassment at work. *Industrial Relations Journal*, 226–236.

Sheppard, D. (1989). Organizations, power and sexuality: the image and self-image of women managers. In *The Sexuality of Organisation* (J. Hearn, D. Sheppard, P. Tancred-Sheriff and G. Burrell, eds). Sage.

Smith, B. (1996). Working choices. In *Beyond Disability: Towards an Enabling Society* (G. Hales, ed.) Sage.

Tancred-Sheriff, P. and Campbell, E. (1992). Room for women: a case study in the sociology of organizations. In *Gendering Organizational Analysis*. (A. Mills and P. Tancred, eds). Sage.

Taylor, P. and Walker, A. (1994). The ageing workforce: employers' attitudes towards older people. *Work, Employment and Society*, **8**, (4), 569–591.

Thornton, P. and Lunt, N. (1995). Employment for Disabled People: Social Obligation or Individual Responsibility? Social Policy Research Unit.

# Chapter 5
# Theorizing equality and diversity approaches

## Aim

To provide the conceptual and theoretical underpinning which is necessary to develop a critical analysis of current understandings of equal opportunities and diversity approaches.

## Objectives

- To outline the variety of meanings attributed to equality initiatives.
- To present the main theoretical explanations and liberal and radical models of equal opportunities approaches.
- To present the more recent theorizing around issues of diversity and mainstreaming.
- To provide an analysis of similarities and differences between equal opportunities and diversity approaches.

## Introduction

Miller identifies four types of equality: ontological equality, equality of condition, equality of opportunity and equality of outcome (Miller, 1996: 203). The first relates to a belief in the fundamental sameness of human beings. The second relates to the extension of ontological equality into the social and economic sphere, seeking to level the playing field by attempting to equalize conditions for those who are disadvantaged in society. It is equality of opportunity and equality of outcome which have come to have been used most frequently in terms of policy and relate to the liberal and radical approaches respectively, which will be discussed later in this chapter. When looking at equality initiatives in the employment sphere, *equal opportunities* has become the most common descriptor or label. In fact it has become a catch-all for distinctly different types of equality initiative. Thus, it is a term that will be used frequently in this chapter, however it is important to recognize that there are problems with using such a term without remaining critically aware of its weaknesses and the fact that it actually encompasses different types of equality initiative. Such issues will be discussed in greater detail in the rest of this chapter.

As an introduction, there is ongoing confusion in the conceptualization of equal opportunities (EO). Indeed, equal opportunities is a difficult area to theorize, primarily because of the wide variety of meanings attached to the concept. Theresa Rees begins her chapter 'Conceptualising Equal Opportunities' with the statement: 'The concept of equal opportunities is riddled with problematic constructs' (Rees, 1998: 26). Looking at the literature, the reader is immediately faced with a huge array of differing concepts and views of what is meant by EO. This also varies depending on the area of equal opportunities which one is looking at. Is the concern with principles of and philosophizing around EO, the ways in which EO should be implemented or the effectiveness of past and existing EO initiatives? Of course, any assessment of the effectiveness of such policies will very much depend on your particular point of view or underpinning conceptualization of equal opportunities, and so the confusing cycle begins again!

Pertinent questions to emerge include: what forms of equality are workplace equal opportunities initiatives intended to achieve, for example, equality of opportunity or equality of outcome? What forms of discrimination are initiatives supposed to overcome and in what ways (Webb, 1997)? Should we be thinking of employees as neutral individuals who contribute the same abilities, and who should receive the same access and be assessed in the same way regardless of social group membership? Alternatively, should we be playing down the differences which exist between people, and valuing the very existence of those differences? Should we be looking at differences between individuals, or does it still make sense to talk about group differences such as between, 'women', 'minority ethnic groups', 'older workers' or 'workers with disabilities', as comprising people who face similar problems and could benefit from similar solutions?

This chapter aims to present a summary of the key conceptualizations of EO although we recognize that this summary is not finite, and that other views and opinions will exist. As Webb (1997) points out, there have been changes during the 1990s in the political meanings attached to ideas about equality. We begin with the emergence of equal opportunities initiatives in Britain, connected to the legislation enacted in the 1970s and the main theorizing around liberal and radical traditions of equal opportunities and their associated initiatives and policies. This discussion also involves a summary of the critique of traditional EO approaches. The chapter then moves on to look at more recent conceptualizations, involving managing diversity and mainstreaming approaches.

The argument is that EO has moved from a focus on 'sameness' to a focus on 'difference', an analytical framework that will be discussed in some detail during the course of the chapter. This will involve a discussion of the critiques of the 'diversity' or 'difference' approach. Finally, there will be a consideration of the existing state of EO theorizing and of possible ways forward for the discussion. There will be a summary of the conceptualizations from a broadly chronological perspective; however, it is important to see how the older, liberal tradition lives on in policy and practice, even if it has been superseded in theory. Thus the account should be read as outlining theorizing and policy-making, which overlap and connect, rather than as separate and distinct entities.

# The equal opportunities agenda 1970s–80s: liberal and radical models

An obvious starting point is to look at perhaps the most acclaimed and cited text in terms of EO theorizing, that of Jewson and Mason's (1986) 'The theory and practice of equal opportunities policies: liberal and radical approaches'. They contrast liberal and radical approaches within existing EO policies and thus provide a useful framework within which to analyse other literature on the subject.

## The liberal tradition

The liberal approach to EO derives essentially from political ideals of classic liberalism and liberal democracy (Jewson and Mason, 1986) and is based around a view of the rights of the individual to universally applicable standards of justice and citizenship (Webb, 1997). Therefore, 'equality of opportunity exists when all individuals are enabled freely and equally to compete for social rewards' (Jewson and Mason, 1986: 307). The model is predicated on a philosophy of 'sameness': that people should have access to and be assessed within the workplace as individuals, regardless of social category (for example, gender, ethnicity, sexual orientation, age group). The focus is based on the individual, where people are required to deny, or attempt to minimize differences, and compete solely on grounds of individual merit (Liff and Wajcman, 1996).

Within a free market philosophy, policies based on the neutral individual are seen as the most efficient means of achieving a fair distribution of resources in the workplace. This has a grounding in theories of free market competition and thus refers back to neoclassical explanations of occupational segregation. Within the neoclassical view, discrimination is not an inherent or intrinsic feature of the capitalist labour market, but is a distortion of an otherwise rational market. Notions of the free market are central to the liberal approach and, therefore, equal opportunities within the liberal approach are focused on what Jewson and Mason (1986) call 'positive action', where efforts are made to remove obstacles to the operation of the free labour market and meritocratic competition. This should not be confused with 'affirmative action' which derives from the US, reflects a more radicalized approach (see Table 5:1) and is more akin to 'positive discrimination' which is discussed later. Positive action might include initiatives such as advertising campaigns reassuring candidates that all applications will be judged solely on their merits, crèche facilities in the workplace, and EO training that emphasizes non-biased procedures in recruitment and appraisal.

The liberal approach to EO underlies the campaign for anti-discrimination legislation in Britain in the 1970s, leading to the Sex Discrimination Act (1975), Race Relations Act (1976) and Equal Pay Act (1970). Here the emphasis is on encouraging employers to develop procedures which formalize fair and meritocratic methods of access to jobs, training and promotion, and will lead to the development of a 'metaphorical level playing field' (Webb, 1997). Thus, the liberal approach to equal opportunities is based on a bureaucratization and formalization of procedures within organizations (Jewson and Mason, 1986).

**Table 5.1** Comparison of types of equality initiative

| Approach | Principle | Strategy | Method | Type of equality |
|---|---|---|---|---|
| Liberal | Fair equal opportunity | Level playing field | Policy statement, equality proof recruitment and selection procedures | Equality of opportunity |
| | Positive action | Assistance to disadvantaged social groups | Monitoring, pre-entry training, in-service training, special courses, elevate EO within management | Equality of opportunity |
| | Strong positive action | Give positive preference to certain groups | Family friendly policies, improve access for disabled, make harassment a disciplinary offence | Moving towards equality of outcome |
| Radical | Positive discrimination | Proportional equal representation | Preferential selection, quotas | Equality of outcome |
| Managing diversity | Maximize individual potential | Use diversity to add value | Vision statement, organization audit, business-related objectives, communication and accountability, change culture | Equality means profit aligned with organizational objectives |

*Source*: Based on Miller (1996: 205, 206).

# The radical tradition

In contrast to the liberal approach, the radical view emphasizes direct intervention in order to achieve not only equality of opportunity (the 'rules of the game' in Jewson and Mason's terms) but also equality of outcome. Thus, the point is not only in achieving fair procedures, but also in achieving fair distribution of rewards. In this aim the focus is not on individuals, recognizing that while discrimination affects individuals, it is at the group level that this discrimination can be identified. The philosophy that all people are equal regardless of social group membership should be actively reflected in the distribution of rewards in the workplace. The absence of fair distribution is, therefore, evidence of unfair discrimination. The radical perspective does not see ability or talent as neutral but, instead, notions of ability and talent contain and conceal a series of value judgements and stereotypes. Discrimination is not, therefore, simply a distortion of the free labour market but is a socially constructed part of the market process (relating to the social identity construction and feminist and gender perspectives presented in Chapter 3). While the aim is to achieve equality of outcome on the same terms, there are elements of a 'difference' perspective in the radical approach. This 'difference' approach recognizes the differential treatment received by members of certain social groups and the social construction of the differential abilities possessed by members of different social groups.

The policies associated with the radical perspective focus around 'positive discrimination' (Jewson and Mason, 1986), where employment practices are deliberately manipulated to obtain a fair distribution of those disadvantaged groups in the workplace (Jewson and Mason, 1986). While the liberal approach emphasizes the need to formalize procedures, the radical approach emphasizes the need to politicize the processes of decision-making. Policies could involve the imposition of quotas or the necessity to employ a minimum percentage of a certain group of workers. Although many such policies are outlawed in Britain, there are elements of the radical approach within existing legislation and employer EO practices and policies (Liff and Wacjman 1996; Miller, 1996).

# Linking liberal and radical perspectives

There are aspects of 'difference' within conventional EO policy, for example recognition, within the legislation, of the concept of indirect discrimination. This is where a condition is applied equally to all, but a larger proportion of people from one social group find it more difficult to comply with than people from another social group. Liff and Wajcman (1996) cite the fact that such provision within the legislation, for example, relating to gender, has been used to remove age restrictions on entry to certain civil service grades as it was disadvantaging women who had been out of the labour force due to domestic responsibilities. Age criteria of 'maturity' can be indirectly discriminatory as the minority ethnic population is comparatively youthful, and so will disproportionately exclude more minority ethnic applicants. The Equal Value Amendment (1984) to the Equal Pay Act also has elements of a radical approach, ruling that men and women in different jobs should get equal benefits in terms of pay where these jobs can be judged to involve comparable skill, responsibility and working conditions. Similarly, policies such as offering childcare and measures to reduce the difficulty of combining domestic responsibilities and waged work, can be seen as direct intervention to influence the outcomes of EO initiatives. Cockburn (1989: 214) in her study of high street retailing identified similar policies where for example, computer programmer jobs were opened to part-time women returners and women and minority ethnic workers were encouraged to attend store managers' training schemes.

On the one hand, this would seem to breach the liberal view that people should receive the same treatment regardless of social group membership. On the other hand, it is clear that such differences are closely associated with group membership, and therefore should be irrelevant in terms of the meritocratic 'free' labour market. Although the legislation and employer policies are primarily based around the liberal approach, elements of the radical approach and acknowledgement of 'difference' have emerged as 'organisations which are proactive on equality issues have stretched and re-interpreted the equal treatment model in a number of ways'(Liff and Wajcman, 1996: 82).

This mix of radical and liberal approaches within EO policy is symptomatic of the ambiguous nature of traditional conceptualizations of EO. In their study, Jewson and Mason (1986) find that individuals and groups frequently invoke various aspects of both conceptions, depending on the time, the circumstances and their needs. While this is often due to overall confusion and misunderstandings around conceptualizations and practice of EO, they also find more conscious and deliberate attempts to mislead and mystify opponents and outsiders.

Moreover, Cockburn (1989) finds that others interpreted certain policies in workplaces differently, depending on what was expected and desired from the EO policies. In particular, in high street retailing, EO is seen as different things in different people's minds. Cockburn identified the interests of the shareholder who had a strong personal commitment to EO, the executive team who saw EO as a profit-making policy relating to marketing technique and customer orientation, the lawyers who wanted EO initiatives to avoid employment tribunal cases of discrimination, the personnel managers who saw EO as part of wider management trends, and the line management who were only concerned with EO of it did not conflict with maintaining work discipline and cost budgeting. Thus, employers do not have only one approach to EO; there is no overall consensus about best practice.

In essence, EO policies are part of the wider, complex and multifaceted nature of workplace relations within the social structures and systems of wider society. As Jewson and Mason state: 'the confused and contradictory deployment of different conceptions of equal opportunities policies can constitute an important aspect of the struggle for control of resources, deference and legitimacy at work' (Jewson and Mason, 1986: 302).

1 There are a variety of meanings approaches attached to the concept of equal opportunities. Key approaches identified include liberal and radical.
2 Discussion around conceptualizations of EO is polarized between approaches based on 'sameness' and those based on 'difference'.
3 The liberal approach based on 'sameness' relates to free market theory, and is predicated on the premise that people should have access to, and be assessed within, the workplace as individuals regardless of social group membership. Policies within this approach are based on formalizing procedures and 'positive action' to ensure that the 'rules of the game' are fair.
4 The radical approach attempts to ensure equality of outcome as well as equality of opportunity and recognizes that discrimination is a socially constructed part of the market process. Policies are based around direct intervention in achieving a fair distribution of advantages in the workplace.
5 Equal opportunities legislation in Britain is based on a liberal, 'sameness' approach, although elements of a 'difference' approach are visible in both recognition of the existence of indirect discrimination and in employer policies designed to improve the position of certain social groups.

# A critique of equal opportunities: dangers of 'sameness'

There have obviously been successes involved with the liberal approach to equality. With regard to gender disadvantage, Webb (1997) points to the rising number of women in the labour force, the increasing number of women in the professions and the growth in the numbers of women achieving some degree of economic independence. Chapter 2 identified the main changes in the British labour market relating to different social groups of workers, some of which have been progressive from an EO perspective. However, there are also obvious criticisms and weaknesses of an EO approach that is largely liberal and focused on procedures and equality of opportunity rather than of outcome.

As Webb (1997) points out, there are two main varieties of criticism: the first looks at the legislation and how it has been weakened in practice. Collinson, Knights and Collinson (1990) and Cockburn (1991) provide accounts of where the legislation and its prescriptions have been ignored in routine practice, looking at the extent to which direct and overt discrimination continues. Considerable segregation, which still exists within, and disadvantage is faced by many workers in the British labour market. Other explanations for these weaknesses, have focused on the lack of political will underlying the legislation, the institutional weakness of personnel managers in organizations (the people largely responsible for implementing employment policy), the lack of support from senior management for EO initiatives (Gooch and Ledwith, 1996) and the limited resources of national bodies such as the Equal Opportunities Commission and the Commission for Racial Equality (Webb, 1997).

The second variety of criticism is the main concern and deals with a critique of the model of EO rather than its effects. As discussed above, at the heart of the liberal perspective is a view that fair procedures lead to fair outcomes (Jewson and Mason, 1986). In particular, the criticisms focus around the fact that a model based on procedural formalization promises more than it can deliver and is no guarantee of fairness (Cockburn, 1991; Liff, 1996; Webb, 1997). Webb (1997) points to the ways that procedures can be evaded, especially with substantial managerial discretion remaining in place and a lack of monitoring of the continual process of EO policies (Dickens, 1994). A reliance on procedures and increased bureaucratization, also seems at odds with the trends towards deregulation and flexibility, and have come to be seen as unfair and restrictive within the *laissez-faire* economy (Rees, 1998). Moreover, Jewson and Mason's (1986) research indicates that certain aspects of work life are very difficult to bureaucratize, pointing to the numerous informal norms and codes which exist, however formalized an organization.

In particular, many writers (Cockburn, 1991; Webb, 1997) have focused on the fact that the liberal approach to EO assumes that issues of acceptability and suitability of candidates for jobs could be separated. In essence, procedures are set up to attempt to ensure that candidates are chosen on the basis of their suitability for the job on meritocratic grounds. However Collinson, Knights and Collinson (1990) point to the fact that acceptability and suitability are inseparable in practice because the labour supply is gendered, racialized, aged and sexualized from the start. For example, stereotypes about groups of workers (statistical discrimination) mean that different workers appear differentially suitable. As Webb points out with regard to gender, 'aspects of masculinity and femininity become established as indicators of suitability' (Webb, 1997: 161). A belief that a woman would not be acceptable as a top manager due to her 'inability' to put in long hours at work (due to domestic responsibilities) means that this gendered characteristic becomes a measure of suitability for her appointment, regardless of her qualifications. Similarly, one can look at stereotypes of minority ethnic workers around attitude and language proficiency which deem them as less suitable for managerial positions (see Chapter 4).

The radical model also has its critics. While on the one hand it seems to recognize the fact that formal procedures have not led to fair outcomes and attempts to intervene to change the status quo, it also carries its own dangers. Cockburn (1989; 1991) identifies how initiatives, which aim to deliberately enhance the position of workers from certain social groups, are seen negatively as meaning 'special treatment'. The women, and workers from minority ethnic groups in Cockburn's research, indicated their dislike of the idea of favouritism, first, because of the fear of a backlash by the dominant group or groups. Rees (1998) discusses the furore over, and negative feeling surrounding, the Labour Party's all-women short lists for nominated candidates in certain seats in 1996. This was a radical interventionist measure designed to address the gender imbalance in the number of Members of Parliament. The policy met opposition from both men and women because it was felt by some to be unfair or to be 'reverse discrimination'.

Perhaps more significantly however, initiatives to deliberately ease the position for a particular group or groups, while they may improve the relative position of that particular group, were not felt to lead to any improvement in the nature of the organization (Cockburn, 1989). The loudest criticism of the traditional EO approach, which can be identified in the literature, is that both the radical and the liberal approach do not challenge the status quo. As Cockburn states, 'it seeks to give disadvantaged groups a boost up the ladder, while leaving the structure of that ladder and the disadvantage it entails just as before' (Cockburn, 1989: 217). In essence, much is left unchanged. While the rhetoric of EO is change, the reality is more static, indeed even if the emphasis on procedures is seen as successful, there has been little development of EO legislation and ideas since the early 1980s. The codes of practice of the EOC and the CRE have not been significantly revised since they were first written (Kandola and Fullerton, 1994).

The EO measures in law focus on rights and procedures, not outcomes, and therefore they stand as attempts to treat the symptoms of disadvantage and discrimination rather than the causes (Rees, 1998). The focus on individuals as part of the model of 'sameness' is also a weakness, suggesting that people should be treated as neutral individuals without recognizing the impact of culturally reproduced and socially constructed group membership. Jewson and Mason (1986) similarly point out that the liberal view ignores or cannot accommodate the structural sources of social capacities and skills. The traditional approach leaves the prejudices and stereotypes unchallenged and so is seen as ineffective in leading to change, but rather reproduces inequalities that exist in the broader context (Rees, 1998). The place of women in the labour force serves as an example. Rees (1998) emphasizes the importance of the fact that within the traditional EO approach, there is a continued separation between the private (domestic) and the public sphere without recognition that the two influence each other. Thus 'granting equal access to men and women will only benefit certain women: those whose cultural capital, experiences, family circumstances and share of domestic responsibilities are similar to those of [white] men as a group' (Rees, 1998: 29). Equality of access is an illusion while the white, male, full-time worker, with few domestic responsibilities is seen as the norm.

It is the lack of this challenge to the status quo, and existing hierarchical division of labour and allocation of resources, which also means that the radical approach and views of 'special treatment' are seen as unfair (Liff, 1996). This is what Cockburn (1989; 1991) is referring to with her view of the 'short' and 'long' agenda of EO. The short agenda characterizes the traditional EO approach based on treating the symptoms of discrimination and disadvantage, or pushing for special policies to protect or enhance the position of certain social groups. Alternatively, the long agenda would seek to respond to, and respect differences rather than seeking to assist people in fitting into existing organizations and cultures.

What is meant by a long agenda is a campaign to change the unequal systems and structures, and to transform organizational cultures. Assessments of the liberal and radical approaches to EO have not found much evidence of this long agenda at work.

In addition, the traditional approach and the analysis of liberal or radical models within this approach have been seen as too simplistic, underestimating the complexity of organizations. As with the discussion of the diverse number of interests in EO policies, the employee interest is also seen as heterogeneous, whereby there were divisions among women, between the young and old, those with children and without. Different ethnic groups had different interests relating to cultural and religious affiliation. Some groups were ignored, for example, the organizational code of practice on equality did not even mention the place of gay and lesbian workers in the company (Cockburn, 1989). The traditional approach based on 'sameness' has been criticized for failing to advance the position of disadvantaged groups of workers, and failing to change the unequal systems, structures and hierarchies that exist. Workers are expected to assimilate, and to dilute or deny their differences in order to meet a norm, predominantly that of a white, non-disabled, heterosexual, man, aged twenty-five to forty years. A move away from this traditional approach is seen in the diversity or 'difference' model of EO.

| **Key learning points** | 1 The traditional approach to EO has been criticized for failing to deliver equality of outcome, and failing to look at the extent to which discrimination continues to exist and suitability criteria continue to be judged against the dominant white, male norm. Radical policies within the traditional approach can be criticized for being seen as 'special treatment'. |
| --- | --- |
| | 2 Most significantly, the liberal and radical approaches based on 'sameness' only benefit a minority of workers from disadvantaged groups who can most easily meet the dominant norm. This is because the traditional EO approach makes no challenge to the status quo, continuing to perpetuate unfair structures and systems within organizations and wider society, such as that responsibility for the domestic sphere is predominantly held by women. |
| | 3 Thus the traditional approach to EO follows a short agenda rather than a long agenda that seeks to change the unequal systems and structures and transform organizational cultures. |

# The equal opportunities agenda 1990s: the diversity model

It is self-evident that policies within the workplace are influenced by wider economic, political and ideological trends. Thus a shift in thought about EO also accompanied the late 1980s and 1990s trend towards deregulation, flexibility, new managerialism and human resource management (Webb, 1997; see also Chapter 9). The strategy of the Equal Opportunities Commission in Britain demonstrated this shift, restricting the EO agenda to employment issues and facilitating the use of disadvantaged groups as a resource to meet governmental priorities (Webb, 1997). There was also a shift in feminist consciousness, on the one hand led by an increasing backlash to feminism and feminists (Cockburn, 1989, 1991; Webb, 1997), leading to a need to downplay the innate 'sameness' of gendered groups and the development of a female interest challenging the male. Second, as discussed in Chapter 3, the black feminist critique of Western feminism, focused on the way that it denied the differences within social groups, fostering a shift in thought towards a 'difference' approach.

As one might expect, there are a variety of ways in which the 'difference' or diversity model of EO has been viewed. The literature finds it variously presented: as an evolutionary step from EO (Kandola and Fullerton, 1994); a sophistication of the EO approach (Rubin, in Overell, 1996a); a repackaging of EO (Ford, 1996); more negatively, as a sanitized, politically unthreatening and market-oriented notion (Webb, 1997); or a 'comfort zone', allowing employers to avoid actively fighting discrimination (Ouseley, in Overell, 1996b). It seems useful first to try to unpack the essential elements of the diversity approach.

Kandola and Fullerton (1994) provide a summary of the development of the concept of 'managing diversity' (MD). They locate the use of the term in the USA from 1987, when an influential report, *Workforce 2000* by Johnston and Packer (1987), identified the increasing heterogeneity of the American workforce, pointing to the fact that by the year 2000 the white male employee would make up a minority of new entrants to the labour force. However, like the experience with conceptualizing the traditional EO approach, Kandola and Fullerton begin their discussion of a definition of the MD approach with the statement: 'managing diversity means different things to different people' (Kandola and Fullerton, 1994: 7) and provide a variety of different statements from different sources about what an MD approach is. Their own definition perhaps provides a starting point:

> The basic concept of managing diversity accepts that the workforce consists of a diverse population of people. The diversity consists of visible and non-visible differences which will include factors such as sex, age, background, race, disability and work style. It is founded on the premise that harnessing these differences will create a productive environment in which everybody feels valued, where their talents are being fully utilized and in which organizational goals are met. (Kandola and Fullerton, 1994: 8)

Other writers converge on the essential ideas of this MD approach. At the heart is the idea that organizations should recognize differences rather than deny or dilute them (Liff, 1996). There is a move away from the idea that different groups should be assimilated to meet an organizational norm. The employer is expected to be committed to creating a workplace which facilitates the inclusion of different social categories and enables everyone to contribute in their own way, to the business (Webb, 1997). In this way, rather than difference being viewed negatively, there should be a recognition of the inherent strengths of employees based on their cultural background, gender or age, or differential experience (Chen, 1992). Difference is thus viewed positively, looking at the benefits to the organization which could derive from different perspectives and approaches and seeing that differences should be nurtured and rewarded rather than suppressed (Liff and Wajcman, 1996).

However, Kandola and Fullerton's model is really an ideal type, for it implicitly presupposes that equality already exists so that difference can be celebrated. As Thomas (1990) points out, you cannot 'manage diversity' unless you have a diverse workforce to begin with; in other words, that equality of outcome already exists and is testified to in a fair distribution of jobs, rewards and resources. In this respect, Liff (1996) perhaps produces a more sophisticated and multidimensional model of diversity than Kandola and Fullerton, particularly in making links between diversity and the liberal and radical approaches. Liff (1996) sees MD as involving four approaches based on 'difference': dissolving differences, valuing differences, accommodating differences and utilizing differences. These approaches have different goals and objectives, and are not mutually exclusive; in other words, more than one approach or elements of an approach can be taken up by organizations.

The first of these, dissolving differences, may seem more akin to the 'sameness' approach of EO. However here, MD attempts to dissolve those group-based differences, emphasizing instead that differences exist between individuals, not as distributed on the basis of social group membership (for example, gender or ethnicity). This is significant because it changes the objectives for equality policies, to focus not on gender or ethnic equality as a goal but on the 'opportunity to be acknowledged for the person one is and to be helped in making the most of one's talents and reach one's own goals' (Liff, 1996: 13).

The valuing differences approach moves on from this, acknowledging that some differences are socially based and are significant in perpetuating inequality (remember this is an issue which the liberal EO approach was criticized for ignoring). The aim is to create an organizational culture where all members feel they belong, rather than having to meet the dominant white, male norm. Examples include training for under-represented groups in overcoming past disadvantages and allowing people to be successful.

The accommodating differences approach is seen as similar to that of the radical approach. However, rather than necessarily providing special policies for one particular group, the emphasis is, for example, on recruitment and an overall policy to ensure that talent is recognized despite social differences and, therefore, may involve specifically targeted recruitment drives.

Finally, the utilizing differences approach is different to the other three in making a specific case for the need to give different treatment in order to recognize the different needs of people within an organization. Therefore, the organization might have policies for women who want to have a family that involves a different promotion track. Liff (1996: 15) sees this as 'policies to accommodate difference but at the expense of equality' (For another viewpoint, there are many similarities between Liff's analysis and Miller's [1996] identification of three approaches to MD: radical transformation, learning organization and individualistic approach.)

In many respects, as the typology above relates, there is a great deal of similarity between EO and MD, and a glance at a practitioner model for MD, such as Kandola and Fullerton (1994), demonstrates that many of the measures involved with an MD approach would not be alien to a conventional EO policy. However, MD is presented as significantly different to EO (Kandola and Fullerton, 1994). First, it has a more positive message, as it seeks to ensure the maximization of potential rather than only focusing on the prevention of discrimination. Second, it involves a broader range of people than the common social categories covered in EO legislation and policies. In this there is a shift of focus, too, on the value of nurturing the individual rather than any particular social grouping. Thus MD initiatives tend to be more individualistic (Liff and Wajcman, 1996). In this way, equality is depoliticized or rendered less sensitive to backlash from already 'advantaged' groups and individuals.

Third, it is presented as not only redressing the balance but as an attempt to change the culture of organizations, meeting one of the major criticisms of the EO approach. There is an attempt in the ideal of the MD organization, that the culture will be significantly changed to view differences as positive. This is one area where various terms within the 'difference' literature converge with MD. Thus Rees (1998) talks about the 'mainstreaming' of equality, a policy advocated within the European Union programmes and initiatives. Mainstreaming equality essentially means the need to include equality issues in every part of strategy and policy, rather than just having specific equality policies. Equality issues are supposed to disseminate through every function of an organization. In that this requires a shift in organizational cultures, similarities between 'mainstreaming' and MD are acknowledged by Rees (1998), seeing them as both potentially moving beyond the narrow definition of EO in seeking to 'transform organisations and create a culture of diversity in which people of a much broader range of characteristics and background may confidently flourish' (Rees, 1998: 27). The objective is thus for Cockburn's (1989; 1991) 'long agenda', where the model seeks to effect outcomes by changing cultures, systems and structures.

---

**Key learning points**

1 The managing diversity model of EO is based around a 'difference' approach and seeks to recognize, value and utilize differences between individuals rather than dilute or deny that the differences exist.
2 The MD model has an individualistic focus, downplaying the differences attached to group membership. The ideal of MD also seeks to effect outcomes by changing cultures, systems and structures, seeing difference as a positive rather than a negative.
3 There are a variety of different conceptualizations of MD, however, including mainstreaming which also seeks to transform organizational cultures. One can also identify short and long agendas of MD policies.

## Activity

### Activity 5.1: Comparison of types of equality initiative

Refer back to Table 5.1 and discuss its utility in adequately mapping the territory of approaches, principles, strategies, methods and types of equality in terms of whether:

- this categorization of the differing approaches and initiatives reflects other writers' categorizations discussed in this chapter (for example Jewson and Mason, Cockburn).
- this helps in understanding changes in conceptions of what equality initiatives should achieve and how these outcomes should be achieved.
- MD represents a new approach from EO.

# A critique of the diversity model: dangers of 'difference'

One of the most significant problems is that, just like EO, the MD approach can promise more than it can offer. Indeed Kandola and Fullerton (1994), for all their positive proclamation of the MD model, recognize that there is a long list of debatable benefits of MD and conclude that much more research needs to be conducted to establish whether their model is successful. While an MD approach has been claimed by numerous organizations, there is a lack of evidence indicating the success of such an approach or that the model has been operationalized so that it becomes more than just a name change. Webb (1997) found that while her case study firm proclaimed an MD philosophy, the policies introduced offered no challenge to the structure and culture of the organization. In fact, as opposed to the rhetoric, the policies tended to reflect more of a 'sameness' agenda, where recruitment and training were open to all and managers saw the lack of women responding and continued occupational segregation along gender lines as evidence of women's choices, rather than recognizing the role of the existing culture.

Thus, the criticisms of the traditional EO approach remain: 'difference' is only valued as long as it contributes to profit or organizational objectives; the persistence of the white, heterosexual, non-disabled, male norm; the division between public and private spheres; and the fact that only certain members of disadvantaged or under-represented groups who are able to meet the norm most easily will benefit from the policies. Clear similarities can be seen between some of the policies associated with the four approaches of MD listed by Liff (1996) and the more traditional EO policies such as positive action and positive discrimination, and therefore also suffer from their criticisms.

The type of polices discussed above would not meet the criteria of the ideal model of MD practice identified by Kandola and Fullerton (1994), and this is partly owing to the way in which MD is interpreted and used rather than what lies at the core of the conceptual model. Rees (1998) states that in practice, there can equally be short and long agendas of MD. Using her term of 'mainstreaming', there is a need for organizational cultures to be 'transformed', building upon the politics of difference. But this is clearly no easy task, especially when organizations face competing pressures from, for example, competition in the market or periods of recession. Thus, many organizations simply have polices of 'tinkering' or 'tailoring' existing initiatives and procedures which do not challenge the inherent inequalities within the structures, systems and cultures. Webb (1997) claims that, overall, what MD tends to mean is a market-driven and politically non-threatening EO, which fits more with the wider trends towards flexibility.

Additionally with the shift in emphasis from social groups to a focus on individuals, MD does not have the collective force of those dis-advantaged groups behind it. In this respect, paradoxically, there is an approach of 'sameness' implicit in the valuing of 'difference' within the ideal model of MD espoused by Kandola and Fullerton (1994). In other words, all differences are viewed on the same or similar terms; none are seen as more salient than others in leading to disadvantage in the workplace. If one takes another look at Kandola and Fullerton's definition of the MD approach presented earlier, they make the case that a wider range of differences are taken into consideration than with liberal and radical EO approaches. However, they are viewed equally, so personal characteristics such as 'workstyle' are seen as being as significant as, and independent of, gender or ethnicity.

This is seen as important by some commentators who believe that the campaign for equality needs the force of political action and collective feeling to have any effect. What an emphasis on differences between individuals does is weaken the ties that people have through common experience that provides the necessary support to push for action, essentially leaving people alone and isolated in their struggle (Cockburn, 1989). In Dickens's (1997) ideal model of EO practice, the role of trade unions, for example, is seen as a vital piece of the 'jigsaw' making up the campaign for equality in the workplace. Rather than being empowering then, the ideal model of MD could be disempowering, dissolving collective identity and strength. Thus, such arguments challenge Kandola and Fullerton's (1991) argument that MD can succeed where EO has failed.

Sir Herman Ouseley, chairman of the CRE, has stated that employers are using the diversity approach as a 'comfort-zone', to protect them, and act as an alibi for avoiding the responsibility of addressing the unfairness which characterizes many employees' experiences (Overell, 1996b). This reflects the fact that there are also inherent dangers with an approach based around difference. This includes the danger that emphasizing the differences which exist will be used to reassert inferiority and justifiable exclusion (Webb, 1997). Indeed, Webb uses a quote from Cockburn (1991) pointing out that there is little room for difference *not* to be constructed as something inferior, 'the dominant group know you are different and continue to treat you as different, but if you yourself specify your difference, your claim to equality will be null' (Cockburn, 1991: 219).

Thus a diversity approach may give ammunition to those who feel that being 'different' to the dominant norm, disqualifies members of certain groups from equality, allowing differences to be used in a way which is detrimental to equality (Liff, 1996). As Liff continues, people may talk about women's skills of 'caring attitudes' but this does not explain why women continue to be at the bottom level of pay and status. The use of difference can often be used to emphasize gendered skill in terms of the current occupational sex segregation. Chris Chen comments that employers should be able to recognize and articulate that certain cultures, backgrounds and gender have inherent aptitudes towards certain skills, for example that 'women do well in social services and education' or that 'Asians, having an aptitude for maths, excel at engineering' or 'it just appears that blacks have some advantage in achieving success in basketball' (Chen, 1992: 33). However, the challenge to such a claim would be that such acknowledgement of difference may not reflect inherent differences but stereotyped and socially constructed differences that are not acknowledged by the 'utilizing and valuing diversity' assertions. Based on social group membership, people are not equally powerful and so the emphasis on needing to recognize the interests and differences of individuals may only serve to maintain the power of the dominant groups (Liff, 1996). Thus, while empirical evidence indicates the equal (if not better) educational qualifications of the Asian population in Britain, this education is not reflected in overall job status.

There are downsides to the diversity debate, particularly when it exclusively focuses on individual differences, allowing the avoidance (in similar terms to Sir Herman Ouseley's earlier comment) of recognizing the more negative aspects of working with diversity, which often involves the realities of discrimination, prejudice and unfair treatment (Ford, 1996). Even Kandola and Fullerton (1994: 104) acknowledge that some of the work conducted in the name of diversity could enhance rather than reduce the effects of stereotypes. As a necessary requirement of MD policies therefore, Ford (1996) suggests that there is a need to ensure that all human resources processes in an organization are intrinsically fair and based on individual ability. However, the question to ask, then, is against what criteria is something judged fair and who develops the criteria?

Liff and Wacjman (1996) state that this reflects a weakness in the dichotomy that opposes 'sameness' and 'difference' when the terms are only relative to each other. In other words, what tends to happen in organizations is that 'sameness' and 'difference' continue to be judged against the dominant norm. In addition, linking to the discussion above about the loss of collective resources, the concepts of 'sameness' and 'difference' are unitary categories. Thus the differences between social groups and also the similarities between people from different social groups are ignored. As Kandola and Fullerton (1994: 107) acknowledge, the danger of ignoring what is similar to emphasize difference may become apparent. In particular, material similarities and differences are significant. For example, women of all ethnic groups typically take on the responsibility for children and are less able to compete for jobs with men, not withstanding qualitative ethnic differences in how women may 'juggle' their multiple roles. The existence of socially constructed stereotypes and prejudices continues if the fundamental systems and structures are not challenged.

The MD approach is also introspective, focusing more on the movement of people within organizations and not the problems existing in the wider labour market (Miller, 1996). There are obviously more factors involved in the perpetuation of disadvantage than direct discrimination at entry level to organizations. Wider workplace values and fundamental human assumptions are very difficult to manage. Thus, the evidence that managers are often unable to disentangle assessments of suitability from assessments of acceptability based on stereotypes continues to thwart MD (Collinson, Knights and Collinson, 1990; Liff, 1996). Kandola and Fullerton comment that MD is not about 'removing our prejudices. It is about recognizing they exist and then questioning them before we act' (Kandola and Fullerton, 1994: 12). While it is obviously a difficult task to remove what are often unconscious prejudices, the fact that there does not appear to be the need for an overt challenge to such prejudices within this MD statement seems to leave a large amount of room for stereotyped discretion, which may be detrimental to equality. It is almost as if it is enough to recognize that the prejudices exist but then not to challenge and aim to remove them.

There are dangers if the MD approach is seen as something totally new and does not require the maintenance of the basic safeguards and protections set up in law and codes of practice within the liberal EO approach. Dickens (1997) emphasizes the problems if equality is left totally to the individual employers responding to the diverse labour market, business cases for equality initiatives always being contingent on such factors as the profitability of the firm or nature of the product market. If MD is presented as an alternative to EO then this threatens to sever the link between organizational strategies and the realities of labour market disadvantage (Miller, 1996). Based on the current assessment of the MD approach, the situation would seem very detrimental to equality within the workplace.

# Possible ways forward

Is the duality between 'sameness' and 'difference' an obstruction to the equality project? As Webb (1997) quotes from Bacchi:

> the 'sameness' alternative is insufficiently critical of the status quo. The 'difference' option *is* critical ... but seems to conjecture that women can exist in some sort of separate world. Seeing women as *the same as men* prevents us from challenging the model, against which women are being compared; seeing women as different prevents us from changing it. (Bacchi, 1990: 262)

While this view is based on a discussion of gender relations, it can be utilized to highlight the difficulty of sameness and difference agendas for other social groups in the workplace. Thus equality initiatives often aim to make those workers from disadvantaged groups fit the dominant norm within the 'sameness' agenda while the focus on differences seems to further enforce the disadvantage. The quote is also useful in pointing to the difficulty of finding a workable solution to the problem of achieving equal opportunities in the workplace.

People may not want to be treated the same, or different, with respect to all aspects of their work lives (Liff and Wajcman, 1996) and, we would add, at different times over their careers. This returns us to a point made earlier about the inseparability of 'sameness' and 'difference'. Thus, people possess what Liff and Wajcman call 'mobile subjectivities' where people share multiple differences and similarities. So, for example, people may want to be treated the same for recruitment purposes regardless of their ethnicity or gender, but may want their rights recognized to have more flexible arrangements to look after a dependant or to have specific arrangements for religious worship without it detrimentally affecting their long-term prospects. In this way people are the same and different simultaneously. But this does not give any explanation as to how such a policy could be constructed without falling foul of the criticisms noted in this chapter. It is difficult to know how to construct criteria which would assess these situations of difference and sameness and what policy would then be appropriate.

## A new norm

Liff and Wajcman (1996) suggest that what is needed is the construction of a new norm based on women's needs and interests, so that women can be assessed in their own right and not as 'not men' or 'other'. It is not easy to define exactly what are 'women's interests'; indeed, the diversity of interests within social categories is a recurring issue in this book. However, it would obviously be helpful if the norm of work was not full-time, uninterrupted service, as this has been seen to disadvantage many workers, specifically those who work part time or who have domestic responsibilities. The experience of Sweden is cited as demonstrating where an equality strategy sees typically female patterns of work as the norm. For example, extensive leave provisions and support for both men and women challenges the male stereotype of the breadwinner role which prevents men from taking more domestic responsibility.

There are, however, obvious problems with such a strategy. The first is that having the opportunity to assume more domestic responsibility does not necessarily mean that men will take it. Indeed, in Chapter 10, the low take-up of paternal leave in Sweden is discussed. For this to work, therefore, at least some of the challenge to the status quo has to come from the dominant group, otherwise the origin of 'differences' remain identified with inferiority (Webb, 1997). Second, and perhaps more importantly, as Liff and Wajcman (1996) acknowledge, a fundamental criticism of the female norm approach is that gender is privileged over other social divisions such as ethnicity, disability, sexuality or class. Any new norm would have to ensure that there was enough space for workers from other social groups. Thus this can only be a partial solution to the overall problem. However, as has been highlighted throughout this book, the issue is not that gender is given parity with these other identities; a new norm has to recognize the overlapping and multiple identities ascribed to and achieved by individuals (see the discussion in Chapter 3).

## An integration of approaches

Perhaps what is more useful is to look for an integration of 'sameness' and 'difference' approaches, rather than seeing EO and MD as opposed and contradictory. It may be more beneficial to integrate diversity and EO initiatives instead of prioritizing one or the other, so that they could work in tandem (Ford, 1996). Certainly, the dangers of embracing diversity without EO legislation and codes of practice have been discussed earlier, and most commentators highlight the need to maintain traditional EO safeguards alongside the new initiatives (Kandola and Fullerton, 1994; Liff, 1996; Rees, 1998). This would fit more with an approach of a long agenda (Cockburn, 1989; 1991), recognizing the need to maintain elements of past policies and aim for continuity of process. Dickens (1997) suggests that collective equality bargaining by trade unions could underpin and generalize employer's initiatives, while the law could generalize and underpin both of these.

---

**Key learning points**

1 There is still limited evidence as to the success of MD policies and initiatives. In addition, there are examples of where the 'difference' approach can be used to reassert the inferiority and justifiable exclusion of certain groups of workers. Therefore, attempts to transform existing structures and cultures have not occurred.
2 There is still a lack of clarity in knowing how to achieve equality in the workplace. Suggestions include recognizing that people are similar and different simultaneously, and that 'sameness' and 'difference' should not be opposed. This leads to the need to maintain traditional EO approaches alongside more recent MD initiatives.

---

# Conclusion

This chapter has summarized the key conceptualizations of EO and MD approaches, pointing to their strengths and weaknesses. What has emerged from the discussion has been the lack of clarity in knowing how to achieve equality in 'sameness' or 'difference'. As a final comment, a search through the relevant literature finds similar concluding remarks at the end of most articles or book chapters on this subject, reflecting on the continuing difficulties, complexities and indeterminacy of the state of the discussion. This chapter will end no differently. There is no clear and undisputed conceptualization of EO or MD and no clear guidance as to the future direction of the equality project. It is, of course, always much easier to find weaknesses and criticisms than it is to construct new ways of doing things. Many of these problems will be discussed further in the following five chapters dealing with the translation of theoretical approaches into policy and practice within the law, trade unions, management thinking and in comparison with other European countries. The theoretical perspectives offered will provide a useful background which can be used to help make sense of, and assess the success of, the various policy initiatives presented.

## Activity

## Activity 5.1: Understanding equality approaches

### Warning signals to keep women on board

In the wake of events on board HMS *Coventry* and a number of other harassment cases, [the Royal Navy] has been taking further steps to improve the environment in which its 850 seagoing Wrens and sometimes junior male ratings work. The introduction of a help line in April this year enables naval personnel to contact an independent adviser or counsellor by phone from anywhere in the world to discuss problems of bullying or other issues. More radically, an experimental warning system has been put in place to enable officers and ratings to make it clear if somebody is overstepping the boundaries of acceptable behaviour. The scheme allows crew members and officers to flourish a yellow card to indicate that a person's conduct is offensive and unwelcome and should stop, and a red card to show that such conduct has gone too far and will be the subject of a formal complaint ... 'We have a determined policy towards equal opportunities for women, race issues and coming down on bullying' the spokesman added. 'The help line complements the system we already have in place. It is all part of the navy's policy of ensuring that it is a good place to work for people of any race or gender.'

*Source*: Edited extract from the *Guardian*, 13 October 1998.

### £44 million childcare boost

The government yesterday announced £44 million of new cash to boost Britain's childcare provision. The money would help create at least 60,000 extra places in playgroups ... the equal opportunities minister, Margaret Hodge, said: 'Good quality childcare makes a real difference to working mums and dads and their children. It helps the youngsters to develop and brings peace of mind to their parents, knowing their children are safe and well looked after.' The money will be used to boost the numbers of childcare places offered by local councils.

*Source*: Edited extract from the *Guardian*, 15 October 1998.

## Age code fails to satisfy campaigners

The government yesterday held out the possibility that workers who suffer age discrimination may be able to claim compensation at employment tribunals, as it faced criticism from unions and age campaigners for failing to stick to an earlier Labour pledge to outlaw ageism. Employment minister Andrew Smith instead unveiled a draft voluntary code of practice to encourage employers to treat staff according to ability, not age. The publication of the code follows the release of an employer-commissioned report estimating that age discrimination is costing the country up to £26 billion a year in lost potential output by older workers forced out of the labour market.

*Source*: Edited extract from the *Guardian*, 17 November 1998.

## Asda in two-for-one jobs offer

Asda, the supermarket group, is to guarantee that 10 per cent of its senior positions will be offered on a job share basis to encourage more women into store management. At the moment just 10 of the 220 Asda general store managers are women, none of the seven divisional directors are female . . . The supermarket has pledged that by April 20 store managers will be allowed to split their workload in two and share it with a fellow employee. 'Both men and women will be encouraged to apply for these positions. There are a host of people who are the best in the market for a particular job but who for personal reasons are unable to do it. We are trying to make these positions viable for the best people', said an Asda spokesman. Jayne Monkhouse, employment policy manager at the Equal Opportunities Commission, said: 'This is a revolutionary move. While many retailers create part-time jobs, which often exclude people from employee rights and training and where women tend to get ghettoised, what we want is for people to realise that any job can be done part time, including senior managerial roles'. . . The first female store manager to share her job [said:] 'This will make an incredible difference to my lifestyle. There is a culture of very long hours in supermarket management, which can make it prohibitive for a parent, especially if their partner also works full time.'

*Source*: Edited extract from the *Guardian*, 1 October 1998.

## Building bricks of tolerance

Charles Allen, the chief executive of catering to television group Granada, as deputy chairman of Business in the Community, the organization set up to foster better relations between business and stakeholders, has taken on the lead role in a three-year-old campaign called Race for Opportunity. He admits the campaign does not offer a quick fix for anti-racism campaigners, mainly because many of the measures that companies can put in place are about changing attitudes, something that takes time. 'At Granada we are structuring a meritocracy and that means that ethnicity should not be a barrier to success. But you are confronting a culture where people tend to promote people like themselves.' He says part of his job has been to force his peers to recognise that they can be racist. 'I took 15 other chief executives to a school in Brixton with over 80 per cent of the kids from ethnic minorities. They found many of their assumptions challenged by the children. These trips make people understand there are things they do which are instinctively racist.

*Source*: Edited extract from the *Guardian*, 22 May 1999.

*Questions*

Presented above are recent examples of EO policies from the government and from employers. Discuss the examples, thinking about the following issues:

1 Do any of the policies fit into either traditional EO or MD approaches?
2 What are the strengths and weaknesses of the policies, reflecting on the arguments made within this chapter?
3 Discuss the fit between the various policies/initiatives and the rationale for them given by those spokespeople from the organizations
4 Critically analyse the potential that each of the policies has for leading to a 'transformation' in organizations.

# Review and discussion questions

1 What are the differences and similarities between the liberal, radical and diversity approaches? What types of equality do they address?
2 What are the strengths and weaknesses of each of the approaches?
3 How does such an analysis help us to conceptualize the direction that equality initiatives will, or should take, as we move into the twenty-first century?
4 '"Managing diversity" is not anything new. It is simply another renaming exercise to enhance the image of existing equal opportunities initiatives' (Hollinshead, Nicholls and Tailby, 1999: 451) Discuss this statement.

# Further reading

Cockburn, C. (1989). Equal opportunities: the long and short agenda. *Industrial Relations Journal*, Autumn, 213–225.

Jewson, N. and Mason, D. (1986). The theory and practice of equal opportunities policies: liberal and radical approaches. *Sociological Review*, **34**, (2), 307–334.

These two articles provide critical analyses of the traditional equal opportunities approach and a starting point for theorising. Supported by original empirical research.

Kandola, R. and Fullerton, J. (1994). *Managing the Mosaic: Diversity in Action*. Institute of Personnel and Development.

This is the key practitioner text for the managing diversity approach in the UK and provides a concise summary of existing models of practice and research evidence. A good starting point for critical analysis.

Liff, S. and Wajcman, J. (1996). 'Sameness' and 'difference' revisited: which way forward for equal opportunity initiatives? *Journal of Management Studies*, **33**, (1), 79–95.

An insightful analysis of the 'sameness' and 'difference' approaches to equal opportunities, identifying the key strengths and weaknesses of the respective approaches and providing ideas for possible future directions for theorizing and policy-making.

Webb, J. (1997). The politics of equal opportunity. *Gender, Work and Organisation*, **4**, (3), 159–167.

Sketches the main movements in conceptualization and practice of equal opportunities since the 1970s, linking changes to the wider economic, political and ideological context. Provides a critical analysis of the managing diversity approach, drawing out the weaknesses of current conceptualisations of equal opportunities.

# References

Bacchi, C. (1990). *Same Difference: Feminism and Sexual Difference*. Allen and Unwin.

Chen, C. (1992). The diversity paradox: personnel management and cultural diversity. *Personnel Journal*, **71**, (1), 32–35.

Cockburn, C. (1989). Equal opportunities: the long and short agenda. *Industrial Relations Journal*, Autumn, **20**, 213–225.

Cockburn, C. (1991). *In the Way of Women: Men's Resistance to Sex Equality in Organisations*. Macmillan.

Collinson, D., Knights, D. and Collinson, M. (1990). *Managing to Discriminate*. Routledge.

Dickens, L. (1994). Wasted resources? Equal opportunities in employment. In *Personnel Management* (K. Sisson, ed.). Blackwell.

Dickens, L. (1997). Gender, race and employment equality in Britain: inadequate strategies and the role of industrial relations actors. *Industrial Relations Journal*, **28**, (4), 282–289.

Ford, V. (1996). Partnership is the secret of progress: equal opportunities policy and diversity programs. *People Management*, **2**, (3), 8 February, 34–36.

Gooch, L. and Ledwith, S. (1996). Women in personnel management-re-visioning of a handmaiden's tale. In *Women in Organisations: Challenging Gender Politics* (S. Ledwith and F. Colgan, eds). Macmillan.

Hollinshead, G., Nicholls, P. and Tailby, S. (1999). *Employee Relations*. Financial Times/Pitman Publishing.

Jewson, N. and Mason, D. (1986). The theory and practice of equal opportunities policies: liberal and radical approaches. *Sociological Review*, **34**, (2), 307–334.

Johnston, W. and Packer, A. (1987). *Workforce 2000: Work and Workers for the Twenty First Century*. Hudson Institute.

Kandola, R. and Fullerton, J. (1991). Equal opportunities can damage your health. *Equal Opportunities Review*, **38**, July/August, 30–34.

Kandola, R. and Fullerton, J. (1994). *Managing the Mosaic: Diversity in Action*. Institute of Personnel and Development.

Liff, S. (1996). Two routes to managing diversity: individual differences or social group characteristics. *Employee Relations*, **19**, (1), 11–26.

Liff, S. and Wajcman, J. (1996). 'Sameness' and 'difference' revisited: which way forward for equal opportunity initiatives? *Journal of Management Studies*, **33**, (1), 79–95.

Miller, D. (1996). Equality management: towards a materialist approach. *Gender, Work and Organisation*, **3**, (4), 202–214.

Overell, S. (1996a). Equality enters the mainstream: interview with Kamlesh Bahl, chairwoman of the Equal Opportunities Commission. *People Management*, **2**, (4), 22 February, 26–28.

Overell, S. (1996b). Ouseley in assault on diversity. *People Management*, **2**, (9), 7–9.

Rees, T. (1998). *Mainstreaming Equality in the European Union: Education, Training and Labour Market Policies*. Routledge.

Thomas, R. (1990). From affirmative action to affirming diversity. *Harvard Business Review*, **90**, (2), 107–112, March.

Webb, J. (1997). The politics of equal opportunity. *Gender, Work and Organisation*, **4**, (3), 159–167.

# Part Two
# Policy and practice

# Chapter 6

# The legislative framework

*Linda Johnson and Sue Johnstone*

## Aim

To critically examine the nature and content of anti-discrimination legislation in Britain and to critically analyse issues affecting the development of the law.

## Objectives

- To examine different approaches to anti-discrimination and equality legislation.
- To explain the role and impact of the EU in the development of legislation in the UK.
- To outline anti-discrimination legislation and mechanisms to support this.
- To discuss contemporary issues arising from recent developments in the law.

## Introduction

As it is recognized that a number of students on equality and diversity modules of management and business studies courses will not have studied the English legal system this introduction provides students with a brief overview of the system, and the impact of European Union (EU) law. The examination of the law in this chapter is valid at the time of going to print (November 1999). It is beyond the scope of this chapter to provide a detailed account of either system, and students who need more detailed understanding are referred to the 'Further reading' section near the end of this chapter.

The sources of English (English law refers to the law of England and Wales, although these laws can be, and often are, extended to Scotland and Northern Ireland) employment law are common law (decisions made by judges), legislation (also referred to as Acts of Parliament or statute law, enacted in the UK's Parliament which includes the House of Commons and House of Lords) and European law (if UK and EU law clash, EU law overrides UK law). There are also codes of practice which do not have the full force of law. Breach of a code of practice can be used as evidence in a court or tribunal. A number of important bodies are involved in the employment law arena including the Advisory Conciliation and Arbitration Service (ACAS), the Central Arbitration Committee (CAC) the EOC, the CRE and the Disability Rights Commission (DRC). The respective roles and power of the main bodies will be explored in this chapter together with the Employment Tribunal (previously the Industrial Tribunal) and Employment Appeal Tribunal (EAT) where legal remedies are sought. The influence and impact of EU law will also be critically examined.

The Employment Tribunal system was set up to process disputes with the minimum amount of legalism and it has been argued that as employment law is dominated by legislation, thereby necessitating statutory interpretation by the courts and tribunals, this results in tension between the aims of the tribunal system and the decisions reached.

## Public policy considerations

Issues of public policy play a significant role in the development of employment law. Legislation is informed by the economic and political climate of the day and by the views of society, and is therefore quite fluid and, at times, responsive to the organizational actors and pressure groups involved.

The employment relationship is generally weighted in favour of the employer, and UK governments have made various attempts to protect employees from unfair employment practices. Economic strategies have varied, however, and some governments have adopted a more interventionist approach while others, such as the Conservative government from 1979 to 1997, adopted a strategy of minimum intervention. The ideology of the Conservative governments was that minimum statutory intervention allows 'flexibility' in the marketplace, allowing businesses to flourish and encouraging competition. Historically, Conservative governments have been more likely to introduce and tighten legislation in collective labour law, however, and from 1979 to 1997 several Acts of Parliament were created which reduced the power of the trade unions (see, for example, Pitt, 1997).

Traditionally, Labour governments have created a more favourable environment for protective employment legislation and collective rights. However, the present Labour government elected in 1997 is quite different from its predecessors. Although it is far more sympathetic than the previous Conservative government to employment protection measures and representations from the unions, 'New Labour' articulated its changing relationship with the unions in its White Paper, *Fairness at Work 1998*. The White Paper clearly stated that 'Employers must and will be free to organize their business in the way they choose' and that trade union collective bargaining mechanisms will not be permitted to interfere with commercial viability. The subsequent Employment Relations Act 1999 is discussed below.

# Legislative approaches to anti-discrimination and equality

The role of governments in upholding the rule of law and protecting vulnerable members of society from discriminatory treatment varies enormously and is often informed by what governments believe their electorate will tolerate, as witnessed by the history of the UK and US race relations legislation discussed below (Bindman and Lester, 1972).

## Different approaches

States vary in their legislative approaches towards preventing discrimination. The complaints-based approach, which concentrates on redressing discrimination against individuals rather than seeking to eradicate social disadvantage, tends to predominate in most European countries. An anti-discrimination law approach uses the law to redress injustice and inequality and protect vulnerable members of particular groups in society. The British system is modelled on this approach.

The White Papers leading to the sex discrimination and race relations legislation in Britain in the 1960s and 1970s, detailed below, acknowledged that there was 'active prejudice' operating against disadvantaged groups in society and that discrimination was 'institutionalised' (Ellis, 1997: 15). The White Paper on the Race Relations Act (RRA) 1976, a piece of legislation modelled on the Sex Discrimination Act (SDA) 1975, aimed to 'reduce discrimination' thereby breaking the 'familiar cycle of cumulative disadvantage'. However, the British anti-discrimination legislation does not really seek to *promote* equality. It has been argued that the White Paper on sex discrimination did not attempt to deal with the social problems facing women (Bamforth, 1996: 49). The race relations legislation has been criticized for failing adequately to tackle institutionalized discrimination (Macpherson Report, 1999). It has been suggested that 'anti' or 'non-discrimination' approaches are negative while an 'equality' approach is more wide-ranging and positive (Lustgarten, 1992: 455).

The use of law as an instrument of social change is a controversial one (Hepple, 1992: 19; Lustgarten and Edwards, 1992: 271). Legislating to change beliefs and attitudes is particularly problematic. The rule of law and legislation can, however, promote and encourage equal opportunities and provide some redress for victims of discrimination. Arguably, it also has a role to play in establishing and shaping acceptable behaviour in society, for example, by outlawing blatant acts of discrimination against particular groups.

The effectiveness of anti-discrimination and equality law may be hampered by the individual nature of the system. The US system of class actions permits individuals who have been affected by identical discrimination to be given the same remedy as the person who was successful in a particular case, whereas in Britain each person affected would have to bring an individual claim. It has been argued that the US system is more forward looking and results in a 'cost maximising' deterrent for American employers as they will have to deal with huge compensation payouts (Lustgarten and Edwards, 1992; MacEwen, 1995).

Remedies and mechanisms for enforcement are vital components. The system in Britain is predominantly enforced through the employment tribunal system. The tribunal system also allows the complainant to claim compensation, which is a more appropriate remedy for victims of employment discrimination. However, individuals may not have the finances to pursue civil claims and access to legal advice from trade unions and agencies such as the EOC and the CRE often provides a valuable lifeline. A study carried out by the Institute of Employment Studies highlights, for example, that success under the Disability Discrimination Act is linked to legal representation, and that lack of finance is the main barrier to claims (EOR, 1999). A Directive on burden of proof, due to be implemented in 2001, states that the burden of proof in sex discrimination cases should be shared. The UK government and EU Commission is of the view that the Directive simply confirms the European Court of Justice (ECJ) decisions in the area rather than grant any new rights, however, some commentators disagree (Croner's Europe Bulletin, 1998).

# Groups in need of protection

Debates continue as to whom should be included in anti-discrimination or equality law. Examples of broader provision from other jurisdictions include Holland, which includes religion, personal conviction and views, political orientation, race, gender, nationality, sexual preference, marital status and duration of employment, and the USA which includes race, religion, age and sexual orientation in some state provision. Anti-discrimination law in Britain, detailed below, currently covers discrimination on grounds of sex, race and disability, and provides limited protection for discrimination on trade union grounds and, most recently, against transsexuals. The law has been significantly influenced by the EU since the latter's accession in 1973.

**Key learning points**

1 Public policy considerations play a significant role in the development of employment law. Legislation is influenced by the economic and political climate of the day and by the views of society.

2 The role of governments in upholding the rule of law varies, as do approaches to anti-discrimination or equality law.

3 Anti-discrimination law attempts to use the law to redress injustice and inequality, and to protect vulnerable members of particular groups in society. An 'equality' approach is wider ranging and includes positive action and the use of quotas.

# The role and impact of EU law on the UK

## Brief background

The EU law-making process and machinery are somewhat complex, and the original European Community (EC) Treaty has been subject to change in recent years via the Single European Act 1986, the Treaty on European Union 1993 and the Treaty of Amsterdam 1997, which came into force on 1 May 1999 resulting in large-scale renumbering of the treaty Articles. This section seeks to introduce the reader to the basic framework of EU law. References to Articles in the EC Treaty are to the renumbered provisions.

European Union member states are bound by the treaties and secondary legislation – Regulations, Directives and Decisions, termed the 'hard law', which can be invoked before the courts. 'Soft law' provisions include resolutions and declarations, which do not have the full force of law. The EU derives its competence from the treaties, and secondary legislation requires a specific legal treaty base to ensure its validity. If there is a conflict between national law and EU law the latter overrides.

Breach of EU law can result in court action being taken by member states, the Commission or even individuals. Some treaty Articles, Directives and certain international provisions, require member states to ensure their national law meets the EU obligations and allows individuals to rely on such rights in their national courts. The courts must give effect to it even if there is no national law on the subject. Directives, the most common legislation used in the social policy and employment field, require national legislation to give them effect. Deadlines are stipulated in the Directive and usually include an eighteen to twenty-four month period to allow member states to transpose the provisions into national law.

## Impact on sex discrimination

Equality of treatment between men and women has occupied a fairly high profile in the EU. For example Article 141/EC, on equal pay for equal work in the Treaty of Rome provided the base for the initial Directive on Equal Pay 1975 and Article 308/EC was used to enact the Equal Treatment Directive 1976, which introduces the principle of equal treatment relating to access to employment, vocational training, promotion and working conditions. Subsequent ECJ judgements have assisted in elevating the principle of equal treatment as one of the fundamental rights protected by Community law (Nielsen and Szyszczak, 1997: 151).

European Union law has had a major impact on sex equality law. Initially, the Equal Pay Act 1970 and Sex Discrimination Act 1975 enacted in Britain were greatly influenced by the American equality legislation. Little regard was given to the Equal Pay and Equal Treatment Directive being drafted at that time, although the UK was keen to be seen to be complying with the broad provisions of former Article 141 as it was seeking entry to the Community. However, by 1979 it was apparent that the British sex equality legislation needed some assistance to challenge the deep-rooted discriminatory practices. European Union law in cases such as *Defrenne* (1971, 1976 and 1978) led the way for further ECJ challenges and the EOC attempted to embark on a litigation strategy, although this was thwart with problems in its early stages (Barnard, 1995: 263). References from national courts to the ECJ relating to the interpretation of EU law, in cases such as *Macarthy's* v *Smith* (1980 – equal pay) and *Jenkins* v *Kingsgate* (1981 – part-time workers and indirect discrimination) resulted from lawyers noticing the potential influence of EU law rather that any grand strategy.

A strategy started taking shape in the 1980s with the EOC funding successful cases such as *Marshall* (1986 – discriminatory retirement age) and *Barber* (1990 – discriminatory occupational pensions). In 1983 (following enforcement proceedings brought against the UK in 1981) the EOC working with the TUC, notified the European Commission that it believed that national legislation on equal pay was incompatible with EU law and this led to changes in national law.

The EOC's Chief Legal Officer declared in 1990 that it would steer a two-pronged strategy in the future in that it would persist in making references to the ECJ and that it would make use of judicial review to challenge national law. However, criticisms have been levelled at the EOC as it was reluctant to fund a number of test cases. For example, Mrs Marshall initially had to fund herself in *Marshall (No. 2)* and Mrs Webb in *Webb* v *EMO Air Cargo* (1994 – pregnancy dismissal) did not receive EOC funding. The role of individual litigants such as Mrs Marshall and Mrs Webb has therefore contributed to the successes championed in the ECJ.

Criticism has been levelled at the ECJ for its 'market ideology' approach (Nielsen and Szyszczak, 1997: 209; see also Chapter 10). The precedence of economic rights over social rights has been witnessed and is seen to have 'a suffocating effect on the development of the principle of equality' (Barnard, 1997: 71).

## Impact on other forms of discrimination

The influence of the EU in other areas of equality such as sexual orientation, disability, age and race has been less marked. Until the Treaty of Amsterdam 1997, which introduced a broad non-discrimination clause (Article 13) as discussed in the contemporary issues section below, the EU continually denied it had the power to intervene in matters such as race discrimination. Arguments centred on amending the treaties or using existing treaty bases, which required a unanimous vote and, as member states could not agree, the EU resorted to 'soft law' provisions, countless Resolutions and rhetoric. Similarly, there has been reluctance to recognize competence (this relates to whether or not there is reference to the subject in the EU treaties) in the area of sexual orientation. European Parliamentary debates and reports, for example, the Squarcialupi Report 1984 on sexual discrimination at work, highlighted the issues relating to sexual orientation and suggested that measures were necessary to protect such disadvantaged groups. The ECJ had the opportunity to pronounce in *Grant* v *South-West Trains* in 1998 but, despite the Advocate General's supportive opinion, the ECJ ruled that discrimination on grounds of sexual orientation did not amount to sex discrimination.

As regards disability, its history is again one of 'soft law' provisions (for example, Council Recommendation and Guidelines on the Employment of Disabled People in the EC 1986). Articles 151 and 308/EC have been used to introduce a number of programmes to support the disabled and the Social Charter 1989 raised awareness of their entitlement. Disability is included in the general equality clause introduced at Amsterdam 1997. In addition, when drawing up measures under Article 95/EC 'the institutions of the Community shall take account of the needs of persons with a disability'.

Minimal concrete action has been witnessed in the field of age discrimination. The year 1993 was designated as the European Year of the Elderly and Solidarity between Generations, and the White Paper in 1994 on social policy made reference to the need for action to protect older workers. A Resolution on the Employment of Older Workers was adopted and member states were requested to acknowledge the barriers to older workers and take appropriate measures to eliminate these obstacles. Discrimination on grounds of age is included in the Amsterdam non-discrimination clause (Article 13).

---

**Key learning points**

1 European Union law has a significant impact on anti-discrimination law in Britain, particularly the law relating to sex equality
2 The ECJ has had a major impact on sex equality law developments, but has been criticized for allowing economic rights to take precedence over social rights. The ECJ has extended protection to transsexuals but stopped short of granting protection on grounds of sexual orientation

---

# Anti-discrimination legislation in the UK

Common law upholds the principle of freedom of contract and the concept of discrimination is not recognized. According to common law, an employer is free to enter into an employment contract with whomsoever they choose, on whatever terms are agreed. The complaints-based system of anti-discrimination law adopted in Britain is founded in Acts of Parliament, which override common law. Anti-discrimination legislation provides rights for specified groups of people who are refused employment or who are in other ways disadvantaged by an employer's discriminatory exercise of that right to freedom of contract.

The main statutes considered here are the SDA, RRA and the Disability Discrimination Act (DDA) 1995. The Sex Discrimination (Gender

Reassignment) Regulations 1999 are referred to, as they extend the SDA to cover transsexuals. Codes of practice are also considered, the most recent code relevant to this area being the 1999 code on age discrimination. Within the legislation the groups who can claim unlawful discrimination are women (or men), married women (or men), minority ethnic groups, people with disabilities and transsexuals. Outside this legislative framework, there is no law to prevent an employer from refusing to employ someone on any grounds they choose; because of, say, their sexuality or their political beliefs, or because they have red hair or a big nose!

The Acts covering the different groups are very similar in their wording and their approach to anti-discrimination. The SDA and the RRA are identical in many respects, and these will be considered together. Discrimination against people with disabilities raises different issues from sex and race, and that Act is looked at separately.

## The scope of the sex and race discrimination legislation

As the wording of the SDA and RRA are almost identical, decisions of the tribunals and courts made under one Act are used to interpret the other, and comments made on one Act apply to the other unless otherwise indicated (the EU law on sex discrimination has therefore indirectly influenced race discrimination laws in Britain). However, the first distinction between the Acts is, of course, the scope of the legislation.

The SDA covers discrimination on grounds of gender, marital status and gender reassignment. The provisions of the Act also apply to men (section 2) and married persons (section 3) (though not to someone who is single!) and new section 2A extends the definition to someone on the grounds that the person 'intends to undergo, is undergoing or has undergone gender reassignment'.

The RRA applies to discrimination on 'racial grounds', defined in section 3 of the Act as grounds of 'colour, race, nationality or ethnic or national origins'. This definition has not been without its problems, particularly in relation to the meaning of 'ethnic origin'. The leading case is *Mandla* v *Dowell Lee* (1983), where the House of Lords decided that 'ethnic origin' was wider than 'racial origin' and that it could cover religious and cultural differences. Applying this test, it has been possible to include some religious groups within the definition, such as Sikhs, whereas others have been excluded. In *Dawkins* v *Department of the Environment* (1993) it was held that Rastafarians did not constitute a racial group as they were not a distinct section within the Afro-Caribbean community. In *J. H. Walker Ltd* v *Hussain* (1996) it was held that Muslims could not be treated as an ethnic group although the decision in *Khanum* v *IBC Vehicles* (1998) adopted a different approach, focusing on the applicant's nationality.

## The definition of discrimination

There are two main forms of discrimination recognized by the SDA and RRA: direct and indirect discrimination. Direct discrimination is where a person from one group is treated less favourably than people not in that group, as defined in the SDA and the RRA. This is the most blatant form of discrimination. For example, where an employer states that they will not 'take on a coloured girl when English girls are available', this is direct discrimination (*Owen and Briggs* v *James* [1982]). Similarly, if a woman is refused employment because she is female, she suffers direct discrimination.

Furthermore, where an employer uses gender-based criteria in their employment practice, that will amount to direct discrimination. The courts here apply a 'but for' test – 'but for' the sex of the complainant they would be treated differently. For example, in the leading case of *James* v *Eastleigh Borough Council* (1990), where a local authority allowed free admission to a swimming pool for people of pensionable age (i.e. sixty for women and sixty-five for men), it was found to be discriminatory as Mrs James was admitted free whereas Mr James, who was the same age, had to pay. 'But for' his sex, Mr James would have been admitted free also. This leading case concerned the provision of services, but the test must also be applied to employment cases.

Indirect discrimination occurs where an apparently neutral employment practice has a disproportionately disadvantageous effect upon a particular group. Indirect discrimination is more covert than the direct form, and is intended to cover those situations where discrimination is institutionalized. The SDA and RRA provide that there is indirect discrimination where an employer imposes a requirement or condition which applies equally to all groups but can be met only by a considerably smaller proportion of a particular group than the proportion of those not of that group. An individual member of the disadvantaged group who suffers as a consequence can claim indirect discrimination, unless the employer can objectively justify the requirement or condition on other grounds. For example, where a school required boys to have short haircuts and applied a 'no turban' rule, it was held that this requirement had a disproportionate effect upon Sikhs, the number of whom could comply with the rule was considerably smaller than the number of non-Sikhs who could comply (*Mandla* v *Dowell Lee*).

There is a third category of discrimination – that of victimization. This applies where an employee suffers less favourable treatment because they have been involved in a complaint under the statutes (SDA or RRA) relating to discrimination, and aims to prevent people from being penalized for using the legislation. There are relatively few cases in this category but it can provide valuable protection for employees who may be in a difficult position bringing a legal action against their employer.

Intention and motive have been discussed in a number of cases, and it is clear that it is not relevant that an employer had no desire to discriminate or did so for the best of motives. The tribunal will look at the *effect* of the discriminatory act. A good example of this is the *James* case on direct discrimination, referred to above. The council in that case argued that their concessionary rates were for the benefit of members of the community who were less well off. The House of Lords found that although the motive for the council's policy was to be applauded, the effect was discrimination and the motive was irrelevant.

The same principle also applies to indirect discrimination. This must be so if the issue of institutional discrimination is to be tackled at all by the legislation. Employers may apply employment policies that unwittingly have the effect of discriminating against a particular group. The law would be undermined if it was found that there was no discrimination in those cases simply because the employer had no intention to discriminate. This may seem harsh on employers, but the repercussions for the employer may be mitigated in the tribunal's decision as to the amount of compensation to be paid by the employer to the complainant. Compensation amounts are discussed, but there is unlikely to be an award for injury to feelings where the employer had no intention to discriminate.

## Problems with applying the definitions of discrimination

Statutory definitions are subject to interpretation by the courts and tribunals, and the wording of the discrimination legislation has given rise to numerous cases establishing the parameters of the law. It has led to some controversial decisions, and circumstances which to the lay person appear to be obviously discriminatory have been excluded from the scope of the Act. For example the pregnancy dismissal cases such as *Turley* v *Alders Department Stores Ltd* (1980) and *Webb* v *EMO Air Cargo Ltd* (1995).

The definition of indirect discrimination has also given rise to problems of interpretation. To fall within the statutory definition of indirect discrimination there are four essential elements. First, there must be a requirement or condition, which is of general application, imposed by the employer. Second, the requirement or condition must have a disproportionate impact upon a particular group (i.e. a considerably smaller number of women or members of a particular racial group can comply with the requirement or condition than the number of men or those who are not members of that racial group). Third, the employer has no objective justification for imposing the requirement or condition, and fourth, it must result in a detriment to the complainant. Restrictive definitions of discrimination have been subject to criticism. Proposals for reform were put forward by the EOC and CRE in 1998. The CRE, for example, called for a change in the definition of discrimination in that indirect discrimination should not depend on a statistical analysis of the numbers of a particular group affected by a condition, but applicants should have to show only that there is a risk that a particular group could be adversely affected. The government has rejected any need for reform. The government's view is that the greater need is for existing law to be better understood and acted upon by employers, and that the EOC and CRE need to work together on practical means of achieving this.

## Is the discrimination unlawful?

If a person establishes that they have been discriminated against, either directly or indirectly, they must then go on to show that the discrimination is 'unlawful'. This means showing that the act of the employer falls within the situations specified in section 6 of the SDA and section 4 of the RRA. These sections apply to discrimination before an employment relationship exists, i.e. in the recruitment and selection process or in the terms offered. Thus, unlike most other employment statutes, their application is wider than just to employees. It is also unlawful to discriminate in the course of employment, for example, in promotion and training, and in relation to dismissal or by subjecting the applicant to 'any other detriment'.

There are exceptions to the rules. Both the SDA and RRA set out circumstances when it is lawful to discriminate, what is termed 'genuine occupational qualifications' (GOQs). These cover situations where the effective performance of a particular job requires a person of a particular sex or race. They cover, for example, physiology or authenticity (for example models or actors), decency or privacy (for example, in the provision of medical or nursing services), or provision of personal services (for example, services promoting the welfare of a particular racial group). Where a GOQ applies, it is a complete defence to a complaint as the discrimination is rendered lawful as in *Lasertop* v *Webster* (1997) where the EAT held it was lawful for a ladies health club to restrict employment to female staff. The exceptions relating to the armed forces, police, immigration service, prison service and local government officers have been subject to challenge by the ECJ and by Macpherson following the Stephen Lawrence Inquiry in 1999.

## Remedies

The main remedy for unlawful discrimination, as may be expected with a complaints-based system, is compensation for the victim of the discrimination. There are two other sanctions available to an employment tribunal: a declaration of the parties' rights in the matter and a recommendation that the employer take action to remove or reduce the discriminatory treatment of the complainant. Neither of these remedies is particularly effective in preventing discrimination, as a declaration simply provides vindication for the applicant and the tribunals cannot enforce recommendations whose only power for non-compliance is the award of additional compensation. As far as the victim is concerned monetary compensation is the best they can hope for, although compensation is awarded in only a small minority of cases – 2.5 per cent of cases in 1998 (EOR, 1999). Following challenges in

**Table 6.1** Compensation awards, 1998 (1997 figures in brackets)

|  | *Average* | *Median* |
| --- | --- | --- |
| Disability discrimination | £11 501 (£3 743) | £3 250 (£2 000) |
| Race discrimination | £6 038 (£8 220) | £3 303 (£3 312) |
| Sex discrimination | £6 873 (£4 556) | £3 000 (£2 073) |
| All discrimination awards | £6 944 (£8 222) | £3 000 (£2 500) |

*Source: Equal Opportunities Review*, (86), July–August 1999.

**Table 6.2** Record breakers: highest compensation awards

| Category | Compensation award | Injury to feeling |
|---|---|---|
| Disability discrimination | £102 717 *Kirker v British Sugar Plc.* | £8 000 *Brown v South Bank University* |
| Race discrimination | £122 464 *Chan v London Borough of Hackney\** | £45 000 *Yeboah v Crofton and London Borough of Hackney* (included £10 000 for aggravated damages) |
| Sex discrimination | £222 755 *McLoughlin v London Borough of Southwark* | £25 000 *Bamber v Fujii International Finance* (included £20 000 for aggravated damages) |

*Note*: \*Originally, the employment tribunal awarded compensation of £113 964. At a subsequent hearing, the tribunal ordered the court to pay additional compensation of £8 500 for failure to comply with a recommendation. The previous record award – £358 289 in *London Borough of Lambeth v D'Souzo* – was set aside by the Court of Appeal at the end of 1998

*Source*: *Equal Opportunities Review*, (86), July–August 1999.

# Activity

## Activity 6.1

Tables 6.1 and 6.2 relate to recent compensation awards. It will be useful in preparation for this activity to have consulted some recent editions of the *Equal Opportunities Review* and the *Employment Law Digest*.

### Questions

1 Examine the figures and identify where the highest awards are being made and what trends can be identified when looking at figures for 1997 and 1998.
2 Comment on possible reasons why in some circumstances, employment tribunals award large sums whilst the average award is relatively low.
3 Drawing on discussion in Chapter 8, discuss the implications of employers on average having to pay higher awards for compensation. Consider how this might affect employer policy and practice.
4 Engage in a general discussion about whether the levels of awards are adequate compensation for the discrimination faced by the complainants.

the ECJ (*Marshall No. 2*, 1993) and the subsequent changes to the law, the levels of compensation have continued to rise, with record amounts awarded in 1998.

# Impact of the law

What does all this mean in practice for employers? In order to avoid complaints of unlawful discrimination and possible high levels of compensation awarded against them, employers need to adopt employment policies and practices that promote and support equality and diversity within their workforce. Although there is no formal requirement to review employment practice, employers need to consider carefully the effect of their employment policies to ensure they are not discriminatory. The intention or motive of the employer is irrelevant – it is the effect that counts. For example, advertisements for posts are specifically covered by the legislation. Thus, an advert for a 'Head Waiter' without further reference to 'male or female' was held to have a sexual connotation, indicating an intention to recruit a man for the job, and was unlawful (*EOC* v *(1) Masser and (2) Carriages Leisure Centre Recruitment*, 1990). Informal methods of recruitment, for example, by word of mouth, may be unlawful as it could result in some minority ethnic groups being excluded from the selection process as they never get to hear of the vacancies. It does raise a problem as far as the potential applicants are concerned, as they cannot complain of discrimination if they have no knowledge of the vacancy in the first place.

In order to avoid legal liability, employers need to ensure good record-keeping and the adoption of formal procedures in their selection processes. Although the burden of proof is formally upon the complainant, and discrimination is difficult to prove, the employer needs to be able to rebut any inferences of discrimination, which the tribunal may draw. Guidance for employers is found in the CRE's and EOC's codes of practice on the elimination of discrimination. Although these codes are not legally binding documents, they provide guidance as to good practice, and breach of the guidelines may be used as evidence in a tribunal.

It is worth noting that employers may also be liable for discriminatory actions 'in the course of employment' by fellow employees under section 41 of the SDA and section 32 of the RRA. A broad approach to such liability has been adopted as witnessed in the landmark case of *Burton and Rhule* v *De Vere Hotels* (1998) where a hotel was found responsible for stand-up comedian Bernard Manning's racially insulting treatment of two waitresses during one of his shows.

## Enforcement of the law

The EOC and CRE play a crucial role in the development and the enforcement of the law. Although they are unable to provide representation for individuals in every claim, both commissions will offer advice to potential complainants. For example, in 1998 the CRE received 10 000 calls for advice and received 1657 applications for assistance (in line with the 1997 total of l661). A 'sharp increase' (60 per cent) in the number of complaints against private employers was noted, overtaking complaints against local authorities for the first time (CRE Annual Report 1998). The EOC and CRE funds are limited but they will support cases that they believe will make some impact on discrimination law. The EOC in particular has pursued a policy of strategic support for cases that have been at the forefront of establishing the boundaries of the law. As discussed above, the EOC has made full use of the EU law in expanding those boundaries, whereas the CRE have not had the advantage of EU law to back up their legal arguments. However, they may adopt a different approach in the future given the changes to the law following the Amsterdam Treaty.

The two commissions also have an investigative role, with power to investigate discrimination in a particular field of employment or a specific employer. However, following the House of Lords decision in *CRE* v *Prestige Group plc* (1984), the powers of the commissions have been curtailed, and an investigation requires prior evidence of unlawful discrimination. Both commissions have sought clarification of their powers and have proposed that more extensive powers be made available to them. The government has given a commitment to provide clarification and to bring them into line with the newly established Disability Rights Commission.

As the commissions do not have adequate powers to tackle the issue of discrimination at an institutional level, it is largely left to individual complainants – an approach that has been subject to criticism (Fredman and Szyszczak, 1992; Lustgarten and Edwards, 1992). This means that the law requires an individual complainant who is prepared to take a case through the tribunals and courts, which is not an easy option. Cases can take many months, if not years, to be settled. It requires a very determined applicant to see a case through to the end. Discrimination cases often last many days or weeks in the employment tribunal, which can be very trying for the complainant – but also very expensive for the employer, as key personnel can be tied up in the tribunal for many days, not to mention the time spent preparing for the hearing and the legal costs incurred (which cannot be recovered unless there are certain exceptional circumstances). It has been argued that the introduction of class actions, as found in the USA, would improve the system (Lacey, 1992; Lustgarten and Edwards, 1997; see also the discussions about the importance of collective action in Chapters 5, 8 and 11).

# The Disability Discrimination Act

The DDA is aimed at discrimination against people with disabilities. Disability is defined as 'a physical or mental impairment which has a substantial and long-term adverse effect on [the person's] ability to carry out normal day-to-day activities' (section 1). Many cases that have reached the tribunal have centred around whether or not the complainant does in fact have a disability within the meaning of the Act. Difficulties have arisen over the meaning of 'substantial' and 'long term'.

One problem lies in the number of different sources available to the tribunals (and parties involved) to ascertain whether or not an applicant is covered by the Act. For example, guidance is given in schedule 1 of the Act as to the meaning of 'long term adverse effect', whilst further help is available in the *Guidance on Matters to be Taken into Account in Determining Questions Relating to the Definition of Disability* (HMSO, 1996) and the *Code of Practice for Elimination of Discrimination in the Field of Employment against Disabled Persons or Persons Who Have Had a Disability* (HMSO, 1996). Guidance on the approach to be taken by tribunals was given by the EAT in *Goodwin* v *The Patent Office* (1999), where it was stated that tribunals should refer to the *Code of Practice* and *Government Guidance* for assistance in interpreting the legislation, but the definitions should not be treated as an additional hurdle for applicants.

The DDA contains a similar definition of direct discrimination to that found in the SDA and RRA, but there are crucial differences. The DDA prohibits 'less favourable treatment' (section 5), but the DDA allows the employer the defence of justification, which is not a valid defence to direct discrimination under the SDA and RRA. Under section 5 of the DDA, discriminatory treatment is justified 'if, but only if, the reason for it is both material to the circumstances of the particular case and substantial'.

In the case of *Baynton* v *Saurus General Engineers Ltd* (1999), EAT stated it is material to consider the circumstances of the disabled employee as well as the employer's conduct when deciding on justification. Baynton became disabled when his thumb was crushed in an accident at work and was dismissed following an absence of twelve months. The employer argued his dismissal was justified as he was unable to perform his job and had long-term absence. Any other employee, it was argued, would have been dismissed in those circumstances. However, the employee argued that he had been dismissed without prior warning and a few days before he was due to see his specialist when he hoped to be declared fit to return to work. The EAT accepted the employee's argument that the tribunal must take account of the position of the employee as well as the employer's conduct.

Under the DDA the definition of discrimination also places employers under a duty to make adjustments. Section 6 refers to 'arrangements' or 'any physical feature of premises' which place a disabled person at a 'substantial disadvantage'. In that case, there is a duty on an employer to 'take such steps as is reasonable, in all the circumstances of the case,' in order to prevent the arrangements or feature from having that effect. Unlike the other Acts, the DDA puts a positive obligation upon employers to take measures to prevent the discriminatory effect. The employer's duty is to do what is reasonable, with the tribunal deciding what is reasonable in all the circumstances.

Section 6(3) also gives examples of steps that an employer may have to take. These include: making adjustments to premises, allocating some of the disabled person's duties to another person, transferring them to fill an existing vacancy, altering their working hours, acquiring or modifying equipment and modifying instructions or reference manuals. In determining whether a step is reasonable, section 6(4) requires a number of issues to be taken into account, including how effective the relevant step would be, the financial costs and the employer's financial and other resources. The Employment Appeal Tribunal has taken a fairly wide view of the extent of this duty. In *London Borough of Hillingdon* v *Morgan* (1999) EAT made it clear that the *Code of Practice* had to be referred to when deciding what is reasonable. In that case, it was decided that the employer had failed to comply with the duty to make adjustments when they did not allow an employee who had become disabled to work from home temporarily in order to assist her transition back into full time employment.

One of the main criticisms of the Disability Discrimination Act 1995 was that it did not provide for a commission with any powers of enforcement similar to those of the EOC and CRE. However, the Disability Rights Commission Act was passed in 1999 which establishes a new Disability Rights Commission. The new commission will have rights and duties similar to those of the EOC and the CRE.

# Age discrimination

Another area of reform to which the Labour Party stated its commitment prior to the 1997 election was the elimination of age discrimination. However, no legislation has been brought forward in this area. There is instead a code of practice. The purpose of the code, according to the draft published in December 1998, is to 'help employers, employees and applicants alike by setting a standard. The Code will show how businesses and employers can take steps to ensure they choose, retain and develop the best person for the job by eliminating the use of age as an employment criterion' (*Code of Practice for age diversity in employment*, 1998).

The code does not, of course, have the force of the law. The government is using the code to urge employers to ensure that age is not a barrier to jobs and opportunities. The incentive for employers to follow the guidance in the code is the benefit to themselves. The Employment Minister, Andrew Smith, in launching the code in the House of Commons, pointed out that by 2000 more than one-third of the workforce will be aged over forty-five (House of Commons Parliamentary Report, 7 December 1998). Thus, it does not make commercial sense for employers to exclude such a large part of the workforce. Whether or not the voluntary approach will be successful in encouraging employers to recognize age diversity in the workplace remains to seen. The government has given a commitment to keep the code under review, with an evaluation of the code's impact by February 2001. The minister made it clear that legislation is still an option.

# Sexual orientation

Discrimination in employment on grounds of sexuality is not covered in any statutes, nor is it covered by EU law as discussed above. It has been argued that the sex discrimination legislation covers discrimination against lesbians or gay men on the basis that a woman dismissed for a relationship with another woman, is being treated less favourably than a man would have been treated in similar circumstances (i.e. in a relationship with a woman). However, as we have seen, the law in Britain requires the treatment to be 'on grounds of her sex', not her sexuality. Therefore the law has been found to be lacking. The ECJ has also confirmed that discrimination on the grounds of sexuality is not prohibited by EU law as seen in the case of *Grant* v *South-West Trains* mentioned in the EU section above.

Despite these setbacks for the homosexual community, there have been successful cases in the European Court of Human Rights. *Lustig-Prean and anor* v *United Kingdom* and *Smith and anor* v *United Kingdom* 1999 has set the scene for changes in the law in future.

## Key learning points

1 Legislation in Britain covers sex (including transsexuals), race and disability. A code of practice on age discrimination has recently been enacted. Codes do not have the full force of the law, but can be used in evidence in a court or tribunal.
2 The law recognizes direct (blatant) and indirect (more subtle and institutionalized) discrimination together with victimization. The Disability Discrimination Act places a positive duty on employers to take measures to prevent the discriminatory effect of indirect discrimination.
3 Intention and motive is not relevant in cases of discrimination. The tribunal will look at the effect of the discriminatory act.
4 The burden of proof is on the complainant, although the tribunals may draw inferences.
5 Remedies are confined to redress for individuals with no real sanctions against employers. Class actions such as apply in the USA, appear to be effective but, there is no precedent for this in Britain.

# Some contemporary issues

## Article 13 EC

Following years of campaigning and pressure from bodies such as the Standing Conference against Racism (seeking to improve rights for ethnic and racial minorities), Stonewall (the lesbian and gay rights group) and the Starting Line Group (a group of international experts seeking to introduce a draft directive on race discrimination), the EU finally introduced a non-discrimination clause at Amsterdam. The introduction of Article 13 in the

Amsterdam Treaty, which came into force on 1 May 1999, will provide fertile ground for the advance of equal opportunities in the EU and its impact is eagerly awaited by civil and human rights campaigners across Europe. It could take some years to witness the impact of the Article as it has no time limit attached and is likely to encounter political resistance from some member states. The Article states:

> Within the scope of application of this Treaty and without prejudice to any special provisions contained therein, the Council, acting unanimously on a proposal from the Commission and after consulting the European Parliament, may take appropriate action to prohibit discrimination based on sex, racial, ethnic or social origin, religious belief, disability, age or sexual orientation.

The future prospects for Article 13 have been vigorously debated in academic circles. Allen (1999) outlines some of the difficulties relating to interpretation including the definition of 'appropriate action', which could be interpreted by some members states as more 'soft law' provision. Bell (1999) has considered the limitations of Article 13 and opined that other provisions in the treaty may provide greater scope for action in the area of non-discrimination, for example, the newly incorporated social provisions in Articles 136–45. Hervey (1999) and Waddington (1999) paint a more optimistic future for Article 13. Waddington argues that the Commission seems to be 'determined' to produce legislation and Hervey argues that its very inclusion demonstrates that member states acknowledge that they cannot retain total control over actions to fight and prevent racism. As the British race relations legislation has been described as the best in the Community (European Committee Against Racism and Intolerance, 1997; Forbes and Mead, 1992,) the impact of EU law in the area of race discrimination is likely to be less marked in the UK than in many other EU member states. The potential in the areas of religion, age and sexual orientation is yet to be tested.

## The Human Rights Act 1998

An examination of international and regional anti-discrimination measures demonstrates that the right to equality on grounds of race, colour, sex, language, religion, political or other opinion, national or social origin, property, birth or other status (see, for example the United Nations Charter of Human Rights, 1948 and United Nations Universal Declaration of Human Rights, 1948) is internationally recognized as a fundamental right. The incorporation of the European Convention of Human Rights (ECHR) into UK law via the Human Rights Act (HRA) 1998 will also have an impact on the field of discrimination as it will require all public authorities to comply with the rights and obligations under the Convention. However, the Convention will not have direct effect and the Act will not therefore allow the courts to strike down national law per se. Any conflicts will have to be resolved by Parliament.

Article 14 of the ECHR addresses the principle of equality: 'The enjoyment of the rights and freedoms set forth in this Convention shall be secured without discrimination on any ground such as sex, race, colour, language, religion, political or other opinion, national or social origin, association with a national minority, property, birth or other status.' The range of rights falling within the remit of the ECHR includes the right to life, right to a fair hearing, rights to privacy, family life, home and correspondence, to marry and found a family and to equality of spouses, right to peaceful enjoyment of possessions, right to education, right to free elections but excludes the right to employment. However, it may be argued that discriminatory acts in employment impinge on other rights, such as the right to privacy. The Act does not grant direct rights against private sector employers but it will indirectly affect the rights of all workers as the courts have to interpret the law so as to be compatible with the Convention (Hepple, 1998: 64).

The legislation is not due to be implemented until October 2000 but it has already been the subject of both praise and criticism, as outlined in a series of papers edited by Markensis (1998). Whether the Human Rights Act will result in improved rights for individuals within the UK has yet to be put to the test. Access to justice should be quicker and cheaper as individuals can seek redress in the national courts as opposed to the Strasbourg court. In addition, the extent of protection granted by the ECHR is broader, as evidenced in *Lustig Prean* v *UK* (1999) which held that the Ministry of Defence's discharge of the four applicants in pursuance of their policy banning lesbians and gays was in breach of the Convention and constituted a violation of their right to private life under Article 8. The EU's ECJ failed to recognize discrimination on grounds of sexual orientation in *Grant* v *South-West Trains*. The full impact of the *Lustig Prean* decision may have to wait until the HRA comes into force as international judgements are difficult to enforce, as outlined earlier. The decision has signalled to the government that this could well be the next area requiring legislative intervention to redress injustice at the workplace. Another area the HRA is likely to have an impact on is religious discrimination. The ECHR recognizes the right to religious freedom but this is generally determined as tolerating or preventing direct discrimination against practising a particular religious faith and does not entitle individuals to equality in religion, which would challenge the preferential rights of the majority religious group (Freedman, 1998: 122).

## Positive action and positive discrimination

There has been an ongoing debate about the need for more effective measures to combat discrimination. This has mainly been in the areas of sex and race discrimination as these are the areas where legislation has been in place for some time and, according to some commentators, has been ineffective (Lustgarten and Edwards, 1992).

There is no agreement as to the pros and cons of positive action or positive discrimination, or whether there should be a legal requirement for such approaches. There is generally support for the idea of positive action – where obligations are placed upon employers to take a proactive stance to eliminate discrimination at the workplace. For example, the Fair Employment (Northern Ireland) Act requires positive action, and legislation in other jurisdictions such as the USA also takes this approach, referred to as affirmative action. Positive action includes monitoring the workforce, identifying areas where groups are under-represented, devising employment strategies to address under-representation, and evaluating the success of those strategies. It could also involve setting targets for the recruitment and promotion of people from the disadvantaged groups.

Positive or reverse discrimination, on the other hand, is more controversial. It involves giving preferential treatment to a member of a disadvantaged group. It means discriminating in favour of that person even though they may be less qualified, in order to redress past discrimination. It is argued that only by favouring disadvantaged groups can true equality be achieved. Parekh (1992) argues that in Britain the policy is being increasingly used in practice (see Chapter 5). On the other hand, Pitt (1992) accepts that the SDA and RRA have not had the desired effect of eliminating discrimination, but argues that reverse discrimination is a violation of the equality principle. She concludes, though, that perhaps public bodies should take the lead in positive action programmes and allow 'limited', closely monitored reverse discrimination programmes.

Under UK law, positive discrimination is unlawful. However there are exceptions. It is lawful to discriminate in favour of women in terms of access to training to help them to do work in an area in which there are no, or very few, people from that group (section 48, SDA). Furthermore, section 49 allows trade unions to reserve seats for women on their governing bodies – a section which the TUC has taken advantage of, reserving twelve seats for women. Outside these narrow exceptions, positive discrimination will be found to be unlawful.

The issues have been brought sharply into focus in the EU. The ECJ's decision in *Kalanke* v *Frei Hansestadt Bremen* (1995), relating to whether EU law permits positive discrimination, caused quite a stir when the ECJ ruled that positive discrimination infringed the Equal Treatment Directive as the law should be used to remove obstacles and not to allow national legislation automatically to permit positive discrimination at the point of selection. However, subsequent Commission communications and the ruling in *Hellmut Marschall* (1998) softened the ruling as the court accepted that a rule which did not automatically entitle positive discrimination was compatible with the Equal Treatment Directive as long as objective criteria applied which did not discriminate on grounds of gender. The most recent case on positive discrimination to come before the ECJ is *Badeck and Ors* v *Hessiche* (1999). The Advocates General's preliminary opinion is that the Equal Treatment Directive does not exclude the use of quota systems as long as women are not given automatic priority. The position on positive action has not yet been clearly answered, although the amendments to Article 141 EC at Amsterdam encourage positive action.

The distinction between positive action and positive discrimination is not always clear cut, as demonstrated by the ECJ cases. Positive action is lawful; indeed, in some jurisdictions it is a requirement of the law. However, there can be a blurring of these concepts. Experience in the US has demonstrated that where affirmative action programmes include positive or affirmative action this can lead to a backlash. Such initiatives have been questioned and tested in US courts. It has been successfully argued that affirmative discrimination is contrary to the American Constitution as it is treating some preferentially rather than 'equal' in accordance with the Constitution. Such viewpoints indicate some of the possible pitfalls of the introduction of positive discrimination measures.

## Key learning points

1 The right to be treated equally is a fundamental human right and the Human Rights Act 1998 which incorporates the European Convention of Human Rights into UK law, could have an enormous impact on the field of discrimination. Although the ECHR does not grant a right to employment, successful actions have relied on other rights contained within the Convention, such as the right to privacy.
2 Article 13EC and other social policy provisions introduced at Amsterdam have the potential to improve equal opportunities across the EU on grounds of sex, race, disability, religion, age, social origin and sexual orientation. Sex equality is given a higher profile in the treaty.
3 Opinions are divided as to the merits or otherwise of positive discrimination in employment. Positive discrimination is outlawed in the UK.
4 Forms of permitted positive action include monitoring the workforce and promoting equal opportunities in the workplace. It is argued that such action should be a requirement of the law.

## Activity

### Activity 6.2

This activity requires you to consider the arguments for and against positive action and positive discrimination.

Parekh argues; 'it [positive discrimination] is one of the few policy tools capable of breaking through the self perpetuating cycle of deeply entrenched inequalities' and 'it is on balance and within limits a valuable tool of public policy . . .' (Hepple and Szyszczak, 1992: 261).

Pitt states:

> the argument that all race-conscious or gender-conscious discrimination is bad has a powerful appeal. After all, the main argument to justify the outlawing of discrimination against women and ethnic minorities is the requirement of formal justice that like cases should be treated alike, coupled with the denial that gender, race, colour or ethnic or national origin are relevant distinctions between human beings rendering them unlike cases. To allow reverse discrimination to help one group seems as much a violation of this principle as the former discrimination to limit its opportunities. (Hepple and Szyszczak, 1992: 280)

*Questions*

1 Distinguish between positive action and positive discrimination.
2 Consider the arguments for and against positive discrimination.
3 In what circumstances might positive discrimination be justified. After reading Chapter 7, consider the arguments for positive discrimination within the trade union context.

# Conclusion

'Managing diversity' involves recognizing, accommodating and valuing diverse cultures and characteristics. It is arguable that if the law is to be used to achieve this, there needs to be all-encompassing legislation which requires employers to justify all their employment practices on objective grounds. The perception might be that this would be too interventionist an approach and too great an imposition on business. Instead, the dominant approach is to provide protection for those groups within society who are recognized as most disadvantaged and in need of legislative support to redress the effects of widespread discrimination. Changing public opinion has resulted in extending protection towards groups such as transsexuals and in limited rights for homosexuals. Euopean Union law has had an enormous impact on equality law as it relates to gender and is set to influence other areas. Other developments are found in the UK government's Employment Relations Act 1999. The government has given a commitment for the introduction of 'family friendly' policies, although the details of those policies are not yet known. The Act provides for changes to maternity leave entitlement and for the introduction of regulations on parental leave. The detailed regulations are not available at the time of writing, but need to be put into effect by December 1999 if the UK is to meet its EU obligations.

Public awareness of race discrimination has been raised by the Macpherson Report (1999), investigating the police handling of the Stephen Lawrence murder, which sparked a public debate on race relations and the law and called for a reappraisal of the RRA. Some of the more controversial proposals put forward by Macpherson, such as making private racist remarks illegal, have met with resistance from the government and the legislative impact of the report is still awaited.

The use of the law as an instrument of social change is controversial. The law does not have mystical powers and is not a panacea. The rule of law and legislation can, however, promote and encourage equal opportunities and provide some redress for victims of discrimination. The UK's Disability Discrimination Act still has room for improvement but the positive obligations incorporated into the legislation are a welcome addition to the legislative portfolio. Forms of positive action, such as the requirement to monitor the workforce and to promote equality, need to be encouraged and rewarded along the lines suggested by the CRE in its 1998 report if change is to occur.

# Review and discussion questions

1 Provide examples of how public policy has influenced anti-discrimination law.
2 Explain the difference between direct and indirect discrimination and give examples.
3 What is the legal significance of the new Article 13/EC?
4 Discuss how the wider social disadvantage and discrimination outlined in the Human Rights Act 1998 might impact upon the employment context?

# Further reading

Dashwood, A. and O'Leary, S. (eds) (1997). *The Principle of Equal Treatment in EC Law*. Sweet and Maxwell.
    A collection of papers from a conference organized by the Centre for Legal Studies.
Dine, J. and Watts, B. (eds) (1996). *Discrimination Law: Concepts, Limitations and Justifications*. Longman.
    A collection of papers from a symposium entitled 'Justifying Discrimination' at Essex University.
Hepple, B. and Szyzsczak E. (eds) (1992). *Discrimination: The Limits of the Law*. Mansell.
    A collection of papers from the Hart Legal Workshop at the Institute of Advanced Legal Studies.
Pitt, G. (1997). *Employment Law*. Sweet & Maxwell.
    Textbook on employment law, which has useful chapters on the impact of EU law, UK employment law framework and changes in trade union legislation.

# References

Allen, R. (1999). Article 13 and the search of equality in Europe: an overview. European Conference document, Vienna.
Bamforth, N. (1996). Limits of anti-discrimination law: legal and social concepts of equality. In *Discrimination Law: Concepts, Limitations and Justifications* (Dine, J. and Watts, B., eds). Longman.
Barnard, C. (1995). A European litigation strategy: the case of the Equal Opportunities Commission. In *New Legal Dynamics of European Union* (Shaw, J. and More, G., eds). Clarendon Press.
Barnard, C. (1997) P and S: kite flying or a new constitutional approach? In *The Principle of Equal Treatment in EC Law* (A. Dashwood and S. O'Leary, eds). Sweet and Maxwell.

Bell, M. (1999). The New Article 13 EC Treaty: a sound basis for European anti discrimination law. *Maastricht Journal*, **6**, 1.

Better Regulation Task Force (1999). *Anti Discrimination Legislation Review.*Central Office for Information.

Bindman, G. and Lester, A. (1972). *Race and Law*. Penguin Books.

Commission for Racial Equality (1998a). *Reform of the Race Relations Act 1976*. CRE.

Commission for Racial Equality (1998b). *Proposals for Legislative Measures to Combat Racism and to Promote Equal Rights in the EU*. CRE.

Commission for Racial Equality (1999) *Annual Report 1998*.

*Croner's Europe Bulletin* (1998). Employment law developments. *Croner's Europe Bulletin*, 65, July.

Dashwood, A. and O'Leary, S. (1997). *The Principle of Equal Treatment in EC Law*. Sweet & Maxwell.

Dine, J. and Watts, B. (1996). *Discrimination Law: Concepts, Limitations and Justifications*. Longman.

Ellis, E. (1997). The principle of equality of opportunity irrespective of sex: some reflections on the present state of European Community law and its future development. In *The Principle of Equal Treatment in EC Law* (A. Dashwood and S. O'Leary, eds). Sweet and Maxwell.

EOC (Equal Opportunities Commission) (1998). *Equality in the 21st Century*. EOC.

EOR (Equal Opportunites Review) (1999). Compensation awards 1998: a record year, *Equal Opportunities Review*, (86), July–August, 14–18.

Forbes, I. and Mead, G. (1992). *Measure for Measure*. Department for Employment.

Freedman, S. (1998). Equality issues. In *The Impact of the Human Rights Bill on English Law* (B. Markensis, ed.). Oxford University Press.

Freedman, S. and Szyszczak, E. (1992). *The Interaction of Race and Gender*. In *Discrimination: The Limits of the Law* (B. Hepple and E. Szyszczak, eds). Mansell.

Hepple, B. (1992). Have 25 years of the Race Relations Law in Britain been a failure? In *Discrimination: The Limits of the Law* (B. Hepple and E. Szyszczak, eds). Mansell.

Hepple, B. (1997). The principle of equal treatment in Article 119EC and the possibilities for reform. In *The Principle of Equal Treatment in EC Law* (A. Dashwood and S. O'Leary, eds). Sweet and Maxwell.

Hepple, B. (1998). The impact on labour law. In *The Impact of the Human Rights Bill on English Law* (B. Markensis, ed.). Oxford University Press.

Hepple, B. and Szyzsczak E. (1992). *Discrimination: The Limits of the Law*. Mansell.

Hervey, T. (1999). *Putting Europe's House in Order: Racism, Race Discrimination and Xenophobia after the Treaty of Amsterdam*. Forthcoming.

Lacey, N. (1992). From individual to group. In *Discrimination: The Limits of the Law* (B. Hepple and E. Szyszczak, eds). Mansell.

Lustgarten, L. (1992). Racial inequality, public policy and the law: where are we going? In *Discrimination: The Limits of the Law* (B. Hepple and E. Szyszczak, eds). Mansell.

Lustgarten, L. and Edwards, J. (1992). Racial inequality and the limits of law. In *Racism and Antiracism* (Braham, P., Rattonsi, A. and Skellington, R., eds). Open University Press.

MacEwen, M. (1995). *Tackling Racism in Europe: An Examination of Anti-Discrimination Law in Practice.* Berg.

Macpherson Report (1999). *Report from the Stephen Lawrence Inquiry.* HMSO.

Markensis, B. (ed.) (1998) *The Impact of the Human Rights Bill on English Law.* Oxford University Press.

Nielsen, R. and Szyszczak, E. (1997). *The Social Dimension of the European Union.* Handelshojskolens Forlag

Parekh, B. (1992). A case for positive discrimination. In *Discrimination: The Limits of the Law* (B. Hepple and E. Szyszczak, eds). Mansell.

Pitt, G. (1992). Can reverse discrimination be justified? In *Discrimination: The Limits of the Law* (B. Hepple and E. Szyszczak, eds). Mansell.

Pitt, G. (1997). *Employment Law.* Sweet & Maxwell.

Waddington, L. (1999). Testing the limits of EC Treaty on discrimination. *Industrial Law Journal*, **18**, (2), 133–151.

# Chapter 7
# Trade unions as agents of change

## Aim

To demonstrate that as one of the three key industrial relations actors, trade unions potentially have a central and strategic role to play in the promotion of equality and diversity issues in employment.

## Objectives

- To examine contemporary union membership patterns, union recognition patterns and collective bargaining coverage.
- To outline the economic and political objectives of trade unions in so far as they relate to equality and diversity.
- To examine the role and nature of trade union activity on equality, for example 'equality bargaining', in particular collective agreements, and representative functions.
- To discuss features of internal trade union organization and democracy, which give rise to constraints on unions' ability to pursue an equality and diversity agenda.

## Introduction

Trade unions are generally regarded as one of the three key industrial relations actors: that is, trade unions play a key role in shaping employment opportunities and outcomes through various strategies and interventions in international, national and local contexts. Broadly speaking, trade unions exist to protect employees and further their interests at the workplace. Their existence is underpinned by the assumption of inequalities of power between employers and employees and the consequent need for employees to have collective representation and to act collectively in order to improve pay and conditions at work through negotiations with management. Chapter 6 has shown the law to be a weak instrument in terms of securing equality at work and eradicating discrimination. This is partly attributable to the lack of any 'class action' provision within British law (Dickens, Townley and Winchester, 1988). Trade unions play a role, therefore, in defending employees' terms and conditions at the workplace, but their broader objective is to work towards a fairer, more equal society. From equality and diversity perspectives, our interest in trade unions lies in both these objectives, which can be said to be economic and political.

Trade unions, however, do not wield the power and influence in the UK labour market that they once did. There has been a continuous downward trend in trade union membership since 1979 and whilst the majority of employees in the UK do not now belong to a trade union, a substantial 30 per cent do (Cully and Woodland, 1998). Thus, trade unions retain a significant and substantial presence, although the extent of union membership varies considerably between employment sectors, occupations and according to organization size, affecting the degree of union influence at an organizational level. Employers do not necessarily act unilaterally to change their policies and practices (Healy and Kraithman, 1991) and consequently 'bottom-up' pressure from employees can be equally as important as 'top-down' commitment from senior management. Dickens, Townley and Winchester (1988: 65) underscore this, arguing that 'review of discriminatory terms and practice is more likely to occur where there is some form of joint regulation than where issues are unilaterally determined by employers'. There is considerable potential for unions to exert pressure on employers to develop policies to combat discrimination and promote equality and diversity. However, unions' ability to influence or develop an equality agenda at an organizational level is not unproblematic for two principal reasons. First, not all employers recognize trade unions for the purposes of collective bargaining. The law on trade union recognition is complex: employers are obliged to recognize unions only if certain conditions are met. Second, unions have traditionally focused their efforts on improving the terms and conditions of employment of their membership according to a unitary conception of members' interests. This unitary perspective has been widely criticized (for example, Cockburn, 1991; Dickens, 1997; Ellis, 1988; Rees, 1992) as being white-male biased and for failing to take account of the diversity of union membership.

Loss of union membership and the consequent decline in both union recognition and collective bargaining coverage combine with white-male domination of union power structures to provide external and internal constraints on unions' ability to pursue effectively an equality agenda. The unions are seeking to tackle both issues by active membership recruitment campaigns and by a variety of methods designed to improve the representation of a diverse profile of members within union power structures. There is also considerable potential for unions to exert pressure on government to develop relevant public policy. Some examples of this are provided below. It is in their economic and political roles that unions can be regarded, along with the state and employers, as one of the three key industrial relations actors.

This chapter seeks to examine and discuss the role of trade unions in promoting an equality and diversity agenda. It describes the economic and political objectives of trade unions and, in order to provide a context against which to set the discussion of unions' role in promoting equality, the chapter also examines contemporary union membership patterns and collective bargaining coverage. The chapter proceeds to discuss the role and nature of trade union activity on equality, focusing on equality bargaining and representative functions. We emphasize the potential for trade unions to promote equality, but also highlight ways in which trade unions have sometimes contributed to reproducing inequalities in employment.

It is worth noting that we recognize that many students of equality and diversity modules on management and business studies courses will not have a grounding in industrial relations. Therefore, this chapter should be viewed as an introduction to the role of unions as a key industrial relations actor. It is the intention that its contents will be comprehensible to those with only a passing acquaintance with trade unions. This may at times result in a simplistic analysis. Interested readers should consult the References at the end of the chapter for a more sophisticated analysis of the issues raised here. The Glossary at the end of the book will help to clarify any unknown terminology.

# Trade union objectives

The TUC was established in 1868 and operates as a co-ordinating body for the trade union movement in Britain. Individual unions can affiliate to the TUC: it currently has more than seventy member unions, including most large unions, and represents almost 80 per cent of total union membership (Cully and Woodland, 1998). Our analysis of trade union objectives focuses on the TUC-affiliated unions and gives examples of what the TUC has done to promote equality. Individual unions are also actively promoting equality at an organizational and political level, although examples from individual unions are not examined here. The TUC represents the trade union movement's principal conduit for influencing governments, thereby influencing social and economic policies of concern to affiliates and, by extension, to trade union members.

The TUC (1998a) suggests that unions' roles in the workplace include giving advice when members have a problem at work, representing members in discussion with employers, making sure that members' legal rights are enforced at work, helping members take cases to employment tribunals, fighting discrimination and helping to promote equality at work. Accomplishing these objectives is a multilayered task, which involves negotiation and advocacy at the workplace, and campaigning and lobbying in the political arena.

During the postwar period until 1979, the government generally consulted the TUC before introducing legislation or policy affecting the interests of the trade union movement (Farnham and Pimlott, 1995). Following the election in 1979 of the Thatcher-led Conservative government, this dialogue was broken until the election of the Labour government in 1997. The eighteen-year period of Conservative government placed the TUC on the margins of British political life, unable to exert direct influence on the social, economic and legal policy of the period. In 1997 the Labour government reopened the dialogue with unions, promising them 'fairness not favours' (Blyton and Turnball, 1998: 127). In the light of the Labour government's commitment to retaining most of the legislation passed under the previous Conservative administration, much of which is inimical to trade union influence and power, the unions are now concentrating their efforts on re-establishing their role as 'social partners' in the political process.

The TUC employs a range of means to pursue its broad political objectives. These include lobbying Members of Parliament and government ministers in order to give voice to affiliates' interests within the political process. For example, the TUC's support of European integration and the Social Chapter have led it to lobby government to legislate on a number of equality issues. A brief examination of the TUC's 1998 'General Council Report' (TUC, 1998b) reveals some detailed examples. During 1998 members of the TUC Women's Committee met various government ministers to argue for action on childcare, reform of equality legislation and maternity/paternity rights. The TUC also constructed a response to the government's consultation on the 'Fairness at Work' White Paper and the EOC's consultation on reforming sex equality legislation. In the latter instance, the TUC argued that any such legislation should cover discrimination on grounds of sexuality. Further, on legal matters, the TUC was closely involved in the government's consultation on the code of practice to combat age discrimination, and on the establishment of the Disability Rights Commission. At a European level the TUC has pressed European Commission officials to begin work taking forward new legislative instruments on race equality.

The TUC also influences the political process in another important way: by nominating trade union representatives to national, regional and local bodies. These include the EOC and the CRE. In addition the TUC publishes and disseminates research papers, discussion documents and policy statements (Farnham and Pimlott, 1995), which reflect the views of and give voice to its affiliates' interests. The TUC uses the media to publicize its views and activities, although media coverage is not always sympathetic to it. Thus, it can be seen that the trade union movement remains influential in public life, contrary to some popular representations of unions as a spent force.

---

1 Trade unions seek to promote equality at work by supporting, representing and negotiating on behalf of employees in the workplace and by influencing politicians and government.

**Key learning points**

# Contemporary union membership patterns and collective bargaining coverage

## Brief background

Union membership figures are an *indicator* of union power and influence at both local (workplace or organizational) and national levels. (There are other indicators, measures and determinants of union power. For a fuller discussion see Kelly, 1998.) The ability of unions to achieve their objectives in relation to employers and government is contingent on their power to influence and apply pressure. In other words, union power rests, in part, on strong union organization and on high union density. It is for this reason that we now provide a brief background against which to set contemporary union membership patterns and against which to set a discussion of the potential for unions to promote equality. It is, however, beyond the scope of this book to provide a detailed history of British trade unionism. What follows is a brief historical excursion, noting the most significant developments along the way.

Early trade unions emerged in the first half of the nineteenth century and were formed largely by skilled male workers. By the end of the century and in the aftermath of the Industrial Revolution, unions of relatively unskilled, general workers had been formed. A concurrent development was the growth of a separate women's trade union movement. This emerged partly because women were often excluded from men's unions and partly because of the growing influence of the feminist movement (Cunnison and Stageman, 1995). There were now well over 1000 separate unions, most of them tiny. Trade union membership grew at a rapid rate before, during and after the First World War, such that by 1920 almost half the British workforce was trade union organized (Farnham and Pimlott, 1995). The 1920s witnessed the emergence of a small number of large, powerful unions which came to dominate the TUC for the next sixty years. This was also a period of merger between separate women's unions and those set up and dominated by men. Between 1920 and the late 1960s union membership waxed and waned in response to the economic and political climate. Women's union membership grew significantly during this period.

During the 1970s union membership increased, particularly among white-collar workers and among women – between 1968 and 1978 women's membership had grown at more than three times the rate of men's (Cunnison and Stageman, 1995). Union membership was becoming more diverse in another important way. During the postwar period, black migration to Britain gathered pace, reaching a peak in the 1960s. From these early days black workers joined trade unions in greater proportions than did white. In the mid-1970s 61 per cent of black male workers were union members compared with 47 per cent of white males (Lee, 1987). However, union membership did not necessarily confer the benefits to black members that might be expected. This is discussed later. Union membership reached a peak in 1979 of 13.3 million members, representing a union density of around 55 per cent (Farnham and Pimlott, 1995).

To summarize, in little more than a century British trade unionism had risen from obscurity to occupy a prominent position in British, social, economic and political life. However, the membership gains of the 1970s were totally nullified by the losses of the 1980s. The question facing trade unions today is whether they can reverse the massive membership decline of the 1980s in order to prevent their returning to obscurity. This question concerns us here in so far as the unions' potential to act as an agent of change and effectively promote equality and diversity at work is contingent upon their strength in numbers.

---

1 Historically, trade unions were set up by and for male workers. Union membership gradually became more diverse as greater numbers of women entered the labour market and joined unions and as a consequence of black migration to Britain.
2 Union density has declined from its peak of 55 per cent in 1979 to around 30 per cent today.

**Key learning points**

---

## Contemporary union membership patterns

During the period 1979–98 trade union membership declined by 40 per cent (Cully and Woodland, 1998). The membership losses were most dramatic in the 1980s and these were broadly equivalent to the gains of the 1970s. Blyton and Turnball (1998) review the various explanations for this decline, but briefly these can be summarized as arising from a complex interaction of features of the political, economic, social, technological and legal context of the period.

According to Labour Force Survey data, total union membership currently stands at 7.94 million, the lowest since 1945 (Cully and Woodland, 1998) and as stated earlier this represents about 30 per cent of all employees. (Union membership figures vary according to the source from which the data are gathered. Labour Force Survey data are based on self-assessment and include non-TUC unions. The TUC data therefore produce a lower overall membership figure.) Yet, paradoxically, according to a 1996 opinion poll, trade unions have never been so popular. Eight out of ten people believed that 'trade unions provide vital protection for many groups of workers'. Nearly seven out of ten believed that 'employees feel more involved in company decisions where employers talk to unions'. Conversely, only a quarter of people agreed that 'trade unions hold back companies in today's competitive world', and only around one in ten people agreed that 'trade unions are no longer relevant in today's world' (Kellner, 1996: 2). These findings, replicated by other surveys (for example, Jowell, Witherspoon and Brook (1990), suggest that there is future potential for trade unions successfully to increase their membership and become more influential in organizational and political life.

One of the most important indicators of union strength is union density. Union density measures the proportion of a workforce that is unionized. The aggregate figure of 30 per cent does not reflect the enormous sectoral and industrial differentials that exist. For example, union density varies considerably from industry to industry ranging from a tiny 7 per cent in hotels to 63 per cent in the utilities (electricity, gas and water supply). There are other industries which have higher than average union density, but generally speaking, union density is higher in the public sector (60.8 per cent) than in the private sector (19.7 per cent) (Cully and Woodland, 1998). Another interesting comparison can be made between the two main sectors of the economy – production and services. Historically, unions have been stronger in membership terms in the production sector, but for the first time, in 1997, union density was higher in services (31.9 per cent) than in production (30.9 per cent) (Labour Research, 1998). As a consequence the characteristics of trade union members have altered over time. This is a phenomenon discussed below.

Union density also varies according to workplace size, standing at just 16 per cent in workplaces with fewer than twenty-five employees (Cully and Woodland, 1998) compared with a higher than average 48 per cent in workplaces with 500 or more employees (Cully et al., 1999). Union density climbs above the average 30 per cent in workplaces with more than a hundred employees (Cully et al., 1999). In other words the larger the workplace, the higher is union density. However, workplace size intersects with sector in that only 9 per cent of employees in small (less than twenty-five employees) private sector workplaces are union members compared with 52 per cent in small public sector workplaces (Cully and Woodland, 1998). It is important to note that despite the increase in numbers of small firms, large firms, of more than 500 workers, employ around a third of all workers. Very small firms employ only a small percentage of the workforce. Thus, although sectoral changes are of deep concern to trade unions (that is the shift from production to services), unions still retain a reasonably strong base.

Within industries there are also significant occupational variations in union density. For example, only 9 per cent of sales staff are union members, compared with 50 per cent of professionals (Labour Research, 1998). Other occupations with higher than average union density are associate professional/technical workers, craft and related workers, and plant and machine operatives (Labour Research, 1998). In all occupations full-time employees are more highly unionized than those who work part time – 34 per cent compared with 20 per cent of part-timers. Thus, we can see how aggregate union membership or density data conceal significant variations across three dimensions – sector, workplace size and occupation. Union members are also differentiated by a range of individual characteristics.

Table 7.1 shows differences in union density by various characteristics and how the characteristics of the 'typical' or 'paradigmatic' (Howell, 1996)

**Table 7.1** Union density by various characteristics (percentage)

|  | *1989* | *1997* |
|---|---|---|
| Male employees | 44 | 32 |
| Female employees | 33 | 28 |
| Full-time employees | 44 | 34 |
| Part-time employees | 22 | 20 |
| Manual workers | 44 | 30 |
| Non-manual workers | 35 | 30 |
| Production industry | 45 | 31 |
| Service industry | 38 | 31 |

*Source:* Cully and Woodland (1998).

trade unionist have changed over time. In 1989, the 'typical' trade unionist was a male, full-time, manual worker in the production sector. By 1997 the profile was less straightforward. Today, the 'typical' trade unionist is just as likely to be female as male, non-manual as manual, more likely to work in services than production and, the one constant, to work full time. These characteristics have important implications for trade union recruitment strategies. In particular, the unions' failure to recruit part-time employees concerns trade union leaders in so far as part-time working is an increasing phenomenon in the contemporary labour market.

One of the interesting trends in union membership in recent years has been the slower rate of decline in density among women when compared with men. This has resulted in the near closure of the historical union membership gender gap. Almost 32 per cent of male employees are union members, compared with 28.4 per cent of female (Labour Research, 1998). This is interesting because it is a reversal of the traditional trend for men to have a far greater propensity to be union members than women. For example, the gender gap was far wider – in 1989 almost 44 per cent of male employees were union members compared with just under 33 per cent of female (Labour Research, 1998). This is a phenomenon related to economic restructuring and the concomitant decline in male employment dating back to the late 1960s. Although there has been a considerable growth in women's employment, most of this has been in part-time work and in the service sector where unions traditionally have been weak. If we compare male employees with full-time female employees, women are now slightly more likely than men to be union members (34 per cent compared with 33 per cent) (Labour Research, 1998).

Rates of union membership also vary according to a number of other individual characteristics. Ethnic origin is one of these. Not all unions can produce reliable breakdowns of membership by ethnicity, because the extent of ethnic monitoring varies (EOR, 1995). Therefore Labour Force Survey data are used here. The Labour Force Survey uses two broad categories of ethnic origin: white and non-white. In 1997 30 per cent of white employees were trade union members, compared with 28 per cent of non-white. The category 'non-white' is further subdivided into black, Indian, Pakistani/Bangladeshi and 'other'. Of these the category 'black' stands out as having higher union density (36 per cent) than the category 'white'. In other words black employees are more likely to be trade union members than are white. The TUC (1998c) states that black women are more likely to be trade union members than are female employees in general. This is partly because black women are more likely than white to be in full-time employment and there is a strong association between full-time employment and trade union membership, as shown earlier.

Of particular concern to the trade union movement is the age profile of membership. Employees aged forty to forty-nine are most likely to be union members (39 per cent), whilst among younger workers aged twenty to twenty-nine only 21 per cent are members. Cully and Woodland (1998) claim that there is now evidence to suggest that the greater likelihood of older employees belonging to a trade union reflects different attitudes to trade unions across age-based cohorts rather than changing attitudes to trade unions over the life course. This means that unions will need to strive to demonstrate their relevance to younger people, who may not share the views of their parents' generation. However, the opinion poll referred to earlier would appear to contradict this claim. What is clear is that unions need to recruit more women, young people and part-time workers if they are to reverse the trend of membership decline (Waddington and Whitston, 1997) and the accompanying loss of influence. This is discussed below in so far as the need to attract diverse groups of employees into membership is reflected in unions' activities around equality initiatives.

What the foregoing analysis of contemporary union membership trends reveals is the uneven pattern of union coverage of sectors and industries, and by certain characteristics. Generally speaking, unions are most able to advance an equality and diversity agenda in those areas where they have the strongest presence.

# Key learning points

1 Union density varies according to several characteristics. These include sector, workplace size, occupation, hours of work. Generally, union density is higher in the public than private sector.

2 Certain characteristics of individual employees are also important determinants of trade union membership, especially gender, ethnicity and age. Thus, collective bargaining coverage is not uniform.

3 The characteristics of the 'typical' trade union member are not static and have changed in line with demographic changes in the labour market and structural and economic changes.

## Collective bargaining coverage

Union recognition is a prerequisite for collective bargaining. Union recognition arrangements formalize the procedures and processes of collective bargaining, at a national, industry, organizational or workplace level. Union recognition is strongly associated with workplace size. Seventy-eight per cent of workplaces with 500 or more employees recognize trade unions, compared with 45 per cent of all workplaces with twenty-five or more employees. To put it another way, the majority (53 per cent) of UK workplaces (with twenty-five or more employees) have union members and over 80 per cent of these recognize one or more trade unions for collective bargaining purposes (Cully et al., 1999). Our principal interest in this chapter lies in unions' ability to have a role in promoting equality in employment. This role is likely to have the strongest potential where unions are recognized for the purposes of collective bargaining. Therefore, the above analysis would suggest that unions have the opportunity to assume this role in 45 per cent of all workplaces, with the exception of the very small. It is also important to note that 8.1 million employees are covered by collective agreements, representing 36 per cent of all employees (Cully and Woodland, 1998). This is a significant proportion of the workforce and is greater than the proportion of the workforce that is unionized. This is because non-union members who work in union-recognized workplaces often benefit from the provisions of collective agreements.

# Equality bargaining

'Equal opportunities, equal treatment and the fight against unfair discrimination are the foundation of trade union activity' (MSF, 1996: B1). This is the claim of one trade union in its *Bargaining Handbook*. In practice trade unions have a 'mixed record' (Dickens, Townley and Winchester, 1988: 65) in challenging discrimination against disadvantaged groups. For example, historically some unions have sought to exclude women from certain trades, whilst others have accepted women but in segregated, low-skill, low-paid jobs (Cockburn, 1991; Walby, 1997). The TUC had supported the principle of equal pay for women since 1888, but had done little to effect it until the 1970s (Walby, 1997). Similarly, other writers give instances of where unions colluded with management in encouraging racist practices, which resulted in Asian and Caribbean workers being confined to low-paid, low-skill jobs (Lee, 1987; Phizacklea and Miles, 1987). Other groups, including disabled and lesbian and gay members, have remained invisible within and to the trade unions until recently (Colgan, 1999; Labour Research, 1996a). Most unions can only produce reliable breakdowns of the composition of union membership by gender, with monitoring by race/ethnicity, disability and sexual orientation being the exception rather than the norm. It is arguable that these gaps in the knowledge of the characteristics of union members impact negatively on a union's ability to represent a diverse constituency.

We turn now to the substance of, and processes involved in, contemporary trade union activity around equality. Bercusson and Dickens (1996) alert us to the fact that some equality (and diversity) issues may be handled within the collective bargaining machinery, whilst others may be subject to unilateral employer action. The scope of the equality bargaining agenda will vary from one organization to another and may be determined by a number of factors. These include the history and traditions of collective bargaining in the industry or organization, management objectives in industrial relations and how these relate to business strategy, and the balance of bargaining power between employers and unions. Therefore collective bargaining is a dynamic process, which is why we discuss it largely in terms of its potential to promote equality. It should be noted that there could also exist other avenues for trade unions to promote equality at an organizational level, in particular joint consultation with management. However, consultation does not result in mutually binding agreements, suggesting that collective bargaining is the most powerful instrument available to trade unions. Also, equality bargaining objectives vary from one union to another, depending upon the composition and characteristics of union membership, the type of employers they bargain with (Kumar, 1993), and those employers' own objectives and strategies in relation to equality.

Traditionally unions have assumed that people working within the same industry, organization or occupation shared the same interests and therefore the same objectives in relation to their employers and their employment. This assumption has led to a unitary conception of union bargaining objectives. Unity of interest among the membership has traditionally been regarded by unions as essential to the building of a solidarity movement, which could effectively challenge and influence management decision-making. Unions have feared that highlighting plurality of interests might undermine solidarity and thereby union power. However, industries, organizations and occupations are composed of diverse groups of employees, whose interests may at times converge, but at others diverge. For example, in a survey of almost 3000 new union members (IRS, 1994) women were twice as likely as men to support union negotiation of career breaks and three times as likely to support union backing for job sharing. This is echoed by another survey (Kerr, 1992), which found female union members accorded a higher priority to rights for part-timers and equality for women than did men. Thus, unions represent sites in which a plurality of interests exists. The challenge to unions is to represent effectively the interests of diverse social groups.

# Activity

## Activity 7.1: Ford halted by 'racism' strike

About 1300 workers at Ford's Dagenham factory in Essex staged a strike yesterday in protest at alleged systematic racism inside the US car group's biggest UK plant.

The stoppage, given immediate but covert backing by union leaders, halted production of Fiestas and Mazda 121s and was expected to be joined by the night shift.

Black, white and Asian employees joined the unofficial strike in the latest flare-up at the plant where 45 per cent of the workforce is non-white. Workers were said to be wearing stickers on their overalls demanding the sacking of an allegedly racist manager, and 'justice and respect'.

Ford said 800 people had taken part, and maintained last night it was unaware of the reason for the action, insisting it practised a policy of 'zero tolerance' towards racism. But insiders said: 'There's a hell of a lot of racist attitudes and actions within Dagenham. It's like a tinder box and takes little to light the fuse.'

Yesterday's action is the latest incident to hit the plant where, for the past six months, union leaders have failed to persuade local managers to hold a joint inquiry into the implications for Dagenham of the report of the Stephen Lawrence inquiry into institutional racism.

Shop stewards who led the walk-out in the paint, trim and assembly areas of the plant said they had lost confidence in local managers to resolve what they called the endemic problem of racism.

Angry union officials accused the local managers of at best turning a blind eye to repeated incidences of racist abuse and bullying, and at worst of complicity.

Sir Ken Jackson, leader of the AEEU engineering union, said: 'Race relations have improved at Ford over recent years but there are still clear examples of outrageous abuse which Ford has signally failed to deal with.'

As shop stewards demanded an urgent inquiry by the Commission for Racial Equality, Bill Morris, general secretary of the Transport and General Workers' Union, reiterated his call for talks with Jac Nasser, Ford president.

In what Mr Morris described as the worst case of racist intimidation his union had experienced, Sukhjit Parma, an engine plant worker, suffered a four-year campaign of racist abuse, culminating in threats to his life.

Two weeks ago at an east London tribunal Ford admitted racial discrimination, harassment and victimization towards Mr Parma.

'Unless people outside the plant get a grip on the situation and put structures in place that the staff have confidence in, there'll be more walk outs', union sources said.

The last straw, one insider said, came last week when an AEEU shop steward, Jaswir Tega, who was working near the production line, was pushed by a white foreman dangerously close to the conveyor belt, it was alleged.

Insiders said local managers had refused to heed demands for the foreman to be suspended and a full inquiry to be held. Instead, he was kept away from the shop floor and returns today.

*Source*: *Guardian*, 6 October 1999.

## Questions

1 Summarize the events that led to the strike by Ford workers.
2 There appears to be a gap between the management policy of 'zero tolerance' towards racism and perceptions on the shop floor. Why might this be? (Chapters 4 and 5 will help you to answer this question.)
3 In what ways do you think the union presence at Ford makes a difference to the tackling of racism?

## Conceptualizing equality bargaining

Developing Colling and Dickens' (1998: 390) definition of equality bargaining beyond a narrow gender focus, we define equality bargaining as 'the collective negotiation of provisions that are of particular interest or benefit to disadvantaged groups and/or are likely to facilitate equality at work'. Following Bercusson and Dickens (1996) we now attempt to analytically distinguish two main approaches to equality bargaining. The first consists of the 'equality dimension' to traditional union bargaining objectives and agendas. As a specific instance of this we consider low pay. Chapter 2 has shown that the labour market differentiates between different social groups and that this produces unequal outcomes. It is the case that much of the disadvantage experienced by some employees relates to basic terms and conditions of employment such as pay, working hours, employment security, redundancy. Low pay among, for example, women is not necessarily a result of direct discrimination by employers (although it can be). Rather, low pay is a feature of certain occupations and industries in which women are concentrated. Therefore, it may appear that the general problem of low pay has no direct relevance to equality. Indeed, tackling low pay is a traditional or 'mainstream' union bargaining objective – that is the eradication of low pay would be expected to be of interest and benefit to the entire workforce. Yet a positive bargaining outcome or improvement in pay levels may be of disproportionate benefit to women in situations where they are over-represented in low paid work. Therefore, tackling low pay promotes gender equality and this may be an intended or unintended consequence of collective bargaining. This can be conceptualized as the 'equality dimension' to traditional collective bargaining. A formal equal opportunities policy need not underpin equality bargaining of this nature, in the sense that advancements towards gender equality, for example, may be achieved without explicitly or self-consciously tackling women's equality issues. However, collective agreements, which do not explicitly promote equality, may themselves be indirectly discriminatory and positive outcomes for disadvantaged groups are by no means guaranteed where the equality dimension remains invisible and unarticulated.

A second conceptualization of equality bargaining is one, which is underpinned by an employer-led equal opportunities policy and/or a union–management negotiated equality agreement. Policies and agreements on equal opportunities have an explicit intention to promote equality and to address discriminatory practice. In this case it would be expected that unions would seek to influence the structures, processes and outcomes of organizational policy. Bercusson and Dickens propose a useful conceptualization of 'good' collective agreements. They make a distinction between agreements which 'of themselves appear good' and those which are 'good when considered in context', (Bercusson and Dickens, 1996: 28). The first category is agreements, which contain a strong and explicit declaration to promote equality and which attempt to address discriminatory practice. We would suggest that to be classified 'good', such agreements should have a broad equality agenda and include action around gender, race, age, disability and sexual orientation.

The second category is agreements which improve on the traditional or historical provision of the particular organization, sector or industry; those which can be deemed 'good' in relation to legal regulation or those which are good in the particular bargaining context.

In this chapter, we deal predominantly with equality bargaining which is underpinned by an equal opportunities policy or equality agreement and those agreements which 'of themselves appear good'. This is in line with our intention to focus on the potential for unions to promote equality. It is recognized, however, that the realization of that potential will be contingent on a complex interaction of a number of macroeconomic and microeconomic, political, social and legal factors.

---

| | |
|---|---|
| 1 There are two main approaches to equality bargaining: that which indirectly tackles inequalities and that which has an explicit intention to promote equality. | **Key learning point** |

---

## The scope of equality bargaining

Bercusson and Dickens identify five key categories for consideration in analysing collective agreements in respect of women's disadvantage in employment. These are pay discrimination/pay equity, sex segregation, job access/security, family–work interface, organizational cultures/ structures (Bercusson and Dickens, 1996: 32). These mirror Ellis's (1988) framework for examining trade union attempts to tackle occupational sex segregation, which we also refer to. Since our analysis extends beyond gender equality, we adapt these categories to analyse equality bargaining from the perspectives of women, minority ethnic groups, older people, disabled people and lesbians and gay men. Using these key categories we now discuss in more detail the substantive content of collective agreements on equality and instances of relevant union activity.

### Pay/benefits discrimination and pay equity

Chapter 2 noted that on average, women earn less than men, with the gender pay gap currently at around 20 per cent. Similarly, minority ethnic employees have lower average earnings than do white employees. Disabled workers and older workers are overrepresented in low-skill, low-status jobs, which are also likely to be low paid. The gender pay gap is particularly marked between the ages of forty-five and fifty-five. Lesbians and gay men also suffer remunerative losses as a result of discriminatory practices. Therefore, the five social groups we focus on potentially have something to gain from union efforts to promote pay equity. There is evidence to suggest that unions have had some success in this respect.

Working in a trade union organized environment appears to confer a pay advantage on employees, known as the union 'mark-up'. After controlling for a number of possible variables (including level of qualification, marital status, employment sector, occupation, class, age and number of children), Main (1996) finds that trade union membership leaves the average male manual wage just over 7 per cent higher than in the absence of union membership. The average female full-time worker's pay is 5.5 per cent higher and the average female part-time worker's pay is nearly 10 per cent higher. This is echoed by the 1998 Workplace Employee Relations Survey, which finds that workplaces where unions were recognized were much less likely to have a quarter or more of the workforce earning below £3.50 per hour (Cully et al., 1999). It would appear, then, that female part-timers gain the most, in pay terms, from working in unionized environments. Paradoxically, this group has lower than average rates of union membership.

Unions have also had some success in tackling the inequitable access to employee benefits experienced by many lesbians and gay men. For example, British Telecom succumbed to union pressure to change its pension scheme so that same-sex partners can benefit. In the same organization and in the civil service union negotiations ensured that all leave and relocation entitlements could be equally accessed by all staff (Labour Research, 1994). This has particular implications for lesbians and gay men, who may be denied bereavement, dependency or carer's leave by some employers. Union pressure does not always result in positive outcomes: despite efforts by rail unions, only London Underground extends the perk of reduced rate travel to same-sex partners (Labour Research, 1994).

To conclude the discussion on unions' role in achieving pay equity, there is evidence which shows that employees in unionized organizations are more likely to be covered by formal job evaluation schemes (Millward, 1995), and that these are likely to reduce bias in grading for pay purposes. Further, employment tribunal claims for equal pay for work of equal value made by individual women are more likely to emanate from unionized workplaces (Colling and Dickens, 1998). A specific example of this is provided by a case study of equal pay in the electricity supply industry (Gilbert and Secker, 1995). The conclusion drawn was that union negotiations, coupled with union-supported tribunal claims by individual women was set to improve the pay of thousands of women in the industry. This underscores the importance of union support in individual cases of discrimination.

## Job segregation

Most of the published work on job segregation concerns women. The terms commonly used are 'occupational sex segregation' or 'gender segregation'. Evidence of job segregation is examined in Chapter 2, whilst Chapter 3 seeks to explain the phenomenon. These chapters also discuss labour market segmentation by race, age and disability. It can be argued that job segregation is a product of discrimination and disadvantage in the labour market, and that in order to promote equality, unions need to concentrate effort on breaking down job segregation. Unions seek to do this by placing a number of issues on the bargaining agenda. First, it is essential to negotiate access to training that will enable under-represented groups either to climb the hierarchical ladder to more senior positions or to enter occupations where they are traditionally not well represented. Second, unions need to audit and monitor recruitment, selection and promotion policies, processes, practices and outcomes to ensure that there are no barriers created either by the bureaucracy surrounding the exercise or by managers' actions. These are not new union objectives. Ellis (1988) describes a range of individual union initiatives that have the objective of breaking down job segregation, showing the potential for unions to play a role.

## Job access/job security

This category contains consideration of redundancy and termination policy and practice, security of hours and contractual status. The union objective is to uncover and challenge discriminatory practice. Chapter 2 has shown women, ethnic minorities, disabled people and older people are overrepresented in insecure, non-standard forms of employment. Although it is true that some people, women for example, choose to work part time, for many people, including women, insecure work is involuntary (Lim, 1996). This suggests that access to high-quality jobs is an important bargaining issue for these groups of employees. Chapter 2 has also shown that lesbians and gay men experience discrimination in recruitment and promotion, denying them access to high-quality jobs.

Job access and job security issues overlap with job segregation, in that training and recruitment and selection are particularly important areas for unions to negotiate around in order to tackle disadvantage. However, only about a fifth of temporary workers and part-time workers are trade union members (Cully and Woodland, 1998). This may attenuate unions' ability and commitment to bargaining in these workers' interests. Nevertheless, TUC General Secretary, John Monks, warned in 1996 that unions would have to recruit more part-timers in order to survive (Labour Research, 1996a). Since there is thought to be a circular relationship between unions' bargaining objectives and employees' propensity to become members, bargaining for non-discriminatory job access and for job security should, in principle at least, take a prominent position on the bargaining agenda.

## Family–work interface

This category includes bargaining around issues such as maternity and paternity leave, childcare, working time, career breaks and employee benefits. The potential here is for unions to develop a progressive bargaining agenda. This would seek to ensure that maternity and paternity leave arrangements allow and encourage both mothers *and* fathers to take an active parental role, rather than following the traditional assumption that the birth and nurture of children is solely women's business. Similarly, another aim could be to ensure access to childcare facilities or subsidies is available to both mothers and fathers. Exemplifying union efforts in this area are proactive campaigns for childcare support mounted by the Manufacturing, Science, Finance (MSF) union and by the British Telecom unions (EOR, 1992). Working-time and career-breaks arrangements, whilst falling within the so-called 'family-friendly' policies, often give rise to disadvantage in pay, conditions or future prospects. Union pressure can help to challenge this situation. Unions further aim to ensure these and other employee benefits are made available on an equal basis to lesbian and gay couples. This is reflected in the model union 'equal opportunities agreement' in Activity 7.2.

In other words union bargaining around the family–work interface seeks to ensure that the needs of employees are fully accommodated. This is important at a time when 'business case' arguments are increasingly driving employer approaches to equality and diversity policy. This is discussed further in Chapter 8.

## Organizational cultures/structures

The key issues in this category are workplace harassment and career paths. Cockburn (1991) views harassment as an expression of power. She goes on to argue that equality policy can expose such power: its use and abuse. Cockburn further suggests that the real test of equality policy is whether or not cases of complaint are encouraged and whether action is taken against offenders. Almost three-quarters of employers have a policy on sexual harassment (IRS, 1996a). Policy action on other forms of harassment, for example racial, lesbian and gay may be lagging behind. Although union pressure does not appear to have been a factor in the introduction of sexual harassment policies (IRS, 1996b), there is nevertheless potential for unions to mount pressure on employers to establish clear policy guidelines on this and other forms of workplace harassment. Indeed, the TUC produces guidance on harassment issues for union negotiators and its website includes a page 'Harassment update', with latest employment tribunal cases and examples of union initiatives. Many large unions have issued guidelines on tackling racial harassment in the workplace. These guidelines are issued to union representatives (EOR, 1995) and include model procedures for monitoring harassment.

Harassment can also be regarded as an expression of organizational culture (there is more discussion of this in Chapter 4). The point to make here is that equality awareness training may help to create a culture that celebrates diversity rather than punishes it. Unions, potentially, can act to push for such training. The issue of organizational structures links, and overlaps, with the fourth category, the 'family–work interface'. The unions' role is to identify possible structural barriers to promotion, transfer and training, which indirectly give rise to discrimination.

**Key learning point**

1 The strength and potential of employer–union equality agreements can be evaluated by analysing their content in five key categories: pay discrimination/pay equity, sex segregation, job access/security, family–work interface, organizational cultures/structures.

## Activity

### Activity 7.2: Model equal opportunities agreement

A management–union agreed statement, as a prelude to an equality agreement, might look something like this:

The parties to this agreement are committed to the development of positive policies to promote equal opportunities in employment regardless of employees' sex, marital status, creed, colour, race, ethnic origin, sexuality, disability or age. This principle will apply in respect of all conditions of work including pay, hours of work, holiday entitlement, overtime, shift work, work allocation, guaranteed earnings, sick pay, pension recruitment, training, promotion, redundancy and other benefits.

The agreement aims to ensure that no job applicant or employee is placed at a disadvantage by requirements or conditions which would have disproportionately adverse effects on his or her particular group and cannot be shown to be necessary for the satisfactory completion of the job. Additionally, entry into the Company and progression within it will be determined solely by the application of objective criteria, personal performance and merit.

To ensure the Equal Opportunities Agreement is effective the overall responsibility for its implementation will be allocated to a senior member of staff, and it will be made known to all job applicants and employees. Contractors working on Company premises will also be expected to comply with the Equal Opportunities Agreement.

*Source*: MSF (1996: B16).

*Questions*

1 Drawing on the previous discussion of what constitutes a 'good' equality agreement, evaluate the strengths and weaknesses of the above example.
2 To what extent does this represent an example of a collective agreement, which 'of itself appears good'?
3 What factors might impair a union's ability to negotiate such an agreement?

# Handling discrimination cases

In addition to negotiating collective terms and conditions with employers, trade unions also perform another function at a workplace level: that of representing individuals who have experienced discrimination. There is evidence that union members highly value union support when they encounter problems at work. In two major surveys (IRS, 1994; Kerr, 1992) more than 70 per cent of union members said they had joined principally in order that the union could support them if they needed advice on grievance and disciplinary matters. The TUC and individual unions issue a range of advice to union representatives on handling discrimination cases (EOR, 1995). This is done via publications and education programmes. However, discrimination is a sensitive issue and it is thought that some members, black people for example, may lack confidence in their unions to handle effectively a discrimination case (TUC, 1991). This may lead some members to seek advice elsewhere, for example the CRE, EOC, Citizens Advice Bureau or law centres. To overcome these barriers to representing effectively a diverse membership, the TUC (1991: 44) recommends that unions negotiate workplace procedures for dealing with cases of discrimination, that union representatives are trained in how to handle discrimination cases and that the assistance available is publicized. The degree to which unions can expect to meet with success in equality bargaining and in handling discrimination cases, when internally unions' decision-making structures remain unrepresentative of the diversity of membership, is something which has increasingly come under scrutiny. It is to this topic that we now turn.

# Internal equality

As democratic membership organizations, trade unions are governed by their memberships by means of formal, local and national representative structures. Trade unions also employ a cadre of paid officials to carry out union business at both local and national levels. The governing bodies and decision-making structures of most unions are dominated by white men (Cockburn, 1991; Dickens, 1997). The unrepresentative nature of union leadership is thought to constrain unions' abilities to promote equality in employment (Cockburn, 1991; Colling and Dickens, 1989; Kirton, 1999; Trebilcock, 1991).

Where a numerically dominant membership group exists, their interests are likely to prevail and be translated into a bargaining agenda. This is particularly so, when the dominant group also monopolizes union positions of power. Organizational power holders are able to influence policy and practice. Conversely, those with little power also exert little influence. Discussing unions' failure to adequately address women's equality issues, Colling and Dickens (1989: 32) suggest that the 'absence of women *at* the table has to be part of the explanation for the absence of women *on* the table'. The irony here is that unions need to be seen to meet the needs of diverse groups of employees in order to boost membership recruitment. The TUC (1997) goes so far as to suggest that positive and successful union actions in the areas of discrimination and equality will be 'major selling points' in the drive to recruit diverse members. In addition, if collective bargaining is to be an effective tool for addressing the concerns of a diverse membership, those groups arguably need to be fully integrated and represented in unions' decision-making structures (Kumar, 1993). This is not the case at the present time: unions' decision-making structures remain dominated by white men. Women and Caribbean men are particularly poorly represented among elected union post holders, when compared with white and South Asian men (Modood et al., 1997).

A body of evidence exists which demonstrates that female trade unionists are especially well placed to understand the particular problems faced by women workers and to identify gendered dimensions to traditional bargaining issues (for example, Cockburn, 1991, Cunnison and Stageman, 1995; Heery and Kelly, 1988; Kirton and Healy, 1999; Watson, 1988). This principle of 'like understanding like' can also be applied to other groups of union members. For example, it can be argued that black trade unionists are well placed to understand the concerns and experiences of black workers (TUC, 1991).

For some years, unions have been striving to reflect membership diversity in the ranks of their national and local leaders and negotiators. Broadly following Trebilcock's (1991) categorization of union efforts to achieve equality, we now examine the nature of those efforts.

## Striving for equality

The first step towards equality within trade unions has often been the adoption of a policy statement. This approach has been strongly encouraged by the TUC (Trebilcock, 1991). However, policy statements, in themselves, do nothing more than declare a *commitment* to equality. Structural and organizational changes are often necessary to *deliver* equality. Unions have not adopted such structural and organizational changes in a uniform way, nor have the unions necessarily accorded equal priority to tackling the equality of diverse groups. For example, women's equality has been pursued more vigorously by unions than equality for other under-represented groups such as disabled and lesbian and gay members. There is a compelling economic imperative encouraging unions to address women's equality, since women are a growing proportion of the labour force and thus a growing proportion of potential new union members (Kirton and Healy, 1999). Nevertheless, most large TUC unions have sought to dismantle the barriers to fully representative leadership. There are seven categories of reform undertaken to a greater or lesser extent by individual trade unions:

- equality conferences
- equality committees
- equality officers
- reserved seats on governing bodies
- electoral reform
- new approaches to conducting union business
- trade union education.

These categories are now considered in greater detail.

### Equality conferences

Some unions hold annual equality conferences with a broad agenda containing a range of equality issues. Others hold conferences dedicated to particular groups including women, disabled members, lesbian and gay members, and black and minority ethnic members. Equality conferences serve the twin purposes of raising awareness and exploring equality issues and of providing a forum in which delegates from under-represented groups can gain experience of trade union processes and procedures. In some cases, equality conferences are empowered to pass motions or resolutions that influence the central governing body of the union.

## Equality committees

Similarly, equality committees provide regular forums, at a regional and/or national level, in which equality issues are discussed. Such committees usually have access to financial resources, which can be utilized for campaigning, educational and other activities. They also represent another vehicle for under-represented groups to gain experience of trade union affairs. There is a danger, however, of equality issues being confined to a separate, powerless sphere. This can be avoided if there is a direct relationship between equality committees and unions' 'mainstream' decision-making structures (Healy and Kirton, 1999), using the vehicle, for example, of reserved seats, discussed below. In some instances, equality committees have been pivotal in achieving some of the internal reforms discussed here (Cunnison and Stageman, 1995).

## Equality officers

Equality officers are usually members of the union's paid staff. They provide administrative support and expertise to the committees and generally assist in raising the profile of equality issues within the union.

## Reserved seats

A minority of UK trade unions has taken the more radical step of introducing reserved seats on governing bodies (usually for women and/or ethnic minorities). Reserved seats are radical (Jewson and Mason, 1992), in that their aim is to intervene in the democratic process to shape outcomes: that is to recast the composition of union government. In Jewson and Mason's terms, reserved seats aim to redistribute rewards: they aim to guarantee certain groups a role in union decision-making. (Chapter 5 explains and discusses in greater depth Jewson and Mason's conception of liberal and radical approaches to equality.) Reserved seats are controversial because they challenge liberal conceptions of fairness and justice, which place the emphasis on ensuring that 'the rules of the competition are not discriminatory' (Jewson and Mason, 1992: 221) rather than reshaping outcomes. For this reason, reserved seats are not always popular with trade unionists. Also, there is the risk that those who occupy reserved seats will be treated as token figures (Trebilcock, 1991) and that they may be accorded legitimacy in speaking of equality issues only (Cockburn, 1995). Thus, reserved seats are not always popular with those they are designed to benefit.

## Electoral reform

Proportionality is a complex electoral reform strategy adopted by some unions in order to increase women leaders, such that women are represented in union governing bodies in the same proportion as in the membership. This innovation is in recognition of women's increasing share of union membership and continued under-representation in union decision-making. The largest UK union, UNISON, has adopted the parallel strategy of 'fair representation' which aims to ensure a broad balance of members in union leadership, including minority ethnic, disabled and lesbian and gay members (Terry, 1996). Achieving fair representation is a rather more imprecise, complex and ongoing process (Colgan, 1999). Within UNISON, self-organization is a key ingredient to achieving the objectives of both strategies. 'Self-organization' is the term used to describe forums in which under-represented groups (such as women, disabled, lesbian and gay and minority ethnic members) meet to share concerns and establish their own priorities. Such forums are less formal and structured than unions' equality committees. In particular, participation is open to any member who self-identifies with the group rather than to members elected to represent a particular constituency. Such concerns and priorities are then fed into mainstream union governing bodies. Self-organization is a strategy adopted by a minority of other unions, but it is most highly developed in UNISON. Support for self-organization among under-represented groups is widespread (Colgan, 1999; Modood et al., 1997).

## New approaches to conducting union business

Trade unions have made changes in the ways in which they have traditionally conducted their business, in order to facilitate participation by diverse groups. These especially relate to removing the barriers to women's participation (Ellis, 1988; Rees, 1990) and include addressing childcare needs, arranging transport to and from meetings, and adjusting the timing and location of union meetings. Efforts have been made by many unions to facilitate the participation of disabled members including disabled access at meetings and conferences, communication aids for members with hearing impairments and documents in accessible formats, braille for example (Labour Research, 1996b).

## Trade union education

Trade union education contributes to the development of union representatives, negotiators and leaders. The TUC and many individual unions provide courses aimed both directly and indirectly at improving participation in union affairs by diverse groups. For example, women-only training courses are offered by a number of unions. Many unions also provide and encourage training on equality issues to any member or representative who wants it. The former type of training seeks to develop leaders from under-represented groups, whilst the latter seeks to raise awareness within the union more generally of equality issues (Cunnison and Stageman, 1995).

---

1 Union decision-making structures are mostly under-representative of the five social groups we are discussing.
2 Unions have initiated various structural reforms in order to promote internal equality. These include introducing equality conferences, equality committees, equality officers, reserved seats on governing bodies, electoral reform, new approaches to conducting union business and trade union education.

**Key learning points**

---

## Activity 7.3: The involvement of black members

This activity uses a survey of ten trade unions undertaken on behalf of the TUC to examine the involvement of black workers in trade unions. The quotations below were made by trade union (paid and lay) officials, who were interviewed as part of the study.

> As far as we are concerned a member is a member. Wherever they come from we want to treat them all the same. We would not want to make the identification otherwise it appears there is a problem. We create a problem.

> I see all kinds of problems about that (i.e., not monitoring). We don't know where our black members are. We are not able to target. We are not able to feed in appropriate support and help. It's not good news. We can't also tell . . . whether you are making progress. You can't tell whether you are going forwards or backwards if you don't know your starting point.

The above statements were made by white officials, the following was made by a black representative:

> In 1985 (the union) agreed to monitor black membership to keep black activists quiet at the time. However, six years later, not only have they done no monitoring, but they have actually not done anything about getting blacks involved – thus the monitoring will always remain as 'pretence', i.e. an attempt to be seen to be doing something.

*Source*: TUC (1991).

*Questions*

1 Discuss the contrasting views reflected in the first statement when compared with the other two statements.
2 Consider the possible advantages and disadvantages of monitoring the diversity of union membership.
3 Consider the implications, for effective representation of members' interests, of the statement 'a member is a member. Wherever they come from we want to treat them all the same'.
4 Return to this activity when you have read the whole book. Look again at the first statement and replace 'a member is a member' with 'an employee is an employee' and discuss the implications of this viewpoint for the promotion of equality and diversity in employment.

# Conclusion

From the discussion of categories within collective agreements, it can be seen that equality bargaining is broad based. It seeks to both enforce and build upon employees' legal rights. The potential of collective bargaining to promote equality is derived from its nature as a collective instrument

(Dickens, Townley and Winchester, 1988), which should widen the focus from individual cases of discrimination to achieving equality for the entire workforce. In practice, collective bargaining achieves a balance between a number of competing, even conflicting, objectives (Kumar, 1993). Equality and diversity issues can easily slip off the bargaining agenda in a hostile economic or organizational climate and if union negotiators have little or no practical interest in them. Ellis described the transformation of union agendas to include equality bargaining as a 'minor revolution' (Ellis, 1988: 156). However, as we can see from Chapter 2, this 'revolution' in intent has had only limited impact on reality. As Ellis commented, the will on the trade union side is strong but the climate is unfavourable. These remarks have a particular poignancy more than a decade later, not least because of the further erosion of union influence and power, and the economic uncertainty now surrounding much labour market activity.

To realize their potential to act as agents of change and promote equality successfully, unions will need to be similarly successful in achieving membership growth. The TUC (1997) confidently predicts that this is possible. The recruitment of women members is thought to be critical, since forecasts of job growth are in the professional and associate professional occupations in which female unionization is highest. Therefore, some of this growth should translate into membership gains for the unions. However, the TUC's optimism must be balanced against the likelihood that much of this growth will occur in sectors with very low rates of unionization, such as hotels and catering. New legal arrangements for union recognition should also assist unions in their aim of reversing membership decline.

We have also shown that unions' decision-making structures are mostly unrepresentative of membership diversity. This is thought to constrain the effectiveness of collective bargaining as an instrument to promote equality. Unions are bureaucratic organizations and as such the pace of change is slow. The unions' strategies and practices described in this chapter have met with varying degrees of success in terms of creating a more representative leadership, and the central governing bodies of most trade unions remain unrepresentative of membership diversity: therefore, the equality project within trade unions is still not completed. Nevertheless, such strategies and practices provide an opportunity to inject an equality perspective into union decision-making and create the conditions whereby the 'democracy deficit' (Cockburn, 1995) in trade unions can be addressed. This is especially important for trade unions today, as it is a widely held belief that 'issues of *internal* equality (the position of women and ethnic minorities and the representation of their interests within unions) are connected to issues of *external* equality' (Dickens, 1997: 288).

# Review and discussion questions

1 Why might it be considered important for unions to monitor the composition of their memberships by a range of characteristics?
2 In what ways does the social, economic and political climate unions are faced with influence the realization of union objectives?
3 What are the main factors that promote or inhibit equality bargaining?
4 How can the under-representation of women and ethnic minorities in union decision-making structures be explained?

# Further reading

Cully, M. and Woodland, S. (1998). Trade union membership and recognition 1996–7: an analysis of data from the Certification Officer and the LFS. *Labour Market Trends*, July, 353–362.
Provides comprehensive data on the determinants of trade union membership and recognition.
Cunnison, S. and Stageman, J. (1995) *Feminising the Unions*. Avebury.
An in-depth analysis of the roles and activities of women in trade unions (women are treated as a heterogeneous group), together with examination of union efforts to achieve internal equality.
Dickens, L. (1997). Gender, race and employment equality in Britain: inadequate strategies and the role of industrial relations actors. *Industrial Relations Journal*, **28**, (4), 282–290.
A short, yet insightful, article summarizing the strategies of the state, employers and trade unions in relation to equality.
Phizacklea, A. and Miles, R. (1987). The British trade union movement and racism. In *The Manufacture of Disadvantage* (G. Lee and R. Loveridge, eds). Open University Press.
Discusses the commitment of Asian and Caribbean workers to the trade union movement and provides a critical view of trade unions' role in perpetuating racial inequalities.

# References

Bercusson, B. and Dickens, L. (1996). *Equal Opportunities and Collective Bargaining in Europe: Defining the Issues*. European Commission.
Blyton, P. and Turnball, P. (1998). *The Dynamics of Employee Relations*. Macmillan.
Cockburn, C. (1991). *In the Way of Women*. Macmillan.
Cockburn, C. (1995). *Strategies for Gender Democracy*. European Commission.
Colgan, F. (1999). Moving forward in UNISON. In *Labouring for Rights: A Global Perspective on Union Response to Sexual Diversity* (G. Hunt, ed). Temple University Press.

Colling, T. and Dickens, L. (1989). *Equality Bargaining – Why Not?* EOC.

Colling, T. and Dickens, L. (1998). Selling the case for gender equality: deregulation and equality bargaining. *British Journal of Industrial Relations,* **36**, (3), 389–411.

Cully, M. and Woodland, S. (1998). Trade union membership and recognition 1996–7: an analysis of data from the Certification Officer and the LFS. *Labour Market Trends,* July.

Cully, M., Woodland, S., O'Reilly, A. and Dix, G. (1999). *Britain at Work.* Routledge.

Cunnison, S. and Stageman, J. (1995) *Feminising the Unions.* Avebury.

Dickens, L. (1997). Gender, race and employment equality in Britain: inadequate strategies and the role of industrial relations actors. *Industrial Relations Journal,* **28**, (4).

Dickens, L., Townley, B. and Winchester, D. (1988). *Tackling Sex Discrimination through Collective Bargaining.* EOC.

Ellis, V. (1988). Current trade union attempts to remove occupational seregation in the employment of women. In *Gender Segregation at Work* (S. Walby, ed.). Open University Press.

EOR (Equal Opportunities Review) (1992). Unions campaign for childcare. *Equal Opportunities Review,* (43), 3–4.

EOR (Equal Opportunities Review) (1995). Trade unions and race equality. *Equal Opportunities Review,* (62), 23–28.

Farnham, D. and Pimlott, J. (1995). *Understanding Industrial Relations.* Cassell.

Gilbert, K. and Secker, J. (1995). Generating equality? Equal pay, decentralization and the electricity supply industry. *British Journal of Industrial Relations,* **33**, (2), 191–201.

Healy, G. and Kirton, G. (1999). Women's, structures, oligarchy and trade union government. University of Hertfordshire, Business School Working Paper.

Healy, G. and Kraithman, D. (1991). The other side of the equation: the demands of women on re-entering the labour market *Employee Relations,* **13**, (3), 17–28.

Heery, E. and Kelly, J. (1988). Do female representatives make a difference? Women full-time officials and trade union work. *Work, Employment and Society,* **2**, (4), 487–505.

Howell, C. (1996). Women as the paradigmatic trade unionists? New work, new workers and new trade union strategies in conservative Britain. *Economic and Industrial Democracy,* **17**, (4), 511–543.

IRS (1994). Why white-collar staff join trade unions. *Employment Trends,* 565.

IRS (1996a). Sexual harassment at work. *Employment Trends,* 615, 4–10.

IRS (1996b), Sexual harassment at work. *Employment Trends,* 618, 7–12.

Jewson, N. and Mason, D. (1992). The theory and practice of equal opportunities policies: liberal and radical approaches. In *Racism and Antiracism* (P. Braham, A. Rattansi and R. Skellington, eds). Open University Press.

Jowell, R., Witherspoon, S. and Brook, L. (1990). *British Social Attitudes.* (Seventh report). Dartmouth.

Kellner, P. (1996). *Trade Unions: The Popular Verdict.* TUC.

Kelly, J. (1998). *Rethinking Industrial Relations*. Routledge.

Kerr, A. (1992). Why public sector workers join unions: an attitude survey of workers in the health service and local government. *Employee Relations*, **14**, (2), 39–54.

Kirton, G. (1999). Sustaining and developing women's trade union activism: a gendered project? *Gender, Work and Organisation*, **6**, (4), 213–223.

Kirton, G. and Healy, G. (1999). Transforming union women – the role of women trade union officials in union renewal. *Industrial Relations Journal*, **30**, (1), 31–45.

Kumar, P. (1993). Collective bargaining and women's workplace concerns. In *Women Challenging Unions* (L. Briskin and P. McDermott, eds) University of Toronto Press.

Labour Research (1994). *Same Sex – Different Deal*. LRD.

Labour Research (1996a). *Unions Must Recruit More Part-Timers*. LRD.

Labour Research (1996b). *Able to Take Part in the Union*. LRD.

Labour Research (1998) *Hard Work Ahead for Unions*. LRD.

Lee, G. (1987). Black members and their unions. In *The Manufacture of Disadvantage* (G. Lee and R. Loveridge, Open University Press.

Lim, L. (1996). *More and Better Jobs for Wo ILO.

Main, B. (1996). Union relative wage gap. In *Trade Unionism in Recession* (D. Gallie, T. Penn and M. Rose, eds). Oxford University Press.

Millward, N. (1995). *Targeting Potential Discrimination*. EOC.

Modood, T., Berthoud, R., Lakey, J., Nazroo, J., Smith, P., Virdee, S. and Beishon, S. (1997). *Ethnic Minorities in Britain. Diversity and Disadvantage*. PSI.

MSF (Manufacturing, Science, Finance) (1996). *The MSF Bargaining Handbook*. MSF.

Phizacklea, A. and Miles, R. (1987). The British trade union movement and racism. In *The Manufacture of Disadvantage* (G. Lee and R. Loveridge, eds). Open University Press.

Rees, T. (1990). Gender, power and trade union democracy. In *Trade Unions and their Members* (P. Fosh and E. Heery, eds). Macmillan.

Rees, T. (1992). *Women and the Labour Market*. Routledge.

Terry, M. (1996). Negotiating the government of UNISON: union democracy in theory and practice. *British Journal of Industrial Relations*, **34**, 87–110.

Trebilcock, A. (1991). Strategies for strengthening women's participation in trade union leadership. *International Labour Review*, **130**, (4), 407–426.

TUC (1991). *Involvement of Black Workers in Trade Unions*. TUC.

TUC (1997). *Women and the New Unionism*. Economic and Social Affairs Department.

TUC (1998a). *Unions at Work*. TUC.

TUC (1998b). *General Council Report*. TUC.

TUC (1998c). *Black Trade Unionists Today*. TUC.

Waddington, J. and Whitston, C. (1997). Why do people join unions in a period of membership decline? Paper to British University Industrial Relations Association, Bath

Walby, S. (1997). *Gender Transformations*. Routledge.

Watson, D. (1988). *Managers of Discontent*. Routledge.

# Chapter 8
# Organizational policy and practice

## Aim

To explore variations in approach among organizations to equality and diversity policy and practice.

## Objectives

- To discuss the ideology underpinning policy approaches.
- To examine the form and content of contemporary equality and diversity policy and practice in different organizational contexts.
- To explore the role of key organizational actors in promoting equality and valuing diversity or in reproducing inequalities.

## Introduction

The development of approaches to equality policy in the UK has been strongly influenced by legislation. The sex and race equality legislation, outlined in Chapter 6, has existed since the 1970s, whilst legislation concerning disability is more recent (1995). More recently still, a government-initiated code of practice concerning age discrimination has emerged. Thus, the unequal labour market outcomes we highlighted in Chapter 2, exist within the context of formal equality of opportunity. (Equality for lesbians and gay men is the exception – this group is not explicitly covered either by legislation or a code of practice.) The equality legislation of the 1970s was, arguably, pivotal in drawing attention to inequalities in employment and in placing equality issues on the policy agenda of employers (Liff, 1995). However, the legislation is essentially liberal and as such, minimalist in nature. By this we mean that it focuses on issues of equal access to and equal treatment in employment, avoiding the more sensitive issues involved in the radical approach of 'redistributing rewards' or in shaping labour market outcomes. In other words, there is little scope within the law for positive action or radical policy measures. We discussed theoretical and conceptual approaches to equality and diversity in Chapter 5 and the present chapter draws on these discussions.

Organizational equal opportunities policies (EOPs) have also tended to reflect liberal and minimalist legal requirements and, thus, have generally been concerned to tackle inequality by the implementation of formal rules and procedures to be applied in a uniform way to all employees, irrespective of gender, race, disability and so on. Such an approach seeks to ensure that the employer stays within the law in its employment policy and practice. Typically, organizations produce a statement setting out their intention to be or become an 'equal opportunity employer'. Some employers do no more than this (Liff, 1995), whilst many others develop a policy with clearly articulated aims and objectives. Whatever form they take, EOPs are widely criticized for their failure to deliver equality of outcome. In Chapter 4, we examined some of the dimensions of organizational culture, which might help to explain why bureaucratic, formalized EOPs have had limited impact on outcomes. From this we can conclude that formal EOP statements are unreliable indicators of the *actual* beliefs and values towards equality issues of organizational members, decision-makers and gatekeepers. For a complete explanation of the continued existence of labour market inequalities, we also need to look to wider society, for example the education and political systems, the gendered division of domestic labour and so on. These are issues, which space limitations do not allow us to address in any detail in this book. The central focus in this chapter is to examine present and emerging developments in employer equality and diversity policy approaches within the context of widespread recognition of the need for new strategies to tackle deep-seated or embedded inequalities.

This chapter begins by examining the ideology underpinning organizational policy approaches. These are broadly conceived of as two seemingly opposing ideologies, that of the 'business case' and of 'social justice'. However, as will be shown, in practice organizations often develop policies containing a mix of elements stemming from different ideological orientations. This section alludes to the advent of 'managing diversity' and the influence of this North American model on UK policy and practice, although for a full discussion of conceptual understandings of 'managing diversity' see Chapter 5. We then examine the form and scope of equality and diversity policy. Finally, the chapter considers the role of key organizational actors in advancing or hindering the equality and diversity agenda.

# Underpinning ideology

An EOP can be defined as 'a commitment to engage in employment practices and procedures which do not discriminate, and which provide equality between individuals of different groups or sex to achieve full, productive and freely chosen employment' (Lean Lim, 1996: 34). Whereas, the concept of 'managing diversity' is generally seen as 'proactively capitalizing on the different skills, qualities and viewpoints that a diverse workforce has to offer' (EOR, 1999a: 14). For reasons which will become clear below, equality and diversity policies can be viewed as complementary and mutually reinforcing, rather than opposing, strategies.

As explained above, the traditional orientation of EOPs in the UK has been towards legal compliance, an orientation that, arguably, has constrained the development of a proactive equality agenda. Recognition of the limitations of the law and legal compliance in tackling labour market inequalities has led to the emergence of two analytically (although not practically) distinct approaches to policy formulation – that of social justice and the business case.

## The social justice approach

From the social justice perspective, labour market inequalities are unjust and unfair and employers have a social duty to develop policy and practice to address disadvantage. This is not to say that economic benefits will not be derived from initiatives designed to promote equality. However, the equality project is primarily an ethical and moral one and in this sense it is an end in itself. From this perspective, we can also assume that diversity is a 'good thing' in itself, in the same way that 'socially balanced communities' are traditionally seen as good (Edwards, 1995), the organization representing a microcosm of wider societal communities. At a policy level, the social justice approach places an emphasis on the 'good employer' (Dickens, 1999) and 'best practice' initiatives to redress inequalities. The approach is traditionally most strongly associated with the public sector and the sector's overall aim to act as a good employer in order to promote good practice more widely among employing organizations. The good employer model influenced public sector policy developments in the field of equality during the 1980s in response to, and underpinned by, the legislation. Employers buying into this approach have typically developed formal EOPs, often containing a mix of liberal and radical policy instruments, designed to eradicate discrimination and promote equality. However, the social justice approach has found little purchase in the profit-oriented private sector. Thus business case arguments are increasingly used to justify policy development and intervention, there and in the public sector also.

## The business case for equality and diversity

As Dickens (1999) states, although the benefits to organizations of tackling inequalities have always formed part of the arguments of those advocating action, during the late 1980s and 1990s, business case arguments increasingly came to the fore as the driving force behind EOPs. This occurred against a background of increasing national and multinational competition facing many UK business organizations, and the consequent need to find ways to enhance competitive edge. Within the business case for equality and diversity, the question being asked is rather different from that of the social justice argument. Instead of asking what can be done to relieve the employment disadvantage disproportionately experienced by some social groups, the question centres on how an equality and diversity agenda can contribute to organizational aims and objectives. The cornerstone of the business case for equality is that inequality is inefficient and uneconomic.

There are three principal arguments in support of this claim. First, it is argued that certain social groups constitute an underutilized human resource. This is especially relevant to demographic change and the shortage of young entrants to the labour market. Discriminatory policy and practice prevent organizations from making best use of the wide pool of labour available to them in the internal and external markets and thus contribute to lack of competitiveness. This argument is often used to promote special training courses aimed at under-represented groups or to target recruitment campaigns at particular groups. British Telecom and the Post Office are examples of organizations which have developed training to increase the numbers of women in senior positions (EOR, 1996; 1999a) and the police force has aimed recruitment campaigns at minority ethnic groups. Second, there is increasing recognition of the diversity of customer groups and the perceived need for workforces to reflect such diversity. Organizations such as the BBC, Grand Metropolitan, Littlewoods, Midland Bank and British Petroleum have all invested in promoting equality and diversity in order to improve service delivery (Healy, 1993). Third, it has also become increasingly recognized that everyday employee relations problems can be the direct or indirect consequence of discriminatory policy and practice – for example, high labour turnover, absenteeism, poor performance, low productivity and so on. Eradicating

---

**Exhibit 8.1 'Race for Opportunity' – a business campaign for ethnic minorities: action areas**

*Employment*: developing employment skills and opportunities for ethnic minority employees. For example, analysing selection procedures to identify possible or actual barriers to equal access; carrying out regular recruitment, promotion and exit audits; and introducing and supporting mentoring, shadowing, self-help networks, secondments and career counselling.

*Marketing*: marketing to ethnic minority customers and involving them in the planning, design and delivery of products and service. For example, producing information in other languages; carrying out regular service delivery audits.

*Purchasing*: supporting the growth of ethnic minority businesses. For example, taking steps to encourage tenders from as diverse a field as possible.

*Community involvement*: building business support for educational and community organizations. For example, encouraging employees' involvement in the wider community.

*Source*: EOR (1995).

discrimination and tackling inequality thus becomes a business imperative, an approach reflected in the nationwide business campaigns for race equality, 'Race for Opportunity', and in that for gender equality 'Opportunity 2000'. Exhibits 8.1 and 8.2 set out the main objectives of the two campaigns. It can be seen that both campaigns advocate a broad business-driven policy approach. Members of both campaigns are required annually to demonstrate how they have met their goals.

As we have shown in Chapter 5, business case arguments are often couched in the language of 'managing diversity', thus marking a distinction between the economic and the social need for equality encapsulated in the term 'equal opportunities'. In this chapter we are concerned with the way this affects employer policy approaches. In practice, many of the policy elements of 'managing diversity' are similar to or drawn from traditional EOP approaches and in this vein we can conceptualize 'managing diversity' as an equality strategy, most readily identifiable with the business case. Indeed, Dickens (1994) argues that the business case approach provides an opportunity to identify equality as a

---

**Exhibit 8.2 'Opportunity 2000': five key goals**

*Demonstrating commitment*: senior managers need to drive change through from the top. They must be seen as role models in leading equal opportunities development and in understanding the economic imperative for addressing these issues as part of their business strategy.

*Making the investment*: investing in the future success of a business needs resources – people and time, as well as finance. Evaluating the impact of investment is equally crucial to the business case.

*Changing behaviour*: employees at all levels need room to innovate, maximize opportunities, do things differently and do them better. Practical programmes that enable women to maximize their individual performance at work will, in turn, support personal and professional development. Positive change will create an inclusive and productive culture within the workplace.

*Communicating ownership*: employees need to know what they and their organization are aiming for and why, and that progress is being made. Achievements should be showcased both inside and outside the business.

*Sharing ownership*: involving everyone in developing new working methods is vital to achieving change. Building shared ownership, through two-way communication and working together to find productive solutions, will enhance business performance.

*Source*: EOR (1998b).

strategic goal, thus facilitating the 'mainstreaming' of equality issues. A mainstreaming approach aims to ensure that equality objectives are injected into the overall policies and activities of the organization, and as such become 'owned' by all managers, rather than remaining the preserve of the personnel or human resource department (Dickens, 1994). This resonates with the three business case arguments described above.

However, although sharing many similarities, arguments under the 'managing diversity' banner also differ from traditional equality arguments in at least one important dimension. The concept of 'managing diversity' sees economic sense not simply in equality, but also in valuing diversity. This is perhaps the most significant of differences between traditional 'equal opportunities' and 'managing diversity'. It provides an opportunity to recognize workforces as heterogeneous. A 'managing diversity' approach fits most closely with the second business case argument described above. Put another way, an organization with a culturally and socially diverse workforce should be able to develop greater understanding of customer requirements, through the sharing and reflecting of customer diversity. Dickens (1994) cites British Airways and British Telecom as two examples of British companies that have moved in this direction. Models of 'managing diversity' tend to eschew positive action initiatives associated with 'equal opportunities' because of their targeting of social groups, whereas it is said that 'managing diversity' is concerned to benefit all employees. The irony here is that business case arguments would suggest that if diversity has economic benefits, then financial expediency should demand positive action, or even positive discrimination, to achieve it in circumstances where certain social groups are underrepresented and where the workforce is relatively homogeneous. However, interventionist measures of this nature aimed at specific social groups do not sit easily with the rhetoric and ideology of 'managing diversity'.

Having set out the goals of and benefits to be derived from a business case approach, on a less optimistic note, it is important now to consider the contingent nature of the business case for equality and diversity. The rhetoric of business case arguments often pays insufficient attention to the wider context in which organizations operate. First, if we consider the context of the labour market, it can be seen that competitive pressures, especially in the form of skills and labour shortages, vary over time and space. There may be particular points in the demographic cycle when employers are forced into seeking to attract under-represented groups by virtue of a shortage of the traditional labour source. For example, women and older people become important sources of potential employees at times when young workers are in short supply and when employers are seeking to fill part-time jobs. This imperative has led some employers to develop polices to attract women – childcare initiatives, flexible hours, for instance. However, these issues have greater salience for some employers than for others. Some UK employers in certain geographical locations, in need of low-skill labour, can attract minority ethnic labour without pursuing diversity or equality policy, simply because minority ethnic workers are over-represented in some local low-skill, low-pay labour forces (Edwards, 1995).

Second, contingent variables can also be found if we consider the wider business context. Taking a long-term view, many types of organization could conceivably benefit from 'getting close to the customer' by ensuring that the workforce is reflective of customer diversity, whereas other organizations, especially those which do not interact directly with individual consumers, can flourish in the absence of equality and diversity (Dickens, 1994). In other words, we have to question how exactly equality and diversity contribute to the 'bottom line', particularly in view of the fact that many UK organizations take a short-term view of performance. Thus, it can be concluded that although in many circumstances a business case argument for equality and diversity can be made, and employers may take action on particular issues, in others a cost-benefit analysis may point away from any action (Dickens, 1994). It is in this sense that the pre-eminence of the business case approach could prove detrimental to the promotion and advancement of a comprehensive equality and diversity agenda.

## Broadening the agenda

Dickens (1994) argues convincingly for a broader definition of business case interests to encompass social and political interests. She offers an example of the increasing consideration of ethical and environmental issues within business decision-making, highlighting the importance of organizational actors, such as employees and shareholders, in bringing pressure to bear on employers to link business interests to wider social issues. From this point of view, employers do have a commercial interest in promoting equality. At a policy-making level, Dickens (1994) suggests that one option open to organizations is to attach greater importance to equality as a factor in corporate reputation. This is likely to arise from shareholder, consumer and employee pressure. Thus, broadening the equality agenda will render the business case 'carrot' more attractive to employers and facilitate a move away from a dichotomous view of business case and social justice arguments. This has echoes of the 'mainstreaming' approach we discussed in Chapter 5 and is a position reflected in the CRE's (CRE, 1995) *Standard for Racial Equality for Employers*. The CRE document sets out the business case for racial equality, but links it to wider issues of social responsibility, thus taking a multifaceted approach with an employer's obligation to contribute to 'sustaining a healthy society', sitting alongside 'making the company more attractive to investors'. The CRE *Standard* includes a checklist, which summarizes the range of action involved in developing and implementing a racial equality programme.

Exhibit 8.3 reproduces the 'commitment' section of the CRE's checklist. It can be seen that by emphasizing the depth and breadth of commitment to the equality project that is required, the underlying intention of the checklist is to move equality/diversity from a vision to reality within the organization. It can also be seen that the pursuance of equality strategies requires considerable effort on the part of organizations. Although the CRE focuses on race equality, its checklist is applicable to a broader equality policy.

**Exhibit 8.3 Commitment**

- Does the organization have a written racial equality policy, or a section on racial equality within an equal opportunity policy, clearly linked to the organization's aims and objectives?
- Is there a clear public commitment at the highest level of the organization, emphasizing the value placed on equality of opportunity?
- Does the organization communicate the policy and programme to:

    employees and their representatives, where applicable;
    applicants and potential applicants;
    customers and clients;
    shareholders;
    suppliers of goods and services;
    external organizations, such as Training and Enterprise Councils etc.;
    the public?

- Does the organization have an action plan covering:

    the role of senior management;
    who is responsible for implementing the policy;
    resources needed to make changes;
    objectives and targets, and who is accountable;
    timetables and time scales;
    methods of measuring progress;
    consultation with all staff and employee representatives, groups and institutions in the wider community, including ethnic minority organizations;
    the role of line managers, and local or devolved units;
    the rights and responsibilities of individual employees?

*Source*: CRE (1995).

## Activity

## Activity 8.1: The business case for equality/diversity

Study Exhibits 8.1, 8.2 and 8.3. Answer the following questions.

*Questions*

1 Discuss the extent to which 'Opportunity 2000' and 'Race for Opportunity' accord broad definitions to the 'business case' for equality/diversity.
2 In what sense does the CRE's checklist on 'Commitment' in Exhibit 8.3 reflect broader understandings of the 'business case'?
3 Give some examples of the types of organizations you might expect to embrace 'Opportunity 2000' and 'Race for Opportunity'.

**Key learning points**

1 There are two main approaches underpinning and informing organizational equality policies: those of social justice and the business case. Within the social justice approach both equality and diversity can be viewed as goals worth pursuing in themselves, whereas a business case orientation requires that interventions be justified on grounds of economic expediency.
2 Business case arguments are highly contingent and therefore fragile. Models of 'managing diversity' tend to share the business case orientation.
3 There is an emergent argument, which ties together business case and social justice arguments, within a broader definition of commercial interests.

# The form and content of equality and diversity policy approaches

Equal opportunities policies have been part of employment policy and standard business practice since the early 1980s (Gibbon, 1990): the majority of UK organizations (at least large ones) now have a formal EOP and many are starting to develop diversity policy too (Liff and Cameron, 1997). The public sector has been widely regarded as leading the way in the development of equality policy, whereas the picture of degrees of commitment to promoting equality within the private sector has been more mixed. However, that is not to say that a uniform approach exists in the public sector either, especially in view of the emergence and ascendancy of a business case strategy linked to government initiated changes in public sector employment and service delivery policies in the late 1980s and 1990s (Dickens, 1999). In fact, these changes have probably resulted in greater convergence in public and private sector equality policy approaches, than has ever existed before. Thus, it is *not* the case that all public sector employers proactively pursue equality strategies and all private sector employers take a minimalist approach. It is more the case that public sector employers are more inclined to underpin their equality and diversity policy with a social justice rationale. In the words of Manchester City Council's head of organizational development: 'we are a democratically constituted organization whose whole raison d'etre is based on the people who live in Manchester. If we can't respond effectively to the broad range we are not doing our job properly. One way to achieve this is to have a diverse workforce'(EOR, 1999b: 16). What this suggests is that public sector policies are less likely to be partial and contingent.

Research conducted in Sheffield has found an association between the degree of organizational bureaucratization of the personnel function and the existence of a formal EOP (Gibbon, 1990). In turn, bureaucratization is associated with larger organizations. However, this is a tentative association because there are exceptions to the norm: for example, the large organization whose policy consisted of a five-line statement, and the small voluntary sector organizations with highly developed policies (Gibbon, 1990). Thus, whilst traditional EOPs are highly developed in the UK (albeit with variations in their scope, form and content), proponents of the 'diversity paradigm' have yet to develop specific policy levers and there is some evidence to suggest that it is organizations with established equality policies that have started to develop diversity policy – see for example, accounts of British Telecom (EOR, 1999a, Liff, 1999).

This section examines the form and content of equality and diversity policy approaches that can currently be found among UK organizations. As stated above, business case arguments have increasingly risen to the fore in both public and private sectors and the form and content of organizational policy often reflects this shift in underpinning ideology, in that policies often contain a mix of traditional equality initiatives alongside business-case oriented diversity initiatives. Yet, there is no evidence in the UK of employers abandoning EOPs in favour of diversity policies, thus it is still relevant to examine equality policy in the context of UK organizations. It can be argued, then, that in the UK, unlike in the US context, employers appear to understand diversity as an equality strategy, complementing and supplementing, rather than substituting traditional EOPs. This is a view espoused by the Institute of Personnel and Development, in its *Position Paper* (IPD, undated: 1), in which the IPD states its belief that 'the management of diversity complements established approaches to equal opportunities'. This twin approach affords an opportunity for the organization to develop a strategy to enable differences between and among groups of employees to be recognized, at the same time as treating them equitably (Liff, 1999). That is not to say that some organizations are not simply adopting the *language* of diversity, rather than making any deep changes to equality strategy. It nevertheless remains pertinent to examine EOPs, and to do this alongside an examination of new and emergent approaches. The purpose of this section is to provide an overview of current organizational attempts to tackle inequalities and to advance a diversity agenda.

## Equal opportunity organizations

The introductory section has highlighted that many, if not the majority, of UK organizations, declare themselves to be equal opportunity organizations. Recent evidence finds that around two-thirds of workplaces are covered by formal written EOPs (Cully et al., 1999). This section seeks to explore the variations in what this means in terms of policy and practice. At present we cannot really talk about 'diversity organizations', because diversity policy is at an early stage in the UK and it is unclear how or if this new approach will diverge from or transform traditional EOPs. However, because of their longer history, we can talk about 'equal

**Exhibit 8.4 Types of equal opportunity organization**

1 *The negative organization*
A negative organization will not have an EOP and it may not comply with the law. It will not claim to be an equal opportunity employer: indeed, it may practise, consciously or unconsciously, discrimination. It will not perceive itself to be an organization standing to benefit from diversity.

2 *The minimalist/partial organization*
This organization will declare itself to be an equal opportunity employer, but in practice equality will have a low profile, as will diversity. It will not have developed a written EOP nor will it have developed procedures designed to overcome discrimination and promote equality. The minimalist organization is likely to adopt a reactive approach and defend claims of discrimination as and when they arise, rather than take action to avoid them.

3 *The compliant organization*
The compliant organization will ensure that it fulfils its legal obligations through a formal policy approach, probably developed and implemented by personnel practitioners. The emphasis is likely to be on recruitment, and procedures will adopt 'good practice' as advocated by the statutory agencies. Also, because anti-discrimination law covers only three principal areas (sex, race, disability), the compliant organization will have a relatively narrow, and in Cockburn's (1991) terms, short equality agenda. Paradoxically, this organization may have switched to the language of 'managing diversity' in order to downplay equality issues and to suggest neutrality towards diverse social groups, thereby signalling that inequality is not an issue within the organization.

4 *The comprehensive proactive organization*
The proactive organization will also ensure it complies with the law, but will also be concerned to monitor the outcomes of policy and practice in order to assess their impact. Positive action initiatives will be a feature of policy here to ensure that the agenda moves beyond tackling discrimination towards promoting equality. We can add that the proactive organization will also have a broad and, in Cockburn's (1991) terms, a long equality agenda, seeking to redress the disadvantage faced by a wide range of social groups. Writing in the late 1990s, the proactive organization may also be developing diversity policy as a complementary strategy to the traditional EOP and playing up the benefits of a diverse workforce. Thus, this type of organization will have a strong sense of social justice, but will also see good business sense in pursuing equality and diversity policy. It is likely that a senior member of the organization will be championing equality and diversity.

opportunity organizations', and attempt to classify organizations according to their orientation towards equality. It is worth reiterating that many organizations who declare themselves to be equal opportunity employers do no more than produce and publicize a statement of intent, whilst others develop and implement a formal and sometimes thoroughgoing policy. Gibbon draws a distinction between what equal opportunity employers do and what the contents of EOPs are. He does this because 'no direct relation between declarations that an organization is an EOE (equal opportunity employer) and possessing a written EOP, let alone implementation of such an EOP' (Gibbon, 1990: 236) can be found in the existing research. Later research (Cully et al., 1999) confirms the low correspondence between policy and practice. Reflecting this view of policy and practice, Healy (1993) constructs a typology of four types of equal opportunity organization, which is useful for classifying and understanding organizational approaches to EOPs. We build on her typology, by injecting a diversity perspective (Exhibit 8.4).

## Equality and diversity policy and practice

The typology in Exhibit 8.4 can also be viewed as a continuum of forms of organizational approaches to equality, moving from approaches which can be characterized as reproducing inequality, to tackling discrimination, through to actively promoting equality. Having classified equal opportunity organizations, we now turn our attention to the nature of equality and diversity policy and practice in the 'comprehensive proactive organization'. We are not attempting to present a picture of the reality of equality within such organizations, rather we explore the ways in which employers seek to tackle equality and diversity issues utilizing a range of policy levers. What follows, therefore, is not a detailed description or analysis of the contents of EOPs within organizations, rather it provides a glimpse at the principal features thereof. Most EOPs focus on the key functions of personnel management, that is, recruitment and selection procedures, training and development policies, and terms and conditions of employment. This is the traditional territory of equality initiatives within the liberal approach. The aim is to develop procedures and practices which do not give rise to unfair direct, or indirect discrimination, in other words to create a fair competition for rewards. However, there are also more radical elements to be found within the positive action initiatives contained in many EOPs, the aim of which are to influence outcomes, without going so far as to favour disadvantaged groups for positions.

### Recruitment and selection

In equality terms, good practice in recruitment and selection is generally taken to mean the development of formalized, bureaucratic procedures (Gibbon, 1990), which are both transparent and justifiable, to guide the processes involved: for example the drawing up of a full job description and person specification based on it; the use of an application form in preference to CVs. It would be expected that both 'compliant' and 'proactive' organizations would give consideration to their recruitment and selection procedures and practices as a basis from which to ensure legal compliance and the elimination of discrimination, as would organizations embracing both social justice and business case arguments, for discrimination is both unethical and uneconomic.

The idea behind formalization of recruitment procedures is that it will enable the objective requirements of the job to be more easily identified and therewith a selection decision based on a person's suitability, rather than acceptability, to be made. Thus, discrimination is less likely to occur (Healy, 1993). Adherence to rigorous procedures can challenge and halt the perpetuation of certain stereotypes and myths: for example, the fact that a job has always been done by a man does not mean that a man is necessary in that position, or the fact that a disabled person has never been employed does not suggest that a disabled person cannot be successfully employed.

Formalization of recruitment and selection usually extends to moving away from reliance on 'word of mouth' methods (Healy, 1993), where family and friends of existing employees are appointed. Traditionally, this method of recruitment is favoured by many small companies and by those operating within local labour markets, because of its cheapness. However, where certain groups of people – minority ethnic workers or women, for example – are under-represented in an organization, it is likely that this method will perpetuate such under-representation. It is, therefore, a method to be avoided by the organization seeking to be proactive. The proactive organization will advertise job vacancies in locations that will reach the largest pool of suitably qualified applicants, particularly those social groups who are currently under-represented in the organization. It may also target advertising in order to reach under-represented groups, for example, by utilizing the minority ethnic press. In addition, advertisements will be carefully constructed so as to avoid deterring certain social groups from applying and to avoid the impression that particular 'types' of candidates will be favoured. In fact there is some evidence of the efficacy of the kinds of approaches described here and found within proactive EOPs: workplaces with an EOP employ proportionately more people from ethnic minorities than do those without (Cully et al., 1999).

The aim of elimination of bias and discrimination in the recruitment and selection process has salience for both the equality-oriented and the diversity-oriented organization. To put it another way, there exist both social justice and business case triggers. In the case of the former, tackling discrimination is a worthwhile project in itself whilst, in the case of the latter, the organization's inability to recruit and select from a wide pool of candidates inhibits organizational effectiveness. It is in this sense, then, that the formalization of recruitment and selection can be viewed as part of both traditional equality strategies and the emerging diversity strategies. However, one must not forget the contingent nature of the diversity approach: for example, if it appears that organizational effectiveness calls for homogeneity of certain sections of the workforce, then diversity strategies will not be justifiable from the business case point of view.

## Training and development

The use of training and development as a vehicle to pursue equality and diversity objectives falls within the ambit of the proactive organization, for this is a form of positive action (see Table 5.1). Within equality/diversity policy, training and development strategies have twin goals. The first is to use training as a vehicle to implement the policy; that is, communicate the aims and objectives of the policy, to raise awareness of equality and diversity issues and to instruct managers and other employees of their roles and duties in relation to the policy. For example, as part of the implementation of an equality policy supervisors and managers involved in recruitment and selection or in appraisal may undergo training in the methods the organization is using in order to eliminate the exercise of bias and prejudice. Alternatively, equality and diversity awareness training may be used to in an attempt to manipulate organizational members' attitudes and behaviour towards disadvantaged and diverse social groups within the employment and customer service contexts, with the aim of winning commitment to equality and diversity. Training in this vein may focus on certain equality levers, such as a harassment policy.

The second objective centres on using specially targeted training programmes to break down various forms of segregation and to achieve a more diverse workforce. Thus, this type of initiative can sit well within both conventional equality and emergent diversity policies. There are a number of organizations adopting this approach in relation to women: the Royal Mail, for example, has devised an in-house training course for women in non-managerial positions who wish to explore personal development opportunities (EOR, 1996). British Telecom has also developed a course for women middle managers who work in male-dominated areas: the aim is to assist women in developing a managerial career (EOR, 1999a). Examples of organizations targeting other under-represented groups are harder to find, although Lloyds TSB (EOR, 1999b) has instituted training programmes for minority ethnic workers and Midland Bank offers summer placements to disabled undergraduates with a guaranteed first interview (Wright and Storey, 1994). Also, organizations which have signed up to the 'Race for Opportunity' campaign, discussed below, are exploring ways of using training to develop the careers of minority ethnic workers.

Utilizing training and development to effect organizational change within the equality and diversity arenas, represents a form of positive action, a strategy that is not universally popular among employers in the UK. What is striking is that articles about equality initiatives in both the academic and practitioner journals tend to use the same few companies as examples, suggesting that the strategies adopted in the private sector, beyond this rather limited list of twenty or so employers, are somewhat less proactive. Nevertheless, it is important to highlight exemplars of good practice in order to provide encouragement and inspiration to key actors in other organizations.

## Terms and conditions of employment

The focus here is on ensuring that terms and conditions of employment are fairly and equitably applied to all employees and to developing positive action initiatives to facilitate the employment of disadvantaged groups. The 'compliant' organization, as well as the 'proactive', may take action in this area: the former to avoid claims of discrimination within the legal framework and the latter to promote equality. Initiatives here may fit within both social justice and business case approaches, contingent upon a range of conditions and circumstances.

Conditions of employment can be taken to relate to the terms of contract as well as to the work environment and to work processes, thus encapsulating a broad range of interventions. Having said this the emphasis is frequently placed upon developing initiatives to facilitate women's participation in employment: for example, childcare provisions, enhanced maternity provisions, career break schemes, flexible hours of work, job share schemes. Essentially these can be categorized as arrangements designed to assist women in juggling domestic work and paid work which, whilst of doubtless value to many women, do not challenge the unequal distribution of domestic work that places this uneven burden on women in the first place. In Cockburn's (1991) terms such policies represent examples of a 'short' rather than 'long' equal opportunities agenda.

Organizations with a broad and progressive equality agenda may also develop measures aimed at other social groups. For example, for minority ethnic workers arrangements for time off for religious observance and extended leave for visiting family overseas may be appropriate, as may flexibility in relation to uniforms and dress codes to ensure that cultural and religious customs can be upheld. In the case of disabled people, an EOP provides a means by which to comply with the law in relation to adjustments to the physical working environment, but also to develop proactive policies and practices such as disability leave, transfer to part-time work or lighter duties following disability. For lesbians and gay men, changes to basic terms and conditions of employment are often necessary to ensure that indirect discrimination does not occur in, for example, access to employment benefits, such as compassionate leave on death of a partner, and other benefits and concessions which traditionally apply only to partners/spouses of the opposite sex.

## Monitoring and auditing

It is widely recognized that the adoption and communication of an EOP will not of itself translate the policy into practice. Therefore, one of the common features of a proactive EOP are arrangements for monitoring and auditing the procedures and outcomes, to determine whether or not the objectives of the policy are being achieved. Auditing provides the evidence required to justify and to plan any further action and initiatives. Monitoring and auditing need not be viewed simply as a bureaucratic exercise or as a process that is only capable of being aligned with a social justice approach to equality. It is a process which also has utility for the business case approach: Cameron (1993) contends that it makes good business sense for organizations to know what their resources are and where they are, in order to link equality and diversity policy with business objectives.

**Exhibit 8.5 An equality audit**

1 *Where are employees located?*
A breakdown by grade, job and site on the basis of gender, race/ethnicity, age, disability, sexual orientation should be produced.
This will help identify patterns of job segregation and inequalities in access to promotion opportunities and help determine the reasons for such patterns. Thus, a simple 'head count' approach is avoided as this would not reveal the qualitative data needed to plan remedial measures.

2 *Is the organization complying with the law?*
This will help identify any practices that could make the organization vulnerable to equal pay and sex, race or disability discrimination claims under the law.

3 *What educational, vocational and professional qualifications do employees hold?*
This will help identify employees who are underemployed and who might be suitable for development and promotion. It will also help to identify any patterns of career under-achievement among diverse social groups.

4 *What skills and experience do employees have?*
This is a complementary exercise to (3) above, which trawls for a wider profile of experience and expertise and is similarly capable of identifying patterns of disadvantage and areas where discrimination may be taking place.

5 *What are the organization's labour turnover rates?*
This will help identify employee relations problems that might be related to equality issues.

6 *Auditing and monitoring access to training resources.*
A review of the routes to promotion will identify any patterns of discrimination and disadvantage. It will also assist the organization wishing to develop an action plan or programme to break down segregation and improve workforce diversity.

7 *Auditing and monitoring appraisal procedures, processes and outcomes.*
This is an exercise linked to (6) above and can help reveal disparities between groups of employees and uncover patterns of discrimination and disadvantage, particularly as regards access to promotion and training.

8 *Auditing and monitoring sickness statistics.*
This can help identify the possible organizational causes of sickness absence, as well as enable analysis by different groups of employees.

9 *Cohort analysis.*
This can help identify disparities in the career progress of different social groups. It could also be used to monitor exit rates and patterns.

10 *Survey of employee opinion.*
This can uncover employee perceptions of barriers and obstacles to equality within the organization.

*Source*: Adapted from Cameron (1993).

Exhibit 8.5 shows the type of questions that an audit exercise might ask and the kinds of information it might collect. The findings of the audit can be used to determine what effects the policy is having and to develop new measures to advance an equality and diversity agenda. However, as can be seen, the audit is likely to cover some sensitive areas: sickness absence, for example, which some groups of employees may fear will be used to justify their exclusion from certain types or levels of work. Where uneven patterns in matters such as sickness absence are uncovered, the objective in the spirit of an equality policy would be to seek to understand any underlying reasons which might relate to equality issues. Exhibit 8.5 focuses on the internal labour market and does not allude to recruitment and selection, which is an area commonly subjected to monitoring in order to assess success rates between and among diverse social groups.

---

1 There are four types of 'equal opportunity organization': the negative organization, the minimalist/partial organization, the compliant organization and the comprehensive/proactive organization. This typology can be viewed as a continuum of forms of organizational approaches to equality, moving from approaches that reproduce inequalities to those that actively promote equality.
2 Most EOPS (and diversity policies, where they exist) focus on the key functions of personnel management, that is, recruitment and selection procedures, training and development policies, terms and conditions of employment.
3 A traditional and comprehensive EOP comprises a mix of liberal and radical policy levers designed to combat discrimination and promote equality. It usually involves the formalization and standardization of recruitment, selection and appraisal procedures.
4 Monitoring and auditing is a means of collecting information on different segments of the workforce to assist in evaluating the success of policy levers and in planning new interventions.

**Key learning points**

---

# Critical appraisal of policy formulation and implementation

What can be seen from the above examination of equality policy form and content, is that some elements of equality policy involve taking steps to ensure that all employees are treated the same, irrespective of gender, race, disability, age or sexual orientation, whilst other elements involve treating different groups of employees differently, in recognition of the disadvantage and discrimination they encounter in employment. (This relates to the concepts of 'sameness' and 'difference', which we discussed in Chapter 5.) Thus, a conceptual muddle is created surrounding the objectives of the various measures: that is, is the aim to ensure that everyone is treated equally, or is the aim to achieve equality of outcome?

Ensuring that everyone is treated equally is a worthwhile aim in itself and as such constitutes good employment practice, however, it does not guarantee fair and equal outcomes (Liff, 1995). On the other hand, if members of certain social groups are targeted for 'preferential' treatment, this practice may be perceived as unfair by those who do not qualify for such treatment and is especially at odds with a 'managing diversity' orientation. Liff and Cameron (1997) note that studies record high levels of opposition to any form of positive discrimination, for practices which base policy action around specific groups violate the principle of treating all individuals the same. These are sensitive issues which can create tensions and conflict, as in the US context, where the discourse of equality has given way to that of diversity, partly because of a backlash effect: white men are starting to complain that progressive equality laws have led to their experiencing discrimination in the search for employment and for promotion (Edwards, 1995). Some organizations may seek to avoid the risk of conflict by adopting the language of 'managing diversity' and by emphasizing the needs of the individual and the organizational benefits to be derived from 'valuing diversity'. Thus, a shift in the moral ground is achieved, for diversity is more about utility than about justice (Edwards, 1995). In this vein, actual policy instruments may or may not change: what is important for policy-makers who fear resistance or conflict, is that the underlying rationale for intervention changes to sit more comfortably within a liberal, individualistic framework, resonant with current management thinking in the search for competitive edge. This approach depoliticizes equality strategies and endows them with a common-sense meaning. Thus, diversity is appealing to some organizations because it does not lay claim to what may look to many like the 'specious moral high ground' (Edwards, 1995: 177) of righting wrongs and promoting justice. However, it should be noted that in the UK context, positive action tends to have focused on equipping disadvantaged groups to compete on equal terms, rather than giving them preferential treatment by 'rigging' the competition. Nevertheless, this debate serves to highlight the eclecticism of equality and diversity policy and practice within UK organizations.

Similarly, if we turn to some of the detailed prescription and common policy instruments, further conundrums are uncovered. For example, the notion that the formalization of recruitment and selection procedures will eradicate discrimination rests on the spurious assumption that there will be a 'best person' for the job and that rational, unbiased procedures can reliably detect who that person is (Gibbon, 1990). It is more likely that any particular job could be performed equally well by countless applicants. In this case, there will be no single best person, yet a selection decision must still be made: the question is, using what criteria? Further, the claim that objective criteria can be constructed by gendered, racialized and subjective human beings, without being viewed through a subjectivist lens, is also likely to prove naive. Collinson, Knights and Collinson's detailed study of insurance sales uncovers the insidious nature of gendered judgements in recruitment and selection: for example, when evaluating male candidates, involvement in sport was a definite advantage, whereas a female's sporting achievements were viewed by selectors as indicative of a 'very narrow existence' (Collinson, Knights and Collinson, 1990: 147). Another example from Collinson, Knights and Collinson's case studies highlights the way that certain personal characteristics are often viewed as appropriate to one gender, but not the other: behaviour described as 'pushy' when exhibited by a female candidate, was described as 'showing initiative' when a male candidate was involved (Collinson, Knights and Collinson, 1990: 101). In short, managers often find it difficult to disassociate characteristics such as leadership from the socially constructed concept of masculinity (Liff, 1995). These problems remain unresolved by the formalization of policy and procedures.

Moving on to interventions falling within the ambit of training and development, the picture is no more straightforward or encouraging here. It can be argued that awareness training is much needed in order to break down the widespread ignorance of issues such as disability, racism, sexism, ageism, sexual orientation and so on, on the basis that such ignorance contributes to the perpetuation of myths and stereotypes which, in turn, result in inequalities. Controversy surrounds some of the *methods* employed, rather than the *aim*. Critics variously argue that approaches such as 'racism awareness training' induce 'white guilt' and therewith defensive behaviour (Shapiro, 1999), stir up conflict where there is none, personalize racism and have not been subjected to rigorous evaluation to determine effectiveness in changing attitudes and behaviour (Iles and Auluck, 1989). Similar criticisms could be made of training focusing on other forms of discrimination. However, in many UK organizations 'awareness training' has been explicitly linked to specific organizational procedures and practices, and used as a lever of change. There is evidence suggesting that well-designed equality training can contribute to the achievement of a number of objectives, including conveying to participants the rationale for equality initiatives, creating a greater awareness of their own stereotypes (Liff, 1996). For example, training often focuses on selection procedures, in particular interviewing, and encourages a reflective approach to challenging one's own biases and prejudices, as well as encouraging strict adherence to formalized measures designed to eradicate discrimination. One of the other main concerns about 'awareness training' concerns employees' attendance: should attendance be compulsory for all employees or for all employees in a specific area of activity, such as recruitment, or should it be voluntary? The former approach risks resistance and hostility; whilst if the latter is adopted, those most in need of the training may not attend. This is a dilemma which is not easily resolved.

There are also dilemmas and controversies surrounding targeted training programmes, which may be no more popular with those they are designed to benefit than with the organizational decision-makers. Being positioned as the recipient of a positive action initiative can be a stigmatizing and lonely experience, for positive action confounds the merit principle and there may always be an air of doubt as to whether the outcome was deserved (Liff and Dale, 1994). This can engender negative attitudes and behaviours among the dominant group towards the under-represented group. Nevertheless, some organizations, especially those associated with the national campaigns 'Opportunity 2000' and 'Race for Opportunity', have reported successes with targeted training interventions. Some organizations have been able to improve the representation of certain groups within their workforces through the provision of targeted training (EOR, 1995; 1996; 1998b; 1999a). The subjective experiences of those who have 'benefited' is an interesting area of enquiry, at present under-researched, which might shed light upon the social processes and relations involved in positive action.

Measures designed to facilitate the employment of women are also often located within the arena of positive action: childcare provision and flexible work hours, for example. The consequence is that these 'family friendly' provisions come to be viewed as benefits rather than entitlements: that it they are constructed as a 'concession for those who cannot conform to "normal" working patterns' (Lewis, 1997: 15), usually women. Those women who take advantage of such 'benefits' are constructed variously as being uncommitted to the organization and to paid work or as being unable to compete without assistance. The alternative approach is for organizations to think about ways in which *they* need to change to adapt to a changing workforce, rather than the converse. Thus, provisions such as childcare, flexible work hours, career break schemes and so on, could become more inclusive and eligibility extended beyond women (Liff and Cameron, 1997), to all employees. For example, men who wish to spend time caring for children, or men and women without children who wish to take time out of employment for personal development, may benefit from such provisions. However, the danger here is that employment policies which treat all employees the same may lead to the absorption and dilution of the equality agenda, rather than to its transformation (Liff and Cameron, 1997). Traditional equality issues may become subsumed under business imperatives. Also, there is doubt that such an approach could have a deeply transformative effect unless men were to take up the 'benefits' in such large numbers as to force a rethink of traditional gendered roles and responsibilities.

Under 'terms and conditions', we also considered inequities in access to other employment benefits and suggested that a proactive equality and diversity policy would seek to ensure fair and equitable access to such benefits and to avoid indirect discrimination. The much publicized case of South West Trains employee, Lisa Grant, is an illustration of the existence of such inequities. Grant complained to the European Court of Justice because she was not entitled to the same travel benefits for her long-term female partner as were her heterosexual colleagues (Prickett, 1998). The high-profile case was pivotal in drawing attention to poor practice, as well as to good: some companies, such as British Airways and London Transport were shown to be operating equitable arrangements. The objective of ensuring equal treatment of all employees can only be met with any degree of certainty if the policy's procedures are regularly reviewed and if outcomes are monitored. Thus, the absence of monitoring and auditing may give rise to a gap between policy and practice, and to the failure of the policy to effect any real change, but its presence does not guarantee success. It is important that auditing and monitoring are not simply exercises used to legitimate procedures, but also to monitor outcomes, as suggested by Exhibit 8.4. Exhibit 8.4 also indicates that extensive qualitative data is necessary in order to move beyond a simple 'head count' approach, (i.e. finding out where different groups of employees are) which reveals very little about the experiences of different segments of the workforce. However, Liff and Cameron (1997: 42–3) caution that the results of auditing are open to conventional interpretation: for example, there are few women in management positions because women do not apply or do not possess the appropriate qualifications, or prioritize their family commitments. This approach does little to identify the reasons for the choices employees appear to be making. Further, some aspects of auditing may be viewed by employees with suspicion and hostility: for example, questions on sexual orientation. Lesbians and gay men who disclose their sexual orientation may fear victimization. Therefore, it is essential that the collection of sensitive information be justified on the basis that it will result in action to tackle the barriers and obstacles to equality that the process uncovers.

1 Within the UK context it is often unclear whether EOPs seek to treat people the same, or whether they seek to redress disadvantage by, on occasion, deliberately treating people differently.
2 There are cognitive difficulties inherent in the process of constructing 'fair and objective' decision-making criteria, which arise from human beings' subjectivist positions and perceptions, such perceptions also being socially constructed.
3 Some 'positive action' measures risk alienating and arousing hostility among dominant groups, who do not see themselves as benefiting.
4 Monitoring and auditing exercises should be able to capture the experiences and perceptions of employees.

**Key learning points**

# The role of key organizational actors: agents of discrimination or champions of equality?

It is widely recognized that fair procedures do not automatically translate into fair and equal treatment in employment. Traditionally, responsibility for the formulation and implementation of equality policy has resided with personnel practitioners. Within the context of the 'flattening' of organizational hierarchies and the devolution of certain human resources responsibilities to line managers (EOR, 1997), it becomes apposite to consider the role of line managers in delivering equality policy, even where human resource practitioners remain the guardians of the policy. These recent debates, emerging from the shift towards 'human resource management' (discussed in Chapter 9), notwithstanding, line managers have always had a role to play at the level of policy implementation. Further, dependent upon the degree of autonomy they have, line managers have always been able to ignore or actively subvert equality policy (Woodall, Edwards and Welchman, 1997), especially as personnel or human resource staff are often weak in organizational terms.

The behaviour and actions of line managers contribute to explaining why EOPs have so frequently failed (Liff and Cameron, 1997) to establish equal treatment, let alone to significantly recast outcomes. In other words, part of the problem lies with organizational decision-makers' lack of commitment to (Liff and Cameron, 1997), and interest in the principles of equality, especially within the social justice approach with its emphasis on redressing disadvantage. Collinson, Knights and Collinson's (1990) in-depth case studies are concerned with the 'power structures' and dynamics, which characterize the social relations and practices of organizations and labour markets. They place the emphasis on human agency (Collinson, Knights and Collinson, 1990: 11), arguing that human beings retain a relative autonomy and a capacity to act in a manner of their choosing, formal procedures notwithstanding. Since line managers are endowed with structural power, they are in a position to either reinforce or resist traditional patterns of disadvantage. Collinson, Knights and Collinson's evidence shows that line managers are more inclined to the former.

If we accept that line managers are active agents in either working for or against equality aims, we need to consider their own objectives and how their commitment to equality objectives can be secured. Line managers' principal concern lies with business objectives and it is in recognition of this positioning that leads proponents of the business case to argue that a crucial element of the business case approach is to transfer responsibility for equality from personnel to line management (Liff and Cameron, 1997). The alignment of equality and diversity goals with broader business goals should, the argument goes, ensure that line managers become committed to their implementation and interested in the outcomes, although there is a lack of empirical evidence supporting this proposition. As we have discussed earlier, the business case for equality and diversity is contingent upon a number of contextual variables, which in some circumstances may point managers away from equality and diversity practice. For example, in the long term a diverse workforce may improve service delivery, but in the short term managers may fear upsetting existing teams and customers by employing hitherto under-represented groups. As another example, Woodall et al.'s (1997) study finds that organizational restructuring has negative implications for equality programmes, because of the added pressures line managers are placed under during and after a period of change.

However, even in the absence of evidence to support the proposition that a transfer of responsibility to line managers engenders a sense of ownership of equality and diversity policy, it remains an important goal, because of the central role supervisors and line managers play in day-to-day implementation. For example, in recruitment and selection the processes are replete with opportunities for decision-makers or gate-keepers to assert bias and prejudice, whether consciously or uncon-sciously, and thereby to perpetuate the very myths and stereotypes that EOPs seek to challenge. Indeed, Noon's (1993) innovative study involv-ing speculative application by two bogus candidates, Evans and Patel, to the UK's top 100 companies, revealed that companies with no EOP were more likely to practise blatant discrimination, but that even companies with an EOP did treat the white candidate more favourably. A recent employment tribunal case involving Marks & Spencer plc found that an applicant was discriminated against on the grounds of her race, because the company's interviewers were guilty of bias. It was recognized that the company had made extensive efforts to implement its EOP, but that there remained an unrecognized climate of discrimination among middle management (EOR, 1998a). Hence, the utility of monitoring and auditing policy, procedures *and* practice discussed above and advocated by the CRE, EOC, trade unions and government.

Similarly, the processes by which individuals are selected for training and promotion also provide ample opportunity for bias and prejudice to guide decision-making, highly formalized procedures notwithstanding. Take, for example, performance appraisal, a process usually carried out by line managers and one which often opens the door to training and promotion opportunities, as well as to performance or merit pay. Despite the rhetoric that equality and diversity policy (Cameron, 1993) should be 'owned' by the people who are able to translate it into practice, there is abundant evidence that managers continue to make decisions on the basis of stereotypes, that they have a predilection for people in their own image and that they hold strongly sex-typed views of job requirements (Liff and Wacjman, 1996). Given that certain groups of employees are under-represented in management, namely women, minority ethnic people and disabled people, this has obvious worrying implications. The commonplace negative stereotyping of older workers and gay men and lesbians is also an issue here. Thus, the central problem is that there exists greater homogeneity among those conducting appraisal than among those being appraised. In the context of gender equality, Woodall et al. (1997) argue that it is doubtful whether line managers can be left with responsibility for managing women's careers. Similarly, the widespread negative stereotyping of disabled people would suggest that non-disabled managers cannot be left to manage disabled people's careers. This is highlighted in one survey where disabled respondents com-mented that they did not feel accepted by middle management as equal members of the workforce; that they seldom went on courses, while those who did were promoted (Bargaining Report, 1998). Another study (Cunningham and James, 1998) found line managers to be inflexible when dealing with cases of disability and that they generally viewed disabled people as a problem or burden.

What the above discussion highlights, is the potentially negative consequence of transferring responsibility for the implementation of equality or diversity policy to line managers, without finding some way of rewarding them for their commitment (Liff and Dale, 1994). It seems unlikely that line management will consent, let alone commit, to equality aims unless their own performance objectives are explicitly linked to equality objectives. One answer to this is to inject equality aims into managers' performance targets or appraisals. Some organizations have stressed the importance of top-level commitment, believing that equality or diversity 'champions' can act as catalysts of change (EOR, 1999a). Although this may well be a worthwhile aim, in itself it does not resolve the problem of how to embed equality policy within everyday organizational practice.

## Key learning points

1 Line managers play an important role in either challenging or reproducing inequalities. It is essential to consider how the commitment of line managers to equality and diversity goals can be won.
2 The under-representation in management of certain social groups – women and minority ethnic employees, for example – gives rise to greater homogeneity among managers than among those they manage. This is likely to be problematic for equality and diversity.

## Activity

### Activity 8.2: Equality award launched

A new award, which aims to recognize the contribution of individuals achieving significant equality breakthroughs in employment, has been launched by the Wainwright Trust. The Breakthrough award, which comprises a specially commissioned trophy together with £1000, will be first presented in 1999, and biennially thereafter. Examples of potentially award-winning initiatives include equal opportunity measures that really make a difference, through to a successful legal case that changes personnel practice.

Eligible people could include law centre workers, trade union officials, individuals who have won discrimination cases, line managers, employees or equal opportunities managers.

In June 1998 the second annual Wainwright Trust lecture was given by Baroness Valerie Amos. Her theme was ethics and equality at work. She argued that the 'business-case approach to the delivery of equality and social justice is insufficient, and that we need a radical rethink of equality strategies which goes beyond the diversity models and encapsulates the complexity of the relationship between societal change, globalization and organizational change'.

In particular, she explored the relevance of developments in current thinking around ethical issues, corporate governance and community responsibility, which is becoming integral to the values of many organizations. Amos saw the development of ethical policies in organizations as a key mechanism for moving equality issues from the margins into the mainstream.

*Source*: Edited extract from EOR (1998: 8).

*Questions*

1 What do you see as the value and utility of the creation of an 'equality award'? In what ways might the award influence organizational policy and practice?
2 What do you think Baroness Amos means when she argues that the business case approach and diversity models are inadequate?
3 Why might the development of ethical policies in organizations move equality issues into the mainstream?

# Conclusion

If we examine aggregate labour market data, what is clear is that patterns of inequality and disadvantage are unevenly spread across occupations and industries, but that overall, inequalities remain widespread and deeply embedded. However, we stated in the introduction to this chapter that our aim was not to examine the reality of equality or diversity within organizations, as that is a task beyond the scope of this book, but to look at policy approaches. We have done this by presenting a typology of equality organizations and proceeding to examine the content of equality policy within those organizations situated towards the proactive end of the continuum. At times, we have intentionally not distinguished between equality and diversity policy. This is because 'managing diversity' strategies are at an emergent stage and, within the UK context at least, can be said to represent a complementary or perhaps evolutionary development in equality policy, rather than a totally separate approach. Most of the initiatives placed by some organizations and writers under the banner of 'managing diversity' would not be out of place within a conventional EOP (Liff and Wajcman, 1996).

However, that is not to say that there are not conceptual and theoretical differences between 'managing diversity' and 'equal opportunities' as debated by the various writers cited in Chapter 5. Our focus in this chapter has been issues surrounding policy formulation and implementation, in other words, the practice of equality. The evidence suggests that diversity policy is usually grown from and on to equality policy. Further, organizations which have eschewed equality policy show no greater liking for diversity policy, thus there is no reason to suspect that 'negative', 'minimalist' or 'compliant' organizations will engage with a diversity paradigm any more strenuously than they have with an equality one (Cunningham and James, 1998). We have also discussed the emergence and rise to pre-eminence of business case arguments in justification of equality and diversity policy. Whilst some writers argue that when a link is forged between equality and commercial objectives, there is evidence of increased resources devoted to equality, as well as raised awareness of equality issues within the organization (Shapiro, 1999), others remain sceptical as to whether the business rationale alone can ever be powerful enough to effect fundamental change (Lewis, 1997). What is evident, is that line managers are structurally and strategically placed to either reinforce or challenge overt and covert forms of discrimination. However, what is also clear is that the 'multiple constraints and pressures' faced by line managers (Cockburn, 1991; Liff and Cameron, 1997: 41), which may lead to their failing to comply with or commit to equality and diversity objectives, must be recognized. Further, line managers' actions and behaviours in reinforcing and reproducing inequalities simply reflect the deeply embedded nature of prejudice, discrimination and disadvantage. Chapter 9 continues the discussion of development in the practice of personnel management in so far as it relates to equality and diversity, by examining in detail the central tenets of 'human resource management'.

# Review and discussion questions

1 How easy is it to distinguish between the equality/diversity policy levers associated with a social justice approach and those associated with a business case approach? Provide some examples.
2 Using your answer to Question 1, in what circumstances might a specific policy lever be justified or informed either by a social justice or by a business case approach, or by both? As an example, start with management training targeted at minority ethnic employees.
3 Discuss the extent to which the formalization of procedures can ever deliver equality of outcome.
4 Identify the possible uses for information gathered by an equality audit.

# Further reading

For a critical evaluation of equality and diversity policy and practice, this chapter draws predominantly on journal articles, rather than texts or edited collections of articles. We recommend the following text, but also signal with an asterisk (*) articles on the list of references which we highly recommend.

Collinson, D., Knights, D. and Collinson, M. (1990). *Managing to Discriminate*. Routledge.
    This text draws on in-depth studies of five employment sectors to offer rich insights into the informal processes, which give rise to the continuance of sex discrimination. Much of what the authors say can be seen to apply to the discrimination experienced by other social groups.

# References

Bargaining Report (1998). Long road to equal rights for disabled. *Bargaining Report*, **179**, January, 10–11.

Cameron, I. (1993). Formulating an equal opportunities policy. *Equal Opportunities Review*, (47), January–February, 16–20.

Cockburn, C. (1991). *In the Way of Women*. Macmillan.

Collinson, D., Knights, D. and Collinson, M. (1990). *Managing to Discriminate*. Routledge.

CRE (Commission for Racial Equality) (1995). *Racial Equality Means Business. Standard for Racial Equality for Employers*. CRE.

Cully, M., Woodland, S., O'Reilly, A. and Dix, G. (1999). *Britain at Work*. Routledge.

Cunningham, I. and James, P. (1998). The Disability Discrimination Act: an early response of employers. *Industrial Relations Journal*, **29**, (4), 304–315.

Dickens, L. (1994). The business case for women's equality. Is the carrot better than the stick? *Employee Relations*, **16**, (8), 5–18.

*Dickens, L. (1999). Beyond the business case: a three-pronged approach to equality action. *Human Resource Management Journal*, **9**, (1), 9–19.

Edwards, J. (1995). *When Race Counts. The Morality of Racial Preference in Britain and America*. Routledge.

EOR (Equal Opportunities Review) (1995). Race for Opportunity: a business campaign for ethnic minorities. *Equal Opportunities Review*, (64), November–December, 24–31.

EOR (Equal Opportunities Review) (1996). Women in the Post Office. *Equal Opportunities Review*, (66), March–April, 13–19.

EOR (Equal Opportunities Review) (1997). Devolution hinders EO in private sector. *Equal Opportunities Review*, (74), July–August, 6–7.

EOR (Equal Opportunities Review) (1998a). Effect of bias by interviewers. *Equal Opportunities Review*, (79), May–June, 48–50.

EOR (Equal Opportunities Review) (1998b). Achieving the winning edge: Opportunity 2000 awards. *Equal Opportunities Review*, (80), July–August, 24–31.

EOR (Equal Opportunities Review) (1999a). BT: championing women in a man's world. *Equal Opportunities Review*, (84), March–April, 14–20.

EOR (Equal Opportunities Review) (1999b). Improving recruitment and promotion opportunities for ethnic minorities. *Equal Opportunities Review*, (85), May–June, 15–20.

Gibbon, P. (1990). Equal opportunities policy and race equality. In *Racism and Anti-Racism: Inequalities, Opportunities and Policies* (P. Braham, A. Rattansi and R. Skellington, eds) (1992). Sage.

Healy, G. (1993). Business and discrimination. In *Strategic Thinking and the Management of Change* (R. Stacey, ed.). Kogan Page.

Iles, P. and Auluck, R. (1989). From racism awareness training to strategic human resource management in implementing equal opportunity. *Personnel Review*, **18**, (4), 24–31.

IPD (Institute of Personnel and Development) (undated) *Managing Diversity. An IPD Position Paper*. IPD.

Lean Lim, L. (1996). *More and Better Jobs for Women: An Action Guide.* International Labour Office.

Lewis, S. (1997). Family friendly employment policies: a route to changing organizational culture or playing about at the margins? *Gender, Work and Organization,* **4**, (1), 13–23.

Liff, S. (1995). Equal opportunities: continuing discrimination in a context of formal equality. In *Industrial Relations* (P. Edwards, ed.). Blackwell.

Liff, S. (1996). Two routes to managing diversity: individual differences or social group characteristics. *Employee Relations,* **19**, (1), 11–26.

*Liff, S. (1999). Diversity and equal opportunities: room for a constructive compromise? *Human Resource Management Journal,* **9**, (1), 65–75.

*Liff, S. and Cameron, I. (1997). Changing equality cultures to move beyond 'women's problems. *Gender, Work and Organization,* **4**, (1), 35–46.

Liff, S. and Dale, K. (1994). Formal opportunity, informal barriers: black women managers within a local authority. *Work, Employment and Society,* **8**, (2), 177–198.

Liff, S. and Wacjman, J. (1996). 'Sameness' and 'difference' revisited: which way forward for equal opportunity initiatives? *Journal of Management Studies,* **33**, (1), 79–94.

*Noon, M. (1993). Racial discrimination in speculative application: evidence from the UK's top 100 firms. *Human Resource Management Journal,* **3**, (4), 35–47.

Prickett, R. (1998). EU permits discrimination against lesbian employee. *People Management,* 5 March.

Shapiro, G. (1999). Quality and equality: building a virtuous circle. *Human Resource Management Journal,* **9**, (1), 76–86.

*Woodall, J., Edwards, C. and Welchman, R. (1997). Organizational restructuring and the achievement of an equal opportunity culture. *Gender, Work and Organization,* **4**, (1), 2–12.

Wright, M. and Storey, J. (1994). Recruitment. In *HRM: A Contemporary Perspective* (I. Beardwell and L. Holden, eds). Pitman.

# Chapter 9
# Human resource management and the equality project

## Aim

To provide an evaluation of human resource management in terms of what it means for policy and practice in the field of equality and diversity.

## Objectives

- To outline why a focus of human resource management is salient to the discussion of equality and diversity approaches.
- To present the main normative models of, and theorizing around, human resource management, looking at what potential advances are offered for the equality agenda within organizations.
- To appraise critically human resource management as a force which can advance the equality project, looking in more detail at specific policy areas.

## Introduction

It is certain that human resource management is one of the most popular management concepts of the 1990s; evidenced by the proliferation of texts bearing the title, and university and management training courses on the subject. However, equality and diversity issues are often absent from the debate, where the theory, policy and practice of HRM tend to assume the 'generic' universal employee. This gap is significant in that looking at HRM is relevant to the study of equality initiatives, first, as the human resource function (personnel/industrial officers and managers) is most likely to hold the main responsibility for the people planning within an organization. There are, however, interesting debates about the extent to which the human resource function is the main driver of progressive change regarding equity issues (Cattaneo, Reavley and Templer, 1994; Cockburn, 1991; or the counter opinion in Gooch and Ledwith, 1996).

Second, many writers agree that there is considerable 'fit' between more recent developments in managerial practice, in particular, HRM and diversity approaches to equality. Indeed, Miller (1996: 206) states that 'Managing diversity can arguably be classed as the HRM approach to equality initiatives in the workplace'. In the *Personnel Journal*'s end of year summary of the '100 toughest challenges facing human resource practitioners' for 1995, diversity appears high on the list (Flynn, 1995: 63). Similarly, in the same year, the recipient of the Society for Human Resource Management Award for Professional Excellence, considers 'diversity as the most important issue in human resources and believes that organizations who neglect diversity will have trouble succeeding in the future'(Thornburg, 1995: 48). Thus the move to 'difference' and diversity approaches to equality matches a move in thought about human resources practice and policy. Webb also points to this sense of 'fit', seeing the move to 'managing diversity' as capturing 'the wider political shift from collective models of industrial relations, state regulation and associated bureaucratic control procedures to deregulation, free market competition and notions of human resource management based on maximizing the contribution of the individual'(Webb, 1997: 164) (There is a large debate dealing with the differences between HRM and personnel management and whether or not HRM can be defined as different to personnel management. See Guest, 1987, for a summary.)

Thus the scene is set for a discussion of what HRM offers the equality project. This chapter begins by briefly presenting the most widely known normative models of HRM. An extensive discussion of HRM will not be presented here as it is out of the remit of the subject matter, however a brief overview is necessary. This is in order to highlight the similarities between HRM and managing diversity (MD) approaches, and to be able critically to appraise HRM as a force for advancing the equality agenda. (We have indicated in the 'Further reading' section of this chapter some key texts offering a more extensive presentation of HRM.) Specific policy areas of HRM will also be analysed in more detail, drawing on Guest's (1987) argument, in order to frame an analysis around some specific dimensions of the HRM approach. Potential advantages and benefits for equality in the workplace will be discussed, as will a critique of the HRM approach, pointing to weaknesses of theory and practice in advancing the position of disadvantaged groups of workers.

# An exploration of HRM

Like the MD approach, HRM originated in the USA, building on theories of motivation and human behaviour (Guest, 1987). The overall approach is a move away from general management theories prescribing policies and styles that should be applied to all employees. Human resource management is predicated on the notion that some workers will seek out and respond to work environments that provide challenging work, levels of autonomy and opportunities for learning and training. Thus, HRM is based on the assumption that managers need to foster this kind of motivation within the workplace through management style or by careful recruitment and selection (Guest, 1987: 511).

Human resource management is also essentially based around a 'business case' approach as discussed in Chapter 8. Increased competition in national and global arenas forced managers to reconsider the management of all resources within the organization. While old approaches to managing people were based on bureaucratic power structures, money-based incentives and Taylorist-style work organization, HRM emphasizes the role of the individual, motivated worker, focusing on fostering a sense of involvement in, and commitment to, the organization. This is felt to lead to increased productivity and more success in meeting organizational objectives, thus making the organization more competitive through effective management of the human resource (Guest, 1987; Storey, 1989, 1992). The link between this and the business case for valuing diversity is obvious. Examples include, looking at the benefits to be derived from making people feel comfortable and motivated at work so that they can be more effective (Copeland, 1988); the competitive advantage to be derived from mixed work teams, drawing on a diverse range of skills and viewpoints and understanding a wider range of customer needs (Greenslade, 1991); the need to manage cross-cultural teams in international settings within multinational companies (Iles and Kaur-Hayers, 1997). All this fits into the remit of the human resource function and the need for effective people planning.

## A normative model and its link to equality

Defining HRM is not an easy task. As Hollinshead and Leat (1995: xi) acknowledge, 'HRM is a term shrouded by rhetoric ... [there is] a general paucity of analysis to examine what the term actually means, whether it has real applicability at workplace level and whether the assumptions underlying it bear up to close scrutiny'. However, perhaps a good starting point is what has been widely viewed as the 'original' conception of HRM from Michael Beer and his colleagues at the Harvard Business School in the early 1980s. At the centre is the view that the human resource should be viewed as being as important to the success of the business as any other resource (product, marketing etc.). Therefore, effective management of human resources was directly linked to corporate success. Beer et al. (1984) place an emphasis on personnel policies such as employee influence, human resource flow, reward systems and work systems. All these policies should be designed to promote the development of flexible, adaptable and highly committed employees. Perhaps most significant, from equality and diversity perspectives, is the emphasis on the need for human resource policies to be integrated within the overall organizational strategy. This has echoes of the mainstreaming approach to equality, except that here it is a concern for the human resource, which should be mainstreamed throughout all policy decisions.

A concern for equality is an explicit element of this concern with the human resource. Beer et al. (1984) point to the positive long-term consequences that HRM could have for individuals and for society. Managers are advised to track the long-term trends in the labour market which will indicate potential opportunities and difficulties in the acquisition of skills in the future. As part of this, equality issues are highlighted and managers are advised to take account of the increased participation of women and minority ethnic groups in the labour force, as well as an ageing population. In addition, managers should recognize the changing values and aspirations of the workforce through education and training that makes employees more resistant to arbitrary authority (Beer et al., 1984: 31). While the primacy of the manager is clearly evoked in this conception of HRM, it also explicitly recognizes stakeholder interests, potentially offering space for equality issues to arise. In other words, management needs to mobilize the support of various stakeholders including, shareholders, employees, unions, the government and community groups.

There are other features of HRM that the MD approach shares. Most significant of these for discussion later in this chapter, is the individualistic focus of HRM. The onus of policies within HRM is directed towards the individual employee, a harnessing of individual commitment and talents, rather than seeing employees as part of a collective (either trade unions or social group membership). Consequently, HRM has commonly been viewed as denying a role for trade unions and, indeed, exemplars of HRM practice have commonly been non-union firms such as Marks & Spencer and IBM (Turnbull and Wass, 1997). Human resource management certainly has been viewed as a threat by many trade unions and has been linked to policies that aim to marginalize the place of trade unions within organizational processes. This matches the individualistic focus of diversity approaches to equality initiatives discussed in Chapter 5.

Second, as with the managing diversity approach to equality, HRM highlights the supremacy of management in initiating action and mobilising support for policies. Indeed Dale (1998) states that a specific parallel can be drawn between MD and HRM here, where HRM is regarded as the discovery of personnel management by chief executives and MD is regarded as the capturing of the territory of equal opportunities by managers. The concept of leadership from the management level is key in many MD textbooks and practitioner guides (see Kandola and Fullerton, 1994).

Many similarities exist between HRM and the MD approach to equality. Characteristics integral to MD echo those of some versions of HRM, notably the strategic integration of people as a resource to be managed towards the achievement of business goals, and the valuing of the growth in the diversity of the workforce as a direct contribution to the success of an organization. The HRM emphasis on the role of the individual and his or her involvement and commitment also has resonance with 'diversity' approaches to equality.

## 'Hard' and 'soft' versions of HRM

Another feature of HRM that should be discussed is the existence of 'hard' and 'soft' models (see Storey, 1992). Beer et al.'s model is widely regarded as 'soft' HRM, where employees are seen as valued assets. Here, human resources policies are directed towards skill development and high levels of commitment, adaptability and competence (Hollinshead, Nicholls and Tailby, 1999). It is perhaps in this version that there is most potential for equality initiatives. However, at the time Beer et al.'s model was published, so too was a different version (Frombrun, Tichy and Devanna, 1984) that has been characterized as 'hard' HRM. Here, principles of cost-effectiveness hold primacy and the human resource system is seen as a business expense like any other organizational resource. Human resources policies are primarily directed towards meeting organizational objectives rather than the development of employees (see Storey, 1992, for a more extensive discussion). As will be discussed in greater detail later, there is some parallel here between 'short' and 'long' agendas of equality initiatives, where 'hard' HRM would be viewed as following a 'short agenda'. Truss et al. (1997) point out that this distinction between 'hard' and 'soft' HRM has led to a paradoxical situation where the term HRM is used to signal diametrically opposed sets of assumptions. Additionally, as will be presented below when looking at Guest's (1987) model, elements of both 'hard' and 'soft' HRM are present in the same model. Referring back, this is also obvious within Beer et al.'s model where there is simultaneously a concern for valuing the individual employee, as well as objectives of cost-effectiveness and adapting to market conditions.

**Key learning points**

1 Human resource management is based on the premise that paying considerable attention to the human resource aspects within an organization, and making use of appropriate personnel policies to engender increased commitment and satisfaction of employees at work would be directly linked to competitive advantage.

2 There are significant links between HRM and approaches to equality and diversity. These include: the link between the need for human resource policies to be integrated within the overall business strategy and 'mainstreaming' approaches to equality; the need to mobilize the support of diverse stakeholders within an organization to be successful using MD approaches; the individualistic focus of HRM and MD.

3 A distinction has been made between 'hard' and 'soft' forms of HRM. It is the 'soft' versions which seem to offer the most potential for equality, with their focus on employees as valued assets and the premium placed on engendering high levels of employee commitment.

# Analysis of Guest's four dimensions of HRM: barriers to and opportunities for equality

Guest's (1987) article provides a useful summary of the evolution of HRM and its relevance to the British context. The article also outlines the framework of a theory of HRM aiming to develop a set of testable propositions and arrive at a set of prescriptive policies (Guest, 1987: 510). The relevance of outlining the main dimensions of this theory is that it provides a useful way of tapping into the constituent parts of an HRM approach, allowing us to appraise each dimension with reference to its utility for gaining greater equality in the workplace. The overlap between these dimensions and the characteristics of the Harvard model (Beer et al., 1984) will be apparent. Guest (1987) views HRM as encompassing four main dimensions or goals: strategic integration, employee commitment, flexibility and quality.

## Strategic integration

The argument is that a corporate strategy is essential for continuing business success. Within this, the human resources dimension must be fully integrated into the strategic planning process (one could see this as a form of mainstreaming as discussed earlier). There is a need for both vertical integration (of human resources with other strategic concerns, for example, sales, production and so on) and horizontal integration (ensuring that the human resources policies form a coherent entity, for example, that selection and training policies complement each other). Additionally, there should be integration of the human resources strategy into the responsibilities of line managers (again ensuring that the issue is 'mainstreamed'). Finally, employees should be integrated within the business by fostering a sense of company identity.

It is clear that an attempt to make effective management of human resources a concern throughout the organization appears to offer potential benefits to the pursuit of equality. At least employees are recognized as an important asset to the organization, which should be nurtured. Indeed, despite her overall pessimism with regard to the ability of new managerial approaches to deliver equality, Webb (1997: 167) points to the fact that there is at least now a better understanding of what is needed for the process of effective organizational change with regard to equality (even if the evidence for successful organizational change in these terms is limited). This includes the need for commitment and resources at senior levels of an organization (where strategy is likely to be formulated) and the need for regular monitoring of progress (a key feature of the ideal 'managing diversity' approach – see Kandola and Fullerton, 1994).

However, there are critiques of this dimension, particularly involving a debate about the possibility of 'strategically integrating' human resources issues into overall business strategy. There is little point debating the potential for equality, of a strategically integrated human resources policy if this strategic integration cannot occur in the first place. The initial criticism concerns the assumption that managers can be rational and strategic. Many of the prescriptions of HRM rest on strong free-market based assumptions where management has the key role in initiating action and mobilizing support. Within the normative HRM model, there is an emphasis on the need to change or manipulate corporate cultures. Thus some of the debates within the corporate culture literature (see Deal and Kennedy, 1982; Thompson and McHugh, 1990) are relevant here. Within this literature (and connecting to HRM models), it becomes the role of the idealized 'symbolic manager' to take the lead in shaping the culture.

However, there is much discussion about whether or not managers are able to be 'strategic'. The general picture is that there is great diversity in managerial activities and that much of managerial work is reactive (Hales, 1986). Thus the notion of the manager as primarily a strategist may be misconceived. Managers often have a varied and opportunistic approach because individual managers have different access to information and resources, due to the nature of organizational hierarchies or routine practices. Thus, individual managers are often limited in their ability to make strategic decisions.

Managers are also not a homogeneous group and may be very divided across functional, spatial or hierarchical lines. Armstrong (1986) states that managerial control originates with the techniques and knowledge possessed by professional groups in competition for key positions and resources within the organization. Different managerial professions (for example, accountants, personnel/human resource specialists) thus aim to maintain their positions of influence by retaining a monopoly of, and excluding others from, such techniques and knowledge. For example, an implicit part of the strategic integration or 'mainstreaming' of human resources issues within HRM, is the fact that personnel/human resource specialists should 'give away' some of their power and responsibility as professionals to other management functions. Guest (1987: 519) discusses the difficulty of managers accepting such an abdication of responsibility. Thus issues of interprofessional competition may prove to be obstacles to the strategic integration of human resource issues within the organization, even if managers are able to act strategically in the first place.

An associated problem again rests with the view of the supremacy of the management function in HRM. This view of the supremacy of management appears contradictory to the simultaneously held view within HRM theory, of the importance of other stakeholder interests, as discussed above. Hollinshead and Leat point out that often the stakeholder interest of, for example, employees, is focused on the need for forms of employee participation in order to gain increased commitment, not in order to allow any real sharing of decision-making (Hollinshead and Leat, 1995: 22; see also Guest, 1987). Thus, what standing do the different stakeholders have?

Another debate relates to the contingent nature of that strategic integration, linking to discussions above about interprofessional competition among managers. The effectiveness of this integration depends on the place of the human resource function within the organization, which often does not hold a priority place in comparison, for example, to marketing, production, finance or sales (Cattaneo, Reavley and Templer, 1994). Gooch and Ledwith (1996) provide a detailed analysis of the way in which equality issues become constrained and controlled when they are anchored within the powerless personnel or human resources function. Cattaneo et al. have identified four different levels of strategic integration depending on the place held by the human resource function. (For a similar conceptualization, see Legge's [1995: 96] presentation of three dimensions of strategic integration). First, an *ad hoc* strategy, where the human resources function holds a place of low prestige. Here, any gains for equality rely on committed individuals who make a concerted effort to ensure that equality remains on the organizational agenda, even if the structures and systems are not encouraging.

The 'traditional' strategy relies solely on the business case argument, where the pursuit of equality initiatives derives from defensive responses to external pressures (for example, legislation, market competition). It involves mainly a 'numbers game' objective, where the aim is to increase the amount of employees from traditionally disadvantaged groups in the organization. The 'results-oriented' strategy is also related to the business case, and is similar to a 'hard' HRM philosophy, where the bottom line concerns of profit remain in primacy. Both of these last two forms of strategic integration are limited in their ability to deliver greater equality, in that they ultimately defend the status quo and do not challenge the existing organizational culture (which has been discussed as a factor perpetuating segregation and discrimination in Chapters 4 and 5).

The final form, the 'transformational' strategy relates more to the ideal of strategic integration within the HRM model, where equality is seen as a strategic imperative in its own right and where equality issues form part of a continual development of, challenge to and adaptation of, organizational culture and processes. Thus one can identify 'short' (*ad hoc*, traditional and results-oriented strategies) and 'long' (transformational strategies) agendas of strategic integration in much the same way as have been distinguished in equal opportunities and managing diversity initiatives (Cockburn, 1991; Rees, 1998).

However, regardless of the place that the human resource or personnel function has within the organizational strategy and structures, this may not be enough to lead to progressive equality advances. Bearing in mind the vertical and horizontal occupational segregation that exists in the wider labour market, there is recognition of the particular gendered and racialized nature of personnel management as a profession (Gooch and Ledwith, 1996). The gender and race politics of the personnel profession itself has consequences.

# Commitment

Linked to the need to integrate employees into the organization is the concern with developing in individual employees a feeling of commitment to the organization. The assumption is that committed employees will be more satisfied, more productive and more adaptable, thus leading to more successful organizational performance (Guest 1987, 513). Beer et al. (1985: 20) comment that commitment is important, leading to 'more loyalty and better performance for the organization ... self-worth, dignity, psychological involvement, and identity for the individual'. This last comment thus has resonance with managing diversity approaches, with the emphasis on the need to nurture the individual worker and focus on job design and intrinsic conditions of work which will allow the individual to be more satisfied with their work.

One could hypothesize how equality issues would fit in here, where a need to allow the individual to feel 'included' in the organization is emphasized. This would have implications in terms of the need to ensure that individual (and differing) needs are taken into account, that unfair discrimination is challenged, and employees have equal opportunities in terms of pay, promotion and training. This points to a range of possible policies including careful selection, job design and management of organizational culture (Guest, 1987: 514). The focus on commitment to the organization also links to 'difference'/diversity approaches to equality with their individualistic ethos where commitment to other social groups, for example class, trade union, gender or ethnicity is de-emphasized.

The first problem with this tenet of the HRM model involves the definition of the concept of commitment. Guest (1987: 513) presents the differing forms of commitment which have been identified, for example, is commitment behavioural (demonstrated through public statements and action) or attitudinal (issues of identity, sharing goals and values and desire to maintain membership)? In addition, HRM focuses primarily on organizational commitment; however, the issue of commitment is likely to be far more complex. There are many other 'commitments' which might play a part within an organizational context, for example, career, job, union, social group. What are the equality implications of prioritizing organizational commitment? One implication is that such a view underestimates the complexity of competing commitments and loyalties within organizations. Human resource management is essentially a unitarist viewpoint (see Edwards, 1995, for a general discussion). Thus, conflicts and competing interests are seen as deviant, rather than accepted as inevitable (consistent with a pluralistic viewpoint). This appears to give a negative tenor to individual employees' differing identities and loyalties rather than 'valuing' differences, which would be consistent with the ideal 'managing diversity' approach. One could anticipate that other loyalties and responsibilities (such as to domestic responsibilities) would not be accommodated and valued if they were seen to conflict with organizational objectives and goals. Thus, one is drawn back once again to the view that only those people who could meet the dominant norm (white, male, full-time, unencumbered employee) would benefit from the focus on commitment within HRM.

Commitment within HRM is also essentially individualistic. It involves commitment between the individual employee and the organization. This has implications for equality issues, looking at the importance of collective action. A unitarist approach has little room for trade unions and indeed HRM has been discussed by many as involving an implicit attack on the place of trade unions within organizations. As discussed earlier, the so-called exemplars of HRM have been firms without union recognition. In comparison, Colling and Dickens (1998) point to the importance of collective bargaining in maintaining a focus on equal opportunities within organizations. They discuss how the equality agenda declined in the firm they studied, when new market imperatives led to restructuring which marginalized the role of the union and narrowed the collective bargaining agenda. The equality agenda is edged out and marginalized, with a move from joint equality bargaining to managerial prerogative.

In addition, the problems associated with the individualistic focus of the 'managing diversity' approach are also applicable to an individualistic focus of HRM. A move towards individual commitment to the organization weakens the ties that people have through common experience. This has negative implications, denying the similarity between people's experiences in the workplace and the importance of the collective, in emphasizing the individual. Thus within HRM practice: 'the position of individual employees is in fact quite precarious, with a high degree of dependency on the benevolence of employers' (Hollinshead and Leat, 1995: 24).

## Flexibility

The ability of managers to implement the (integrated) strategic plan requires a capacity to adapt and respond to pressures from both inside and outside the organization. Thus the organization must avoid rigid bureaucratic structures and, more significantly for a discussion of equality issues, must avoid the development of powerful interest groups which might lead to divisions and demarcations between groups of employees (Guest, 1987: 514). There is also a requirement for employees to be both numerically flexible (hours of work) and functionally flexible (types of task) so that a multiskilled workforce can be developed which can adapt and respond to changes in production and demand and, therefore, gain the competitive edge (Geary, 1992; Horstman, 1988; Walsh, 1990). Thus within the business case for HRM, one of the solutions to the challenges facing organizations lies in the flexibility and adaptability of labour (Pollert, 1988). There is coherence within the dimensions of HRM, for example, a functionally flexible workforce links to commitment, where the employee identifies with the organization rather than their craft or work group (and subsequently their trade union, traditionally built on craft demarcations).

The move towards flexibility initiatives need not necessarily be negative from an equality perspective and, indeed, holds potential benefits for promoting equality in the workplace (Dickens, 1997). For example, acceptance and encouragement of more flexible working arrangements could be a challenge to the dominant norm of the full-time employee, able to work unlimited hours if necessary. This would potentially have particular advantages for women, facilitating women's integration into the labour market (Dickens, 1997: 283). Widespread encouragement of numerical flexibility could allow a reconceptualization of what is seen as 'standard' working time, avoiding the negative categorization of part-time and temporary workers (predominantly women and minority ethnic workers) as 'atypical' or 'non-standard'. This reconceptualization might then bring about a more equal distribution of paid and unpaid labour between men and women, and ending the pay and status differential between full-time and part-time work. Encouragement of functional flexibility could potentially challenge the existing job segregation, where job territories are racialized and gendered.

The opportunities for beneficial equality outcomes from flexibility policies do not appear to have been taken. Indeed, much research indicates the adverse implications of flexibility policies on equality in the labour market (Dickens, 1997; EOR, 1996; Purcell, 1997; Walby, 1997). Numerical flexibility has not been used as an equality measure, but conversely part-time work has been increasingly 'ghettoized' as low-paid, low-grade jobs, further perpetuating the divided, gendered and racialized labour market (Dickens, 1997: 284). Inequality in terms of pay, employment rights and opportunities for promotion and training are seen as the price which women and minority ethnic workers are expected to pay for flexible jobs. Even the trend for 'family friendly' policies has not attempted to challenge the existing predominance of childcare as a female responsibility. While the 'family-friendly' lobby stresses that the issues are of concern to all employees, the evidence of the introduction and implementation of such policies suggests that this is still seen as a woman's issue (Purcell, 1997).

Thus flexible working tends to operate to the disadvantage of the women and men employed on this basis, evidenced by poorer pay and conditions, and limited access to training and promotion (EOR, 1996). In addition, this is flexibility on employers' terms, with numerical flexibility encouraged to meet employers'/organizational needs. Thus, the situation is 'flexibility *by* workers to suit operational needs, and not flexibility *for* workers or families' (Dickens, 1997: 284). Again, there has not been a transformational approach involved with this part of HRM policy, the status quo of the segregated labour market remains. As Walby (1997: 74) similarly comments, 'the strategy of numerical flexibility . . . is one which provides employment opportunities . . . albeit under worse conditions of service'.

With regard to the experience of functional flexibility, most of the evidence points to approaches centred on job enlargement and work intensification, rather than the multiskilling which would potentially have broken down traditional gendered and racialized demarcations. While the erosion of demarcations is of importance to managers (particularly those which might encourage employee solidarity or trade union resistance), multiskilling has not necessarily been a key issue (Tomoney, 1990). The qualitative benefits of training are often secondary to meeting organizational objectives, thus offering higher wages to gain skilled workers might be preferred to training up existing employees (Atkinson, 1986). Most so-called multiskilling initiatives have involved the addition of lower level tasks (such as cleaning the area) rather than upskilling (Pollert, 1988). Where attempts have been made to break down traditional craft demarcations, the focus has been on breaking down segregation *within* rather than *across* boundaries (Dickens, 1997: 284).

Atkinson's (1986) model of the 'flexible firm' identifies the implications of flexibility policies in the perpetuation of a segregated labour market. This model identifies a core group of full-time, functionally flexible employees, while managers will also actively pursue a policy of developing peripheral groups of numerically flexible employees who will have a more precarious and disposable status. It certainly appears that this differentiation matches the division within the labour market, where the core workforce would be predominantly white and male, and where the peripheral workforce would account for many of those workers seen as facing disadvantage in the labour market. Walby (1997) concludes that if employers are seeking to increase numerical flexibility, the evidence indicates that they are likely to create categories of employment which will be filled by less protected workers. Within this, critics of Atkinson's flexible firm have observed that the tendency has been towards increasing the use of the peripheral workforce rather than on nurturing the development of the core.

This is because flexibility polices can be seen to sidestep equality issues and rights embedded in equality legislation, by increasingly employing workers on contracts which do not qualify for state-backed protection, a practice which enforces less job security on those workers who fall outside the protection of the legislation. Chapter 6 discussed the role of the recent legislation, which seeks to address this problem and extend employment rights to those workers with flexible hours. However, the importance here is that abundant evidence indicates that much HRM practice does not use flexibility in a way that promotes equality. Thus there is a need for regulation by this more recent legislation, as is clearly demonstrated by the fact that survey evidence indicates that the encouragement of flexibility by employers tends to reflect business requirements rather than being motivated by the need to promote equality. The most important reasons for having flexible working arrangements include being able to respond to variations in trade, to reduce labour costs and new developments in technology. Only a few organizations mention equality issues as factors in moving towards increased flexibility (EOR, 1996). The focus on the need to move towards a flexible workforce to reduce labour costs supports Walby's (1997) assertions of the way in which employers attempt to avoid having to pay the costs involved with statutory employment rights.

## Quality

Quality here refers to quality of employees, quality of performance and quality of human resource policies. It thus brings together many interrelated elements and connects the other three tenets of Guest's model. The emphasis is on the fact that considerable attention should be placed on recruitment, selection, rewards, training, appraisal and goal-setting so that high-quality staff are attracted and retained (Guest, 1987: 515). High-quality staff in HRM terms involves those who are committed to the organization and therefore are strategically integrated, and those who are flexible and adaptable. In assessing the role that such an approach can play in promoting equality, arguments discussed earlier can be reiterated; for example, the potential benefits to come from recognition that employees are an important resource which should be developed and nurtured. Consequently, if the organization has a reputation for high-quality treatment of the workforce, this will have potential implications in terms of future recruitment of staff and may impact upon customer choice. This relates to the business case for HRM and the ways in which a focus on developing and retaining quality staff can aid organizational competitiveness.

However, while the benefits of attracting and retaining 'quality' staff seem unquestionable, there are problems with the theory and practice of attention to quality within HRM. We refer back to a statement made earlier about the evolution of HRM: that HRM is predicated on the notion that some workers will seek out and respond to work environments that provide challenging work, levels of autonomy and opportunities for learning and training. Inherent to this statement is a desire to recruit a particular 'quality' of employee. The free market assumptions underlying HRM assume that this 'kind' of employee will actively seek out such jobs or will be attracted by a particular kind of recruitment or advertisement for work. However, HRM is insular in that many of the policies and initiatives relate to dealing with issues internal to an organization; thus, if there are to be any equality benefits from HRM, it will tend to affect those already within the organization. Thus in similarity to the critics of the 'managing diversity' approach, HRM will only help those within an organization rather than seek to challenge disadvantage outside of the workplace (Miller, 1996).

The significant point is that HRM policies often ignore the wider societal structures and systems that perpetuate disadvantage in the labour market (discussed in Chapters 3, 4 and 5). First, that the gendered, aged, sexualized and racialized roles within the labour market, reflect segregated roles in wider society. We have already discussed the ways in which people are 'socialized' into segregated roles seen as appropriate. Thus, for example, HRM initiatives may not benefit all workers. Indeed, there is evidence of a class or sectoral divide here, with studies indicating resistance to so-called enriched jobs (multiskilled, increased autonomy) because they often mean extra work without increased pay and the addition of unwanted extra responsibility (Corbett, 1994; Maher, 1971; McKenna, 1987). The belief that all workers want an enriched job (of the HRM 'quality' type) makes generalized assumptions about personal characteristics and motivation, which are viewed as invariant across people. In addition, such a view ignores the fact that people's choices are constrained by the existence of socialized roles and responsibilities such that, for example, women's choice of part-time jobs derives from time management concerns to fit work around childcare responsibilities

(Scheibl, 1996). Similarly the human capital debates around people's preferences within work can be discussed.

Second, the statement that 'quality' employees will seek out 'quality' jobs and will be attracted by 'quality' human resource practices belies this insular view of disadvantage in the labour market. It may not be a question so much of whether people *seek* out or are *attracted by* 'quality' jobs, but more whether traditionally disadvantaged workers will *get* those kind of 'quality' jobs if they do seek them out. This relates back to discussions in Chapters 5 and 6 about the stereotypes of 'acceptability' criteria which still characterize recruitment and selection. Organizations and wider societal values continue to be gendered, sexualized and racialized. Therefore, we argue that it is those people who can most easily meet the dominant norm of the full-time, under forty, white, male, able-bodied employee who will benefit most from HRM policies within this framework. The four elements of Guest's model do not sit well together. If, as Truss et al. (1997) assert, 'hard' and 'soft' forms of HRM derive from diametrically opposed approaches, the 'soft' quality and commitment aspects do not seem to coexist well with the 'hard' strategic and flexibility aspects within Guest's model. They appear to be competing and contradictory aims.

## Key learning points

1 The main dimensions of HRM summarized by Guest (1987) involve strategic integration, commitment, flexibility and quality. These dimensions offer potential advances for equality in the workplace but also forces obstructing the advance of equality.

2 Potential benefits include the need to mainstream human resource issues within organizational strategy. However, such benefits are obstructed by competing demands on managers, issues of interprofessional competition, and the status of the human resource function.

3 The emphasis placed on highly committed, satisfied and motivated employees has resonance with equality. However, potential benefits are often prevented from being realized owing to competing commitments which lessen the success of HRM initiatives, and the individualistic nature of commitment expected within HRM.

4 Flexibility policies within HRM offer opportunities to make real challenges to the segmentation of the workforce, however, the practice of functional and numerical flexibility tends to be more detrimental to many groups of workers.

5 Human resource management policies, in their focus on the organizational level, often ignore the wider societal systems and structures that perpetuate disadvantage.

# Additional weaknesses of HRM models

## Lack of evidence

Any potential benefits that HRM may seem to offer at least in theory for promotion of equality, seem undermined by the lack of evidence that distinctive HRM even exists within organizational practice (Guest, 1987; Hollinshead and Leat, 1995; Legge, 1989). Research supporting the claims of HRM (in similarity to that of 'managing diversity') is scarce and largely anecdotal, with much of the evidence stating that successful firms do practise many features of HRM, coming from case studies of 'excellent' companies. These firms are usually foreign owned and on greenfield sites, and are not perhaps considered to be typical of British firms. Evidence indicates that while the rhetoric of HRM is often 'soft' (which would have most potential for the promotion of equality), the more frequent 'reality' is of 'hard' HRM (Legge, 1989; Storey, 1989; Truss et al., 1997), beacuse 'hard' HRM is seen to fit more with the prerogatives of a business case approach.

## Dangers of the business case

This section extends from the discussions in Chapter 8. In line with the business case, many of the prescriptions which underlie Beer et al.'s model rest on strong free-market based assumptions, where firms need to be flexible and responsive to the market (Hollinshead and Leat, 1995). Human resource management policies should be designed and implemented around the existing situational factors. Thus the practice of HRM is contingent to the particular company or organization and the internal and external influences and challenges faced by that organization. As discussed previously with regard to flexibility, matching HRM policy to business strategy, calls predominantly for labour costs to be minimized rather than treating employees as a resource whose value may be enhanced by increasing their commitment, functional flexibility and quality (Legge, 1989). For example, in their eight case study firms, Truss et al. (1997) identified training policies that demonstrated the significant gap between HRM rhetoric and reality. Training was tailored to meet specific organizational objectives rather than to create a 'quality', multiskilled workforce. Training and development initiatives were seen as necessary investments in human capital only in so far as they improved the bottom-line competitive advantage. In none of the firms, did human resource concerns take precedence over other strategic business considerations. This relates to Catteneo, Reavley and Templer's (1994) assertions about the importance of the place of the human resources function within the organization discussed earlier.

Linked to the 'managing diversity' approach, the bias within the HRM paradigm is to put organizational needs before those of the disadvantaged employees and, therefore, under these terms the potential for

HRM to promote equality will be limited (Miller, 1996). Colling and Dickens (1998) point to the fact that the business case agenda for HRM emphasizes those areas of the equality agenda which are tackled most easily: cleaning up procedures and concentrating on external image, rather than the more difficult issues of access, power, low pay, part-time rights and so on. The business case offers maintenance of the status quo, with the emphasis on tailoring employees to the needs of the organization rather than the other way around. In addition, the business-case orientation of HRM leads to the practice that diversity is only valued if it leads to market advantage; there is no conception of a wider social justice concern for equality (Liff, 1996; Webb, 1997). There is a danger that relying solely on HRM as the force for equality could lead to informality that is likely to be to the detriment of equality goals. Human resource management is based on organizational contingencies, not a wider societal problem that needs to be regulated by law. Thus there are dangers here (as discussed in Chapter 5) if the formal liberal approaches to equality initiatives do not exist alongside the more informal organizational approaches.

The business case approach is also focused on the short term, particularly in the British context, whereas equality initiatives that aim for a transformation in organizational culture need a long-term viewpoint (Colling and Dickens, 1998). The contradictions within the model are indicated again as the focus on strategic integration within the HRM model has the rhetoric of a longer-term approach. The primacy of the business case focuses on more short-term organizational objectives and, therefore, will in practice only result in 'tinkering' and 'tailoring' approaches to equality (Rees, 1998) – the short, rather than the long agenda. This fits with the short-termist tradition of British business where the priority is often to satisfy performance and cost controls enforced by a corporate centre comprising investment trusts relying on short-term results (Guest, 1987).

Paradoxically therefore, the primacy of the business case within HRM can lead to the support of occupational segregation. For example, Biswas and Cassell (1996) investigated HRM initiatives within the hotel industry and located requirements for particular characteristics of staff as forming part of the business case within the arena of HRM strategy. Thus, the 'quality' of employees required from the business objectives encouraged the perpetuation of 'acceptability' stereotypes in recruitment, where, for example, 'attractive' women were seen as a necessary requirement of the role of receptionist. The equality implications of such a policy are clear for those 'faces which do not fit', be that a disabled, older, or minority ethnic worker.

Thus, HRM initiatives will tend to help only certain groups of traditionally disadvantaged workers from an equality perspective. For example, Miller (1996) usefully coins the phrase that the business case helps those at the 'glass ceiling' rather than those at the 'sticky floor'. In other words, the objective is based on a 'numbers game', increasing the proportion of certain types of worker (the short agenda) rather than seeking to challenge organizational and societal values (the long agenda) (Cockburn, 1989). The discussion above about flexibility focused on how this 'numbers game' could be seen to increase the number of numerically flexible and vulnerable workers without addressing equality issues. In addition, HRM has most to offer for those 'high fliers' at the top of the scale (for example, increasing the numbers of women and minority ethnic managers) rather than meeting the diverse needs of the wider workforce at all levels. For example, so-called 'family friendly' policies are often restricted to certain levels of the organization and, so, only benefit certain types of employee, perhaps those who are usually less disadvantaged to begin with (Colling and Dickens, 1998).

Such a concern can be effectively demonstrated by the development of the 'feminine-in-management' literature that links the HRM concern with the managerial role, and 'managing diversity' approaches which seek to value differences in pursuit of business effectiveness (Calas and Smircich, 1993; Rosener, 1990; Webb, 1997). The feminine-in-management thesis aims to emphasize that women's unique 'feminine skills' can make important contributions to organizational management in the new competitive and demanding external context. Such 'feminine' skills include those of communication and co-operation, interests in affiliation and attachment, and female views of power as transforming and liberating rather than controlling (Calas and Smircich, 1993). The theory then proceeds to state that such 'feminine' skills make women managers more 'suitable' for flexible, non-hierarchical structures, teamworking and high-trust employment relationships (fitting with the HRM goals of commitment and flexibility) (Rosener, 1990).

However, there are serious problems with such a thesis. Some of these relate to the discussion in Chapter 5, debating how an emphasis on the differences between individuals could enforce stereotypes and segregation within the labour market that is not helpful for the promotion of equality. Second, the feminine-in-management thesis is a business-case oriented model where such diversity is only valued if it offers the employer more efficient, committed labour. Thus: 'the appropriation of "women's difference" discourse by management writers is merely another episode in a long history of economic reasoning that ends up valuing women out of economic necessity' (Calas and Smircich, 1993: 75). It does not challenge the wider causes of female disadvantage, and those women who are successful have to follow the dominant norm of a 'self-interested pursuit of market opportunities' (Webb, 1997: 166). It is thus chiefly middle-class, white, women who have made the gains from such an approach; precisely the same group who also gain the most advantages from the liberal, legislative approach to equality (Dickens, 1997; White, Cox and Cooper, 1992). In addition, further evidence of the lack of challenge offered to the structures and processes perpetuating disadvantage comes in the fact that the 'feminine' skills advocated as part of the feminine-in-management thesis encourage the fulfilment of a public version of the patriarchal-defined woman (Webb, 1997). It focuses on the stereotype of the woman as caring, nurturing and co-operative. Such an approach thus does nothing to challenge the existing divisions between paid and unpaid labour, or between the domestic and public sphere, and only supports the existence of segregated male and female jobs.

## Key learning points

1 There is a lack of evidence that HRM exists within organizational practice, particularly the 'soft' version which offers most space for equality initiatives. The practice of HRM more often follows the 'hard' version.

2 The primacy of the business case within HRM means that there is often no wider social justice concern attached to equality. The business case results in a short rather than long agenda of equality/diversity.

3 Human resource management initiatives tend to help those who have less need for assistance in the first place – those at middle managerial level – and may have most to offer for those who most easily can meet the dominant norm of the white, male, full-time worker.

4 The feminine-in-management thesis focuses on the detrimental characteristics of HRM practice based on the business case, where stereotypes and segregation within the labour market and wider society are further perpetuated rather than challenged.

# Conclusion

This chapter offers a relatively negative appraisal of the potential that HRM theory and practice have for the pursuit of equality in the workplace and wider labour market. This is not to deny the potential advantages that HRM could have for promoting equality, most notably because of the recognition within HRM, of the importance of paying attention to the way in which employees are managed within an organization. The strength of HRM is in highlighting the importance of the human resource for organizational effectiveness. However, the evidence of organizational practice of HRM does not seem to match up to the ideals of the model. Some of this derives from the *way* in which HRM is practised within complex organizational contexts.

This chapter has discussed briefly the gap between the rhetoric and reality of HRM (Legge, 1989, 1995; Truss et al., 1997) and the issues of power and resources which can undermine the potential that HRM may have for equality, particularly where the rationale for HRM practice is based on the business case. However, there are also fundamental weaknesses inherent to the theories/models of HRM. This chapter has presented the major contradictions and inconsistencies within the models, most notably the distinction between 'hard' and 'soft' forms of the approach. Additionally, linked to the discussions in Chapters 5 and 8, there are serious problems connected to the individualistic and business-case assumptions that undermine the equality agenda within HRM practice, perpetuating predominantly only the 'short' rather than 'long' agenda of equality.

## Activity

### Activity 9.1: The example of Marks & Spencer

The following extract presents a response by the high street retail company, Marks & Spencer, to the recent problems that it has been facing in the marketplace with a significant fall in profit margins and a round of redundancies. This has led to a change in policy based on a focus on equal opportunities.

We suggest that, in preparation for this exercise, the student reads Turnbull and Wass (1997), Sisson (1989) or Legge (1995: 36–8) as background to the literature surrounding non-union firms such as Marks & Spencer. Read this extract and the subsequent commentary, and consider the questions below:

Diane Thomas, a sales assistant in the formal wear department at the Leeds Briggate store, is a member of the company's regional equal opportunities team . . . She explains that there has been a problem finding recruits from the Afro-Caribbean community. *'A lot of black people thought that Marks & Spencer wasn't the kind of place they could work' she says . 'People have come up to me on the shopfloor and said: How come you're working here? I didn't think Marks & Spencer employed black people'* . . . Christine Evans, deputy supervisor in personnel for the Leeds region, who has been with Marks & Spencer for 23 years, admits that she knew little about equal opportunities when she was asked to chair the regional committee two years ago. *'The idea of equal opportunities has always been accepted here, but it wasn't promoted as actively as it should have been'*, she says . . . The key, she says, has been to raise the awareness of equal opportunities issues from top to bottom throughout the stores . . . The equal opportunities strategy now being rigorously promoted in the Leeds stores, has reaped tangible rewards on the recruitment front. When it was launched in 1997, only 3.4 per cent of its employees at stores in the area came from ethnic minorities . . . The latest figure shows that the proportion has risen to 6.7 per cent, comparing favourably with the 6 per cent average for the Leeds population as a whole.

. . . the [equal opportunities] policy was driven not only by the humanitarian values espoused by Michael Marks (founder of the company), but by hard-headed business imperatives. In a world where ethnic diversity was becoming an accepted reality, Marks & Spencer needed to lose its image as a white, middle-class, English department store and attract customers from the whole of society. In 1992, the company appointed its first equal opportunities manager. *'We wanted this to be seen as an issue for everyone'* says Frances Cutts, corporate communications manager. *'Equal opportunities was seen solely as a personnel function but that's obviously not the case. It's everyone's responsibility to put the policy into effect, as it affected all areas of the business'*.

The company began to monitor its employees' backgrounds to find out whether different ethnic groups were being properly represented, and store managers were encouraged to analyse the diversity of their local communities. Now, once a year, head office examines every store's figures to check that things are moving in the right direction. Any store manager whose recruitment statistics fail to reflect the make-up of their local community has to explain why.

Three years ago, Marks & Spencer sent a guide on equal opportunities to every employee. *Equal Opportunities and You* spells out the company's policy, the legal requirements and definitions of discrimination, harassment and victimisation. It explains that equal opportunities is everyone's responsibility and sets out what staff should do if they believe they are experiencing discrimination. A booklet entitled *Welcoming Ethnic Minority Customers* provides background information for staff on the cultures and religions of ethnic minority groups they may be working alongside, managing or serving. And *Welcoming Disabled Customers* explains the importance of delivering goods and services on equal terms to people with disabilities. Other initiatives have included hiring consultants to work with staff to further their understanding of disability.

Marks & Spencer has suffered major setbacks in the past couple of years, with financial problems leading to rounds of redundancies. Its latest annual results, published last month, have piled on the pressure, with profits cut in half and a sharp decline in sales and market share. But the company believes that it can regain its position, and that equal opportunities is a key part of the strategy ... According to Ashish Poddar, senior executive officer at the Commission for Racial Equality, large retailers have bought into the equal opportunities message in a big way. The 'business case for action' is promoted throughout industry and commerce, but has really made its mark in this sector. *'More and more companies are looking at their marketing, their advertising and their staff to see what kind of message they are sending out'*, he says. *'Diversity and equality messages are becoming increasingly important in the marketplace – and the first point of contact for the public is the workforce.'*

*Source*: Whitehead (1999: 54–6).

Non-unionized firms are frequently cited as models of 'soft' HRM, and the sophisticated human relations practices of firms such as Marks & Spencer are typically held up as examples of a concern to maintain a commitment to people as a resource within the organization (Sisson, 1989). Indeed Turnbull and Wass (1997) have coined the term 'Marksist management', to characterize their exploration of the Marks & Spencer approach to managing people. They outline four tenets of the Marksist management model:

● Good human relations (treat workers as individuals with respect and honesty)
● Good communications (open and honest at all levels)
● Equal opportunities (full and fair regardless of sex, race, age or disability)
● Good conditions of employment (high standards and a share in the company's success). (Sieff, 1990, quoted in Turnbull and Wass, 1997: 101).

However, the contradictions within this model are highlighted within Turnbull and Wass's (1997) study of a retail firm following a Marksist approach, reflecting many of the weaknesses of the HRM approach developed in this chapter. Women are still under-represented at senior management level. Older and more experienced staff were over-represented at the least senior levels. There is also a significant gap between the rhetoric of commitment to good human relations and employee development (the 'soft' approach), and the reality of employee commitment based on the cash nexus, strict discipline, unsociable working hours and the need for employees to be flexible around organizational aims, in the face of intensified competition (the 'hard' approach).

## Questions

1  Consider the approach to managing the human resource which is advocated within this policy response. Does it fit into a 'soft' or 'hard' model?
2  What is the fit between the tenets of a 'Marksist' approach outlined by Turnbull and Wass (1997) and this equal opportunities policy?
3  What are the potential benefits of Marks & Spencer's approach for the equality agenda within the organization?
4  How far is the business case a justification for Marks & Spencer's current emphasis on equal opportunities? What are the implications of this for a discussion of how HRM can advance equality?

# Review and discussion questions

1 What benefits do you think there would be in ensuring equity within an HRM culture? Think about how equality/diversity issues fit into a business case orientation and the benefits of greater equality in the achievement of HRM objectives.

2 Think about the fit between HRM and equality and diversity approaches discussed in Chapter 5. Discuss the HRM model from different equality perspectives, that is, liberal, radical, diversity. To what extent are HRM and equality agendas compatible?

3 Which segments of the workforce benefit most from HRM? What spaces are left within the ideal model for each different social group of workers facing disadvantage (for example, part time, disabled, women, minority ethnic, older workers)?

4 Discuss the difference between 'hard' and 'soft' versions of HRM and the potential that each offers for equality in the workplace. Think about 'soft' and 'hard' elements of the four dimensions of HRM presented.

# Further reading

Cattaneo, R., Reavley, M. and Templer, A (1994). Women in management as a strategic HR initiative. *Women in Management Review*, 9, (2), 23–28.
A useful article dealing with the issue of strategic integration and HRM. Focused around gender inequality, it does have wider implications: highlighting the difficulty of strategic integration and the impact of the differing status of the HR function in equality initiatives.

Dickens, L. (1997). Gender, race and employment equality in Britain: inadequate strategies and the role of industrial relations actors. *Industrial Relations Journal*, **28**, (4), 282–289.
Focuses on a discussion of the potential benefits of flexibility initiatives in advancing equality and analyses why this potential has not been realized.

Guest, D. (1987). Human resource management and industrial relations. *Journal of Management Studies*, **24**, (5), 503–521.
The key article for the HRM model in Britain. Summarizes the evolution of HRM and its distinctiveness from personnel management. Presents the key elements of the HRM model and provides empirical examples of policy and practice.

Truss, C., Gratton, L., Hope-Hailey, V., McGovern, P. and Stiles, P. (1997). Soft and hard models of human resource management: a reappraisal. *Journal of Management Studies*, **34**, (1), 5–73.
This article deals with the rhetoric versus reality debate within the HRM literature. It provides an exploration of 'hard' and 'soft' approaches, a good background from which then to investigate the potential equality benefits of HRM. Empirical evidence is provided indicating the 'hard' reality of much HRM practice.

# References

Armstrong, P. (1986). Management control strategies and interprofessional competition. In *Managing the Labour Process* (D. Knights and H. Wilmott, eds). Gower.

Atkinson, J. (1986). Four stages of adjustment to the demographic downturn. *Personnel Management*, September, 26–29.

Beer, M., Spector, B., Lawrence, P., Quinn-Mills, D. and Walton, R. (1984). *Managing Human Assets*. Free Press.

Biswas, R. and Cassell, C. (1996). Strategic HRM and the gendered division of labour in the hotel industry: a case study. *Personnel Review*, **25**, (2), 19–35.

Calas, M. and Smircich, L. (1993). 'Dangerous liaisons': The 'feminine-in management' meets globalisation. *Business Horizons*, March–April, 73–83.

Cattaneo, R., Reavley, M. and Templer, A. (1994). Women in management as a strategic HR initiative. *Women in Management Review*, 9, (2), 23–28.

Cockburn, C. (1989). Equal opportunities: the long and short agenda. *Industrial Relations Journal*, **20**, 213–225.

Cockburn, C. (1991). *In the Way of Women: Men's Resistance to Sex Equality in Organisations*. Macmillan.

Colling, T. and Dickens, L. (1998). Selling the case for gender equality: deregulation and equality bargaining. *British Journal of Industrial Relations*, **36**, (3), 389–411.

Copeland, L. (1988). Valuing diversity. *Personnel*, Pt 1, June; Pt 2, June/July.

Corbett, J. M. (1994). *Critical Cases in Organisational Behaviour*. Macmillan.

Dale, K. (1998). Book review article. *Industrial Relations Journal*, **29**, (1), 92–3.

Deal, T. A. and Kennedy, A. A. (1982). *Corporate Cultures*. Addison-Wesley.

Dickens, L. (1997). Gender, race and employment equality in Britain: inadequate strategies and the role of industrial relations actors. *Industrial Relations Journal*, **28**, (4), 282–289.

Edwards, P. (1995). The employment relationship. In *Industrial Relations: Theory and Practice in Britain* (P. Edwards). Blackwell.

EOR (Equal Opportunities Review) (1996). Flexible working: the impact on women's pay and conditions. *Equal Opportunities Review*, (65), 19–24.

Flynn, G. (1995). Personnel Journal 100: the year's toughest challenges – and the HR pros who tackled them', *Personnel Journal*, **74**, (12), 63–77.

Frombrun, C. J., Tichy, N. M. and Devanna, M. A. (eds) (1984). *Strategic Human Resource Management*. John Wiley.

Geary, J. (1992). Employment flexibility and HRM. *Work Employment and Society*, **6**, (2), June, 251–270.

Gooch, L. and Ledwith, S. (1996). Women in personnel management – re-visioning of a handmaiden's role? In *Women in Organisations* (S. Ledwith and F. Colgan, eds). Macmillan.

Greenslade, M. (1991). Managing diversity: lessons from the US. *Personnel Management*, December, 28–32.

Guest, D. (1987). Human resource management and industrial relations. *Journal of Management Studies*, **24**, (5), 503–521.

Hales, C. (1986). What do managers do? A critical review of the evidence. *Journal of Management Studies*, **23**, (1), 88–116.

Hollinshead, G. and Leat, M. (1995). *Human Resource Management: An International and Comparative Perspective*. Financial Times Management.

Hollinshead, G., Nicholls, T. and Tailby, S. (1999). *Employee Relations*. Financial Times Management.

Horstman, B. (1988). Labour flexibility strategies and management style', *Journal of Industrial Relations*, September, 25–40.

Iles, P. and Kaur Hayers, P. (1997). Managing diversity in transnational project teams: a tentative model and case study. *Journal of Managerial Psychology*, **12**, (2), 1–17.

Kandola, R. and Fullerton, J. (1994) *Managing the Mosaic – Diversity in Action*. Institute of Personnel and Development.

Legge, K. (1989). Human resource management: a critical analysis. In *New Perspectives in Human Resource Management* (J. Storey, ed.). Routledge.

Legge, K. (1995). *HRM Rhetorics and Realities*. Macmillan.

Liff, S. (1996). Two routes to managing diversity: individual differences or social group characteristics. *Employee Relations*, **19**, (1), 11–26.

Maher, J. (1971). *New Perspectives in Job Enrichment*. Litten Educational.

McKenna, E. (1987). *Psychology in Business*. Lawrence Erlbaum.

Miller, D. (1996). Equality management: towards a materialist approach. *Gender Work and Organization*, **3**, 4, 202–214.

Pollert, A. (1988). Dismantling flexibility. *Capital and Class*, **34**, Spring, 42–75.

Purcell, K. (1997). The implications of employment flexibility for equal opportunities. Paper presented at the BUIRA Conference, Bath, 4–6 July.

Rees, T. (1998). *Mainstreaming Equality in the European Union: Education, Training and Labour Market Policies*. Routledge.

Rosener, J. (1990). Ways women lead. *Harvard Business Review*, November–December, 119–25.

Scheibl, F. (1996). Part time workers: grateful slaves or rational time maximising individuals? An examination of fact and fiction in recent explanations of women's preferences for part time working. Employment Studies Unit Paper 4, University of Hertfordshire.

Sisson, K. (1989). Personnel management in perspective. In *Personnel Management in Britain* (K. Sisson, ed.). Blackwell.

Storey, J. (1989). *New Perspectives in Human Resource Management*. Routledge.

Storey, J. (1992), *Developments in the Management of Human Resources'*, London: Routledge.

Thompson, P. and McHugh, D. (1990). *Work Organizations: A Critical Introduction*. Macmillan.

Thornburg, L. (1995). Sue Ann Tempero: 1995 winner of the Society for Human Resource Management Award for professional excellence. *HR Magazine*, **40**, (9), 48–51.

Tomoney, J. (1990). The reality of workplace flexibility. *Capital and Class*, Spring, 42–72.

Truss, C., Gratton, L., Hope-Hailey, V., McGovern, P. and Stiles, P. (1997). Soft and hard models of human resource management: a reappraisal. *Journal of Management Studies*, **34**, (1), 5–73.

Turnbull, P. and Wass, V (1997). Marksist management: sophisticated human relations in a high street store. *Industrial Relations Journal*, **29**, (2), 98–111.

Walby, S. (1997). *Gender Transformations*. Chapter 3, pp. 66–79. Routledge.

Walsh, T. J. (1990). Flexible labour utilisation in the private service sector. *Work, Employment and Society*, **4**, (14), December, 350–375.

Webb, J. (1997). The politics of equal opportunity. *Gender, Work and Organization*, **4**, (3), 159–169.

White, B., Cox, C. and Cooper, C. (1992). *Women's Career Development: A Study of High Fliers*. Blackwell.

Whitehead, M. (1999). A time for buy-in. *People Management*, 3 June, 54–56.

# Chapter 10

# State policy, social provision and attitudes:
## comparisons with and between member states of the European Union

## Aim

To place the preceding discussion of the equality and diversity issues in the UK within a wider European context, identifying similarities and differences in policy approaches and practice.

## Objectives

- To examine the occupational distributions and labour market participation rates of different social groups in the member states in comparison to the situation found in the UK.
- To discuss similarities and differences in the equality and diversity policy approaches together with employment outcomes between countries.
- To appraise the importance of social and employment policy, wider societal attitudes and the agency of collective groups, in encouraging or discouraging advance of equality and diversity agendas.

## Introduction

This book is clearly set within the UK context, however it is important to compare policy and practice with other European countries. First, the UK is a member state of the EU and of the Single Market. As discussed in Chapter 6, the directives, recommendations, action plans and rulings of the European Court of Justice (ECJ) have already driven substantial parts of UK legislation in the area of equality. This chapter provides an overview of the labour market trends and patterns across the EU, which can be compared with those of the UK, discussed in Chapter 2. We also examine the different social and employment policy approaches adopted by governments, identifying the variety of models which exist and their implications for the advance of equality in the labour market. Some countries have very different approaches to that of the UK, the consideration of which allows us to broaden our perspectives of equality, and to indicate where there are examples of more positive or more negative equality outcomes. Are there models of policy and practice which could be successfully implemented within the UK context and, equally, does policy and practice in the UK offer any lessons or examples for other European countries?

# European trends of labour market participation

The aim here is briefly to examine the employment trends and patterns across Europe of the social groups that have been the focus throughout this book. However, there is not the space within this chapter to do any more than present a very brief sketch. There is also an imbalance in the statistics and data between member states, and readers will note that there are far more examples and much more detailed information about the Northern European countries. This partly reflects the amount of research carried out in the various European countries and partly differences in accounting and monitoring procedures in those countries, which allow only some comparisons to be made. Note also that the discussion is limited to those member states of the EU, plus those that remain outside such as Switzerland and Norway. We do not deal with the Eastern European countries, even those currently applying for entry to the EU. As Hurst (1995) argues, however, their future will very much depend on what happens in the rest of Europe. An attempt to sketch broad patterns and trends, albeit brief, does allow at least some situation of the UK patterns within a broader European context. A final gap that the reader will immediately notice is that there is no discussion of gay and lesbian workers. This reflects the paucity of information that is available, meaning that at the present time an attempt to discuss the employment situation across Europe would be so limited in comparison to the other social groups as to seem tokenistic. We have thus decided to reserve judgement on this issue until a later time.

## Patterns and trends in women's employment

There is considerable similarity between the patterns of women's labour market participation in the UK and those on a broader scale across Europe. Female participation rates have soared across all member states and now stand at an average of 70 per cent (of all women) (EC, 1997a). This represents a ranking from a high of 80 per cent in Sweden to the lowest rate of 28.8 per cent in Italy. Projections for the future indicate that this trend towards increasing female participation is set to continue into the twenty-first century. This compares with long-standing trends that indicate that the number of men in employment across the whole EU declined slightly. Indeed, increasing rates of unemployment in the EU have been a primary concern of the European Commission's Agenda 2000. At first glance it appears that it is women who are benefiting from the new jobs which have been created – almost two thirds of the net additional jobs created in the EU over 1994 – 6 went to women (EC, 1997a).

However, this increased participation has not led to increased equality for women within the labour market. Chapters 2 and 3 discussed how some of the disadvantage of women within the labour market is accounted for by occupational segregation by sex, which relegates women to the lowest paid, lowest status and most vulnerable jobs. In line with the situation in the UK, the expansion of women's employment has mainly been in part-time jobs. Indeed, across Europe, part-time jobs accounted for most of the rise in women's participation during 1996, with nearly 32 per cent of all women in employment working part time (EC, 1997a: 20). This compares with the 6 per cent figure for men (only an increase of 2 per cent since 1990). It should be noted, however, that the growth in temporary and fixed-term working is also a common trend across the EU, with an almost equal take-up by both men and women (EC, 1997a: 51). This indicates that the move to flexible and short-term contracts is a wider feature of future labour market trends. However, the significance of the high numbers of women in part-time work is the lesser status which part-time work continues to be afforded in most member states.

Women still face horizontal and vertical segregation, with women continuing to work predominantly within occupations deemed to be 'female' and within female-dominated professions (Hakim, 1992). Plantenga and Tijdensk (1995) find that the increasing number of women within the European labour market has had little, if any, effect on occupational segregation by sex. Vertical segregation is pronounced across all European countries, including the so-called egalitarian countries with the highest female participation rates. Indeed Platenga's (1995) research indicates that the highest level of occupational segregation by sex is found in Denmark, a somewhat surprising finding, given Denmark's generally positive record on equality issues, as will be discussed later. As the report *Employment in Europe, 1997* for the European Commission states, 'while part-time work has enabled many women to enter the labour market, it has not yet contributed to a greater equality of treatment between part-time and full time workers' (EC, 1997a: 15).

Finally, evidence of the consequences of such segregation is also found in the fact that a considerable pay gap between men's and women's pay continues to exist across Europe (Schippers, 1995). Perhaps the widest gap was found in Luxembourg, where women doing manual work earned only around two-thirds of the equivalent men's wage. Indeed Pillinger (1992: 1) identified two trends in the labour markets of Europe, the feminization of the labour market and the 'feminization of poverty'.

In summary, as was the case with the UK data, the overall picture of patterns in women's employment is not particularly positive. However, it does place the position of the UK in perspective. While the game of 'we might be bad but look at them' does not justify the disadvantage that women face or advance the equality agenda, the UK by no means has the worst record. There is, however, evidence of some change; Platenga (1995) identifies four patterns of female participation across Europe. The two-phase pattern characterizes Ireland and Luxembourg and found women working until they had their first child. A three-phase pattern, with working interrupted by a child-rearing period from twenty-five to thirty-four years characterizes the UK, Germany and France. A pattern common to Greece and other agricultural societies is characterized by women transferring paid employment in the labour market to employ-ment for a family firm upon marriage. What is seen by Platenga as a positive trend indicates that a new pattern had emerged over the 1990s, where there were more women who had unbroken employment records and thus could have a single-phase participation similar to men.

## Minority ethnic employment patterns and trends

On a European scale, identifying different ethnic groups is a more complex task than looking at the figures for the UK. Europe as a whole, is a continent of migration. Some 5 per cent of people of working age resident in the EU are non-nationals. However, a majority of these come from other EU member states and other parts of Europe. Workers from outside Europe account for a not inconsiderable segment of those non-nationals, with workers from Africa accounting for a quarter of that 5 per cent and from Asia, over a tenth (EC, 1997a: 21). Wrench (1998) provides a useful summary of the historical background to the migration of labour within Europe, focusing on the encouragement of foreign workers to cover labour shortages during the post-1945 period of employment boom. A distinction should be made between those non-nationals moving from country to country, predominantly for work – migrant workers – and those non-nationals who intend on residing permanently in the country of migration – immigrant workers.

Such groups of non-EU minority ethnic workers tend to be concen-trated in the most vulnerable and unprotected groups of workers in the EU. Wrench (1998: 3) outlines five groups of worker in the EU:

1 Citizens living and working within their own country.
2 Citizens of an EU member state who work in another country in the EU (EU denizens).
3 Third-country nationals who have full rights to residency and work in a member state (non-EU denizens).
4 Third-country nationals who have leave to stay on the basis of a revocable work permit for a fixed period of time.
5 Undocumented or illegal workers.

The overall picture of minority ethnic employment patterns in the EU is similar to the UK, with minority ethnic groups having lower economic activity rates, facing dramatically higher rates of unemployment than the white population and segregation within the lowest paid and lowest status jobs in the economy (Wrench, 1998). Workers from minority ethnic groups tend to be concentrated in certain sectors, particularly manufacturing, which has faced dramatic decline over the last two decades. Herzing (1995) illustrates how gender and ethnicity interconnect, with comparative research in the Netherlands, Belgium, Germany and the UK indicating that minority ethnic women have a particularly unfavourable position in terms of pay and status compared with men and women of the 'majority' culture. As in the UK, the heterogeneity of ethnic groups is highlighted, where Herzing was able to identify ethnic groups that were worse off than others. For example, particularly low participation and high unemployment rates were found among Moroccan, Turkish, Pakistani and Bengali women, while higher rates were found among Surinamese, Antillean, Italian, Yugoslav and West Indian women. However, similar education levels among the latter, still did not lead to parity of pay and status with the white population. As in the UK, explanations for this disparity were largely focused around discrimination by employers and within wider society, as will be discussed later in this chapter. It should be noted that certain countries stand out as markedly different in this regard; notably Sweden, which, as will also be discussed in detail later, has traditionally placed much weight on equality within immigration policy. Therefore, net wage differentiation between ethnic groups in Sweden is particularly small in comparison to other countries (Hibbs, 1990).

Later sections of this chapter will elaborate on how existing immigration policies and procedures of gaining citizenship and denizenship, which define eligibility for social and legal protection, have been found to be both formally and informally discriminatory against minority ethnic groups. The presence of illegal workers (group 5) is seen as an expanding problem, particularly in the countries of Southern Europe. Estimates of numbers indicate around 350 000 in Greece alone (8 per cent of the registered workforce), while in Spain illegal workers are estimated to account for as much as 60 per cent of workers from non-EU countries. This is significant when considering occupational status, as illegal workers have no rights to employment protection; indeed, in Portugal, around half of minority ethnic workers have no employment contract, legal protection or welfare rights.

## Workers with disability

The difficulty in the definition and classification of types of disability, identified in Chapter 2, is increased when a view across Europe is taken. It is clear that different countries define disability in a variety of ways. The report *The Employment Situation of People with Disabilities: Employment in Europe, 1997* notes that 'there is no consistent series of comparable and reliable data on disability in the Union, partly because of a plethora of definitions used in each Member State to classify the disabled population for the receipt of benefits' (EC, 1997b: 100). However, bearing in mind the differentiation in definition across Europe, taking data from the above report (EC, 1997b), we find that workers with disabilities account for approximately 17 per cent of the EU's working-age population. With regard to participation in the labour market, this stands at an average of only 44 per cent, much behind the overall rate of participation of 63 per cent (EC, 1997a: 23). The report cautions that rates vary considerably between member states. Indeed, looking back at the UK figures, we find that the economic activity rate for workers with disabilities meets the overall European average, however, the difference between disabled and non-disabled workers is more marked in the UK, as the overall economic activity rate is much higher than the European average. We should also note that a significant proportion of workers with disabilities who are in employment, tend to be people who have become disabled while working and who remain with the same employer. This highlights that the labour market participation of workers with disabilities may actually be more disadvantaged from a recruitment perspective.

The high rate of unemployment for workers with disability in the UK was noted in Chapter 2, however, across Europe, the average rate of unemployment is only two percentage points higher than for the total workforce (EC, 1997a: 24). This does not necessarily reflect increased equality, as this statistic does not take into account those who are inactive (capable and willing to work but who favour the alternative of long-term social security benefits (Hyde, 1996). It is noted that this category of workers with disabilities accounts for a higher proportion of the total workforce in countries like Greece, Spain, Ireland, Portugal and Italy, possible reasons for which are discussed later in this chapter. In terms of occupation, a significant segregation is seen: a disproportionate number of men and women with disabilities employed in lower-paid, lower-status and lower career opportunities sectors such as: agriculture (particularly marked in member states where farming is still a major source of jobs, for example, Greece, Ireland and Portugal), construction and, to a lesser extent, in health and personal services. A disproportion-ately small number are employed in manufacturing, business services, finance and education. A higher proportion of workers with disabilities are employed in lower-skilled occupations (for example, only 26 per cent of men with disabilities worked as managers and professionals compared with 39 per cent of workers without disabilities). The pay gap for workers with disabilities stands at an average of 19 per cent across the whole EU, ranging from a high of 35 per cent in Denmark and Portugal to a low of 10 per cent in Belgium and the Netherlands (EC, 1997b: 108).

There also appears to be similar segregation by sex as exists for workers without disabilities (EC, 1998: 104–5). As with the overall rate within the workforce as a whole, women with disabilities were more likely to work part time (30 per cent of women compared with 5 per cent of men), with all the disadvantages which this brings bearing in mind the existing social and legislative framework.

## Older workers

In direct connection with the last section, the link between disability and age is highlighted (EC, 1997b). Indeed nearly half of workers classified as having disabilities are within the fifty to sixty-four age group. The problems of how to encourage increased participation is likely to become more pressing, given the indisputable trend towards an ageing population in Europe. Hugman (1994: 1) identifies three major trends in this regard: an increase in the proportion of people aged over sixty-five years, an increase in the absolute numbers of older people and an overall improvement of life expectancy. While over the past decade there has been a decline in the relative numbers of fifteen to twenty-four-year-olds, projections suggest that by 2015, well over half of the working age population in almost all member states will be forty years old or over (EC, 1997a: 17). The ageing of the population also has major consequences both for the labour force and for social protection and benefits budgets. In the longer term, beyond 2015, an accelerating trend towards a decline in the working-age population is projected.

Perhaps more importantly, these projections have significance when one considers the existing and future changes in labour market participation rates. There is evidence for concern about these trends to be found in employment statistics. Moore, Tilson and Whitting (1994: 1) find that while the number of people in the fifty to sixty-four age group is increasing, overall labour market participation rates of older workers (here defined as over fifty-five) have conversely been decreasing across the EU. Economic participation rates for older men are only on average 60 per cent (with the UK and Ireland standing at 65 per cent while Sweden and Norway see economic activity rates of 79 per cent). On an international comparison (OECD, 1992), Italy stands as having the lowest participation rates of older workers in the world at 10 per cent (compared to Japan at 44 per cent). Overall, there has been a worldwide decline in rates of around 12.5 per cent 1965 to 1990. It should be noted however, that this decline is largely concerned with older men, indeed while Moore, Tilson and Whitting (1994) admit to the difficulty in assessing activity rates for women given the existing statistical databases, participation by women in all age groups has been increasing over time.

---

1 Women's employment has been rising in all EU countries and is projected to continue rising over the next twenty years. However, as a group, women across Europe continue to suffer from vertical and horizontal segregation into lower-paid, lower status jobs. As in the UK, women are disproportionately part-time workers.

2 Wrench's (1998) five-fold classification is a useful tool in identifying the various categories of worker. This highlights the particularly vulnerable position of illegal workers in the EU, most of whom are from non-European minority ethnic backgrounds and are predominantly segregated to the worst paid and lowest status jobs, with little or no employment protection.

3 While differences in definition can skew the statistics in cross-EU comparisons, people with disabilities are more likely to be unemployed or inactive in the labour market, and to hold lower-paid and lower-status jobs than people without disabilities.

4 Demographic statistics identify the accelerating trend towards an ageing population in all EU countries. This is of concern because the labour market participation of older workers is disproportionately low and there are fears that if older workers are not gaining employment, or retirement ages are not raised, then there will be a significant decline in the working age population.

**Key learning points**

# Social and employment policy: the role of the state

This section considers the impact of a range of government policies and interventions on the labour market participation of the social groups we have been studying.

## Citizenship and immigration policy

It is clear that the immigration policies of different countries play a significant part in the differential treatment of ethnic groups. In particular this has implications for defining who is eligible for social benefits, including legislative protection. Exhibit 10.1 offers a classification for major public policy perspectives on immigration and ethnic diversity in European countries, which we have drawn from Wrench (1998), Castles (1995) and Bryant (1997).

One should remember that the classification in Exhibit 10.1 relates to ideal types, indeed, in the case of Germany, there has been a shift towards multicultural policies in education. In the UK now, there is really a mix of assimilationist and pluralist models (Wrench, 1998). However, elements of such ideological models are translated into policy (Bryant, 1997; Wrench, 1997). For example, in France, an assimilationist perspective sees initiatives to encourage recruitment of minority ethnic workers as linked to broader equal rights for all citizens, rather than in the specific form of anti-racism policies. In fact, typical equal opportunities policies common to the UK (see Chapter 5) would run counter to French philosophies of universalistic treatment. In contrast, Dutch pluralism sees separate institutional provision (for example, trade unions, schools, universities, political parties) for people with different religious and secular world-views (Bryant, 1997). The ethnic nature of citizenship in Germany is evidenced in the continued effectiveness of definitions of kinship and race as established by the Nuremberg Laws; for example, former East Europeans who want to be recognized as ethnic Germans often have no proof other than the membership of their father or grandfather in a Nazi organization (Wilpert, 1993).

The significance for us of immigration and citizenship policies resides in their effect on the treatment of minority ethnic workers in employment. Despite the framework of the EU and the Single Market, the differences in the underlying ideologies of different nation states in Europe have implications for the extent to which diversity can be accommodated (Bryant, 1997: 170). For example, the differential exclusion model of Switzerland translates itself into a view of foreign workers as a way to meet short- to medium-term economic needs within the labour market. Switzerland has a labour market that is characterized by a 'guest worker' policy where employment is fundamental to the acquisition of a residential status. The exact status of guest workers however, depends on the category of work permit held – many on shorter-term work permits are only allowed to stay for a maximum of nine months in any one year

**Exhibit 10. 1 Public policy perspectives on immigration**

*Differential exclusion*

Immigrants are seen as guest workers without full social and political rights. Citizenship is defined by descent with proof of descendants having been citizens required. Naturalization is possible for non-nationals but requires the renunciation of other citizenships and evidence of meeting the criteria for the national way of life and affiliation to the country. Civil society is suspicious of ethno-pluralism.

Categorizes Germany, Austria, Switzerland and Belgium.

*Assimilation*

Immigrants are awarded full rights but are expected to assimilate to cultural norms. Citizenship is defined by a mixture of birth in the country, descent and residence. Unlike the differential exclusion model, citizenship is to a territorial community rather than based on descent. Dual nationality is not encouraged.

Categorizes France, Denmark, and the UK in the 1960s.

*Pluralism/multiculturalism*

Immigrants have full rights but maintain some cultural differences. Citizenship is based on a mixture of descent, birth and residence. Dual nationality is allowed. Unlike the two models above, different group identities are officially recognized. The accommodation of different ethnic cultures and norms is encouraged although requires a basic loyalty to the nation.

Categorizes the Netherlands and Sweden.

*Pragmatist pluralism*

Immigrants have full rights and maintain some cultural differences. However, there is a lack of a defined policy perspective. A civic nation (rather then an ethnic nation as with the differential exclusion model) in which the emphasis is placed on the accommodation of different groups. This is similar to the pluralist model but has come about in a *de facto* way rather than legally defined. Citizenship is officially based on birth but naturalization is available for those legally resident for five years, and dual nationality is allowed.

Categorizes the UK since the 1970s.

and there are restrictions on family and spouses joining them. Given the restrictive citizenship laws in Switzerland (differential exclusion model), this guest-worker group predominantly comprises workers from minority ethnic groups. Similarly, strict limits on the numbers of workers allowed to hold temporary work permits in Austria forces more workers into the realm of illegality, compelling foreign workers to accept the lowest paid and lowest status jobs to try to ensure they gain a permit, and encouraging the occupational segregation that exists between national and foreign workers (Wrench, 1998).

Fekete (1997) points to the inherent racism within policies towards greater use of guest workers as part of the push towards more flexible working in the EU. Indeed, the use of labour on temporary work permits allows the government to exclude these workers by removing rights of residence which permanent residents are entitled to. Thus, while Germany relied heavily on guest workers (*gastarbeiter*) during the period of labour shortages in the post-1945 reconstruction, the 1990s has seen a number of incidences where the government has attempted to take residency rights away from groups of immigrant workers. For example, in 1994 the German government revoked residence permits for Vietnamese workers who immediately became part of Wrench's (1998) group 5, illegal workers. Estimates indicate that of around 500 000 construction workers in Germany, one in four is an illegal worker (Fekete, 1997: 8). Similarly, the French Pasqua laws introduced in 1993 reversed measures which previously allowed migrant workers to renew their permits at regular intervals and allowed citizenship after a certain period of years. Thousands of previously legal migrant workers were rendered illegal. Similar examples can be found in the Koppelingswet Law in the Netherlands and the Vande Lanotte Act in Belgium 1996 (Sivariandam, 1997). Legal attempts to limit levels of immigration have come about fairly recently, particularly in Southern Europe. In Spain and Italy there was a complete vacuum of guest-worker policy until the late 1980s and 1990s (Fekete, 1997: 9). As an overview of Europe, Fekete (1997) concludes that what is desired by many governments is the 'work tourist' rather than the guest worker. In other words, the labour is desired but not the labourer. It is such patterns which have led to the term 'Fortress Europe', denoting the barriers and disadvantage faced by minority ethnic groups in Europe.

Other policies appear to offer a better chance of equality of treatment. For example, the multicultural model of Sweden has been held up as almost unique, offering the most comprehensive set of rights to migrant workers (Blos, Fischer and Straubhaar, 1997). This involves the explicit rejection of granting residence permits on the basis of economic grounds (such as in the Swiss example above), instead emphasizing the long-term integration of foreigners admitted to the country for other non-economic reasons (for example asylum) (Blos, Fischer and Straubhaar, 1997). Foreigners can enjoy the same legal privileges as Swedish citizens and the overall ethos is a quest to create social equality amongst ethnic groups, respecting cultures and providing resources (Alund and Schierup, 1993). It has been noted that Sweden stands out in Europe with regard to the wage differentiation between national and minority ethnic workers.

However, even Sweden does not seem immune to the wider trend within Europe, Alund and Schierup (1993) point to the subtle change occurring in Swedish public policy since the late 1980s, meaning that in the 1990s, foreign workers still have lower participation and higher unemployment rates than Swedish citizens. Official policy has begun to change from multicultural accommodation to 'peaceful coexistence', a subtle but significant change of direction and emphasis.

It is difficult to increase the amount of voluntary measures at organizational level, if one of the major barriers to employment is the legal status of the workers to begin with (Wrench, 1998). However, some organizations (albeit a minority), can set examples of how policies aiming to increase the recruitment of minority ethnic workers can be introduced despite legal status and state policy. Wrench (1997) provides twenty-five case studies of good practice in this regard from the fifteen EU countries (see also Wrench 1998: 36–60). These include the example of an electro-coating company in Belgium which specifically recruited via an agency set up to provide assistance to unemployed miners in the region, including an extensive training programme designed to establish a respectful working climate among the multiethnic workforce. Special provision was made for religious practices of the different cultures. Another example illustrated how a shopping centre in France managed to introduce an initiative which benefited minority ethnic workers, without it running counter to the philosophy of universalistic treatment of French state policy. The initiative was based on local preference for recruitment which, being an urban area of Marseilles, included a high percentage of minority ethnic workers. Thus it did not challenge the philosophy of equal treatment for all, as it might have done had the initiative been based around increasing the number of minority ethnic workers. Retailers were asked to give preference to applicants from local districts, forming a strong and effective positive action policy which was not controversial because it was framed not as positive action for minority ethnic groups but for local people (Wrench, 1998: 52).

---

**Key learning points**

1 Immigration and citizenship policies have a significant effect on the differential treatment of ethnic groups, where the different ideological approaches can be identified in policy.
2 The immigration and citizenship policies of some countries can be identified as inherently racist and mean that foreign workers, especially those who are working illegally, face the most vulnerable and unprotected employment contexts.
3 The multicultural model is identified as providing the most opportunities for equality of treatment and opportunity for minority ethnic workers in Europe.

# Activity

## Activity 10.1: The rights of minority ethnic workers

While this chapter does not discuss the employment patterns within the central and east European countries, developments in these countries obviously have an impact on EU member states. The following article involves the migration of Roma populations from the Czech Republic, and the UK government's attempt to restrict and regulate this migration.

### Roma have rights here

Prejudice against Roma/Gypsy people is deeply ingrained in all European societies, but it is particularly problematic in those former communist states (Czech Republic, Slovakia, Hungary, Romania, Bulgaria), where Roma make up 5 per cent of the population. Jack Straw's threat (in the UK) to impose visas if the Czechs do not 'halt the flow' of Roma refugees is futile because it fails to tackle the causes of why Roma feel forced to leave. The Czech government cannot cope with the mammoth task of reintegrating Roma into the economy and society, and thus seeks to manage their exclusion. Substantial investment is needed in health, housing, education, culture, training and employment. Only the EU has these resources and the ability to turn Roma populations into assets for central-east European states, thus strengthening their commitment to tackle discrimination . . .

Quite apart from any claim to asylum they may have, these people have the legal right under EU law to come (to the UK) as economic migrants. All Czech and Slovak citizens are fully entitled to come to the UK (or any other EU country) and to work as long as they remain self-employed. The only restriction that may be imposed on them is that they may not enter the labour market and they are of course subject to the same requirement as other European nationals: they must not represent a threat to public policy, security or health.

*Source*: Edited extract from the *Guardian*, 1 September 1999.

### Questions

1 Consider whether the legal right to work in any EU country is sufficient to allow equality of treatment for those Roma workers.
2 Link back to discussions in Chapters 5 and 8 about the need to make a good business case for tackling discrimination. Would the recommendation that the EU 'turn Roma populations into assets' fit into a 'managing diversity' model, and what are the possible consequences and implications of this?

## Family-friendly provision

The extent to which the state takes an interventionist role in social policy differs from country to country, which is relevant when the position of the most disadvantaged groups in the labour market are considered. There are many different versions of a classification of the welfare systems existing in Europe (see Esping-Andersen, 1990; Langan and Ostener, 1990; Liebfried, 1990) which we can draw upon to gain a general idea of the models available (Exhibit 10.2).

## Exhibit 10.2 Classification of European welfare systems

*Scandinavian/Social Democrat*: Labour market policies should be at the heart of the welfare state based on universal notions of individual citizenship. Thus the focus is the individual rights of workers so that the costs of raising a family should be made a state concern in order to maximize individual capacity within the labour market. (Denmark, Finland, Sweden, Norway.)

*Conservative/institutional*: Traditional corporatist model based on provision of social policy by the state only where the family is unable to provide. The state thus takes the role of financial compensator, where the cost of raising a family cannot be borne by the family itself. (Germany, Austria, France, Italy.)

*Anglo-Saxon/liberal*: Belief in the self-regulatory capacity of the free market. No group needs special treatment or services. Those who cannot enter the labour market will be offered means-tested state support. (UK.)

*Latin rim*: Rudimentary state welfare support for the non-working population, but rights to welfare are not necessarily guaranteed. Supported by the welfare tradition of the Catholic Church. (Spain, Portugal, Greece, Italy.)

Langan and Ostner's (1990) analysis of these models suggest the different implications that they have for the support of women in the labour market. While the Scandinavian model does take the emphasis away from the traditional family, in giving support as a universal individual right, the welfare regime is still gendered; it does not challenge the domestic division of labour; the liberal rather then radical approach. The Conservative and Latin rim models also support the traditional family structure and gendered roles, while the UK model, in seeing men and women as economic free agents and focusing on the need to avoid special treatment, creates inequalities by continuing to support the traditional norms but does not offer any state support for these gendered roles, unlike the state in the Scandinavian countries.

Family-friendly measures include childcare, care of the elderly, parental and other family leave, and monetary benefits or tax rebates. The EC has emphasized the need to move away from models of informal, unpaid care (such as in the Anglo-Saxon, Conservative and Latin rim welfare models) towards formalized state and private provision of facilities and resources (that is, towards the Scandinavian model). A major area of concern here is the fact that women account for 95 per cent of the care sector, recognized as being poorly paid, offering little prospect for career development and little or no formal qualifications (EC, 1998). The exceptions are those countries that have an integrated system of services for young children under compulsory school age, such as

Sweden, Denmark, Finland, Germany, Spain and Austria. Parental leave and care services are of significance to facilitating women's participation in employment, given that the care function remains predominantly the responsibility of women.

Pot (1995) draws on large-scale survey evidence from the EC to identify significant national differences in childcare provision and benefits between the UK, the Netherlands, Denmark and Belgium. In addition, the EC (1998) report on *Reconciliation between Work and Family Life in Europe* offers a wider comparative analysis across the member states. The outstanding position of Denmark is highlighted in terms of quality and quantity of services. This includes paid family care leave (including the unemployed who get a proportion of their unemployment benefit), statutory minimum maternity leave, paternity leave, pre-school nursery and after-school services. These services are predominantly provided by the public sector; there are very few private facilities. When the link between family-friendly provision and women's labour market participation is taken into account, Denmark also sees the percentage of working mothers about equal to the percentage of working women without children. However, it should be noted that Danish women with children still tend to work part time. Despite positive examples in Sweden and Denmark, in general, state-supported care provision is low everywhere else in the EU. Indeed, while female employment has increased throughout Europe, there does not seem to have been a corresponding increase in state provision of care services, which further forces women into part-time, temporary and generally low-paid, low-status occupations.

However, there is a trend towards providing more publicly funded childcare, for example, in Austria, Germany, the Netherlands and Spain which did not traditionally provide a high level of publicly funded services (EC, 1998). There is also hope for change seen in individual cases, where policies follow a long agenda, attempting to follow a different norm of gender regime. Such an example is of the City-Time policies in many Italian cities (Franco and Ponzellini, 1997). In Modena, one project aims to improve the extent to which services meet citizens' needs in terms of content and accessibility. Women are expressly identified as the people for whom restricted opening hours and services are a problem, making the interface between work and family life very difficult. Changes to the opening hours of private and public services, the setting up of a health services booking centre, the opening of a playschool and a daycentre for elderly people were all introduced. The project is a relatively successful attempt to arrange time to accommodate a female norm of activity rather than that of a male. It could be said, on the one hand, that this initiative still does not challenge the balance of gender roles, but just accommodates them, and one can note that, for its successful implementation, it relies on the existence of women in senior institutional positions in the city council. However, on the other hand it does illustrate that service provision can be built around an alternative view of activity, and also illustrates the importance of gaining women in senior positions for the advancement of equality initiatives.

There is an imbalance between provisions for children and those for dependent adults, especially older people. There have been developments, for example, Finland, Austria and France have recently introduced new financial benefits devoted specifically to the care of older people (EC, 1998: 11). The Scandinavian countries (and the Netherlands) again stand out as having the greatest provision where older peoples' rights to services are laid down in legislation. This compares with the other member states where there are no clear entitlements to a minimum level of service. Given that the ageing of the population is occurring at the fastest rate in the Southern European countries, it is of particular concern that these southern countries have the lowest public provision of either institutional or home-based care.

With regard to monetary benefits and tax rebates for care, there are only a limited number of countries which offer such provision (EC, 1998) – where they exist, they are fully taken up, however, they tend to reinforce a female-centred model of care provision. Such a policy is typified by Austria where leave provisions, part-time work and financial compensations allow a woman to stay at home for care purposes, but the same provision is not available for men. Similarly gendered provisions are found in Germany, Greece, Belgium and France, the last of which sees benefit given to parents at the birth of their second child (Allocation Parentale d'Education) and which has been directly related to a decline in the activity rates of *mothers* of two or more children (EC, 1998: 10). In addition, with regard to care of the elderly, in most EU countries, trends are in favour of home based care and away from institutionalization (EC, 1998: 12). Given the existing imbalance in the gender responsibility for care and domestic work, this trend does not bode well for facilitating women's employment participation. Once again the policy can be criticized for doing little to challenge the status quo; indeed, the continuing gender imbalance in the entire approach to caring is perceived to be an area where future action must be taken (EC, 1998).

Finally, linking back to earlier discussion, the position of migrant workers in gaining access to such services should also be considered. Given the citizenship and immigration policies of many European countries, such resources and facilities will only be available to those workers who are citizens, reinforcing once again the double disadvantage faced by migrant women.

---

1 Different models of family-friendly state policy can be identified which have different implications for the division of domestic labour and care services. The predominant pattern in each of the models however supports a female-centred provision of care.
2 The UK compares negatively with provision and policy in many other European countries. However, despite outstanding examples such as that of Denmark, with its integrated system of state-supported services and provisions, women are still primarily responsible for care and the need to manage the interface between work and family life across Europe.
3 Trends are towards further accommodation of women's care roles rather than challenging the status quo. There is little evidence that there is a change in the existing sexual division of labour.

**Key learning points**

## Policy on older workers

Moore, Tilson and Whitting (1994), in an international overview of employment policies towards older workers, identify similarities and differences between countries. All countries are trying to develop provisions to cope with demographic changes as the costs of supporting inactive elderly people increases. Most countries have aimed to make retirement ages higher and to make pensions more flexible, indeed there has been a clear trend away from encouraging the exit of older workers through early retirement, to one where retention of older workers is increasingly favoured.

However, there are clear differences between approaches to retirement and pensions, and legislative protection against age discrimination. On a European-wide comparison, specific age-related legislation is limited, but there are some examples: Germany and Austria, have legislation requiring employers to report any planned redundancies of older workers to ensure against discrimination. In France, workers aged fifty to fifty-four who are made redundant are excluded from the state pension, and the employer is forced to bear the cost. With regard to measures to retain older workers, specific training and skills courses can be found in France and Austria while wage subsidies are available for employers recruiting older workers in Germany, Austria and France. Scandinavian countries have established health-at-work initiative schemes targeted at older workers such as the 'FinnAge' programme in Finland. This is in contrast to most other countries, including the UK where training for older workers tends to fit into the framework of general state provided vocational training; most with age limits. However at least in the UK, the age limit for this training has been increased to sixty-three in 1994, while other countries have narrower age limits, for example, twenty-nine in Italy and forty-six in Greece (Moore, Tilson and Whitting, 1994). Europe still has a long way to go to meet the examples of Japan which has the strongest tradition of measures for older people, where 85 per cent of people aged fifty-five to sixty-four work (Moore, Tilson and Whitting, 1994), and the USA with the most long-standing and wide-ranging legislative provisions (since 1967) and a range of agencies for advice, guidance and support to older people.

Stronger state/public policy on older workers can encourage employers to develop their own further strategies at organizational level. Indeed, examples of organization-level initiatives in Europe tend to be found in those countries with more developed state policies for older workers (Moore, Tilson and Whitting, 1994). However, initiatives tend to focus on the need to rehabilitate older workers already in employment who are no longer able to continue in their present position. Much still has to be done about the lack of recruitment of older workers and age-related discrimination.

It is difficult to assess the possible and likely effects of age-related anti-discrimination legislation, because discrimination is only a contributory factor to the low level of older worker participation. Interconnecting with employer discrimination are health problems associated with some older workers, the firm's economic performance, and the pension and retirement rules of the various governments. Albeit in a US context, Rix (1993) found that anti-discrimination legislation has little effect at all on employer practices or, more importantly, on attitudes towards older workers. This is largely because age-related legislation is seen as generally poorly defined and weak where it exists, or relating to a very narrow and limited range of activities, for example, in France, it only relates to job advertisements.

There is also personal choice to be considered. People do not always want to work in their fifties, let alone past official retirement age. Thompson (1991) found in the UK context that there was a lack of applications from older workers in many recruitment campaigns, and it should be remembered that the 1980s and early 1990s trend towards early retirement schemes was also supply led. Indeed, early exit from employment is generally welcomed by employee groups as an individual right, especially by trade unions. For example, in the Netherlands, trade unions impeded moves by the government to abolish early retirement arrangements (Moore, Tilson and Whitting, 1994).

Finally, as with many of the equality measures discussed throughout this book, the economic motive or business case is always prominent. Measures to increase the participation of older workers come from a concern for the demographic trends in Europe which seem to predict an accelerated decline in the working-age, economically active population, rather than concern for the ethical issue of equality or the need to value diversity in the workforce.

---

1 All countries are trying to develop policy to cope with the ageing population. A shift from encouraging the early exit of older workers through the 1980s towards recognition of the need to retain older workers can be identified.
2 Legislation around age-related discrimination is limited across Europe and compares negatively with that enacted in the USA and Japan.
3 The issue of individual choice to retire early and opposition against increasing retirement ages must be considered as a possible future impediment to current policy initiatives.

**Key learning points**

---

## Policy on disability

Hurst (1995) divides Europe into three subdivisions. The Nordic countries and the Netherlands, countries with powerful colonizing traditions (UK, France, Germany, Spain) and poorer, underdeveloped countries such as Portugal, Italy, Ireland and Greece. The Nordic group stands out in Europe in having a long reputation of concern for human rights and equality of opportunity, resulting in financial commitment to service provision for disabled people. This also includes a high level of integrated education and housing within the community rather than institutions. However, these countries are weak on legislative rights of disabled people. The 'colonizing countries' are weaker on social provision but stand out with their anti-discrimination legislation. The 'underdeveloped' group stand out in a negative way with their overall lack of provision, whether involving services or legislation.

In general, a significant criticism of public policy in all countries of Europe, is the way in which disabled people are isolated and separated from mainstream society. Policy is often made on the basis of a 'charity ethic' rather than policy being discussed, decided and initiated by disabled people themselves. Legislation aiming to ensure that disabled people have rights to equal treatment, as opposed to only receiving assistance has been adopted in most member states (EC, 1997a: 112). However, that which exists is seen as lacking enforcement measures, while there is little attempt to ensure that all aspects of society are accessible to disabled people. This affects chances of employment if disabled people cannot live and work in the mainstream of society. In addition, anti-discrimination legislation tends to achieve much more for those people already in work, rather than encouraging further recruitment (EuroFoundation, 1998: 83).

There has been a general shift in state policy towards disabled people, notably the move from a medical (focusing on the disability as residing in the person) to a social model (focusing on the disability as residing in society's attitudes towards the person) (EC, 1997b: 111). There has also been a shift away from quota systems, the primary legal tool in the EU to assist employment, where there is a mandatory obligation on firms to employ a minimum proportion of disabled workers. Although such systems still exist in over half the member states, it has been recognized since the mid-1980s that they have failed to deliver real gains. Indeed, quota systems have been abandoned in the UK, and restricted in five other countries (EC, 1997b: 112; Thornton and Lunt, 1995: 9). Explanations range from the negative 'backlash' effects of positive discrimination discussed in earlier chapters (particularly Chapter 5; see also Hurst, 1995: 531) to the way in which the systems were operated. For example, the now abandoned UK system of quotas was 'uniquely odd in its conception' (Thornton and Lunt, 1995: 11) having no enforcement of penalties for non-compliance and relying on numbers of those officially registered as disabled when the trend was towards a decline in registration as disabled due to the stigmatization it was felt to bring. Quota systems that still exist in other countries operate within a climate of recognition of rights and are not reliant on national disability registration. Additionally, fines for non-compliance were replaced in Germany, France and the Netherlands by voluntary contributions to special funds supporting disabled causes, thus encouraging the social responsibility of firms (Lunt and Thornton, 1993).

Other trends within state policy, include the move away from compensatory principles towards increased recognition of employment rights, increased attention to equal opportunities and a shift from state intervention to individual responsibility (Lunt and Thornton, 1993).

This last aspect has been a trend which has been encouraged by the demands of the disabled movement such as the 'Independent Living Movement' in the UK which has argued against the 'charity ethic' policy of many countries (Hurst, 1995; Thornton and Lunt, 1995). Largely because of the comparative strength of the disabled movement in the UK (and one might suggest, the fit between the overall emphasis on the individualization of the employment relationship and focus of legislation – see discussion in Chapters 5 and 9), such policies as the 'Access to Work' scheme in the UK have aimed to give the disabled worker control over decisions about the best way to meet their needs in employment, meeting Hurst's (1995) criticisms of much of European policy.

Moving on to welfare packages, in the UK and Ireland, the system of state benefits is seen as a major barrier to employment for the disabled person. Taking up paid work depends on the feasibility of the complete financial income package, which means that often, only very part-time work might be a feasible option (EuroFoundation, 1998: 76). This can explain the high level of inaction by choice referred to earlier in this chapter, at least for the UK and Ireland. In other countries, the social security system does not militate against paid work for disabled people in the same way. However, the fact that similar levels of occupational segregation, economic inaction and unemployment exist over Europe as a whole, indicate that other strategies must also be failing to deliver real gains. There is evidence that subsidies for employing disabled workers (for example, in France, Spain, Germany) are often not taken up, and their appropriateness is questioned by employers in a similar way to positive discrimination initiatives (EuroFoundation, 1998: 79). Research also found that employers were often unaware of, or were unconcerned about, other publicly funded aid and adaption schemes such as grants to improve access and improve training (EuroFoundation, 1998).

It should also be remembered that there are restrictions on eligibility for legislation and the variety of state-sponsored schemes. First, in many countries, eligibility is restricted to legal citizens or denizens, highlighting once more the disadvantaged position of those millions of guest workers, especially those who are illegal workers. Second, much of the legislation is not applied to small- and medium-sized enterprises, those that employ less than 500 people (accounting for two-thirds of EU employment), leading to concern with the position of disabled workers within these smaller workplaces and the production by the EC of the report on *The Employment of People with Disabilities in Small and Medium-Sized Enterprises* (EuroFoundation, 1998).

When comparing the UK with other European countries, current UK policies may be more effective in delivering real gains for people with disabilities because the disabled movement is so strong compared with in other EU countries. However, the major difference is that the statutory code of practice in the UK is still not supported by mechanisms to ensure compliance, unlike in many other countries where the mechanisms for ensuring good practices, are legislative (Thornton and Lunt, 1995: 33).

**Key learning points**

1 While different national models, with their respective strengths and weaknesses can be identified, state policy across Europe can be criticized for failing to take into consideration the views of disabled people themselves.
2 There has been a lack of integrated attempts to ensure that all aspects of society are accessible to disabled people with obvious consequences for employment opportunities.
3 State policy can have a detrimental effect on the labour market participation of disabled people. In particular, the state benefits system in the UK and Ireland are seen as major barriers to employment.

# Wider social attitudes

This section aims to consider what significant trends exist in Europe with regard to wider social attitudes. This relates to a social identity approach to looking at equality and diversity in employment, emphasizing the way in which wider social attitudes impact upon, and intersect with, the experience of different groups in the labour market.

## The rise of European racism

A particularly worrying trend involves the current resurgence of racist and extreme nationalist movements in a number of European societies (Wrench and Solomos, 1993). The Front National in France is perhaps one of the most conspicuous of racist groups and there are similar political groups in other EU countries such as the British Nationalist Party, Italy's Northern League, the German People's Union and Austria's Freedom Party. As evidence of increasing popularity, the Freedom Party is now the third largest political party in Austria, (Fekete, 1999) and has come closer to gaining a place in national government than any other far-right European party after coming second in the polls in the recent Austrian election (Castle, 1999).

In addition, Deland (1998) points to the rise of many smaller extreme right groups all over Europe, for example, the Research Group for Studies of the European Civilization in France, the Salisbury Group in the UK, Vesta Nueva in Italy, the Young Forum in Germany. Even in Scandinavia, countries held up as models of egalitarian values, there are similar trends, for example, the Norwegian People's Movement Against Immigration, the Danish League and the Swedish Homestead Party. These smaller groups base their arguments not around biological bases which cause more immediate criticism and rejection, but in cultural terms, arguing about the impossibility of cultural integration, the threat posed to national cultures by diversity and the need to separate ethnic groups. In Italy, this has seen divisions between the rich North and poorer South emphasized, with direct campaigns against immigrants and Gypsies in northern cities (Fekete, 1999: 193). Such attitudes have also begun to filter through into public discourse in Sweden (see Alund and Schierup, 1993: 106–8; Deland, 1998; Pred, 1997). Relating to the discussion of immigration and citizenship policies above, moves away from Swedish multicultural and pluralist ideologies could have significant negative implications for minority ethnic groups in these countries.

Wider social attitudes intersect with legislation and state policy, where the recommendation is that there must be a change in the legal status of workers as well as attempts to change social attitudes towards race. On the one hand, as was argued earlier, changing state policy and citizenship rights will not guarantee equal treatment if the society is divided on ethnic/racial grounds. On the other hand, nor will more open recruitment by employers, if foreign workers are denied the rights of residence and free movement. Legal citizenship may be of limited value if there are structural and cultural impediments, such as discrimination and racist attitudes, to the exercise of such rights and responsibilities (Bryant, 1997). Wrench (1998) takes a similar line in his argument that making citizenship easier will not necessarily help those millions of workers not covered by EU legislation, particularly the most vulnerable 'group 5' workers stating that 'formal membership ... is by no means a guarantee of "equal opportunity" or an answer to a society divided along ethnic/racial lines' (Wrench, 1998: 28). As an illustration of this, a recent newspaper report included the following story:

> A Viennese acquaintance, born and bred, has a successful job as a computer programmer. He sounds Viennese, but does not look it: both parents are from Ghana. The affluent programmer lives in a slum, because every time he calls round to view a flat, his dream home is immediately – and temporarily – withdrawn from the market. Though he has an Austrian passport, he will not answer adverts that state: 'For Austrians only'. (Karacs, 1999)

What is clear from this example are the detrimental effects which wider social attitudes can have if minority ethnic workers, regardless of legal status or background, are classified and identified by other people as 'migrant' or 'immigrant': the case of 'Fortress Europe' once again. It is clear that all ethnic groups do not receive equal treatment in the labour market, or wider society. Such an example illustrates a key underlying theme throughout this book, that workplace and labour market inequality cannot only be an employment policy issue. Inequality in the labour market reflects inequality throughout society and the effect of wider social attitudes on the labour market.

---

1 A current resurgence of racist movements can be identified across Europe. Widespread racist attitudes impede the employment opportunities of minority ethnic workers by impacting upon state policy. In addition, wider attitudes intersect with state policy on citizenship and immigration, to further disadvantage workers from minority ethnic groups regardless of their legal status.

**Key learning point**

# The continuing gender regime

On the issue of the balance of responsibilities between domestic and paid work, there are signs of change. Kiernan (1992) finds that there is a clear change in sex-role attitudes since the 1970s, with men and women increasingly espousing more egalitarian attitudes. Indeed, Van der Lippe and Roelofs (1995) find that while, overall, women still spend more time than men on domestic activities, across all of the countries studied, women are devoting less time to domestic duties including childcare.

On the other hand, both studies also find that if one parent has to give up work to care for a child, it is almost always the woman (Van der Lippe and Roelofs, 1995). Similarly with regard to the interface between work and family life, the implicit assumption is that if some adaptation and flexibility is required the onus is on the family to adjust to the workplace rather than the other way round, (Kiernan, 1992: 497) and within families, on the woman to adjust. There are still wide disparities between countries with regard to who takes responsibility for domestic tasks. For example, men take on the least proportion of domestic work in Italy where women do 84 per cent of domestic activities (remember that, correspondingly perhaps, Italian women have the lowest employment participation rates in the EU) while Danish women do the least domestic work (they still do 66 per cent however). The UK stands at 67 per cent. However, the trend for women to do less domestic work is not accounted for by the increasing role of men in the domestic sphere, indeed while Danish women do the least domestic work, Danish men do not appear to do any more work, reflecting the wider use of state facilities. A clear illustration of this involves the take-up of paternity leave which few men make use of, even if their failure to use it results in its loss or in financial penalties (EC, 1997b). In Finland for example, the take-up rate is only 64 per cent while in Denmark, it is 58 per cent – both countries which are held up as having good family-friendly provision. The low male take-up undermines the objective of equality, since it means that it is still women who take time off to fulfil parental responsibilities.

In summary, on the one hand there appears little change to the predominant view that domestic work is women's work and that legislation, and public policy initiatives, appear to have done little to change social attitudes. While social attitudes on the sexual division of labour within families do not appear to be changing in themselves, there is also little legislative pressure for change in this domain either. Relating back to the discussion of women's labour market patterns and evidence of the growth in the number of women with unbroken career patterns (Plantenga, 1995), it is notable that as qualifications to her finding, Platenga added the note of caution that the new pattern of female participation required a specific social infrastructure to allow paid and unpaid work to be combined. Only Denmark reflected this model and, given the contradictory evidence of continued occupational segregation, even in Denmark, were these uninterrupted female careers characterized by low-status, vertically segregated, low-paid jobs? Also, as has been discussed at various points in the book, should the aim be to increase women's uninterrupted career paths; ultimately meeting the dominant norm of work, or would the most radical aim be that alternative forms of working, including broken career paths and part-time work, are also valued?

However, such a negative conclusion should not divert attention away from the positive examples of change and progress. For example, the City-Time policies in Modena which are attempting to change the way in which the interface between work and family life is structured, indicate that there are other models which can be followed. There are also other social models of a different gender contract, where structures and facilities are in place which allow men to take on more of the domestic responsibilities if they so choose. Indeed, while the low take-up of paternal leave in Finland and Denmark was highlighted, it should be remembered that more fathers take paternal leave than do not in these countries. Link this with overall views of a shift (albeit small) in domestic roles, then perhaps we can have a more positive view of future prospects.

## Key learning points

1 There is evidence that women are spending less time on domestic duties and more time in the labour market. However, the balance of the sexual division of labour has been little altered, with wider social attitudes largely supporting the existing gender regime.

2 We need to question whether the trend towards increased childcare and other measures designed to allow women (predominantly) to better manage the interface between work and family is a positive development. Policy such as this continues to support the status quo rather than leading to a radical transformation in gender roles.

## Activity

### Activity 10.2: Equality failing in France

Read these two newspaper articles and discuss the questions below, drawing on issues and themes within this chapter but also from Chapters 5 and 8.

*Boost to equality in French politics*

French women scored a major victory yesterday when the senate passed a controversial motion calling for a constitutional amendment to boost sexual equality in parliament. Under the motion, the constitution will be changed to include a phrase stating: 'The law will encourage equal access for women and men to political life and elected posts.' Women occupy just 10.4 per cent of the seats in the 577 member national assembly, the worst record of any EU country except Greece.

But many feminists fear that legislating for women MPs, far from creating equality, will create a category apart. France is alone in trying to use the constitution to achieve parity between the sexes in public life, and the better path was that taken by Sweden, where growing pressure from women led to gradual change, with the result that women now hold 40 per cent of the seats in the Stockholm parliament.

*Source*: edited extract from the *Guardian*, 6 March 1999

### Drive for equality failing in France

A government inquiry has found that sexual discrimination in the workplace is flagrant and requires radical political remedies. According to the inquiry . . . France has one of the worse records in the EU on women's employment. French women have more difficulty than men in finding posts, receive less training and earn lower salaries. Women also face higher unemployment and more restrictions of their careers.

All left-wing and most right-wing parties are committed to parity in political appointments but there is still resistance to appointing women to certain posts. [The inquiry] will recommend a 'complete rethink' of all reforms intended to protect women or help them balance professional and home life, for she says that they have sometimes created a backlash. Among the restrictions on careers are measures that prohibit night work and allow an extended parental leave of three years, which makes it difficult for women to re-enter the world of work.

*Source*: Edited extract from the *Guardian*, 14 August 1999.

### Questions

1 Discuss the way in which government policy intersects with wider social attitudes. What consequences does this interaction have for the experience of women in the French labour market?
2 Consider the ways in which government policy can support and uphold discrimination and disadvantage in employment, drawing out the key examples from these articles and more widely within this chapter.
3 Consider the various factors leading to the increased equality within the Swedish Parliament.

# European Union

## Strengths

Equality issues do have an emphasis within the official EU rhetoric and find a place within the many Directives, Recommendations and Action Plans of the EU. Indeed, the principle of equal treatment for men and women was enshrined within the 1957 Treaty of Rome, particularly concerning the principle of equal pay, long before it became an issue of significance within the member states (Rees, 1998: 1). The EU and the European Economic Community (EEC) before it, have acted as catalysts to the development of an equality awareness through their legislation (details of which have been discussed in Chapter 6; for a summary see Rees, 1998:

52). Ireland, for example, was forced to bring about a fundamental change in the status of married women in order to meet the European Directive on the subject of equal treatment (Rees, 1998: 54). The ECJ has also had a direct impact in supporting the cause of individual cases against employers or member states which have made significant contributions to the formulation, understanding and delivery of EO policies (see Hoskyns, 1996, for a detailed list of such ECJ contributions). Apart from the legally binding Directives, the EC also publishes Recommendations and Council Resolutions aiming to offer advice and frameworks of policy initiatives. In addition, there have been a number of EC Medium-Term Action Programmes, establishing frameworks within which EC legislation could be enacted, projects funded, progress monitored and networks developed between countries to encourage the flow of information and expertise (Rees, 1998: 59; see Singh, 1997, for specific details about the Fourth Programme). Issues of primary concern have involved women's vocational training, the link between family and work lives (EC, 1998), working time (EIRR, 1997b) and sexual harassment (EIRR, 1997a).

The monitoring function has also been a serious consideration, for example, a progress report of the Third Programme on sexual harassment in the EU in July 1996 found that while some progress had been made in terms of legislation and collective bargaining, the EC Code of Practice and Recommendations had not seen sufficient progress to ensure the effective prevention of sexual harassment. Therefore, within the following Fourth programme, the EC started the process of proposing an instrument on combating sexual harassment at work and proposing possible legislation (EIRR, 1997a). On race issues and racism, growing concerns within the EC led to declarations in 1986 and 1991 calling upon member states to act unambiguously against racism within their countries and, in addition, 1997 was declared European Year Against Racism (for details see EIRR, 1997b), in which racism in the workplace was of particular concern.

Initiatives based around equality issues have also been developed and funded by the EC and member states; for example, New Opportunities for Women aims to help women with their own enterprise development or to reintegrate them into the labour market. The initiative for the Handicapped and Disadvantaged Persons Inter-university cooperation programme (HORIZON) has been targeted in a similar way at workers with disabilities. In Chapter 7, there was a discussion of the need to 'mainstream' equality issues in order to challenge norms of attitude and behaviours and existing structures, rather than marginalize them to particular departments, programmes of action or individuals within organizations. This has also been a concern of the EC, where the Third and Fourth Medium-Term Action Programmes on equal opportunities have aimed to make equal opportunities an integral part of all EU policies (Rees, 1998: 63).

## Weaknesses

All these policy and legislative initiatives are and have been a significantly positive influence on the equality agenda within member states. However, there are a variety of criticisms regarding the impact of the EU at member-state level, not least that there is the widespread continued existence of underlying patterns of disadvantage. Indeed, the continued vertical and horizontal segregation, and inequalities of pay on gender grounds, indicate that even the starting point for equal treatment within the Treaty of Rome is far from gained (Rees, 1998: 69). The main difficulty is how EU Directives and Recommendations are implemented by individual member states. As discussed in Chapter 6, although Directives are binding and take precedence over national law, member states have discretion over how to achieve the desired results; the follow-up recommendations of the EC do not have to be implemented. The impact that EC legislation has depends very much on the legislation and policy within the individual member state. For example, the law in Ireland was perhaps the least favourable in all Europe to women on many variables and so women probably benefited from EU measures; but Danish women are likely to have gained little from the EU legislation and policy initiatives (Roelofs, 1995). Rees (1998: 53) discusses how some member states have been able to 'level down' their rights in line with EC Directives, for example, raising women's retirement age to that of men rather than vice versa.

There are other weaknesses inherent to advancing the equality agenda through EU instruments. First, the financial resources given to policy initiatives such as HORIZON and New Opportunities for Women are insufficient given the numbers of people involved. Issues of cost are obviously at the forefront of decisions to introduce equality initiatives. While much is made of the fact that the Article 119 of the 1957 Treaty of Rome had the principle of equal treatment enshrined within it, more sceptical commentators point to the fact that considerations of competition played an important role in motivating these first policy steps. The French government insisted on a set of regulations as it was the first member state to introduce legislation on equal pay and was afraid that major differences in pay between the sexes would turn out to be economically disadvantageous to France (Rees, 1998: 51; Roelofs, 1995). The vast majority of areas that the EC has dealt with in the realm of equality have had an economic dimension and, so, behind most measures can be found the economic or business-case rationale. For example, one can identify that it is the demographic trends and the threat of a falling working-age population which has led to calls for policies to remove barriers to older workers in the labour market. With the existence of the Single Market, the concern is that part of the drive towards convergence of the various national economies will contain an imperative to reduce public spending (welfare benefits), which will disproportionately affect those who are most disadvantaged within the labour market (Sivar-iandam, 1997). A strong theme of discussion which has run through many chapters of this book (particularly Chapters 5 and 8) has involved the weaknesses of a business-case perspective in advancing the 'long agenda' of equality.

Second, making policy that will appeal to all member states is difficult. Trying to get a Recommendation let alone a legally binding Directive accepted by all member states is a very slow process. The European Industrial Relations Review (EIRR) report on the sexual harassment initiative (EIRR, 1997a) details the lengthy process and the way in which lack of co-operation by certain countries halts progress. With regard to minority ethnic workers, while the Evrignis Report of 1985 set forth forty recommendations for combating racism and xenophobia in Europe, only two have since been realized in full (Herzing, 1995). One could also point to the UK's persistent (but eventually unsuccessful) opposition to the introduction of the Working Time Directive (EIRR, 1997b).

Third, in line with the overall trend for equality policies to become individualized (see discussion of diversity approaches in Chapter 5), the mainstreaming approach of the Third and Fourth Action Programmes places an emphasis on the need for women to integrate themselves; the implication being that women need to be aware of their rights and opportunities. The focus is not on the need to remove barriers to women's employment from social attitudes and discrimination.

One can also criticize other aspects of the content of equality initiatives coming out of the EU. Apart from the legislative Directives, they are based largely around raising awareness and the dissemination of information rather than positive action: the liberal rather than the radical model (see Chapter 5). As with the criticisms of equality policy within the UK context, the lack of challenge to the status quo within the EU policy framework is highlighted as a significant weakness. The onus is on allowing people to change and adapt to fit in with the dominant status quo, 'there is no suggestion of changing the patterns, values and priorities of the mainstream in order to accommodate a more diverse workforce' (Rees, 1998: 68). The emphasis is on the dominant white, male, full time, non-disabled, aged twenty-five to forty, norm of employment. Equal treatment means equal to that male norm. Rees (1998: 67) points out the striking sentence used in the foreword to the EC document outlining its role in developing equal opportunities where 'Women are men's equals'. In Rees's terms, the aim is to 'tailor' the mainstream rather than 'transform' it: Cockburn's (1991) 'short' rather than 'long' agenda. There is no attempt to change the patterns of paid and unpaid work, for example, the ECJ has made it clear that its role is not to invade the private, family sphere and aim to alter the balance of domestic responsibilities (Rees, 1998: 55; Singh, 1997: 70). This is a particular weakness where the position of women in the labour market is concerned, given the discussion in Chapter 3 which highlighted the fact that much of the disadvantage faced by women is rooted in restrictions on their freedom to fully enter into the labour market and education and training in the first place.

Another significant criticism that can be levelled at EU policy is that it is almost exclusively focused on equality between men and women. The legislative framework is designed predominantly to address inequalities between the sexes. For example, disabled citizens are overlooked and ignored in the Treaty on European Union, which is significant because this then limits the EC to non-binding measures, as legislative measures are restricted to areas referred to in the treaty (Waddington, 1997). In addition, commentators have noted the way in which the EC has therefore developed limited competences to address disability-related issues (Hurst, 1995; Waddington, 1997). In particular, the focus of the EC Recommendations is misplaced. Hurst (1995) points out that the traditional perspective of EC Recommendations has seen disability only in relation to rehabilitation rather than also recognizing the concept of the rights of disabled people.

Perhaps most alarmingly, Waddington (1997) identifies that disabled people are denied rights associated with EU citizenship. For example, limited access to education and discrimination adversely affects disabled students who wish to study in a different member state while, more generally, disabled persons have difficulty gaining access to accessible transport, housing and workplaces. Thus the right to freedom of movement is curtailed. With regard to freedom to receive services and purchase goods, disabled people find they cannot access many service providers such as cinemas, shops and bars. Discriminatory practices such as inaccessible polling stations or failing to provide Braille polling papers deny many disabled people the right to vote.

This is clearly also an issue for minority ethnic groups. First, the Treaty of Rome and the Single European Act also did not confer any competence on the EU in the field of racial or ethnic discrimination (Wrench, 1998: 29). There has been some progress with the 1997 Draft Treaty of Amsterdam introducing a clause that, for the first time, allows European institutions to take action to combat racial and ethnic discrimination but there is no provision to ensure that measures are implemented (Wrench, 1998: 31). Linked to the discussion about disabled workers and EU rights are also questions relevant to minority ethnic groups about who is eligible for protection by, and can take advantage of, the facilities of EU legislation and initiatives. Rights to equal treatment only apply to EU citizens. As a rough estimate there are an estimated 13 million workers who would not be eligible (Rees, 1998), including those group 5 workers who face the most precarious and vulnerable employment in the EU (Wrench, 1998). This provides the starting discussion for the way in which different government policies in different EU countries can influence the position and status of different groups in the EU labour markets.

## Key learning points

1 Equality issues have held a central place in the policy-making of the EC and ECJ, with Directives, Recommendations and Action Programmes having a direct influence on policy developments within the member states.

2 The EU is, however, more or less influential depending on the way in which EU policy is implemented at member-state level, and there is continued evidence of underlying patterns of disadvantage. Other weaknesses include limited financial resources and the individualizing emphasis of EU policies.

3 The main weaknesses of the EU with regard to equality issues involve the predominance of the liberal model with its lack of challenge to existing structures and norms, and the fact that policy is almost exclusively focused on equality between men and women.

# Trade unions and equality bargaining

Previous chapters have highlighted the importance of collective action in playing a role in advancing the equality agenda; indeed, the possible detrimental consequences of the individualizing focus of the diversity model of equality initiatives and of HRM have been discussed. The overall conclusion has been that collective methods need to be included in a wider long-term goal of equality, alongside legislative and policy initiatives coming from government, EU and at the organizational level. This can be collective action by self-organized groups such as the disability movements discussed earlier (Hurst, 1995), or by trade unions, the subject of this discussion.

Trade unions have become increasingly involved in EU consultation and policy-making as part of the 'social dialogue' process. This involves on the one hand, unions across Europe coming together as a 'united' body within the European Trades Union Congress (ETUC), and on the other, the ETUC meeting and consulting with other social partners: employer federations and their representative bodies (Cockburn, 1995). Trade unions at the European level have thus become involved with the equality and diversity initiatives of the EC. Cockburn's (1995: 217) research indicates how meeting at the European level has indicated to national trade unions the differences in working conditions between countries, and has encouraged improved European legislation and European collective agreements, a new strategy for unions in the UK. At a European level the involvement of the ETUC in 1994 within the social dialogue was a key element in pushing for a declaration on measures to combat racism and xenophobia, encouragement of anti-racist activity to encourage action in all twenty-two countries where the ETUC has affiliates and in the launch of the 1997 European Year against Racism (EIRR, 1997b; Labour Research, 1994). Joint actions such as this reflect the increasing realization that unions throughout Europe need to mobilize against racist violence (Labour Research, 1994).

In terms of representation, there are a number of women's structures within the ETUC, as there are for the UK TUC, which aim to draw women into decision-making processes. The UK TUC is better than most national trade union confederations in regard to women's representation (Braithwaite and Byrne, 1993). However, few women fill senior, negotiating or specialist officer roles and the structures at European level remain male dominated; indeed, the ETUC executive committee is 93 per cent male (Cockburn, 1995: 220). Overall, it is usually men who represent the women members of national trade unions at a European level. Where women are involved, it is usually over specific 'women's issues'. And representation is likely to be by a white man, or a white woman: minority ethnic workers are under-represented at European level and there are no corresponding structures designed deliberately to draw minority ethnic workers into the ETUC decision-making structures.

With regard to equality bargaining (see Chapter 7), whether or not equal opportunities is seen as a collective bargaining issue by trade unions and employers in different countries can have an effect on its primacy in policy at national and organizational level (EuroFoundation, 1997). A report titled *Equal Opportunities and Collective Bargaining in the European Union* found that: 'it is only if equal opportunities are integrated into collective bargaining at the highest level that pay differentials can be reduced and the 'discriminatory function' of bargaining can be curbed' (EuroFoundation, 1997: xii).

Comparing different countries, the study finds that in Denmark, Finland and Sweden equality issues are integrated into the collective bargaining process, which also coincides with a positive record on equality issues. However, even where equality bargaining is most established, the bargaining agendas remain short rather than long, focusing on accommodation of difference rather than challenging the status quo. Another conclusion of the report finds that 'bargaining remains overwhelmingly dominated by a traditional outlook which has been rendered obsolete by social and economic developments' (Euro-Foundation, 1997: 26–28), highlighting again the white, male hegemony (see Chapter 4) that continues to dominate structures, and the traditional attitudes that continue to dominate wider attitudes.

Europe and the EU offer an alternative level of campaigning and collective action around equality issues for national trade unions. However, there are still weaknesses in terms of representation and the focus on accommodation of diversity rather than challenging the status quo, which limit the effectiveness the European trade union movement can have (see discussion in Chapter 7).

**Key learning points**

1 National trade unions are becoming increasingly involved in 'European' matters, both through the formation of the ETUC and through discussion and consultation with social partners as part of the 'social dialogue'.

2 Although there are examples of ways in which the ETUC has encouraged equality policies and initiatives, European trade union structures remain male dominated and underrepresent minority ethnic groups.

3 Equality issues need to be mainstreamed within collective bargaining agendas in order to gain the most effect, and these suffer from an approach that is based on liberal rather than radical aims.

# Conclusion

This chapter has presented a Europe-wide overview of the situation of those groups identified as being disproportionately disadvantaged in the UK context. Generally, the same groups are seen as facing a similarly disadvantaged position within all countries of the EU, however, the context of each country is different. What has emerged is a picture of differing legal positions of workers, varying approaches to citizenship and immigration, and differing welfare ideologies and service provision. All of these factors are significant influences on the position of different groups of workers within their specific country-contexts. Overall, the Scandinavian countries are highlighted as having the most progressive and egalitarian of systems, where women and minority ethnic workers in particular have the most chance of coming closest to gaining equality within the labour market and wider society (although the shortcomings of even these systems have been discussed).

We have also discussed the way in which such social and employment policy positions intersect and overlap with wider social attitudes. Common themes across the EU have been the worrying rise of racist groups and the continuing gender regime that impedes the equality project. However, such developments will have more or less effect depending on their intersection with state policy; for example, extreme right-wing political groups pose more of a threat to the position of minority ethnic workers where the immigration and citizenship policies also discriminate against them (for example in Austria). We are also able to see how the UK stands in comparison to the rest of the EU. For example, the positive effects of the strong disability movement in the UK compared with that in other countries, and the comparatively accommodating nature of the UK's immigration and citizenship policies. On the other hand, we can see how far behind other EU countries are the UK's legislative protection, its family-friendly provision and services for older workers.

In some respects, the overall picture is somewhat disappointing, with trends towards increasing inequality and breakdowns even in the egalitarian social models of the Scandinavian countries being identified. However, we should not forget that there are examples of positive practice, and a comparative view across different countries allows us to see other models and approaches which may further advance equality and diversity projects.

# Review and discussion questions

1 Consider where you think the UK equality record stands in relation to other countries in Europe.
2 Reflect on the position of illegal workers, both from a point of view of state and EU policy, and of wider social attitudes. Consider the statement that their treatment stands as: 'the super-exploitation of migrants suffering conditions which would not be tolerated by native workers but which they are not in a position to reject' (Wrench 1998: 11). Are there models or countries that provide more opportunities for equality for this group of workers than others?
3 What are the implications of the maintenance of the existing sexual division of labour? How do state and EU policies contribute to support for the status

quo? From the reading in this chapter, what models or policy examples offer opportunity for change or more radical initiatives?
4 'The prevailing society is what discriminates against us – how that society works directly impinges on its treatment of and attitudes to disabled people', (Hurst: 1995: 529). Discuss this statement, drawing on reflections about the impact of state policy and wider social attitudes on the position of disabled workers. (Also draw on discussions in Chapter 3.)

# Further reading

Cockburn, C. (1995). Redrawing the boundaries: trade unions, women and Europe. In *Gender, Culture and Organisational Change* (C. Itzin and J. Newman, eds). Routledge.
Examines the involvement of UK trade unions at a European level. Critically evaluates the structures and practices of the ETUC in representing a diverse workforce. Concentrates on the gender balance.
EC (European Commission) (1997). *Employment in Europe, 1997*, Employment and Social Affairs, European Commission.
Survey findings and information on a variety of trends and patterns in European labour markets.
Hurst, R. (1995). Choice and empowerment – lessons from Europe. *Disability and Society*, **10**, (4), 529–535.
Critically evaluates models of social provision for people with disabilities in Europe and of the role of the EU.
Moore, M., Tilson, T. and Whitting, G. (1994). *An International Overview of Employment Policies and Practices towards Older Workers*. Research Series 29, Employment Department.
A comprehensive study of state policy on and provision for older workers. Includes in-depth case studies of France, Germany and the UK, and some examples at the organization level.
Wrench, J. (1998). *The EU, Ethnic Minorities and Migrants in the Workplace*. Kogan Page.
A comprehensive study of minority ethnic workers across Europe, including theoretical analysis, comparison of state policy and case study examples at the organization level.

# References

Alund A. and Schierup, C. (1993). The thorny road to Europe: Swedish immigrant policy in transition. In *Racism and Migration in Western Europe* (J. Wrench and J. Solomos, eds). Berg Publishers.
Blos, M., Fischer, P. A. and Straubhaar, T. (1997). The impact of migration policy on labour market performance of migrants: a comparative case study. *New Community*, **23**, (4), 511–533.

Braithwaite, M. and Byrne, C. (1993). *Women in Decision-Making in Trade Unions*. European Trade Union Confederation.

Bryant, C. A. (1997). Citizenship, national identity and the accommodation of difference: reflections on the German, French, Dutch and British cases. *New Community*, **23**, (2), 157–172.

Castles, S. (1995). How nation states respond to immigration and ethnic diversity. *New Community*, **21**, (3), July, 10–30.

Cockburn, C. (1991). *In the Way of Women: Men's Resistance to Sex Equality in Organisations*. Macmillan.

Cockburn, C. (1995). Redrawing the boundaries: trade unions, women and Europe. In *Gender, Culture and Organisational Change* (C. Itzin and J. Newman, eds). Routledge.

Deland, M. (1998). The cultural racism of Sweden. Special issue of *Race and Class*, **39**, (1), 51–60.

EC (European Commission) (1997a). *Employment in Europe, 1997*, Employment and Social Affairs, European Commission.

EC (European Commission) (1997b). *The Employment Situation of People with Disabilities: Employment in Europe, 1997*. Employment and Social Affairs, European Commission.

EC (European Commission) (1998). *Reconciliation between Work and Family Life in Europe*. Employment and Social Affairs, European Commission.

EIRR (European Industrial Relations Review) (1997a). Sexual harassment at the workplace: part one. *European Industrial Relations Review*, **287**, December, 13–18.

EIRR (European Industrial Relations Review) (1997b). European Year against Racism. *European Industrial Relations Review*, **278**, March, 27–31.

EIRR (European Industrial Relations Review) (1997c). Racial discrimination and trade union policy. *European Industrial Relations Review*, **277**, February, 26–28.

Esping-Anderson, G. (1990). *The Three Worlds of Welfare Capitalism*. Polity Press.

EuroFoundation (1997). *Equal opportunities and collective bargaining in the EU*. European Foundation for the Improvement of Living and Working Conditions.

EuroFoundation (1998). *The Employment of People with Disabilities in Small and Medium-Sized Enterprises*. European Foundation for the Improvement of Living and Working Conditions.

Fekete, L. (1997). Blackening the economy: the path to convergence. Special issue of *Race and Class*, **39**, (1), 1–17.

Fekete, L. (1999). Popular racism in Europe. *Race and Class*, **40**, (2–3), 189–198.

Franco, M. T. and Ponzellini, A. M. (1997). *City Time Policies: The Italian Experience*. A report commissioned by the TUC.

Hakim, C. (1992). Explaining trends in occupational segregation: the measurement, causes and consequences of the sexual division of labour. *European Sociological Review*, **8**, (2), 127–152.

Herzing, A (1995). The labour market position of women from ethnic minorities: a comparison of four European countries. In *Women and the*

*European Labour Market* (A. V. Doorne-Huiskes, J. Van Hopf and R. Roelofs, eds). Open University.

Hibbs, D. A. (1990). Wage dispersion and trade union activity in Sweden. In *Generating Equality in the Welfare State* (I. Persson, ed.). Oslo University Press.

Hoskyns, C. (1996). *Integrating Gender: Women, Law and Politics in the European Union*. Verso.

Hugman, R. (1994). *Ageing and the Case of Older People in Europe*. Macmillan.

Hurst, R. (1995). Choice and empowerment – lessons from Europe. *Disability and Society*, **10**, (4), 529–535.

Hyde, M. (1996). Fifty years of failure: employment services for disabled people in the UK. *Work, Employment and Society*, **10**, (4), 683–700.

Karacs, I. (1999). Austrians have never been taught not to hate foreigners. *Independent* (review), 4.

Kiernan, K. (1992). The roles of men and women in tomorrow's Europe. *Employment Gazette*, October, 491–499.

Labour Research (1994). *European Unions Tackle Racism*. February. Labour Research.

Langan, M. and Ostner, I. (1990). Gender and welfare: towards a comparative framework. Paper presented to the Social Policy Conference, July, Bath.

Liebfried, S. (1990). Income transfers and poverty policy in EC perspective: on Europe's slipping into Anglo-American welfare models. Paper presented to EC seminar 'Poverty, Marginalisation and social exclusion in the Europe of the 90s', Alghero, April.

Lunt, N. and Thornton, P. (1993). *Employment Policies for Disabled People: A Review of Legislation and Services in Fifteen Countries*. Research series 16, Employment Department.

Milne, S. and Gow, D. (1999). Ford President signs pact to end Dagenham racism. *The Guardian*, 26 October.

Moore, M., Tilson, T. and Whitting, G. (1994). *An International Overview of Employment Policies and Practices towards Older Workers*. Research Series 29, Employment Department.

OECD (Organization for Economic Co-operation and Development) (1992). Labour market participation and retirement of older workers. *Employment Outlook*, July.

Pillinger, J. (1992). *Feminising the Market: Women's Pay and Employment in the European Community*. Macmillan.

Plantenga, J. (1995). Labour market participation of women in the EU. In *Women and the European Labour Market* (A. V. Doorne-Huiskes, J. Van Hopf and R. Roelofs, eds). Open University.

Plantenga, J. and Tijdensk, E (1995). Segregation in the EU: developments in the 1980s. In *Women and the European Labour Market* (A. V. Doorne-Huiskes, J. Van Hopf and R. Roelofs, eds). Open University.

Pot, L. (1995). Policies for children and parents in four European countries. In *Women and the European Labour Market* (A. V. Doorne-Huiskes, J. Van Hopf and R. Roelofs, eds). Open University.

Pred, A. (1997). Somebody else, somewhere else: racisms, racialized spaces and the popular geographical imagination in Sweden. *Antipode*, **29**, (4), 383–416.

Rees, T. (1998). *Mainstreaming Equality in the European Union*. Routledge.

Rix, S. (1993). Older workers in the United States: conditions of work and transitions to retirement. Paper presented to the International Congress of Gerontology, July.

Roelofs, E. (1995). The European equal opportunities policy. In *Women and the European Labour Market* (A. V. Doorne-Huiskes, J. Van Hopf and R. Roelofs, eds). Open University.

Schippers, J. (1995). Pay differences between men and women in the European labour market. In *Women and the European Labour Market* (A. V. Doorne-Huiskes, J. Van Hopf and R. Roelofs, eds). Open University.

Singh, R. (1997). Equal opportunities for men and women in the EU: a commentary. *Industrial Relations Journal*, **28**, (1), 68–71.

Sivariandam, A. (1997). Introduction. Special issue of *Race and Class*, **39**, (1), 1.

Thompson, M. (1991). Last in the queue: corporate employment policies on older workers, *IMS Report*, **209**, July.

Thornton, P. and Lunt, N. (1995). *Employment for Disabled People: Social Obligation or Individual Responsibility?* Social Policy Research Unit Report, 2.

Van der Lippe, T. and Roelofs, E (1995). Sharing domestic work. In *Women and the European Labour Market* (A. V. Doorne-Huiskes, J. Van Hopf and R. Roelofs, eds). Open University.

Waddington, L. (1997). The European Community and disability discrimination: time to address the deficit of powers? *Disability and Society*, **12**, (3), 465–479.

Wilpert, C. (1993). Ideological and institutional foundations of racism in the FDR. In *Racism and Migration in Western Europe* (J. Wrench and J. Solomos, eds). Berg.

Wrench, J. (1997). *European Compendium of Good Practice for the Prevention of Racism in the Workplace*. Office for Official Publications of the European Communities.

Wrench, J. (1998). *The EU, Ethnic Minorities and Migrants in the Workplace*. Kogan Page.

Wrench, J. and Solomos, J. (eds) (1993). *Racism and Migration in Western Europe*. Berg.

# Chapter 11
# Destination diversity?

## Aim

To provide a summary of issues raised throughout the book and an exploration of the future direction of equality policy and practices.

## Objectives

- To highlight and identify key themes and issues raised in Chapters One to Ten.
- To explore the prospects for a 'diversity' paradigm eclipsing the present 'equality' paradigm.

## Introduction

One of the ways in which any piece of academic writing, is always assessed, is the extent to which it meets the objectives set out by the authors. In this we can refer back to Chapter 1 where the primary aim of the book was to fill the gap identified within the broad field of equality and diversity, helping readers to 'manage' more effectively, the study of the diversity of society within the context of employment. This focused on current and emerging equality and diversity debates and issues within the context of the UK labour market, providing conceptual and theoretical underpinning, and broadening the agenda of the discussion to examine the social and economic contexts within which labour market activity takes place. Other aims included the desire to stimulate debate and critique, of theory, policy and practice in the area of equality and diversity, and the need to trace developments in equality and diversity approaches, in order to identify possible future directions as we enter the new millennium – in particular, whether 'managing diversity' is to be seen as a new way forward. This chapter summarizes the key themes of the ten chapters in this book and indicates how these objectives have been met.

# Summary of themes and issues

## Continuing patterns of disadvantage

Perhaps the most predominant finding of the book, is the continued pattern of disadvantage faced by many social groups within the UK labour market. However the statistics are looked at, the labour market of the twenty-first century is going to be characterized by continued segregation, disadvantage and discrimination, which disproportionately affects some groups, on average, more than others (Chapter 2). This discrimination and disadvantage is reflective of wider societal attitudes, institutions and structures, and the overall picture across Europe is very similar, as highlighted in Chapter 10.

In an interview with well-known feminist writer Germaine Greer, Jeremy Clarkson (BBC2, October 1999) commented that the position of women had progressed far during the 1980s and 1990s, indeed, the UK had elected a woman Prime Minister and the producer of his programme was a woman; did this mean that the fight for equality had been won? As Germaine Greer went on to argue, and as the evidence presented within this book illustrates, the fight for gender equality within employment appears far from over. Perhaps more importantly, the agenda of the answer to this question needs to be broadened, as the fight is not restricted to women and gender relations in the UK labour market; equality is far from met for many other groups, particularly, minority ethnic, older, disabled and gay and lesbian workers.

There are countless examples of sexism, racism, ageism and homophobic discrimination within the policies and practices of organizations and governments. Chapters 4 and 8 identified that organizational structures and practices are gendered, racialized and sexualized. Chapters 6 and 10 highlighted the role of the state, both legislatively and in terms of social provision, in contributing to the discriminatory character of labour markets. Chapters 3 and 5 indicated how free-market philosophies of competition and supply and demand factors are not sufficient to explain the continuing patterns of labour market disadvantage. Indeed, explanations need to reflect the significance of social identity categorizations. Wider social attitudes, stereotyping and discriminatory practices are connected to the processes and exercise of individual agency and to identity formation (Collinson, Knights and Collinson, 1990). Such social identity issues have implications at the labour market level, for example in recruitment and selection decisions (Chapter 8). The newspapers and television programmes are full of incidents of employment-related discrimination and efforts to combat it. In the area of race, for example, highly publicized events such as the Stephen Lawrence Inquiry and the associated MacPherson Report, have highlighted the extent to which racism is embedded within our society and its institutions. This has generated considerable debate and 'soul-searching' by organizations in the UK, for example, recent admissions by the Fire

Service of their institutionalized racism (Beckett, 1999), the recent disputes over racism at the Ford plant in Dagenham (Milne and Gow, 1999) and recognition of the need to rectify unrepresentative structures within trade unions (Chapter 7).

## Continuation of the white, male norm

Chapter 5 traced the recent changes in thinking on equality issues and the shift towards conceptualizing workforces as composed of diverse social groups ('difference' rather than 'sameness' approaches). Liberal approaches to equality focus on the need for formalization of procedures to ensure equal treatment and include an emphasis on legislation. Chapter 6 pointed out the weaknesses of the legislative framework in the UK, largely restricted to combating race and sex discrimination, with newer legislation on disability and codes of practice of ageism remaining limited in its ability to advance the equality agenda. Within this, the tenacity of the male norm (Fredman, 1995) and, we would say, the white, male, non-disabled, aged twenty-five to forty norm, weakens the impact of the legislation.

This reflects a key theme emerging from the book, relating to the weaknesses of both equality and diversity approaches because they remain within a liberal and 'short' agenda. Overall, the evidence presented in this book indicates that policy and practice at both national and organizational level, pose little challenge to the existing status quo, existing social attitudes or the existing norm of work, which we have established is gendered, racialized and sexualized. This raises the question of whether 'managing diversity' is a *new way forward* for equality within the UK labour market. With regard to whether 'managing diversity' is a *new* approach, Chapters 5 and 8 highlighted the change in emphasis within the MD approach, towards a recognition of the diversity of workforces and the need to view difference in a positive way, including a broader range of people than in traditional liberal approaches. In addition, the rhetoric of MD appears to encourage the culture change or mainstreaming perspective, which might lead to more radical challenges to existing structures and attitudes. However, what is emphasized overall, was that MD in practice represents little change from the liberal model, with many of the measures involved in an ideal MD approach also being part of a conventional EO policy (Kandola and Fullerton, 1994; Webb, 1997). In the UK in particular, as Chapter 8 discussed, employers have not really taken up MD in the same way as in the USA, so that MD becomes more of a supplement to EOPs rather than posing a new and radical challenge to the organizational structures and cultures.

Managing diversity may not even be seen as a way *forward*. Indeed Chapter 5 indicated the negative implications of the emphasis on 'difference' approaches in reinforcing stereotypes and ignoring similarities between groups. In particular, the MD approach individualizes the policy approach which many commentators see as detrimental (Dickens, 1997). As Chapter 9 discussed, this reflects the similarity between HRM and MD approaches. The unitarist and individualist focus of HR, can be seen as a challenge to the role of collective groups such as trade unions which, as Chapters 7 and 10 highlighted, have an important role to play in encouraging policies and structures that enhance the pursuit of equality issues at workplace and societal levels.

The link between MD and HRM also raises the issue of a business-case approach to equality as discussed in Chapter 8. Our argument is that the business case is not a fruitful basis on which to frame policies, encouraging only the 'short' agenda of equality and only a minimal or compliance approach to EOPs, rather than encouraging the development of comprehensive, proactive, organizations where a strong sense of social justice will also underpin policy and practice (Healy, 1993). As Chapter 8 went on to debate, MD orientations may actually encourage the avoidance of more radical and 'long' equality agendas because what might be seen as 'preferential' treatment will be at odds with an MD orientation (Liff, 1995).

In general, it must be admitted that this is all fairly depressing reading. However, such a critical perspective is valuable, we feel, in order to combat the overly optimistic viewpoints which can be gained from conventional textbooks and practitioner texts. It is certainly important to recognize that many social groups within the labour market are far from achieving equality. With regard to women, the 'you *can* have it all' literature, such as that which perpetuates the 'superwoman' image of the woman being successful within the male norm of work, we feel, is detrimental to the position of women in the labour market. Those women who are able to achieve 'superwoman' status are predominantly in better paid, higher status, and usually professional jobs, but are held up as examples to all other women who are trying to juggle work and family responsibilities. As Chapter 9 discussed, liberal equality approaches tend to help only a small segment of those facing disadvantage, arguably those who are in a considerably better position to begin with (Dickens, 1997; Webb, 1997; White, Cox and Cooper 1992). Such views significantly underplay the power structures, power positions and identity constructions, which are evidenced in the chapters of this book.

On the other hand, it is certain that there have been improvements over the last twenty-five years for many of the groups that we have considered in this book. Diversity within the workforce is commonly recognized, incidents of discrimination cause public outrage, and legislation continues to improve (if only in a limited way) the protection of the rights of a diverse workforce. While the overall picture is of continued patterns of disadvantage, there are many incidents of 'good' practice and more progressive models and structures discussed within this book. Indeed, it is obvious that people need not only be seen as victims of the structures and cultures of which they are part. As stated in Chapter 1, individuals are makers of their own histories and some individuals can and do overcome socially constructed barriers and obstacles generally encountered by their own social group.

Also, there is evidence in the foregoing chapters of organizational and government models and practices which do attempt to challenge (in a more radical or 'long'-agenda sense), those socially constructed barriers and obstacles. For example, Chapter 10 offered some alternative models of state policy and provision that potentially allow more opportunities for equality within the labour market, such as those in the Scandinavian countries. Chapter 8 provided some examples of organizations where a much more comprehensive, proactive approach to equality policy and practice is taken. Such evidence can soften the pessimistic tone of the summary of equality and diversity issues within the UK.

However, what we feel is important is that there is recognition that continued patterns of disadvantage are far more prevalent than the patterns of equality. And as Jenkins (1996: 174) points out: 'Not everyone is equally well placed to resist the compulsion and degradation which many organizational hierarchies routinely inflict upon their members, particularly those at the bottom of the heap.' This alerts us to the fact that there is still much work to be done in advancing equality within the employment arena. The question now, is how can we move forward? What does the evidence presented in this book indicate about the models, practices and policies, which appear to offer the most potential for advancing equality?

# Possible ways forward

As stated in Chapter 1, our objectives in writing this book do not include making recommendations or drawing prescriptive conclusions from our discussions. However, the evidence discussed does highlight models, approaches and practices that appear to either impede or facilitate progression along the road to equality of different groups in the labour market. We are not suggesting a prescription for future practice, but are suggesting elements which, we feel, should play an important part in policy and practice. Four themes appear important in potentially facilitating this progress: first, the need to maintain a collective focus within equality policies and to encourage self-organized groups and collective action. Second, the need to broaden the business case for equality. Third, the need to integrate 'sameness' and 'difference' approaches, rather than seeing EO and MD as opposed and contradictory and, fourth, the need for a significantly revised view of what paid work means and of its centrality in our lives.

## Collective action

Discussions drawn out of many chapters in this book highlight the importance of a collective focus in equality and diversity policy and practice. We suggest that the individualistic focus of MD and 'difference' approaches is not a fruitful basis on which to frame equality policies. While we acknowledge that categorizing individuals in reference to their social groupings may be constraining, we also feel that individuals can never entirely escape their socially constructed positioning, and this needs to be recognized as a fundamental contributing factor to patterns of disadvantage.

Thus we focus on the potentially detrimental effects of equality approaches based on the individual. Chapter 6 indicated the weaknesses of a legislative framework in the UK which places the onus on the individual having to fight their case, or uphold their individual rights, unlike the 'class action' approach of the USA. To us, this seems only to further victimize the individual, focusing on their own experiences and failure to succeed within the discriminatory structures, rather than recognizing that those structures are part of the essential problem. Given the financial resources necessary to fight legal cases, again, this liberal approach will tend to benefit a minority of people. Here the importance of collective groups is emphasized, first, because it is collective groups, such as trade unions, which can provide those essential resources to the individuals concerned.

More significantly than resource issues however, collective groups provide essential support for those facing disadvantage in the labour market. Chapter 4 highlighted the importance of networks and role models for people in organizations in dealing with discriminatory structures and practices. Chapter 7 indicated the important role that trade unions can play in pushing for equality issues as part of the bargaining agenda. What an emphasis on differences between individuals (characteristic of MD approaches) does is weaken the ties that people have through common experience, that provide the necessary support to push for action, essentially leaving people alone and isolated in their struggle (Cockburn, 1989). In Dickens' (1997) ideal model of EO practice, the role of trade unions, for example, is seen as vital in the campaign for equality in the workplace. Such an emphasis on collective social groupings needs to be maintained within diversity approaches.

## Broadening the agenda of the business case

One of the themes emerging from our discussions involves the potentially detrimental effects of a purely business-case approach to equality and diversity (Chapter 8 and 9). While we must recognize that the 'bottom line' is what most organizations will be concerned with, they are, after all, business organizations. However, we suggest that a more fruitful way forward, following Dickens (1994), is to have a broader definition of business-case interests. Business cases for equality should be linked to wider issues of social justice and social responsibility, in essence having a more pluralist conception of the organization. As discussed in Chapter 8, consumer, shareholder and employee pressure may be the catalyst to this broader agenda. This also connects to wider structures and policies, drawing on those models of state provision and policy that offer most potential for equality within the labour market (Chapter 10). Those of Scandinavia, for example, are based more around social justice and ontological equality (Chapter 5) rather than economic necessity.

## Integrating EO and MD approaches

Is MD a *new way forward*? Whilst we have made some attempt to deal with this issue, even engaging with this question does not appear particularly useful and may actually be counter-productive. Why should we think of new policies and approaches as necessarily eclipsing the old? Not only is this often detrimental (as will be discussed), but it is also quite obvious that this does not happen in reality. Just as HRM techniques are tagged on to the end of more traditional industrial relations and management practices (see Pollert, 1996), the older, liberal EO tradition lives on in policy and practice, even if it has been partly superseded in theory. In addition, there are further reasons why it would actually be more practical and useful to integrate EO and MD, liberal and radical approaches. All have weaknesses and strengths as have been discussed at depth in the previous chapters. This may be an idealistic aspiration, but why could the strengths of both not be integrated, so that EO and MD are seen as a complement to each other (Liff, 1999). This would fit more with an approach of a 'long' agenda, recognizing the need to maintain elements of past policies and aim for continuity of process. The MD approach, for example, suffers from its individualistic focus, but also is much more forward-looking than liberal EO in its view of difference and diversity as positive features which should be valued and utilized. Dickens (1997), for example, suggests that collective equality bargaining by trade unions could underpin and generalize employer's diversity initiatives, while the law could generalize and underpin both of these. It is important that in taking up some of the MD approaches, the support and protection offered by legislation and formalized procedures are not lost, or are still fought for. There is still much progress to be made in the legislative and procedural arena (Liff, 1996; Rees, 1998). Managing diversity approaches offer challenges to organizational cultures and EO policies based on accommodating or assimilating difference, but need to be underpinned by more positive action policies which ensure that the diversity inherent in the labour market is reflected in the workforce to begin with (Miller, 1996).

## A new model of work

Finally, we believe that changes in the patterns of disadvantage in the labour market can only come through radical revision of what is considered to be the norm of work. The existing norm, based on the white, male, full-time, non-disabled and heterosexual worker, offers little chance for facilitating a labour market which values diversity rather than attempts to accommodate and assimilate difference. This involves the need for radical changes in wider social attitudes, but also in state provision and organizational structures and practices (Liff and Wajcman, 1996).

This book has examined changes in wider social attitudes, and while on the one hand there is, for example, increasing evidence of more egalitarian attitudes to sex roles and acceptance that discrimination should be outlawed, on the other hand, there is also evidence to the contrary, indicated by the rise of racism within Europe, the tenacity of the traditional gender regime and continued incidents of discrimination. Changing such wider social attitudes is obviously not simple, and is unlikely to happen rapidly. However, we should not necessarily feel that attitudes will, or can never, change. Indeed as Jenkins states:

On the face of things, social identities are neither remorselessly permanent nor frivolously malleable. The most adamantine identity has some leeway in it, if only as a sense of possibility . . . Arising within and out of bilateral processes of mutual recognition which are often rooted in specific situations, social identities are generally contingent, 'for the time being', and somewhat tolerant of inconsistency and contradiction. (Jenkins, 1996: 62)

Existing policies at national and organizational levels still appear to uphold the dominant norm of work, and this has been repeated as a fundamental criticism of policy and practice throughout this book. Chapter 10 engaged with the discussion about the way in which state (and we would add organizational) policy interacted with wider social attitudes, so that neither is sufficient in itself in bringing about change. However, it is important that policy and practices do not simply uphold and continue to perpetuate dominant and inherently discriminatory structures. So for example, the UK Employment Relations Act, introduced in 1999, involves recommendations and legislation supplying family-friendly provisions such as childcare support, parental leave and domestic leave. However, this legislation has been met with disappointment by trade unions and other interest groups because it continues to uphold the mother as the primary carer, despite bearing the label 'parental leave'. As Fredman argues:

Comprehensive provision for childcare would not in itself bring sufficient structural change. The underlying problem is that current patterns of work make no accommodation for participative parenting . . . A real commitment to the value of parenting . . . would require a restructuring of working patterns to accommodate childcare. Change would include provisions for leave to care for babies and children; and the availability of flexible and part-time working at decent levels of pay and status. It is crucial that such provisions be available to both mothers and fathers and that they attract proper payment, funded by a partnership of the State, the employer and the individual. (Fredman, 1995: ii)

We would extend this 'restructuring of work patterns' beyond incorporating only childcare but, as Liff and Wacjman (1996) suggest, a new norm has to recognize the overlapping and multiple identities ascribed to and achieved by individuals. The existing norm of what is considered to be 'work' is predominantly full time, and long hours, with commitment to the job taking primacy over alternative commitments such as to family or religious practice. While part-time and other forms of more flexible working are on the increase and are being encouraged by employers and the government, as Fredman (1995) states, this does not achieve equality, especially when flexible workers face lesser paid, lesser status and less-protected jobs. Chapter 8 discussed the detrimental effects on the five social groups, of work as defined by this hegemonic norm. Changes in the status, pay and protection of more flexible forms of working would be a significant progressive step.

Once again the interaction between attitudes and policy and practice is highlighted. While social attitudes continue to perpetuate the dominant norm, state and organizational attempts to challenge it are limited in their effects. One could look at the failure of Swedish models of welfare to lead to a more equal division of domestic responsibility even though the opportunities for this exist within the structures and provisions. Change at only one level will not be sufficient to enact transformation in the patterns of disadvantage. This needs a combined effort at state, organizational and societal levels: some might say an impossible venture. However, without such fundamental change, the equality project will continue to be piecemeal and limited, and there will be relatively little alteration in labour market patterns over the next twenty-five years. Nevertheless, this should not cause total despondency, the utility of enquiry and critique as in this book is to offer alternative conceptualizations and to point out the areas in which reflexive practice is needed. Organizational actors, legislators, state policy-makers and all of us as individuals, need to take a reflexive approach with regard to our actions and policies, aiming to consider whether these uphold or challenge a status quo which currently supports a segmented and very unequal labour market.

# References

Beckett, A. (1999) Engine trouble. *The Guardian*, 6 October.

Cockburn, C. (1989). Equal opportunities: the long and short agenda. *Industrial Relations Journal*, Autumn, **20**, 213–225.

Collinson, D. Knights, D. and Collinson, M. (1990). *Managing to Discriminate*. Routledge.

Dickens, L. (1994). Wasted resources? Equal opportunities in employment. In *Personnel Management* (K. Sisson, ed.). Blackwell.

Dickens, L. (1997). Gender, race and employment equality in Britain: inadequate strategies and the role of industrial relations actors. *Industrial Relations Journal*, **28**, (4), 282–289.

Fredman, S. (1995). *Women in Labour: Parenting Rights at Work*. Institute of Employment Rights.

Healy, G. (1993). Business and discrimination. In *Strategic Thinking and the Management of Change* (R. Stacey, ed.). Kogan Page.

Jenkins, R. (1996). *Social Identity*. Routledge.

Kandola, R. and Fullerton, J. (1994). *Managing the Mosaic: Diversity in Action*. Institute of Personnel and Development.

Liff, S. (1995). Equal opportunities: continuing discrimination in a context of formal equality. In *Industrial Relations* (P. Edwards, ed.). Blackwell.

Liff, S. (1996). Two routes to managing diversity: individual differences or social group characteristics. *Employee Relations*, **19**, (1), 11–26.

Liff, S. (1999). Diversity and equal opportunities: room for a constructive compromise? *Human Resource Management Journal*, **9**, (1), 65–75.

Liff, S. and Wajcman, J. (1996). 'Sameness' and 'difference' revisited: which way forward for equal opportunity initiatives? *Journal of Management Studies*, **33**, (1), 79–95.

Miller, D. (1996). Equality management: towards a materialist approach. *Gender, Work and Organisation*, **3**, (4), 202–214.

Milne, S. and Gow, D. (1999). Ford President signs pact to end Dagenham racism. *The Guardian*, 26 October.

Pollert, A. (1996). Team work on the assembly line: contradiction and the dynamics of union resilience. In *The New Work Place and Trade Unionism* (P. Ackers, C. Smith and P. Smith, eds). Routledge.

Rees, T. (1998). *Mainstreaming Equality in the European Union*. Routledge.

Webb, J. (1997). The politics of equal opportunity. *Gender, Work and Organisation*, **4**, (3), 159–167.

White, B., Cox, C. and Cooper, C. (1992). *Women's Career Development: A Study of High Fliers*. Blackwell.

# Glossary of terms and abbreviations

**ACAS**  Advisory, Conciliation and Arbitration Service.

**Business case**  A justification of equality/diversity initiatives based upon economic rationality.

**CAC**  Central Arbitration Committee.

**Class action**  US system which permits individuals, who have been affected by identical discrimination, to be given the same remedy as the person who was successful in a previous case.

**Codes of practice**  Government guidance providing recommendations on employment practice, which are not legally binding. May be used as evidence at employment tribunal.

**Collective bargaining**  The method of determining working conditions and terms of employment through negotiations between an employer and a trade union. A **collective agreement** is the outcome of such negotiations.

**Concrete ceiling**  The term used to describe the seemingly impenetrable barriers preventing the progress of people from minority ethnic groups.

**CRE**  Commission for Racial Equality set up by the Race Relations Act 1976. Its duties are to work towards the elimination of race discrimination, to promote equality and good relations between people of different racial groups. It issues various guides for employers on good practice.

**DDA**  Disability Discrimination Act 1995.

**Demand-side**  An economic term. Demand-side factors are those which influence employers' requirements for labour.

**DfEE**  Department for Education and Employment.

**Domestic sphere**  A term used to denote unpaid work in the home and family responsibilities.

**Downward occupational mobility**  The term used to describe the tendency for women to enter lower status employment following a break for childbirth/care.

**DRC**  Disability Rights Commission.

**EAT**  Employment Appeal Tribunal.

**EC**   European Commission.

**ECHR**   European Court of Human Rights.

**ECJ**   European Court of Justice.

**Economic activity rate**   The proportion of the workforce which is either in employment or registered as unemployed.

**EEC**   European Economic Community.

**EIRR**   European Industrial Relations Review.

**Employment tribunal**   Employees can complain to the employment tribunal when they suspect that a statutory employment law has been breached by an employer. The tribunal system operates like an informal court of law.

**EO**   Equal Opportunities.

**EOC**   Equal Opportunities Commission set up by the Sex Discrimination Act 1975. Its aim is to work towards the elimination of sex discrimination, promote equality between the sexes. It issues various guides for employers, encouraging good practice.

**EOPs**   Equal Opportunities Policies.

**Equality bargaining**   Collective agreements on equality issues.

**ETUC**   European Trades Union Congress

**EU**   European Union.

**Family-friendly policy**   Employment policies facilitating the balancing of work and parental/caring responsibilities.

**Feminine-in-management**   A thesis emphasizing women's unique management skills, also termed as 'women in management'.

**Gender pay gap**   The term frequently used to describe the earnings disparity between women and men. If the 'gap' is 20 per cent, then women earn 80 per cent of men's average earnings.

**Glass ceiling**   The term refers to invisible barriers preventing women from advancing to higher levels within organizations.

**GOQ**   Genuine Occupational Qualifications.

**HRA**   Human Rights Act 1998.

**HRM**   Human Resource Management.

**Human capital**   The term used to describe the skills, education, training, abilities and experience possessed by individuals.

**Indirect labour costs**   Costs other than direct remuneration associated with the employment of labour, for example maternity/parental leave, and training.

**Institutional racism**   The term used to describe the existence of policy and administrative processes within social institutions, which result in the adverse treatment of minority ethnic people.

**IPD**   Institute of Personnel and Development, the professional body for those involved within the field of personnel or human resource management. It produces various guides for human resource practitioners, which encourage good employment practice.

**Mainstreaming**   The inclusion of equality issues in every part of business strategy and policy.

**MD**   Managing Diversity.

**MSF**   Manufacturing, Science, Finance – Britain's fifth largest trade union. Membership is predominantly in the private sector, consisting of skilled and professional workers.

**Occupational segregation**   The tendency for certain social groups to be disproportionately situated in certain occupations or status positions.

**OPCS**   Office for Population and Census Surveys.

**Patriarchy**   has been defined as 'a system of social structures and practices in which men dominate, oppress and exploit women' (S. Walby [1990]. *Theorizing Patriarchy*, Blackwell, p. 20).

**Positive action**   Refers to efforts to remove obstacles to the free operation of the labour market. The aim is to promote free and equal competition among individuals.

**Positive discrimination**   Involves the deliberate manipulation of employment practices with the intention of achieving a proportional distribution of disadvantaged social groups within the workforce.

**Public sphere**   A term used to denote paid work in the labour market.

**RRA**   Race Relations Act 1976.

**SDA**   Sex Discrimination Act 1975.

**Social Chapter**   Seeks to pursue Europe-wide regulation of the labour market, including working conditions, dialogue between management and labour, protection of workers.

**Social identity**   The process of achieved or ascribed categorization, which occurs within societal relations.

**Statistical discrimination**   Discrimination against groups of workers, relating to perceived characteristics of that particular group.

**Supply-side**   An economic term. Supply-side factors are those which shape the nature of the labour supply, that is the workforce; including demographic and skill variables, personal preferences.

**TUC**   Trades Union Congress, the co-ordinating body of Britain's trade union movement.

**Union recognition**   An employer may 'recognize' a trade union either as the representative of employees who are members (in cases of grievance or discipline, for example) and/or for the purposes of collective bargaining.

**UNISON**   Britain's largest trade union. Membership is located in the public services.

# Index